D0803170

Computer Simulation in Human Population Studies

STUDIES IN ANTHROPOLOGY

Under the Consulting Editorship of E. A. Hammel,
UNIVERSITY OF CALIFORNIA, BERKELEY

Andrei Simić, THE PEASANT URBANITES: A Study of Rural-Urban Mobility in Serbia

John U. Ogbu, THE NEXT GENERATION: An Ethnography of Education in an Urban Neighborhood

Bennett Dyke and Jean Walters MacCluer (Eds.), COMPUTER SIMULATION IN HUMAN POPULATION STUDIES

Robbins Burling, THE PASSAGE OF POWER: Studies in Political Succession

Piotr Sztompka, SYSTEM AND FUNCTION: Toward a Theory of Society

William G. Lockwood, EUROPEAN MOSLEMS: Economy and Ethnicity in Western Bosnia

Günter Golde, CATHOLICS AND PROTESTANTS: Agricultural Modernization in Two German Villages

Peggy Reeves Sanday (Ed.), ANTHROPOLOGY AND THE PUBLIC INTEREST: Fieldwork and Theory

Carol A. Smith (Ed.), REGIONAL ANALYSIS, Volume I: Economic Systems, and Volume II: Social Systems

Raymond D. Fogelson and Richard N. Adams (Eds.), THE ANTHROPOLOGY OF POWER: Ethnographic Studies from Asia, Oceania, and the New World

Frank Henderson Stewart, FUNDAMENTALS OF AGE-GROUP SYSTEMS

Larissa Adler Lomnitz, NETWORKS AND MARGINALITY: Life in a Mexican Shantytown

Benjamin S. Orlove, ALPACAS, SHEEP, AND MEN: The Wool Export Economy and Regional Society in Southern Peru

Harriet Ngubane, BODY AND MIND IN ZULU MEDICINE: An Ethnography of Health and Disease in Nyuswa-Zulu Thought and Practice

Computer Simulation in Human Population Studies

Edited by

Bennett Dyke

Department of Anthropology
The Pennsylvania State University
University Park, Pennsylvania

Jean Walters MacCluer

Department of Biology
The Pennsylvania State University
University Park, Pennsylvania

Proceedings of a Conference
Sponsored by the Social Science
Research Council and Held at
The Pennsylvania State University
June 12-14, 1972

ACADEMIC PRESS, INC.
New York San Francisco London 1973
A Subsidiary of Harcourt Brace Jovanovich, Publishers

ACADEMIC PRESS, INC.
111 Fifth Avenue, New York, New York 10003

United Kingdom Edition published by
ACADEMIC PRESS, INC. (LONDON) LTD.
24/28 Oval Road, London NW1

Library of Congress Cataloging in Publication Data
Main entry under title:

Computer simulation in human population studies.

(Studies in anthropology)
"Proceedings of a conference sponsored by the Social Science Research Council and held at the Pennsylvania State University, June 12-14, 1972."
Bibliography: p.
1. Population–Congresses. 2. Computer simulation –Congresses. I. Dyke, Bennett, ed. II. MacCluer, Jean Walters, ed. III. Social Science Research Council.
HB849.C57 301.31′028′54 73-5320
ISBN 0–12–785185–2

PRINTED IN THE UNITED STATES OF AMERICA

To the Memory of

MINDEL C. SHEPS

CONTENTS

PREFACE

Over the past decade, a small but growing number of workers in anthropology, demography, and human population genetics have been developing computer simulation models of human populations. Although such models have been used for diverse purposes, certain common characteristics are evident: social, demographic, and biological parameters and their interactions are implicit in most models; and no matter what the purpose of the simulation, there is a remarkable similarity in the computer programs and basic decision techniques involved.

Simulation models are usually so complex that investigators cannot publish detailed accounts of simulation techniques, but we have found from conversations at professional meetings and from reading between the lines of published results that a number of similar (perhaps identical) problems have been encountered and independently either solved or dismissed at the expense of considerable duplication of time and effort. Because of the small number of workers using simulation in human population studies and their varied professional specialties, it has been difficult to exchange useful information at the meetings of the larger professional associations. Consequently, we approached the Social Science Research Council with the idea of their sponsoring a conference intended to provide a critical audience for the discussion of simulation models and their results, and to disseminate information otherwise difficult to transmit. The plan was met with favor, and with the aid of Dr. David Jenness, SSRC Staff Associate, the generous financial support of the Population Council and the National Institute of Child Health and Human Development was secured. The conference was held at The Pennsylvania State University on June 12 to 14, 1972.

The conference was divided about equally between discussions of method and technique, and the presentation of substantive results. Sessions and their chairmen were as follows:

Anthropology and Social Systems:	*Eugene A. Hammel*
Genetics and Adaptive Systems:	*William J. Schull*
Demography:	*Hannes Hyrenius*
Simulation Methodology:	*B. V. Shah*

This volume is organized in approximately the same manner as was the schedule of the conference.

Space limitations in most professional journals preclude the publication of detailed descriptions of simulation programs. We therefore felt that a volume such as this was an appropriate place for such descriptions, and several authors have included them as appendices to their papers. The bibliography at the end of the volume, which is kept on file in an information retrieval system developed at The Pennsylvania State University, includes references to 169 books and articles, most of which are concerned with the application of computer simulation techniques to anthropology and social systems, human genetics, and demography. Although it is obviously incomplete at present, we hope to improve and update it periodically.

ACKNOWLEDGMENTS

Financial support for the conference and for preparation of this volume was provided by Grant Number T72.019C from The Population Council, and Grant Number 1 R13 HD06677 from the National Institute of Child Health and Human Development.

In addition to these organizations, a number of individuals deserve our special thanks: Dr. Jenness; Jane A. Menken and Hilary Page for their help in translating into English the paper by Jacquard and Léridon; Trixie V. Glasgow for her excellent job of typing the final manuscript; Ann C. McGarvey for preparation of some of the drawings; and the many members of the staff of the Penn State Computation Center who bore with us during a period of excessively heavy demand on computer facilities.

LIST OF PARTICIPANTS

Numbers in parentheses indicate pages on which authors' contributions begin. Asterisks designate contributors to this volume.

**J. C. Barrett* (383), London School of Hygiene and Tropical Medicine, Keppel Street (Gower Street), London, W.C. 1E 7HT, England

**Alice M. Brues* (129), Department of Anthropology, Hellums 98, University of Colorado, Boulder, Colorado 80302

**Alice S. Clague*[1] (329), International Institute for the Study of Human Reproduction, Columbia University, New York, New York

**Bennett Dyke* (59), Department of Anthropology, The Pennsylvania State University, University Park, Pennsylvania 16802

Frank Godley, National Center for Health Statistics, 5600 Fisher's Lane, Rockville, Maryland 20852

**E. A. Hammel* (1), Department of Anthropology, University of California, Berkeley, California 94720

[1] *Present address:* Center for Population Research of the Joseph and Rose Kennedy Institute for the Study of Human Reproduction and Bio-Ethics, Georgetown University, Washington, D. C. 20007

LIST OF PARTICIPANTS

**Gerhard J. Hanneman*[2] (97), Division of Communication, University of Connecticut, Storrs, Connecticut 06268

Ivar Heuch,[3] Department of Human Genetics, University of Michigan, Ann Arbor, Michigan 48104

**John H. Holland* (161), Logic of Computers Group, University of Michigan, 611 Church Street, Ann Arbor, Michigan 48104

**D. G. Horvitz* (261), Statistics Research Division, Research Triangle Institute, Research Triangle Park, North Carolina 27709

**Nancy Howell*[4] (43), Office of Population Research, Princeton University, Princeton, New Jersey

**David Hutchinson* (1), Department of Anthropology, University of California, Berkeley, California 94720

**Hannes Hyrenius* (251), Demographic Institute, University of Göteborg, Vasagatan 7, Göteborg C, Sweden

**Albert Jacquard* (241), Institut National d'Etudes Démographiques, 27, Rue du Commandeur, Paris 14e, France

Florence Koons, National Center for Health Statistics, Room 8-51, 5600 Fisher's Lane, Rockville, Maryland 20852

**Peter Kunstadter*[5] (435), East-West Population Institute, The East-West Center, Honolulu, Hawaii 96822

**Henri Léridon* (241), Institut National d'Etudes Démographiques, 27, Rue du Commandeur, Paris 14e, France

**Francis H. F. Li* (221), Department of Human Genetics, University of Michigan, 1137 East Catherine Street, Ann Arbor, Michigan 48104

[2] *Present address:* Annenberg School of Communications, University of Southern California, 915 West 37th Place, Los Angeles, California 90007

[3] *Present address:* Gabels Gate 18, Oslo, Norway

[4] *Present address:* Department of Sociology, Scarborough College, University of Toronto, West Hill, Ontario, Canada

[5] *Present address:* Department of Epidemiology (SC-36) University of Washington, Seattle, Washington 98195

LIST OF PARTICIPANTS

Jean Walters MacCluer (197), Department of Biology, 208 Life Sciences I, The Pennsylvania State University, University Park, Pennsylvania 16802

Jane A. Menken, Office of Population Research, 5 Ivy Lane, Princeton, New Jersey 08540

Kenneth Morgan[6] (15), Department of Anthropology, University of New Mexico, Albuquerque, New Mexico

Newton E. Morton, Population Genetics Laboratory, University of Hawaii, Honolulu, Hawaii 96822

James B. Pick (397), Department of Population and Enrivonmental Biology, School of Biological Science, University of California, Irvine, Irvine, California 92664

Jeanne Clare Ridley[7] (329), International Institute for the Study of Human Reproduction, Columbia University, New York, New York

David L. Rossmann[8] (143), Department of Human Genetics, University of Michigan, Ann Arbor, Michigan 48104

James M. Sakoda (457), Department of Sociology, Brown University, Providence, Rhode Island 02912

William J. Schull (143), Center for Demographic and Population Genetics, Graduate School of Biomedical Science, University of Texas, Houston, Houston, Texas 77025

B. V. Shah (421), Statistical Methodology Group, Statistics Research Division, Research Triangle Institute, Research Triangle Park, North Carolina 27709

[6] *Present address:* Department of Genetics, The University of Alberta, Edmonton 7, Alberta, Canada

[7] *Present address;* Center for Population Research of the Joseph and Rose Kennedy Institute for the Study of Human Reproduction and Bio-Ethics, Georgetown University, Washington, D. C. 20007

[8] *Present address:* Center for Demographic and Population Genetics, Graduate School of Biomedical Science, University of Texas, Houston, Houston, Texas 77025

*_Mark H. Skolnick_ (167), Department of Genetics, Stanford University School of Medicine, Stanford University Medical Center, Stanford, California 94305

Dean O. Smith, Physiologisches Institut der Technischen, Universität München, 8 München 80, Federal Republic of Germany

*_A. M. Sorant_ (305), School of Public Health, Department of Biostatistics, University of North Carolina, Chapel Hill, North Carolina 27514

Ralph Spielman, Department of Sociology, Bucknell University, Lewisburg, Pennsylvania 17837

*_William M. Stiteler, III_[9] (447), Department of Statistics, The Pennsylvania State University, University Park, Pennsylvania 16802

Roy C. Treadway, The Population Council, 245 Park Avenue, New York, New York 10017

Kenneth W. Wachter, St. Catherine's College, 8.1, Oxford University, Oxford, England

*_Anthony Williams_ (71), Department of Geography, 409 Deike Building, The Pennsylvania State University, University Park, Pennsylvania 16802

*_F. Paul Wyman_[10] (481), Department of Management Science, The Pennsylvania State University, University Park, Pennsylvania 16802

[9] _Present address:_ Bray Hall, College of Environmental Science and Forestry, Syracuse University, Syracuse, New York 13210

[10] _Present address:_ Dynamic Simulation Section, Hydro and Community Facilities Division, Bechtel Corporation, P.O. Box 3965, San Francisco, California 94119

OTHER CONTRIBUTORS TO THIS VOLUME

J. R. Batts (261), Statistics Research Division, Research Triangle Institute, Research Triangle Park, North Carolina 27709

R. C. Bhavsar (261), Statistics Research Division, Research Triangle Institute, Research Triangle Park, North Carolina 27709

Arthur S. Boughey (397), Department of Population and Environmental Biology, School of Biological Science, University of California, Irvine, Irvine, California 92664

C. Cannings (167), Department of Probability and Statistics, University of Sheffield, Sheffield, England

P. A. Lachenbruch (305), Department of Biostatistics, School of Public Health, University of North Carolina, Chapel Hill, North Carolina 27514

Q. W. Lindsey (261), Statistics Research Division, Research Triangle Institute, Research Triangle Park, North Carolina 27709

John Longfellow (71), Department of Geography, The Pennsylvania State University, University Park, Pennsylvania 16802

OTHER CONTRIBUTORS TO THIS VOLUME

Charles Monroe (71), Department of Geography, The Pennsylvania State University, University Park, Pennsylvania 16802

James V. Neel (221), Department of Human Genetics, University of Michigan, 1137 East Catherine Street, Ann Arbor, Michigan 48104

A. V. Rao (261), Statistics Research Division, Research Triangle Institute, Research Triangle Park, North Carolina 27709

Gordon N. Schick (397), Department of Population and Environmental Biology, School of Biological Science, University of California, Irvine, Irvine, California 92664

M. C. Sheps (305), Department of Biostatistics, School of Public Health, University of North Carolina, Chapel Hill, North Carolina 27514

Computer Simulation in Human Population Studies

TWO TESTS OF COMPUTER MICROSIMULATION: THE EFFECT OF AN INCEST TABU ON POPULATION VIABILITY, AND THE EFFECT OF AGE DIFFERENCES BETWEEN SPOUSES ON THE SKEWING OF CONSANGUINEAL RELATIONSHIPS BETWEEN THEM

E. A. HAMMEL
and
DAVID HUTCHINSON

INTRODUCTION

Let us begin by saying a few words about the origins of this project, of which the two tests described here are but a part and only a beginning. Hammel's interest began in the early 60's and centered on the effects of endogamy and residence rules on frequencies of cousin marriage (Gilbert and Hammel 1963, 1966). Similar problems were attacked by Kunstadter and his colleagues (1963). Subsequently, Hammel's work in the social structure of mediaeval Serbia led him into historical demography and a close cooperation with Laslett and others at Cambridge, one of the results of which was a determination to develop and use computer simulation to solve ethnological, historical, and policy problems that are sufficiently complex to make approach by other means quite difficult and often unreliable. In addition to the topics named in the title to this paper, there are others that concern the loose consortium of investigators at Berkeley and Cambridge (and here we include Kenneth Wachter, who is officially at Oxford).

One of these, in which the anthropologist Jack Goody is primarily interested, is the simulation of lack of appropriate heirs under particular systems of inheritance, the way in which the odds of having no appropriate heir vary with different birth and mortality rates, and the way in which populations can be expected to modify their reproductive behavior as vital rates and systems of inheritance change. A second topic of interest is the simulation of household composition under varying vital rates to determine whether stem families or extended families, lauded in cultural symbolism (Homans 1941, Laslett 1971), can ever really have been common in fact. A third is the effect on reproductive behavior of varying systems of taxation, given some assumptions about benefits to be derived from child labor or in social security, costs in maintenance and education, as well as maximization of inheritance for heirs. In brief, the research is concerned with two general categories of relationship: the effects of vital rates on social structure and its cultural symbols, and the effects of social structure and its cultural symbols on vital rates.

What follows here is only the simplest demonstration of a crude beginning, based on problems for which the answers are already known in some respect, whether intuitively or through prior empirical research or construction of deterministic models. We have been working on these simulations for only a bit more than six months, and that we have had even the minor success we hope to demonstrate is due largely to the generosity of Dr. Horvitz, who made the closed model of POPSIM available to us for revision and expansion to fit our particular needs (Horvitz *et al.* 1971), and the helpful advice from Nathan Keyfitz, Etienne Van de Walle, and especially Sam Preston. The program was rewritten by Hutchinson to run on the CDC 6400 at Berkeley and ultimately revised to run using extended core storage rather than disc storage to save machine time. Ultimately we hope to use only high speed core when population size permits, which should result in a drastic reduction in running time. Hutchinson has also made a very considerable number of modifications, principally in the event routines and in the construction of a genealogical reckoning subroutine to permit computation of consanguineal relationships of variable depth and to insert incest prohibitions. Even so, we foresee more extensive rewriting involving the basic logic of the program. Ultimately we hope to take into consideration relative status, wealth, and location in computing vital events, to pay heed to the death of a child and the length of lactation in computing the probability of a next child, and so on. The "sociological" portion of our intended simulation must take into account rules of residence, of bride price or dowry, and similar phenomena in which anthropologists and sociologists are always interested. (As this goes to press in April 1973 we can report successful total revision of POPSIM and reorganization into a new program, SOCSIM, which is itself now being expanded.) What we have to say here will, we know, be changed in its particulars. Nevertheless, we are intuitively confident about the general outlines.

THE INCEST TABU

The origin of the incest tabu has been hailed by several generations of anthropologists as the foundation stone of human culture and society, and damned by others as a problem incapable of solution and unworthy of consideration. Since we have no intention of making a detailed reconstruction of the evolutionary process, but only of suggesting the constraints under which it operated, we feel no qualms about sidestepping the anti-evolutionists. Commentators on the incest tabu and its corollary of required exogamy have noted the benefits to internal social peace and psychic harmony derived from the lack of competition for women and the permanence of role relationships within the family or band, as well as the political advantages of alliances with other groups. From its apparent benefits, the incest tabu was clearly something that could hardly wait to be invented, so important was it for the creation of human society as we know it. Slater (1959) has suggested that some kinds of matings would have been quite rare because of lack of temporal overlap of reproductive spans, but instituting the tabu was still crucial.

There are, however, some other problems associated with an incest tabu or with any restriction on mating, because all such reduce the size of the breeding population (Gilbert and Hammel 1963, 1966). The magnitude of the difficulty must of course be a function of two things - the extent of the tabu and the size of the population. All reconstructors of the life of early man are agreed that early human populations were small and scattered and that they increased very slowly in the aggregate, so that on the average they were on the knife edge between demographic success and failure most of the time. (Of course, some were going up while others were going down.) If early human populations were small on the average, we may ask what the effects of introduction of an incest tabu would have been, and how these effects would have varied with tabus of differing extent.

To examine this problem, we created a population of 65 persons by running a suitable "initial" population (in the sense used in POPSIM) 100 years without any incest tabu. Mortality was determined by the Maghreb epipaleolithic rates given by Acsadi and Nemeskeri, made sex-specific by using the Intercisa and Bregetio Roman schedules furnished by the same authors (1970). Fertility was set at 80 per cent of the Cocos-Keeling Island rates (Smith 1960); this was the factor necessary to achieve near-stability for the mortality schedule. Marriage rates maximized the exposure of women to risk of pregnancy. All rates were modified to achieve near stationarity and conditions thought typical of "early man." I do not, by the way, believe that the problem is sensitive to the particular rates except as these affect population size, but these rates are useful in adding to the reality of the simulation. If others are thought to be more accurate in reflecting actual demographic conditions, they could be used instead.

The initial population, having run for 100 years in order to establish a genealogy but with no incest tabu, constitutes what we may call the test population.

The test population of N = 65 was run five times at each of four levels of incest tabu - 20 test runs in all. Each run, although it began with the same 65 persons and used the same vital rates, employed a different starting random number for the event routines. Each run was for 100 years (or until the population was extinct, if that occurred before 100 years had elapsed). The four levels of incest tabu were: 0, namely no tabu, just as in the creation of the 65-person population; 1, namely a tabu on mating between any two persons having a common kinsman in the first ascending generation (this prohibits sibling, half-sibling, and parent-child matings); 2, a tabu on mating if there is a common kinsman in the second ascending generation (this prohibits first-cousin marriages as well as those of level 1); and 3, a tabu on mating if there is a common kinsman in the third ascending generation (this prohibits second-cousin marriages as well as those of levels 1 and 2).

The results of these runs are given in the accompanying graph, in which the level of incest tabu is plotted against the mean rate of population increase (in per cent). It can be seen that a population hovering near stationarity at tabu level zero could be seriously affected even by a first-degree tabu and would almost certainly become extinct eventually, given the same mortality, marriage, and fertility rates. If the tabu were extended beyond that, decline would be very rapid indeed.

The first conclusion to be drawn is that the simulation is working in a reasonable way - the results are in the direction predicted. It is because this problem is so simple that we picked it, and we would have been quite distressed if the results had been otherwise. The second conclusion is that the incest tabu was not likely to have been successfully invented, adopted, and maintained very many times. Of course, this conclusion depends on one's estimate of the severity of demographic conditions, but if they were as severe as is generally thought, it is only with luck - that is, in those populations experiencing

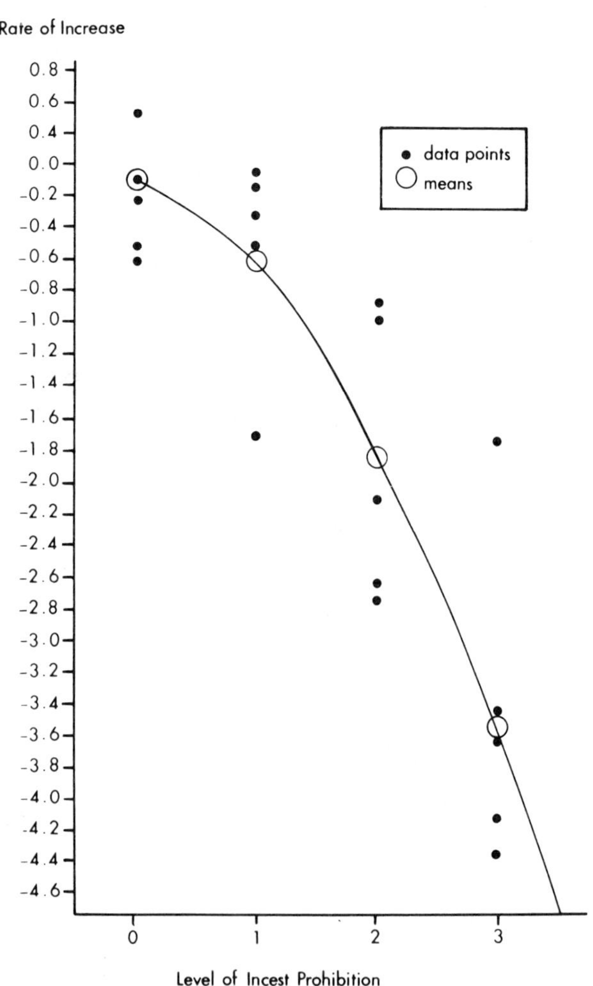

Figure 1. EFFECTS OF VARYING INCEST PROHIBITIONS ON MEAN RATE OF POPULATION INCREASE

rates favorable for expansion - that the tabu could have been instituted successfully. It is, of course, quite possible to run test simulations to see what those rates must have been for the tabu (at various levels) to have been instituted without throwing the population into decline.

We cannot know how rapidly the favorable results of an incest tabu might have taken hold - how rapidly internal strife was diminished, or how soon inimical relations with other groups developed into those of exchange of women, trade of goods, and the building of larger social structures. The immediate effects on population, as in the case of lower homicide rates, might not have been great at all. But the long term effects in the development of the human psyche through permanence of role relationships, on the symbolism of new and complex relationships, and on more intense development of language through increased intergroup communication were doubtless enormous - everyone seems to agree about that, even if they refuse to think about how it might have happened. I do not want to speculate much on how it happened - no further than to point out that these developments must have rested on one, single horseshoe nail - demographic conditions that allowed the destructive effects of the tabu to be overcome, so that the benefits could accrue. Slater (1959) makes a similar argument but on different grounds.

It goes without saying that this argument is sensitive to N and that the population of 65 is a breeding population, not necessarily an entire social group. The simulation is crude, since it ought to have treated actual social groups in occasional contact, with different probabilities of intermarriage. You will see of course that subdivision of a population of size 65 into smaller discrete groups in occasional contact diminishes breeding population size and thus makes institution of the tabu still more "difficult" in these demographic terms. On the other hand, 65 is very likely much too small a number for a total primitive breeding population, alive at the same instant in time, over all ages. It is more likely that the size of the breeding pool would be on the order of two or three hundred. However, such a pool would consist of more than a single group, and if account were taken of only occasional contact between these groups and probabilities of intermarriage of less than 1, the effective breeding pool size would be smaller than two or three hundred. At this moment in our work we do not know how much smaller it would be, although we hope to draw on Nancy Howell's Bushman data, and to refine the simulation accordingly. In any case, the general relationship between the scope of the incest tabu and population viability should remain as demonstrated.

A further problem with this simulation stems from the fact that POPSIM (as of this writing) does not permit polygyny. If polygyny were unrestricted, any woman who might be excluded from the breeding pool by an incest tabu could be included immediately by marrying someone else and would lose no portion of her reproductive span. (Almost all the women in this simulation eventually married, but some were delayed by the incest tabu.) One can skirt the difficulty by giving unmarried women in the POPSIM simulation the same fertility rates as married women; of course, the incest tabu would then have no effect whatever. But polygyny is never unrestricted, and this model would be misleading. At this point we can only say that the presence of polygyny would diminish the strength of the effect noted, to a degree as yet unknown and dependent on the actual achievement of immediate polygyny, but that it would not affect the direction of the relationship.

ASYMMETRICAL MARRIAGE SYSTEMS

The second problem has a longer history of quantified research and has to do with the effects on the distribution of consanguineal marriages, of asymmetry, or bias, in the distributions of certain characteristics of spouses, particularly bias in age.

Let me begin with age. The first observations on this problem, to my knowledge, were made by Jane Goodale in her doctoral dissertation on the Tiwi (1959) and a subsequent paper in *Ethnology* (1962), in which she pointed out that the high frequency of matrilateral cross-cousin marriage (as opposed to patrilateral cross-cousin marriage) was attributable to the extreme difference in age between husbands and wives. Frederick Rose came independently to the same conclusion in 1960 in his work on Groote Eylandt. In his dispute with Leach (1965) over the nature of asymmetrical exchange, he made a cryptic remark (which he unfortunately did not follow up) that it did not matter if the men were older than their wives or the wives older than their husbands (I will come back to this point later). Both Goodale and Rose used simple, mechanistic models, predicting direction but not intensity of effect. Most readers are probably familiar with Hajnal's third independent discovery and his important paper in 1963, which did attempt to predict the intensity of the effect; he did not, however, observe that the direction of the age bias did not affect the consanguineal skewing (for example, marriages between matrilateral cross-cousins will be more frequent than those between patrilateral cross-cousins, not only when males are on the average older than their wives, but also when females are on the average older than their husbands). MacCluer and Schull did a computer simulation of this same problem in 1970, commenting on Hajnal's model. I came rather late to the problem, having stumbled on the solution in an investigation not of bias in age, but of the kind of asymmetry of flow of mates from one social group to the next, which Gilbert and I demonstrated in 1966 using simulation, and which Salisbury showed empirically (1956, cf. Leach 1957). It turns out that if you try a number of possible approaches (1) the direction of the bias does not affect consanguineal skewing; (2) any source of the bias (e.g., age, residence, etc.) produces consanguineal skewing of the same kind, provided that the children of a marriage are all implicated in some regular degree by the existence of the bias between their parents; (3) kinship types, characterized by the source of the bias, distribute in successive generations according to the cells of the Pascal triangle; and (4) transformational rules (in the sense that the phrase is used by linguists and analysts of kinship terminology) can be written to reduce these types in any column of the triangle, to the uppermost cell of each column. For an explanation of (3) and (4) above, see Hammel (1973).

These attributes are all quite regular, and of course have profound implications not only for biased (i.e., anisotropic) gene flow but also for theories of social structure, kinship, and cultural symbolism. Most of us who have ventured a materialistic explanation for asymmetric exchange, like Rose, Salisbury, and myself, have been stung by Leach's lash for our pains (1957, 1965, personal communication), but I think he is avoiding a very real problem in the development and maintenance of symbolic systems (Hammel 1971, 1973).

All of this, of course, is an anthropological problem and not one just in simulation, but the two are connected. The mechanistic models proposed by most of us have been much too rigid, and Hajnal's seems difficult to apply to biases other than age, since it presupposes a knowledge of the variances involved. It would be most useful to see by simulation whether the source and direction of bias between spouses has an effect on the degree of consanguineal skewing.

In anticipation of our hoped-for ability to compute on the basis of status, or wealth, or territorial position, or skin color, we made a few test runs at two levels of age bias: husband averaging 2.6 and 17.1 years older than wife. The results are given in Table 1; it can be seen that marriages between matrilateral cross-cousins are more frequent when the difference is 17.1 years than when it is 2.6. The apparent patrilateral bias at the 2.6 level is probably the result of chance. We would have tested at a mean

Population	Mean age difference (o-^{o}) (years)	Cross-cousin types Matrilateral	Patrilateral	Total (number of marriages)
I	2.6	25	33	(133)
II	17.1	27	5	(172)

$\chi^2 = 12.8$, d.f. = 1, $p < .0005$ (one tailed)

Table 1. NUMBERS OF FULL FIRST AND SECOND COUSIN MARRIAGES IN TWO POPULATIONS, SPOUSES IN SAME GENERATION*

*Incest prohibitions: parent-child, sibling, half sibling, uncle-niece, aunt-nephew

age difference of zero and at several levels of difference of the opposite direction, with wife older than husband, but POPSIM as yet handles that kind of manipulation only with difficulty, a matter which we hope to remedy soon.

Again, in this simple problem we can see that the simulation is working in the right direction, and our confidence in it is sustained. But we can also see that some kinds of problems require careful attention to detail. For example, this particular simulation does not lead us to expect any effects on fertility of an increasing difference in age between husband and wife (husband older), provided that remarriage of widows is relatively easy. But in reality we ought to expect fertility to have some inverse relationship with age difference, particularly if the kind of marriage and remarriage found among the Tiwi and on

Groote Eylandt is any guide. Women in their years of maximal fecundability are coupled with men of diminished virility - whether we take virility to mean viability and quantity of sperm or capacity for sexual relations; on the other hand, men of full virility have their first marriages to women already in their declining years, whom they have inherited from some deceased male kinsman. There is some wife-stealing and philandering in these groups, but the accuracy of the spears of offended husbands evidently keeps extramarital relations from becoming an important demographic factor. Here we see that for the accurate modeling of some kinds of relationships it is necessary to specify demographic rates at a lower level than usual, and rates about which we have poor knowledge - ovulation and implantation, viability of sperm, frequency of intercourse, miscarriage - in other words the rates of biological events that combine to give us fertility. The expense of programming, and of running the simulations, goes up with its reality, as we might expect.

But if accuracy can be achieved at reasonable expense, and if the problems to be attacked justify the effort, then the game is worth the candle. The problems mentioned here - incest and consanguineal marriage skewing - are of little interest to any but a few specialists. But there are problems of wider range involving household structure, the efficacy of changes in inheritance or tax laws in altering reproductive behavior, the efficacy of different methods of contraception, and many others. For these, the problems of the incest tabu and of matrilateral cross-cousin marriage are just a beginning and a means to test the techniques of simulation.

REFERENCES

Acsadi, G. and J. Nemeskeri 1970. History of Human Life Span and Mortality. Budapest: Akademiai Kiado.

Gilbert, J. P. and E. A. Hammel 1963. Computer analysis of problems in kinship and social structure. Annual Meeting of the American Anthropological Association, San Francisco, November 1963.

Gilbert, J. P. and E. A. Hammel 1966. Computer analysis of problems in kinship and social structure, American Anthropologist 68: 71-93.

Goodale, J. C. 1959. The Tiwi women of Melville Island, North Australia. Ph.D. dissertation, Univ. of Pennsylvania.

Goodale, J. C. 1962. Marriage contracts among the Tiwi, Ethnology 1: 452-466.

Hajnal, J. 1963. Concepts of random mating and the frequency of consanguineous marriages, Proceedings of the Royal Society, B, 159: 125-177.

Hammel, E. A. 1971. On the false consciousness of man: Levi-Strauss in the Miocene. Annual Meeting of the American Anthropological Association, New York, November 1971.

Hammel, E. A. 1973. The matrilateral implications of structural cross-cousin marriage. Paper presented at Advanced Seminar in Anthropology and Demography, School of American Research, Santa Fe, N.M., January 1973.

Homans, G. 1941. English Villagers of the 13th Century. Cambridge, Mass.: Harvard Univ. Press.

Horvitz, D. G., F. G. Giesbrecht, B. V. Shah and P. A. Lachenbruch 1971. POPSIM, a demographic simulation program, In Monograph 12, Carolina Population Center, Univ. of North Carolina.

Kunstadter, P., R. Buhler, F. Stephan and C. Westoff

1963. Demographic variability and preferential marriage patterns, American Journal of Physical Anthropology 22: 511-519.

Laslett, P. 1971. The World We Have Lost (second edition). London: Methuen.

Leach, E. R. 1965. Unilateral cross-cousin marriage--reply to Rose, Man, No. 12.

Leach, E. R. 1957. On asymmetric marriage systems, American Anthropologist 59: 343.

MacCluer, J. W. and W. J. Schull 1970. Frequencies of consanguineous marriage and accumulation of inbreeding in an artificial population, American Journal of Human Genetics 22: 160-175.

Rose, F. G. G. 1960. Classification of Kin, Age Structure and Marriage Amongst the Groote Eylandt Aborigines. Berlin: Akademie Verlag.

Salisbury, R. 1956. Asymmetrical marriage systems, American Anthropologist 58: 639-655.

Slater, M. K. 1959. Ecological factors in the origin of incest, American Anthropologist 61: 1042-1059.

Smith, T. E. 1960. The Cocos-Keeling Islands: a demographic laboratory, Population Studies 14: 94-130.

COMPUTER SIMULATION OF INCEST PROHIBITION AND CLAN PROSCRIPTION RULES IN CLOSED, FINITE POPULATIONS

KENNETH MORGAN

INTRODUCTION

In classical population genetic models, little attention is given to details of population structure. In recent years, however, it has become apparent that the student of human population genetics will often have to be a student of the mathematics of population as well (for example, Cavalli-Sforza and Bodmer 1971). The body of theory concerned with changes in the genetic structure of finite populations does not adequately treat certain natural population phenomena such as age-and-sex dependent vital rates, changing age composition, and stochastic fluctuation of vital rates occasioned by small population numbers. Furthermore, in the study of inbreeding in human populations, it has become apparent that even such basic concepts as "random mating" may not apply in the formal, classical sense of population genetics (MacCluer and Schull 1970). Interest in the genetics and demography of technologically primitive populations and also those undergoing cultural transition has contributed additional complexities to genetic model building by the inclusion of socio-cultural parameters. Computer simulation of such complex systems is a useful approach in both model building and hypothesis testing, especially where there as yet exists no complete and tractable mathematical formulation of the system.

In this article I will report on demographic results obtained with a general microsimulation model for populations of small size. These experiments focus on the effects of social structure, marriage rules, and stochastic processes on the growth and evolution of initially small and slowly growing populations. The primary impetus for the modeling came from an intensive historical-demographic study of a Navajo Indian community in New Mexico from the period of its re-establishment, around 1870-1890, to recent years (Morgan 1968, 1973). This population, like other Navajo communities, has experienced very rapid population growth over the last one hundred years as it moved away from more traditional modes of local adaptation towards inclusion in the wider American society in an economically and socio-politically marginal position. It appears that under aboriginal conditions the growth rate of the Navajo (and Apache) could not have been great. One can extend this statement to primitive culture, in general, during the paleolithic era.

It is this much earlier phase of cultural evolution, of apparent slow population growth, that I have attempted to model. This has been undertaken with the somewhat unrealistic assumption of a closed human population, and with a somewhat arbitrary choice of density- and time-independent birth and death schedules for the results reported here. There presently exists no reasonably efficient procedure for comparing different models in stochastic population simulation. Investigators will differ over the significance of certain variables for inclusion in or exclusion from a model. Not only will the logical structure and complexity of the models strongly reflect a given set of research interests, but the logical structure and flow of instructions of the computer programs will vary as well.

The initial phase of experimentation is concerned with the survival of small, closed populations and does not involve sociological constraints that may operate in addition to an age correlation among mates. For this purpose I have chosen fertility and mortality schedules which would imply a very slow rate of growth (of the order of five per thousand per year) in a stable model population. The initial sizes of the age-structured populations were 100 and 200 with equal numbers of males and females. Of primary interest are the effects of different levels of mortality and fertility (but a constant rate of natural increase), of total size, and of initial age composition on the survival of such small populations. The second set of results are from experiments on the genetic-demography of incest prohibitions and clan proscription rules, mating constraints of a type found consistently only in human societies (Aberle *et al.* 1963).

A brief description of the computer model and input data will be presented, followed by discussion of the experimental results. I would like to emphasize at this juncture that the results are essentially still in the descriptive stage; satisfactory explanation of the observations awaits additional experiments and analyses. Thus the interpretation of such general simulation experiments on the effects of incest prohibition on population viability should be viewed with caution, especially in view of the discrepancy between my results and those obtained by Hammel and Hutchinson (this volume). The genetic results from the second set of experiments will be discussed elsewhere.

THE COMPUTER MODEL

Briefly, the computer model may be characterized by its emphasis on Monte Carlo procedures and overlapping generations in a two-sex population process. Only one population is considered in a given run; the sampling unit is the individual and the unit of time corresponds to a year, as does the unit of age. The model is an approximation to a general age-dependent birth-and-death process, with interaction between the sexes through mating and marital fertility, in which the time-scale and the age-scale are discrete. Similar microsimulation models have already been well documented in the literature (for example, MacCluer 1967). A more detailed description of the computer program is available from the author in addition to a brief description which has already been presented

(Morgan 1969). It will be sufficient to point out that the mating procedure is male-dominant; the maximum number of times a male searches the pool of available females during any year and a histogram of preferred age-difference between prospective mates are specified as input data. Finally, with regard to genetic parameters, the average inbreeding coefficient is easily calculated at any census as the proportion of individuals in the population who are homozygous at a marker locus by virtue of the fact that the two alleles are identical by descent. Since every individual in the initial population is assigned a unique pair of these markers, all members of the initial population are heterozygous, non-inbred, and unrelated.

THE INPUT DATA

Mortality schedules approximating the data provided by Coale and Demeny (1966) for "South" model life table levels 1 (S-01) and 24 (S-24) were used in the first set of experiments (Figure 1). The fertility schedules for married females were chosen for each of the two mortality levels in such a way as to approximate a stable population with an intrinsic rate of natural increase of about five per thousand per year (Figure 2). The age structures of each of the initial populations for the experiments approximate the corresponding stable population as tabulated (Figure 3). Since, however, the fertility schedules as utilized here were not adjusted by the proportion of married females, and because of the interaction of the sexes, the realized rate of growth would be expected to be less than five per thousand (see below, especially in regard to discussion of results given in Table 3). In addition, except for the proportion dying prior to exact age one, no yearly graduation of schedules was undertaken. Furthermore, the probabilities used for the mortality schedules are not those of the life table five-year probabilities of dying but, instead, are the death rates (or number of

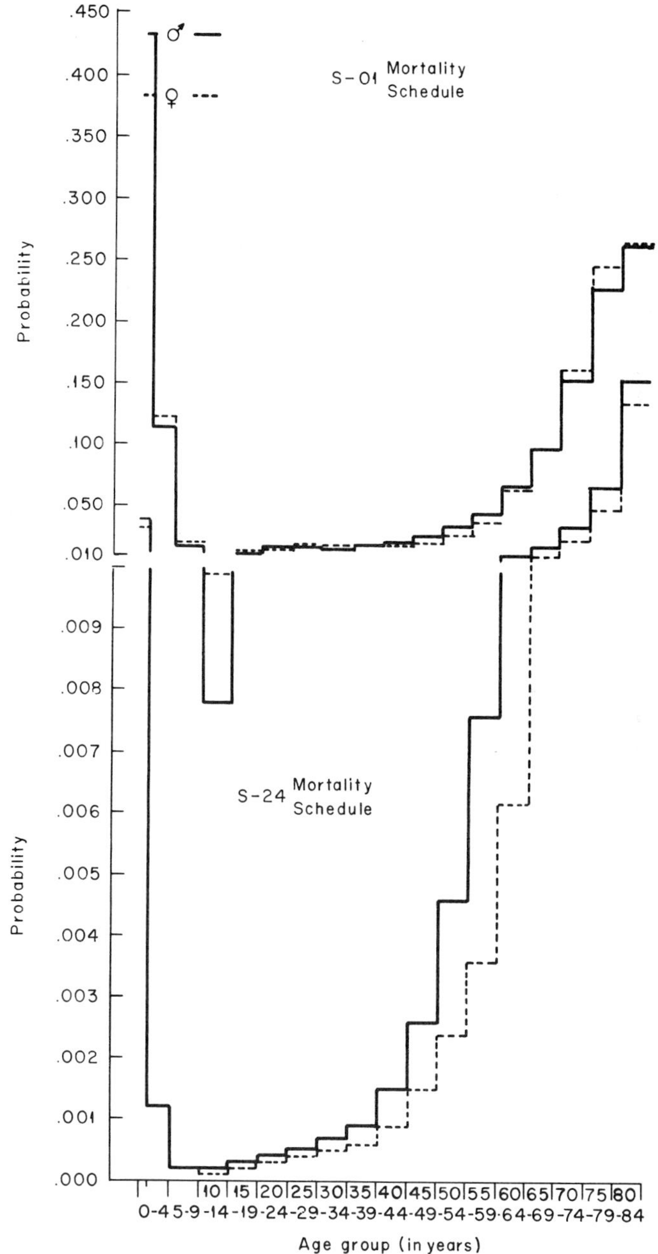

Figure 1. AGE-AND-SEX SPECIFIC MORTALITY SCHEDULES (Note change in scale for .0000-.0100)

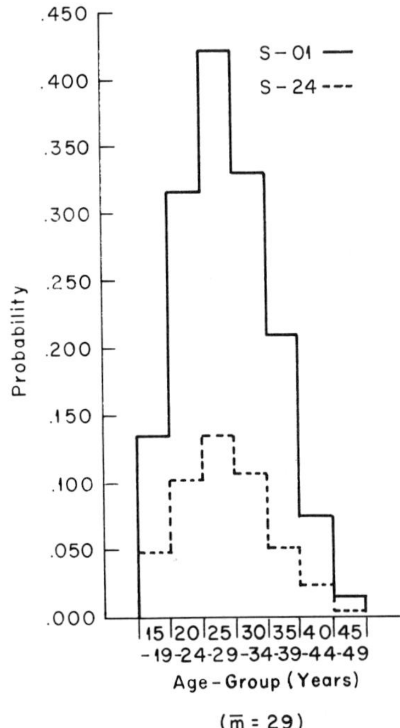

Figure 2. AGE-SPECIFIC FERTILITY SCHEDULES (For married females)

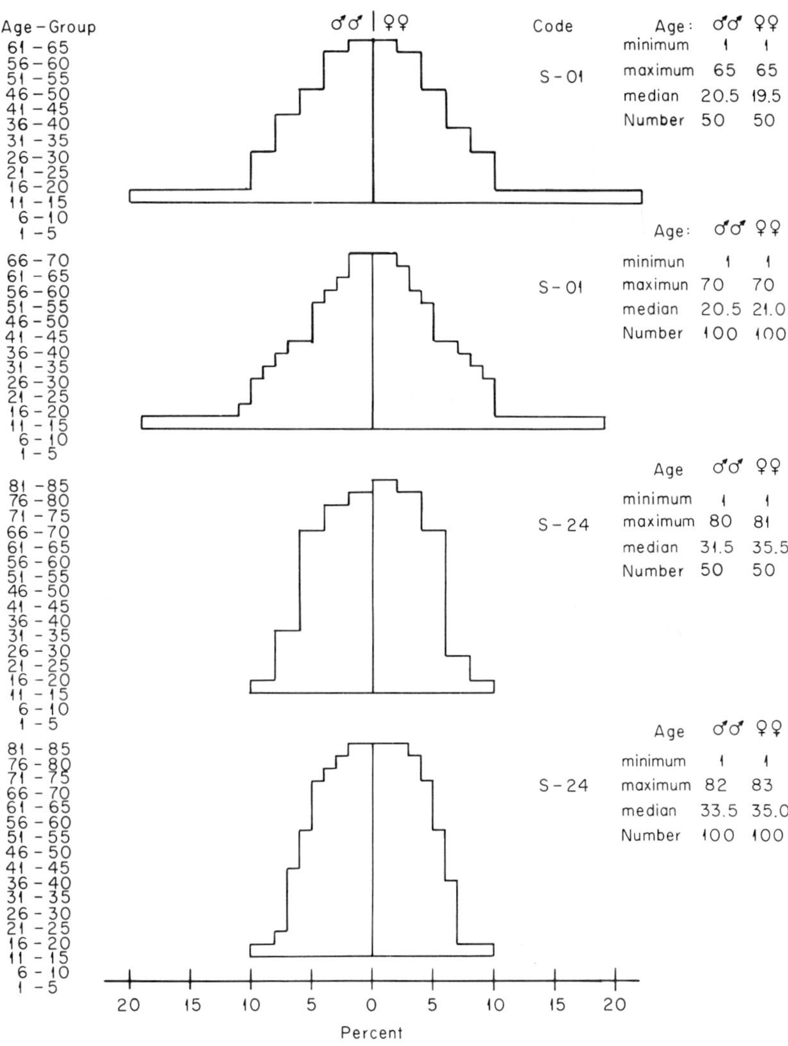

Figure 3. AGE-SEX PYRAMIDS OF INITIAL, ARTIFICIAL POPULATIONS

deaths per person-years lived) in the life table populations. The two mortality levels, S-01 (high mortality) and S-24 (low mortality), matched by corresponding levels of fertility were chosen to investigate one "regional" pattern of extremes of rates on the survival of finite populations.

All members of the input populations are unmarried; and during the first year of the run only the operation of mortality and the contraction of "marriages" among eligible surviving adults are permitted. Each eligible male is allowed (arbitrarily) a maximum of five chances each year regardless of his age to draw a value at random from the input histogram of age differences for prospective mates (Figure 4) and searches the female pool for an appropriate mate. The histogram for preference of age differences of mates approximates a normal distribution, males being on the average four years older than females, with a standard deviation of about the same value. The minimum ages for mating are 14 for females and 15 for males; the maximum ages are 48 and 53, respectively. For reproduction, the minimum and maximum ages chosen for females are 15 and 49, respectively, while the male reproductive period extends from 16 through 54 years of age. The maximum length of life is set at 85 years.

For the first set of experiments, widowed males immediately returned to the pool of eligible mates if they were not over the maximum age for mating. Widowed females, on the other hand, could not return to the pool of eligible mates until the next year following the death of their spouses. All marriages were monogamous. Since there were no other limitations placed on the acceptability of a chosen mate other than those discussed above, "incestuous marriages" were not explicitly prohibited.

For the second set of experiments, the following sets of conditions in all possible combinations were compared for populations of initial size 200 with S-24 age compositions and subject to the S-24 fertility and mortality schedules: incest prohibition versus consan-

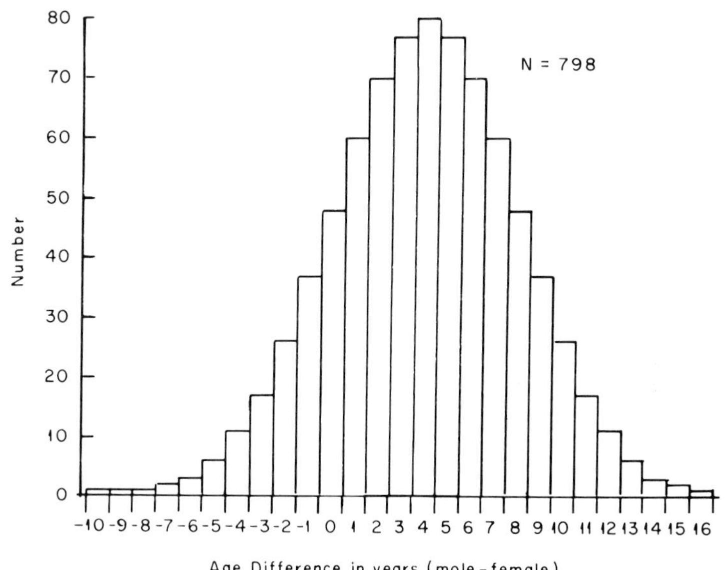

Figure 4. HISTOGRAM OF AGE-DIFFERENCE PREFERENCE FOR PROSPECTIVE MATES
(Age of male minus age of female)

guinity ignored; clan exogamy versus clan affiliations ignored; and remarriage possible versus no return to the pool of eligible mates if ever married (see below for codes of these treatments).

Each run was started with a different initial integer value as input to the random number generator. (The generator was a slightly modified version of the one described in the IBM System/360 Scientific Subroutine Package manual [IBM 1967: 54].) The maximum number of years for any run was set at 1000 for the first set of results. Most runs either did not survive through even half of this period, or terminated prior to the time limit because the growing population exceeded the storage capacity of certain arrays in the program. Summary output data were provided either every ten years or every 100 years.

For the second set of experiments, runs were terminated at the end of year 700 (the initial year being 100), or when the population exceeded 800 individuals, or when the population decreased to some fraction (usually one-fourth) of its initial size. Calculations and summary information were provided on a ten-year basis.

Abbreviations and Codes

To simplify presentation of the results and discussion, the following notation will be used:

For the first set of experiments,

> S-01(100)A stands for the initial age-structured population of size 100 (50 males and 50 females) approximating the stable population of the model South mortality level 1 life table with an implied annual rate of growth of five per thousand;
>
> S-01(200)A is defined as above, but with an initial population size of 200 individuals;
>
> S-24(100)A and S-24(200)A refer to the

initial age-structured populations for the model South mortality level 24 life table; and

S-01-P and S-24-P refer to the fertility and mortality schedules for the two different levels of mortality.

EXPERIMENTS SET 1: RESULTS AND DISCUSSION

None of the populations exposed to the high fertility-and-mortality regime (S-01-P) survived much beyond 400 years (Table 1). Initial populations of size 200 took almost twice as long to go to extinction as those of size 100 for the combinations S-01-A/S-01-P (see Set A, Table 1). In general, differential growth rates of the sexes shorten the time to extinction as suggested by the data of Set B in Table 1 where the conditional probability of a male live birth was set in favor of males, at 0.5041. This undoubtedly reflects unfavorable conditions for the realization of the maximum number of monogamous marriages. The inability of S-01-A/S-01-P runs to survive may in part result from strong stochastic effects during the initial year of the run when only mortality and marriages among eligible survivors can take place. A high probability of extinction is expected because of the closely matched and very high crude birth and death rates.

The data provided by the runs of Set C in Table 1 for the low fertility-and-mortality regime (S-24-P) also suggest that the initial size of the population is of some importance in determining the fate of the population experiencing stochastic variation of vital rates. A smaller population implies a smaller pool of eligible mates for a given individual, especially when criteria for eligibility are not relaxed. Furthermore, that segment of the population (married females of certain ages) which is solely responsible for renewal via the production of births may very likely contain too few or even no members during the early years of the population, especially under a

Run Code No.	Initial Population			Termination of Run	
	Year	Total Size	Number Deaths	At Year	Total Size
Set A; S-01-A/S-01-P; P(♂/LB) = .4959					
1	0	100	4	233	1[a]
2	0	100	4	214	7[a]
3	0	100	4	210	3[a]
4	0	100	6	285	2[b]
5	0	100	6	204	1[b]
6	0	200	11	446	1[b]
7	0	200	15	405	5[b]
8	0	200	2	426	1[b]
9	0	200	3	441	2[a]
10	0	200	10	360	7[b]

Run Code No.	Initial Population			Termination of Run	
	Year	Total Size	Number Deaths	Year	Total Size
Set B; S-01-A/S-01-P; P(♂/LB) = .5041					
11	0	200	8	326	5[b]
12	0	200	9	540	5[b]
13	0	200	11	331	2[b]
14	0	200	10	339	1[a]
15	0	200	10	395	3[b]
16[c]	0	200	7	366	1[b]
Set C; S-24-A/S-24-P; P(♂/LB) = .5021					
17	0	100	2	350	7
18	0	100	0	645	4[a]
19	0	100	1	313	2[b]
20	0	100	1	229	3[b]
21	0	100	1	365	2[a]
22	0	200	1	915	2[a]

[a]Number of males = 0.

[b]Number of females = 0.

[c]Number of chances for eligible male to search female pool for mate of chosen age raised to 6 from 5 for each year.

Table 1. SUMMARY DATA ON NON-SURVIVING, CLOSED POPULATIONS (All initial populations have equal numbers of males and females) (See text for explanation of code symbols)

regime of continuing high mortality. No runs of combination S-24(100)A/S-24-P survived, but the time to extinction was longer as well as more variable than that for S-01(100)A/S-01-P. One population out of five of combination S-24(200)A/S-24-P did die out during the time allotted (run number 22, Table 1) but not until after more than 900 years. The younger age distributions of the S-01-A initial populations were more favorable to immediate growth of the population, in comparison to the older S-24-A sets, when both were subject to the same S-24-P regime (for example, see Table 2).

With regard to the behavior of surviving S-24-P runs, the data in Table 2 demonstrate a fair amount of variability (also shown in the runs discussed in the next section) in vital rates over time, and often a substantial difference between the sexes in crude vital rates during the same time periods (data not shown). From the one-sex model life tables of level S-24, the crude birth rates should have been of the order of 15.7 per thousand for females and 16.4 per thousand for males, with corresponding crude death rates of 10.7 and 11.4 per thousand for females and males in the stable model population. In another set of experiments in which the interaction between the sexes was removed by making reproduction solely dependent on the age of females (marriage no longer being a part of the computer program) and processing the males as a "passive" subpopulation (see Table 3, next section), the expected rate of natural increase of five per thousand per year was obtained, on the average, after about 300 years of run.

Experiments are planned for the study of minimum limits of population size which would permit small populations, subject to stochastic processes and low rates of growth, to survive over long periods of time, of the order of 1000 years. Opening the populations to small amounts of inmigration will be explored as a means to counteract not only population extinction, but also drift of gene frequencies. As many human population biologists have remarked, it is doubtful

Run Code No.	23			24			25		
Initial Population Size	S-24-A 200			S-24-A 200			S-01-A 200		
	Average Annual Crude Rates of Ten-year Periods ($^{o}/oo$)								
	Birth Rate	Death Rate	Natural Increase	Birth Rate	Death Rate	Natural Increase	Birth Rate	Death Rate	Natural Increase
Years of Run (after initial year)									
1-100 Minimum	11.5	10.1	-1.3	12.4	8.5	0.4	10.3	0.9	-3.4
Maximum	16.9	13.9	5.3	18.8	14.2	7.5	22.2	13.8	18.7
Mean	14.6	12.6	2.0	15.9	11.6	4.3	15.6	9.7	5.9
101-200 Minimum	6.6	10.0	-7.0	12.3	10.4	-1.9	10.9	8.3	-2.3
Maximum	20.5	15.2	7.0	15.4	15.4	4.7	16.7	15.6	5.1
Mean	14.6	12.8	1.7	13.8	13.2	0.6	14.1	12.6	1.5
201-300 Minimum	7.5	10.5	-8.3	7.6	8.1	-5.1	11.4	12.0	-1.5
Maximum	17.4	18.8	3.7	19.1	17.2	11.1	16.3	16.3	4.3 [b]
Mean	12.7	13.9	-1.2	14.6	13.7	0.9	14.4	13.5	0.9
301-400 Minimum	12.2	10.8	-5.5	12.9	9.7	-3.1			
Maximum	18.7	18.4	8.0	17.2	16.4	6.8			
Mean	15.4	14.3	1.1	15.1	12.9	2.2			
401-500 Minimum	10.9	9.3	-1.4	12.8	10.9	-0.6			
Maximum	17.9	15.3	7.1	18.7	13.4	6.5			
Mean	14.8	12.0	2.8	15.1	12.1	3.0			
501-600 Minimum	10.3	12.2	-3.6	12.7	10.5	0.0			
Maximum	17.4	16.2	5.2	17.4	16.4	5.4			
Mean	14.0	13.9	0.1	15.2	12.5	2.7			
601-700 Minimum	11.4	10.3	-4.1	14.2	10.7	0.8			
Maximum	16.7	15.5	6.4	18.0	13.4	6.2 [a]			
Mean	14.2	13.4	0.8	15.9	12.1	3.7			
701-800 Minimum	11.6	9.8	-1.5						
Maximum	18.1	14.8	7.3						
Mean	15.4	11.8	3.7						
801-900 Minimum	13.1	11.5	-0.7						
Maximum	16.6	16.2	5.1						
Mean	15.0	12.8	2.3						
901-960 Minimum	13.0	10.0	-0.8						
Maximum	18.7	14.0	7.7						
Mean	16.6	12.5	4.1						

[a]Ten-year average values for years 601-660.

[b]Ten-year average values for years 201-240.

Table 2. SUMMARY DATA ON GROWTH OF THREE POPULATIONS EXPOSED TO LOW MORTALITY AND LOW FERTILITY RATES (S-24-P) (Values given are for sexes combined; rates are per thousand)

that human populations remain closed to migration for any significant number of generations.

The results obtained so far are consistent with the expectation of greater survival probabilities under low versus high rates of birth and death. For the simple birth-and-death process where λ is the birth rate and μ the death rate in a stable population, then in the limit as time increases indefinitely, the Malthusian rate is found to be $R^* = 1/\mu$ and the probability of extinction is found to be $p(0) = \mu/\lambda$ for μ less than or equal to one, and $p(0) = 1$ otherwise (Goodman 1967; Keyfitz 1968: 366-368). Of course this latter model is overly simplified with regard to the experiments at hand, since we are more properly dealing with a modeling of an age-dependent and sex-dependent birth-and-death process (see Goodman 1967 for derivation of explicit equations for the probabilities of extinction under different models of birth-and-death processes; also, Keyfitz 1968: 399-412). Nevertheless as a crude illustration, we note that the birth and death rates from the model life table data imply a probability of extinction for the S-01 schedules of 0.913 for males and 0.912 for females; for the schedules from level S-24 the corresponding probabilities are 0.696 and 0.682. Both regimes have annual rates of natural increase of five per thousand. Clearly, we have only approximated the model life tables and, furthermore, have the additional complexity of interaction of the two sexes via marriage. Stochastic variability of the vital rates and numbers of marriages, thereby affecting the numbers and composition of future cohorts, contributes to the amplitude of oscillations in the age classes which results in increased variability of population numbers while the population is small and far from age-structure equilibrium.

EXPERIMENTS SET 2: RESULTS AND DISCUSSION

The second set of experiments was designed to test the effects of mating rules on the demographic behavior of closed populations of composition S-24(200)A/S-24-P. The two kinds of mating rules investigated overlap in their effects on the frequency of consanguineous matings (see, also, Kluckhohn and Griffith 1951). They are as follows: Incest prohibitions were formulated to exclude matings among individuals related within three generations of each other - that is, first cousins, grandparents and grandchildren (which is rather unlikely anyway because of the great discrepancy of age), uncles and nieces along with aunts and nephews, and closer relatives were prohibited from mating with each other. Results of simulations incorporating incest prohibition are coded with a numeral "2" in the first position of a 3-tuple code. Based on the matrilineal clan proscriptions against marriage observed among the Navajo (Kluckhohn and Leighton 1962; Spuhler and Kluckhohn 1953), a second set of rules was tested: One may not marry a member of one's own clan nor may one marry a member of one's father's clan. Members of the initial population are all clan "heterozygotes" and are distributed approximately equally among four clans. Clan exogamy is indicated by a "2" in the second position of the code. Additionally, the effect of permitting return to the pool of eligible mates after the death of a spouse (contingent upon age) was tested. This is indicated by a "-1" in the last (right-most) position of the code. Thus, eight different kinds of mating restrictions were investigated using the same initial age-structured population of size 200 and low mortality and low fertility rates. Usually, five runs were initiated for each treatment and were followed for varying lengths of time but generally not exceeding 600 years. The treatments are summarized as follows:

0,0,0 = incest permitted, clan rules ignored, no remarriage;

0,0,-1 = incest permitted, clan rules ignored, remarriage possible;

0,2,0 = incest permitted, clan exogamy only, no remarriage;

0,2,-1 = incest permitted, clan exogamy only, remarriage possible;

2,0,0 = incest prohibited, clan rules ignored, no remarriage;

2,0,-1 = incest prohibited, clan rules ignored, remarriage possible;

2,2,0 = incest prohibited, clan exogamy only, no remarriage;

2,2,-1 = incest prohibited, clan exogamy only, remarriage possible.

Thus, for example, all of the various runs from the first set of experiments would be coded (0,0,-1) differing only in initial age distribution, size, and schedules of vital events. For the second set of experiments, we can consider the runs coded (0,0,-1) as control runs.

The results of these experiments for the first two or three hundred years of run are summarized in Table 3 with respect to average population growth. Results of different treatments were combined on the basis of the outcome of the analysis of variance (ANOVA) on the split factorial design given in Table 4, to be discussed later. The effects of the interaction of the sexes via marriage on the average growth rate may be appreciated immediately by comparing the results of a simple, modified one-sex model (discussed previously, above) with the other results in Table 3. All of the runs are graphed and compared in Figures 5 through 9.

At these low rates of growth almost all the populations subjected additionally to the clan proscription rules died out by around 400 years of run. These results are not unexpected, given the small number of

Combined Runs			Estimated Ten-Year Period Growth Rates	
Codes	Number of Runs	Years	Average of Means	Average of Sample Standard Deviations
2,0,0 2,0,-1	10	0-100	0.029	0.0026
		100-200	0.020	0.0024
		200-300	0.034	0.0022
0,0,0 0,0,-1	10	0-100	0.031	0.0033
		100-200	0.004	0.0031
		200-300	0.020	0.0027
0,2,0 0,2,-1 2,2,0 2,2,-1	20	0-100	0.015	0.0042
		100-200	-0.046	0.0047
Modified Model One-Sex Fertility	5	0-100	0.047	0.0030
		100-200	0.039	0.0038
		200-300	0.051	0.0022

Table 3. AVERAGES OF TEN-YEAR PERIOD GROWTH RATES OBTAINED BY LINEAR REGRESSION OF LOG_e TRANSFORMATION OF TOTAL POPULATION SIZE AT TEN-YEAR INTERVALS

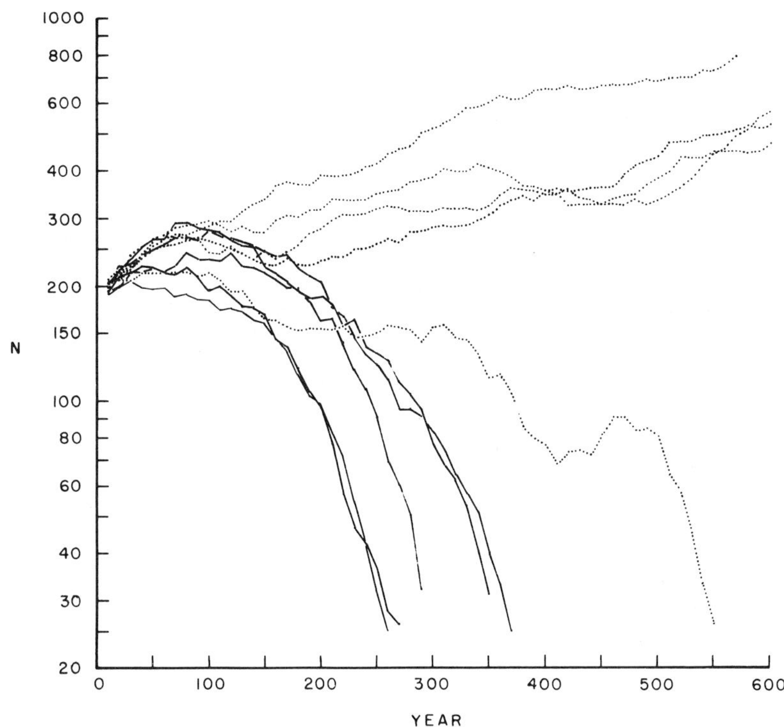

Figure 5. POPULATION SIZE IN FIVE POPULATIONS OF TYPE (0,0,0) (····) AND FIVE POPULATIONS OF TYPE (0,2,0) (——)

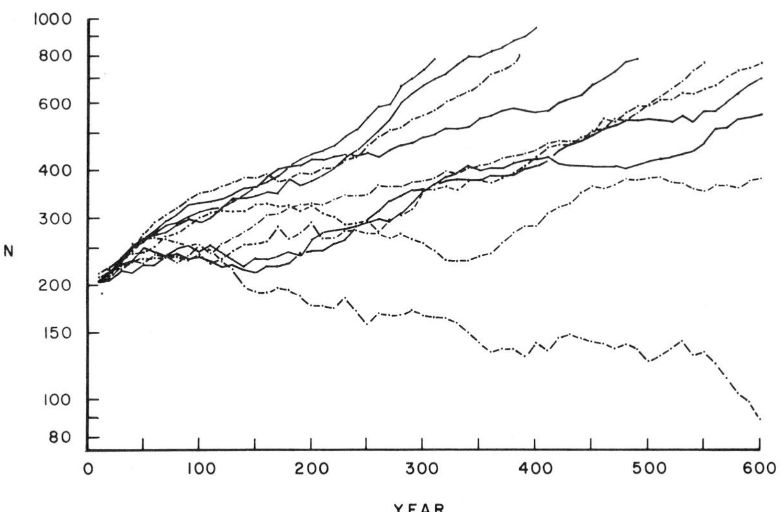

Figure 6. POPULATION SIZE IN FIVE POPULATIONS OF TYPE (0,0,-1) (-·-·-) AND FIVE POPULATIONS OF TYPE (2,0,-1) (——)

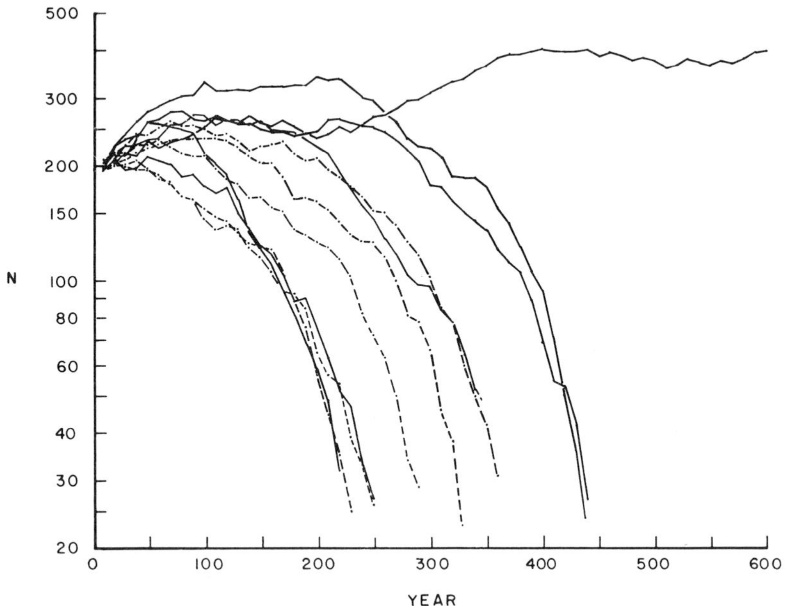

Figure 7. POPULATION SIZE IN FIVE POPULATIONS OF TYPE (0,2,-1) (-·-·-) AND SIX POPULATIONS OF TYPE (2,2,0) (——)

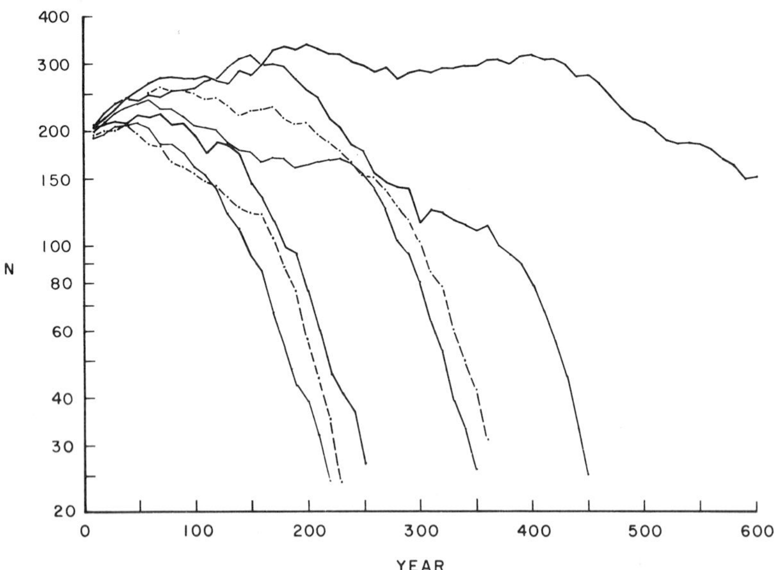

Figure 8. POPULATION SIZE IN TWO POPULATIONS OF TYPE (0,2,-1) (-·-·-) AND FIVE POPULATIONS OF TYPE (2,2,-1) (——)

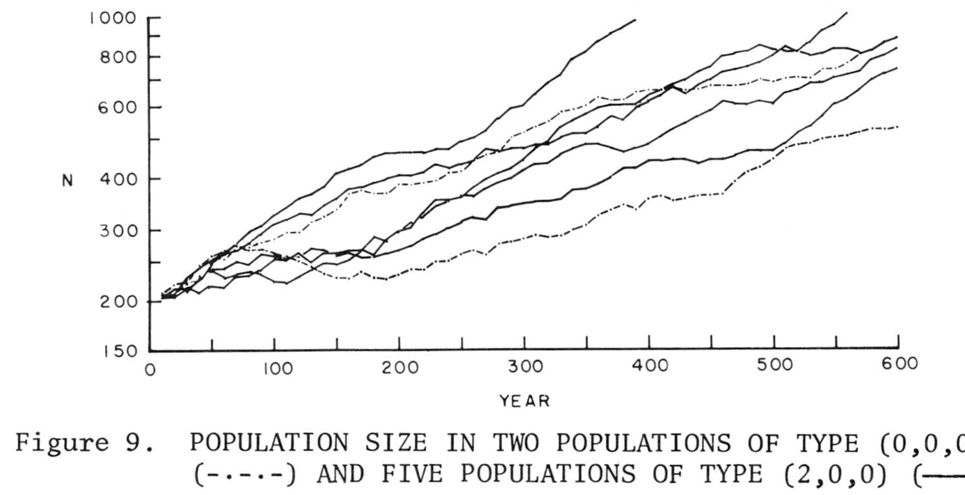

Figure 9. POPULATION SIZE IN TWO POPULATIONS OF TYPE (0,0,0) (-·-·-) AND FIVE POPULATIONS OF TYPE (2,0,0) (——)

exogamous clans to begin with and the probable loss of clans, stochastically, over time. For a somewhat analogous situation that has been discussed in the demographic literature, McFarland (1970) derives explicit expressions for the effects of group size on the availability of marriage partners under the conditions of monogamy, and endogamy and equal numbers of males and females. As the group size increases, the expected proportion of group members who are unable to find eligible mates decreases monotonically towards a limit of zero. The procedure used by McFarland would appear to be applicable to analysis of simple exogamous clan systems after some redefinition. Thus, one could consider as one's "endogamous" group, all those individuals of the opposite sex who are, at the same time, *not* members of ego's clan. It should be obvious that to maximize the proportion of marriages under this system, and in the simplest way, we would require equal numbers and sex ratio in all clans along with a very large number of clans. As the number of clans grows very large while population size remains constant, each individual tends to become the sole representative of a clan for his or her sex and the proportion of individuals who are unable to find eligible mates because of clan exogamy should decrease. The "marriage market" in any real population is obviously more complex than this. Marriages are not always monogamous in primitive populations and among the Navajo, at least, divorce and remarriage are frequent (for example, Kluckhohn 1966). Furthermore, an indefinitely large number of exogamous clans defeats the function of such a system as a means to organize a number of families into a cooperative group for certain social functions (on the sodality and other aspects of primitive social organization, see Service 1962). Also, family alliances as well as clan membership may affect marriage preferences in the Navajo system as indicated by Reichard (1928) and Kluckhohn (1956). As the number of female members of a clan becomes small, stochastic variation in the birth-and-death process will result in extinction of the clan. The problem of clan extinction should find a direct analogy in the extinction of a line of descendants in a Galton-Watson branching process (on the latter, see, for example, Keyfitz 1968: 399-412).

Prohibiting remarriage has only a small effect on population growth, as is to be expected when mortality rates are low and the breaking of marriages occurs only upon death of a spouse (see Table 4, ANOVA).

Where clan affiliation does not count in choosing a mate (Tables 3 and 4), the effect of prohibiting incest (as formulated for these experiments) is to maximize population growth and survival during the second and third hundred-year periods. It is not at all apparent, however, that the asymptotic growth rates differ on the average for the surviving populations among the four treatments which ignore clan rules (see figures). Additional experiments will be necessary to determine whether, contrary to intuition, incest prohibition actually can result in an increase in population growth rate, and if so, under what conditions. When clan proscription rules are also in operation, the additional incest prohibitions cannot be shown to have a statistically significant effect during the first two hundred years of run (Table 4). These results are not unexpected, since a large proportion of incestuous matings would involve individuals who were members of the same clan. It is perhaps more realistic to consider the behavior of these experimental populations from a shorter rather than a longer time perspective since, as we have mentioned before, it is doubtful that human populations remain closed for more than a few generations.

In microsimulation experiments reported by MacCluer (1968), the runs without sib mating grew more rapidly than did runs in which sib mating was not prohibited, on the average. However, the difference between the two sets of five runs each is not statistically significant ($p = 0.274$, one-tailed, Mann-Whitney U test; data were provided by J. W. MacCluer). There are a number of differences

Source of Variation[a]	Sums of Squares	Degrees of Freedom	Mean Squares	Probability
		Clan Affiliations Ignored		
I	0.00289	1	0.00289	less than 0.005
M	0.00012	1	0.00012	NS
IM	0.00004	1	0.00004	NS
C	0.00410	2	0.00205	less than 0.005
IC	0.00090	2	0.00045	NS
MC	0.00002	2	0.00001	NS
IMC	0.00042	2	0.00021	NS
Error	0.01482	48	0.00031	
Total	0.02332	59		
		Clan Exogamy Required		
I	0.00150	1	0.00150	NS
M	0.00227	1	0.00227	NS
IM	0.00015	1	0.00015	NS
C	0.03716	1	0.03716	less than 0.005
IC	0.00000	1	0.00000	NS
MC	0.00022	1	0.00022	NS
IMC	0.00004	1	0.00004	NS
Error	0.04426	32	0.00138	
Total	0.08561	39		

[a]I = Incest prohibition rules
M = Remarriage
C = Hundred-year interval

Table 4. ANALYSIS OF VARIANCE OF TEN-YEAR PERIOD GROWTH RATES FOR DIFFERENT COMBINATIONS OF MATING RULES

between her experiments (and model) and the ones reported on here including a much faster average rate of growth expected for her runs during the initial density-independent phase; less severe incest prohibitions (at least formally); and a more highly age-structured pool of eligible mates (at least for the males).

Additional experiments are needed to determine the extent to which the incest-prohibition effect observed here is robust to reasonable changes in birth and death schedules and to alternative programming of mating routines. We note the different results of Hammel and Hutchinson (this volume) in their micro-simulation study of the effects of the incest tabu. A satisfactory explanation of the apparent discrepancy between their results and the behavior of the present experiments has yet to be offered.

Other parameters of mating, such as age at marriage and the correlation of ages of mates at first marriage, have yet to be analyzed from these runs. Cursorily, it appears that the average correlation among mates with regard to age approaches zero in this data for surviving runs over time. Whatever mechanism is primarily responsible for the observed incest effect, it does appear that there results a decrease in the variability of the growth process during the first few hundred years within the runs. (Compare the average sample standard deviations of the regression coefficients, that is, the estimated period rates of growth, in Table 3.)

REFERENCES

Aberle, D. F., U. Bronfenbrenner, E. H. Hess, D. R. Miller, D. M. Schneider and J. N. Spuhler 1963. The incest taboo and the mating patterns of animals, American Anthropologist 65: 253-265.

Cavalli-Sforza, L. L. and W. F. Bodmer 1971. The Genetics of Human Populations. San Francisco: W. H. Freeman.

Coale, A. J. and P. Demeny 1966. Regional Model Life Tables and Stable Populations. Princeton: Princeton Univ. Press.

Goodman, L. A. 1967. The probabilities of extinction for birth-and-death processes that are age-dependent or phase-dependent, Biometrika 54: 579-596.

Hammel, E. A. and D. Hutchinson 1973. Two tests of computer micro-simulation: The effect of an incest tabu on population viability, and the effect of age differences between spouses on the skewing of consanguineal relationships between them, In Computer Simulation in Human Population Studies, B. Dyke and J. W. MacCluer (eds.) New York: Seminar Press.

IBM 1967. System/360 Scientific Subroutine Package Version II Programmer's Manual. Third edition. White Plains: International Business Machines Corporation.

Keyfitz, N. 1968. Introduction to the Mathematics of Population. Reading, Mass: Addison-Wesley.

Kluckhohn, C. 1956. Aspects of the demographic history of a small population, In Estudios Anthropologicos, J. Comas (ed.) Mexico City, pp. 359-379.

Kluckhohn, C. 1966. The Ramah Navaho. Smithsonian Institution, Bureau of American Ethnology, Anthropological Papers, Bulletin 196, No. 79, pp. 327-377.

Kluckhohn, C. and C. Griffith 1951. Population genetics and social anthropology, Cold Spring Harbor Symposia on Quantitative Biology 15: 401-408.

Kluckhohn, C. and D. Leighton 1962. The Navaho, Revised Edition. New York: Doubleday.

MacCluer, J. W. 1967. Monte Carlo methods in human population genetics: a computer model incorporating age-specific birth and death rates, American Journal of Human Genetics 19: 303-312.

MacCluer, J. W. 1968. Studies in genetic demography by Monte Carlo simulation, Ph.D. dissertation, Univ. of Michigan.

MacCluer, J. W. 1973. Computer simulation in anthropology and human genetics, In Methods and Theories in Anthropological Genetics, M. H. Crawford and P. L. Workman (eds.) Albuquerque: Univ. of New Mexico Press.

MacCluer, J. W. and W. J. Schull 1970. Frequencies of consanguineous marriage and accumulation of inbreeding in an artificial population, American Journal of Human Genetics 22: 160-175.

McFarland, D. D. 1970. Effects of group size on the availability of marriage partners, Demography 7: 411-415.

Morgan, K. 1968. The genetic demography of a small Navajo community, Ph.D. dissertation, Univ. of Michigan.

Morgan K. 1969. Monte Carlo simulation of artificial populations: the survival of small, closed populations, Paper presented at the Conference on the Mathematics of Population, Berkeley and Asilomar, California.

Morgan, K. 1973. Historical demography of a Navajo community, In Methods and Theories in Anthropological Genetics, M. H. Crawford and P. L. Workman (eds.) Albuquerque: Univ. of New Mexico Press.

Reichard, G. A. 1928. Social Life of the Navajo Indians. Columbia University Contributions to Anthropology, volume 7. New York: Columbia Univ. Press.

Service, E. R. 1962. Primitive Social Organization: An Evolutionary Perspective. New York: Random House.

Spuhler, J. N. and C. Kluckhohn 1953. Inbreeding coefficients of the Ramah Navaho population, Human Biology 25: 295-317.

ACKNOWLEDGMENTS

The author wishes to acknowledge the National Science Foundation for post-doctoral support under Training Program NSF-GZ-418 during the period 1968-1970. I would also like to acknowledge Professor R. C. Lewontin for encouragement and for computer funds provided through a Ford Foundation grant for Population Biology during my work at the University of Chicago. The Computing Center at the University of New Mexico also deserves my gratitude for computer support.

AN EMPIRICAL PERSPECTIVE ON SIMULATION MODELS OF HUMAN POPULATION

NANCY HOWELL

There are at least two kinds of wrong ways to go about studying populations of "primitive" people, either contemporary or prehistoric. One wrong way to go about it is to be excessively theoretical, treating a simulation only as a problem in computer programming; the other wrong way is to be excessively empirical, attempting only to measure some aspects of the population. The correct way, of course, is to use the model of population processes that corresponds to reality and then provide the accurate parameters to fit the model, thereby demonstrating the actual dynamics of population ebb and flow over time. My most valuable contribution at this point seems to me to be to share my experiences on the path of excessive empiricism, and to show how the need for models arises directly out of the inadequacy of empirical data. It may also be useful to demonstrate some of the uses of the Coale-Demeny "stable population models" as an alternative to Monte Carlo simulation for some kinds of problems.

My plan for this paper is to describe briefly the population which I studied, describe the data collection processes, and then discuss the analysis procedure and the use of models. The lessons that seem to emerge from this study for model builders will conclude this paper.

!KUNG OF THE DOBE AREA OF THE KALAHARI DESERT, BOTSWANA

The population under consideration is relatively well known, having been investigated during the 1950's and early 60's by Lorna Marshall (1957, 1960, 1961), John Marshall (1956), Elizabeth Marshall Thomas (1959), and others who accompanied the Marshall family on their expeditions, and by Richard Lee (1969), and Lee and Irven DeVore (1968) from 1963-64 and again from 1967-72 by Lee, DeVore and, at various times, twelve other investigators including me. The people in question lived traditionally by hunting and gathering wild foods, with no domesticated animals except the dog. Before establishing contact with Bantu and European settlers into the area, the people lacked settled villages, metal working, pottery, basket-making and agriculture. For some time the !Kung speaking people obtained some of the advantages of civilization, such as metal for arrow points, from long range trade networks. During this century, the process of culture contact has accelerated as both Bantu speaking (especially Tswana and Herero) and European people have moved into territory which previously was occupied by !Kung only. The majority of the !Kung now live in close association with other peoples, and are engaged in agriculture, herding or both, in addition to traditional ways of food collecting. In some areas, hunting and gathering is difficult or impossible on a large scale because of the density of occupation. The region of the research, however, was selected as the area where the !Kung way of life is most intact. The "Dobe area" on the Botswana side of the international border and the "Tsum!we area" on the Southwest Africa side of the border are a contiguous area occupied by what was probably a single group of about 1000 people before the border was fenced and patrolled in the middle 1960's. During the period 1963-69 we registered about 800 people on the Botswana side of the territory, including people who were born and died during the period, and people who came for visits as well as those who lived permanently in the area. During the same period several hundred Bantu people lived in the same area, and many of these people kept cattle and goats. Relatively speaking, the !Kung in this area are unacculturated: Most of them live by hunting and gathering most of the time; their survival skills in food collecting, hunting, and water finding are undulled; and they continue, by and large, to live in small grass-covered huts, dressed in animal skins, moving often and practicing the ways of their ancestors. They are far from the "pure" state of the Pleistocene, however. One of their possible responses to bad conditions is to move to a Bantu cattle post where they receive milk in exchange for working with cattle; one possible response to sickness is to go to the clinic at Tsum!we, where on a few occasions people have been flown out to the hospital at Grootefontein; and one alternative open to young men who become restless is to go into wage work, either with cattle or in the Johannesburg mines.

There is no physician or other source of European medicine in the Dobe area. People are still born and die lying on animal skins on the ground, with the aid of a kind of medical care that operates on magical principles (Lee 1967). Some people were vaccinated against smallpox after an epidemic that swept Botswana during the 1950's, but most people had not been in contact with a western doctor prior to the examinations performed by physicians associated with our expedition (Truswell and Hanson, in press). The doctors concluded that while they saw evidence of tuberculosis, rheumatic heart disease, malaria, venereal disease and intestinal parasites, by and large the people seemed to be in very good condition. They were particularly struck by the absence of obesity and degenerative disease, on the one hand, and the absence of signs of nutritional deficiency diseases on the other.

THE DATA COLLECTION

Between August 1967 and May 1969, a variety of demographic information was collected in the field. This relatively long period for data collection permitted the development of sufficient ability in the

!Kung language so that data could be collected without an interpreter, and the sufficiency of time permitted an elaborate procedure of checking, cross-checking and repeat cross-checking of items of information that seemed not to be consistent or completely understood on the first attempt. Data collected can be summarized under three headings: 1) population register and vital statistics; 2) reproductive and marital history interviews with adult women and men; and 3) relative age-rankings.

The population register was started by R. B. Lee in 1963, and continued by both of us during the 1967-69 field trip. Each person was assigned an identification number and described by name, area of residence, approximate age and physical appearance, and the names of parents, spouse and children. The register was designed to provide a positive identification of each person in the area, and was secondarily the sampling frame for the demographic study. Vital events were recorded, each birth and death being attributed to the proper person in the register. Migration was more difficult to keep track of, as usual. People were entered in the register when they were encountered, even if they only came for a short visit to the area, and notation was made on the register of news that a person was outside the area, visiting others or working. Since the people themselves have elaborate procedures for transmitting this kind of information and since R. B. Lee consistently and conscientiously collected this kind of information, it seems likely to me that the register is complete and correct for all deaths, emigrations and live births during the recording period, although there may be some omission of short term immigrants and pregnancy wastage.

Reproductive and marital histories were collected one at a time, in public, from the man or woman involved, always in the !Kung language and usually with the promise of a small gift in appreciation of cooperation. Most of the women were both truthful and accurate as far as could be ascertained from cross-checks with other people. A few people would reveal their reproductive and marital history only when it had been clearly established from others.

Finally, considerable effort was devoted in the field to collecting a rank-order of the people by age. Determining absolute age was out of the question for people born before 1963. Not only were there few outsiders in contact with this non-literate population prior to the coming of the anthropologists, but many of the outsiders didn't know what year it was either. R. B. Lee invested considerable effort in the attempt to construct event calendars, and succeeded to the extent of finding a series of events that local people knew of that could be dated outside of the area. But, as usual with event calendars, people can relate events in their adult life to datable events, but not to their own birth. Lee succeeded in establishing the important point that people who looked old by physical criteria were indeed old by event calendar reckoning. I abandoned the event calendar approach and used the older-younger feature of their kinship address system to try to place everyone in one or another local age-ranking. People know and are taught by others the correct age-ranking between themselves and all other !Kung to the extent to which anyone knows it. Most of the self placements in the age-rank seemed to be completely consistent, although there were more than a few cases where everyone agreed that A was older than B; B was older than C; and C was older than A. Such ties, which invariably involved people who seemed to be very close in age, were broken by the opinion of a respected !Kung if noticed in the field, or by a flip of a coin if not noticed until back in the U.S. Numerically more important than ties were cases where the people involved refused to offer an opinion about which one was older because the two were not acquainted and had never established a pair of kin terms. It came as a considerable surprise to me that a substantial minority of natives of the same area (consisting of several thousands of square miles of desert) did not know one another, although they might know many people who are located farther away. The !Kung kinship network is not a tightly woven one (Howell, in manuscript). To handle this problem, several different rank-orders were constructed, each for a small enough area that everyone in it was likely to know all of the others, and then the several rank-order lists were interwoven through the placement of some people in more than one list. Finally, with a bit of pushing, a single rank-order list was constructed which included everyone in the Dobe area at a target date.

Data Analysis

This, then, was the inventory of information available upon return from Africa: an age-ranking with perhaps a dozen points roughly correlated with an event calendar; an interview with each woman and each man, so that the number of pregnancies, live births and survivors to the present could be established; and a highly accurate account of the births and deaths of the previous six years. When these data are matched up with the standard techniques of demographic analysis, a disappointingly small harvest of results can be produced. These consist of Crude Birth Rates for each year 1963 to 1968, which fluctuate widely, from 18 to 70, as could be expected from the small number of births per year. The Crude Death Rates also fluctuate widely, and are likely to be artificially low due to the interference by the members of our expedition with the health of the area. Similarly the Immigration Rates are likely to be affected by the attractive or repulsive aspects of our expedition's presence in the area. In the absence of age estimates, the only retrospective measure of fertility that can be constructed is the number of children born to the women who say that they have completed their child bearing years.

In order to proceed with the analysis, an estimate of the age of each individual is needed. While the levels of fertility and mortality of the past are precisely what we want to investigate, we can work with the knowledge that whatever those levels were in the past, they produced a population which now has an age distribution which is a product of them, and that population is internally connected in a way that has to be consistent with them. To give a concrete example, whatever the shape of the age distribution (and one usually thinks of a regular pyramid, with males on one side, females on the other, and the youngest at the bottom) the difference in age between mothers and their first born children should not differ systematically over the life span. In other words, if there is a 20 year difference on the average between mothers and young children, there should be about the same difference in age between adults and their aged mothers. Finding that there is a 30 year difference or a 10 year difference according to a method of estimating ages should cause us to doubt the method.

The strategy used to estimate the ages of the !Kung has been to fit a stable population model age distribution over the rank-order of ages that was collected in the field. The model chosen was selected on the basis of an estimate of completed family size, a judgment about the point in the rank-order of ages that separates those ten years old and younger from those older, and a guess about the level of mortality that one would find in a population like this one. The preliminary estimates were based upon "West Model 5" in the Coale-Demeny series (Coale and Demeny 1966).

The percentages at each 5-year age group and younger were then applied to the age-ranking, and an exact estimate of age was determined for every person in the ranking. When subjected to the tests of internal consistency, such as the difference in age between mother and oldest child, this first approximation seemed to be acceptable. These age estimates, therefore, were attached to the data on individuals and an almost conventional demographic analysis could begin (for results of this analysis, see Howell, in press).

Before considering the reasons why the analysis is "almost" conventional (primarily due to the small numbers involved), it may be useful to consider the assumptions which have been made by the use of stable population theory, and the extent to which these assumptions have to be accepted blindly or conditionally. The assumptions of stable population analysis may seem strong to those who work with Monte Carlo models. One has to be willing to specify that the population is closed to migration, which is unlikely to be true in any real-world population. The weaker form of the assumption, that net migration is zero, may be applicable in some places, and probably is so in an area like the !Kung region where the migrants are likely to be whole families on both sides of the border. Where the age-distributions of immigration and emigration differ, as typically is the case in rural-urban migration, the failure of this assumption may make the stable population models inapplicable, or a special adjustment for the processes of migration may have to be made.

A less obvious assumption that is required by stable population theory is that the population in question is characterized by the same biological parameters as those populations that the models are based upon, which are essentially all of the adequately studied national populations. This assumption does not require that the population in question have the same levels of fertility and mortality that the well-studied populations have: One can guess that any population where these estimates are needed will have higher fertility and mortality than the relatively advanced nations which can afford to collect accurate demographic information. What one must assume is that the underlying fertility of the population is established at approximately the same ages and that relative fertility varies over the life-cycle in approximately the same way, reaching a maximum during the women's twenties, declining during their thirties and becoming negligible during the forties.

The assumptions concerning the age-distribution

of mortality are similar to those of fertility, and are the area where stable population theory has the most to contribute to the discussion of simulation of human populations. Stable population models require the acceptance of the age-specific pattern of mortality described in the family of model life tables that is being used. There are four patterns (or "families") of model life tables presented by Coale and Demeny, which were constructed from actual life tables from regions of Europe. Coale advises use of the "West" family of models for the study of areas outside of Europe, as it is based upon the largest number of cases and adequately describes some populations in Asia that are equally well-studied. Coale would not attempt to argue that these four are the only age-specific patterns of mortality in the world: in fact there are probably an infinite number, depending upon the size of the deviation from other patterns that is considered critical for establishing a new type. But worry about the choice of one family of models over another should not be allowed to distract attention from the much more powerful finding of the essential similarity between the four models (and presumably others yet to be established) in the age-specific pattern of mortality. Plotting the age-specific probability of death for the four families at the same overall level of mortality (i.e., same expectation of life at birth) reveals large similarities and small differences between the patterns. All of the model life tables show a probability of death that is relatively high at birth, and which declines regularly until it reaches the life-time low point, around the age of ten. From about ten to about fifty, the probability curve is basically flat, rising very slowly. After the age of fifty, the probability of death during each year increases sharply and it goes on increasing until there is no one left to be at risk of dying. The differences between model life-tables by *level* of mortality are primarily differences in the probability of dying at each age, that is to say, the height of the probability curve. Differences between families of curves have to do with the relative distribution of mortality at different ages, in such matters as the slope of the decline during the early childhood years, the relative amount of increase during the fifty-year-old decade as opposed to the sixty-year-old decade.

These overwhelming similarities in the age-specific propensity to die raise the biological question of what are the causes of these similarities. In a simple sense, it seems to be clear that the age-specific mortality curves are a product of the interaction of an organism with an age-specific set of weaknesses and vulnerabilities with a large set of causal agents of death. It seems very likely to me that the reality behind the different families of life tables is different mixes of causal agents of death, rather than differences in the genetic composition of the populations, but I am not qualified to judge this question. A useful tool for people interested in pursuing the differences in mortality has been provided by a new series of life tables for national populations by cause of death, analyzing the age-specific pattern of death from one single cause at a time (Preston, Keyfitz and Schoen 1972).

The reason I stress the usefulness of the assumptions that one has to make about mortality in order to use model life tables is that it seems to me that one has to come to terms with the empirical finding that mortality schedules do not vary widely over time, although single years which involve special conditions such as an epidemic or conscription into war may show atypical age-patterns of death. In general, however, patterns which have sometimes been posited to apply to "primitive" people, such as low mortality during the breast-feeding period followed by high mortality at weaning, or low mortality for females from birth until child-bearing, or "early senility" whereby people die of exhaustion during their 30's have nowhere been seen to exist as a regular feature of mortality.

The final assumption that one makes in using

stable population models is that of the long-range persistence of the particular level and pattern of fertility and mortality. One does not have to assume that fertility and mortality are equal, that the population is stationary, but one does have to assume approximately 200 years of persistence of these conditions. This assumption may be known to be false and yet stable population models may be useful for some purposes. In my own studies, I have explored this question as an empirical one.

To return now to a consideration of the problems of studying the !Kung population, the strategy taken after using the model to assign ages was to test the hypothesis that the empirical population did not differ from the model which was chosen. This strategy has proven to be a productive one, directing attention away from questions where the empirical data would never be sufficient to reject the hypothesis of "no difference" (for instance on questions such as the sex ratio at birth, or the seasonality of birth, both of which would require thousands of observations for any chance of rejecting the null hypothesis). The null hypothesis is not so inclusive that it can never be rejected: empirical results clearly required adopting a higher level of expectation of life at birth than we originally guessed at, and the hypothesis that there was no time trend in the level of fertility for different cohorts was clearly not acceptable. The outcome of the study has been that stable population models provided a template by which it was possible to explore the empirical data sufficiently to develop a more refined view of the history of the population and its vital processes. A late stage of the research has consisted in using estimates for ten-year cohort fertility and mortality to construct a new age-sex pyramid and reassigning ages to individuals, again going through a process of successive approximations as the estimates of cohort fertility affect the age estimates, which in turn change the boundaries of the cohorts so that the cohort fertility schedules have to be recalculated.

It may sound more difficult than it is: once the data is prepared for computer processing, age readjustments are a manageable problem.

My empirical perspective on simulation, therefore, is that a model is essential for building up a picture of the reality of a small population. The data will not "speak for itself" when one is dealing with such a small scale phenomenon. The fluctuations due to small numbers alone, without any real differences in the underlying probability of vital events, will blur the outlines of a "primitive" population beyond recognition. And the fact that one is dealing with a "universe" of observations rather than a sample does not really help, since most of us are really interested in the long-range processes of the population, out of which the contemporary experience is a sample. Relying upon empiricism alone, therefore, one can produce the kind of results that may be true for the time of the study but which are internally inconsistent. For example, Neel and Chagnon (1968) reported very low fertility for the Xavante and Yanomama peoples, along with a high level of infant and childhood mortality. In the long run, this combination would produce a population which would be growing very slowly or would be declining in size, and which would have an age distribution with a relatively large proportion of the population at the older ages and a small group of young people. The age distribution given, however, is one of a young population, with the large proportions of children and young people that a rapidly growing population produces. These facts may all be true at a particular moment in history but they aren't being brought to bear upon one another in the absence of a model of their interrelationship. No doubt it was due to the same kind of dissatisfaction with the empiricism of small numbers that they joined forces with MacCluer to explore the situation via simulation.

With all my appreciation of the need for models, however, I also feel the need to remind the simulation builders that these models are going to have to correspond closely with the real world in order to teach us anything about human populations. I become alarmed when I hear discussion of simulation of populations of 50 or 60 people, because I don't think human beings live in populations that small except momentarily in the process of a society going out of business. The size of groups of people who call themselves by a name meaning something like "us" (the !Kung of the Dobe area call themselves *zun/wasi*, which means "real people," and this term includes the Southwest African people studied by the Marshalls, and excludes many other !Kung speakers who are called various derogatory names) tends to be in the range of 500 to 1000 as far as I can see, and if I were engaged in simulating population processes I would try to start with a population of 500. Following the same principle, I would use model life tables and scorn *ad hoc* mortality curves as a waste of time. When the mortality experience of hundreds of human populations is known in detail, it is wasteful to postulate patterns that have never been observed and study their implications in detail. Similarly, fertility should be simulated by curves that resemble human age-specific fertility schedules or some good reason why an alternative pattern is used should be established. The demographic study of human population, which has tended at times to be atheoretical to a fault, can both profit by and contribute to the explorations of human populations that simulation opens up.

REFERENCES

Coale, A. J. and P. Demeny 1966. Regional Model Life Tables and Stable Populations. Princeton: Princeton Univ. Press.

Howell, N. The population of the Dobe area !Kung, In Kalahari Hunter-Gatherers, R. B. Lee and I. DeVore (eds.) Cambridge: Harvard Univ. Press. In press.

Howell, N. Kinship as connectivity. In manuscript.

Lee, R. B. 1967. The sociology of Bushman trance performances, In Trance and Possession States, R. Prince (ed.) Montreal: McGill Univ. Press.

Lee, R. B. 1969. !Kung Bushman subsistence: Input-output analysis, In Environment and Cultural Behavior: Ecological Studies in Cultural Anthropology, A. P. Vayda (ed.) Garden City, New York: Natural History Press.

Lee, R. B. and I. DeVore (ed.) 1968. Man the Hunter. Chicago: Aldine.

Marshall, J. 1956. The Hunters (16mm film). Cambridge: Film Study Center of the Peabody Museum, Harvard Univ.

Marshall, L. K. 1957. The kin terminology system of the !Kung Bushmen, Africa 27: 1-25.

Marshall, L. K. 1960. !Kung Bushmen bands, Africa 30: 325-355.

Marshall, L. K. 1961. Sharing, talking and giving: Relief of social tensions among !Kung Bushmen, Africa 31: 231-249.

Neel, J. V. and N. A. Chagnon 1968. The demography of two tribes of primitive relatively unacculturated American Indians, Proceedings of the National Academy of Sciences 59: 680-689.

Preston, S. H., N. Keyfitz and R. Schoen 1972. Causes of Death: Life Tables for National Populations. New York: Seminar Press.

Thomas, E. M. 1959. The Harmless People. New York: Knopf.

Truswell, A. S. and J. Hanson. Biomedical studies of the !Kung, In Kalahari Hunter-Gatherers, R. B. Lee and I. DeVore (eds.) Cambridge: Harvard Univ. Press. In press.

ACKNOWLEDGMENTS

The fieldwork upon which this paper is based was conducted under a grant from The National Institutes of Health to Harvard University. Analysis was carried out at Princeton University, at the Office of Population Research, in part supported by the Population Council. The support and assistance of the Office of Population Research, and especially the director, Ansley Coale, are gratefully acknowledged. I would also like to acknowledge the help of my friend and colleague, Jane Menken, of O.P.R. at many points in this paper.

ESTIMATION OF CHANGING RATES BY SIMULATION

BENNETT DYKE

In a recent publication we have reported the use of computer simulation as a means of estimating vital rates in a small population isolate (Dyke and MacCluer 1973). In that paper we estimated mortality rates using both deterministic and stochastic simulation procedures. Then, incorporating these mortality rates in a more complex stochastic model developed by MacCluer (this volume), we made estimates of age-specific fertility rates. At that time much of our effort was spent in validating the model which had previously been used with non-European and model populations (MacCluer 1967, 1973; MacCluer and Schull 1970a, 1970b; MacCluer *et al.* 1971), and in matching selected demographic characteristics of the simulated population with those of the isolate. Much of this procedure was carried out under the assumption of constant vital rates applied to the artificial population over the entire 50-year period simulated. However, it was shown that a better match of final population structures could be achieved when simulation input fertility rates were changed periodically through time. This paper reports the details of the latter procedure, that is, changing simulation input fertility rates through time, and gives estimates of secular change in fertility which result.

THE POPULATION

The population studied is a French-derived isolate on St. Thomas, U.S. Virgin Islands (see Morrill and Dyke 1966, Dyke 1970, 1971) which was founded by immigrants from the island of St. Barthélémy, French West Indies. Immigration from St. Barthélémy began in the middle of the 19th Century, rose steadily until the turn of the Century, and then declined so that by 1966 all but ten per cent of the living population had been born on St. Thomas. The time period of interest was 1916 to 1966, during which migration in and out of the population was minimal, and growth was rapid.

PREVIOUS ESTIMATION PROCEDURES

As described in our previous work, the structure of the population in 1916 was ascertained with as much accuracy as possible, both prospectively and retrospectively. Given this "initial" age distribution, it was possible to select a mortality schedule which, in conjunction with numbers of births recorded in each subsequent year, would produce the age structure of the population as ascertained in 1966. A series of model mortality schedules from Coale and Demeny (1966) was tried until a set was found which gave the closest match between real and simulated populations with respect to age-sex distribution and total numbers. Figure 1 shows the age structure of the real population superimposed on that obtained from Coale and Demeny's Level 19 West for females and Level 20 West for males. The relatively close fit between the two pyramids implies that a constant mortality rate is not a bad approximation for the time period in question.

With these estimates of mortality, it was then possible to make estimates of fertility using the larger simulation program. Input to this program was as follows:

(1) The initial 1916 pedigree (N = 201).

(2) Probabilities of dying as a function of age and sex (Coale and Demeny Level 19 West for females, Level 20 West for males).

(3) Probabilities of searching for a mate for males as a function of age and previous marital status.

(4) Mean and standard deviation of desired age of wife as a function of male age.

(5) Probabilities of reproducing as a function

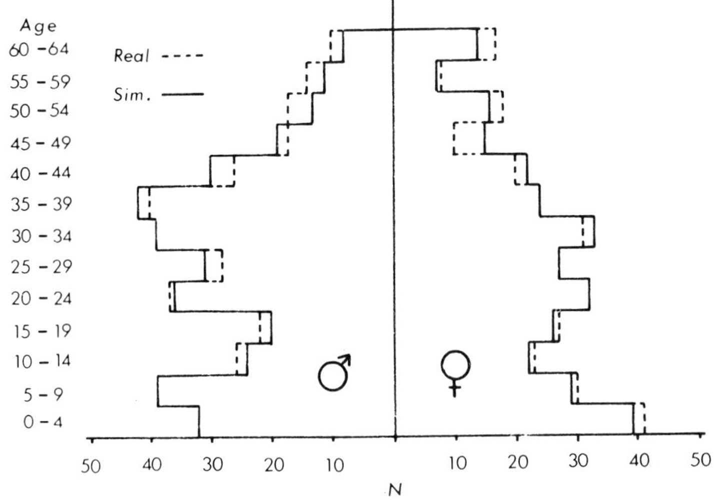

Figure 1. AGE STRUCTURE OF THE REAL POPULATION, AND THE MEAN FOR SIMULATED POPULATIONS WITH PRE-DETERMINED NUMBER OF BIRTHS PER YEAR

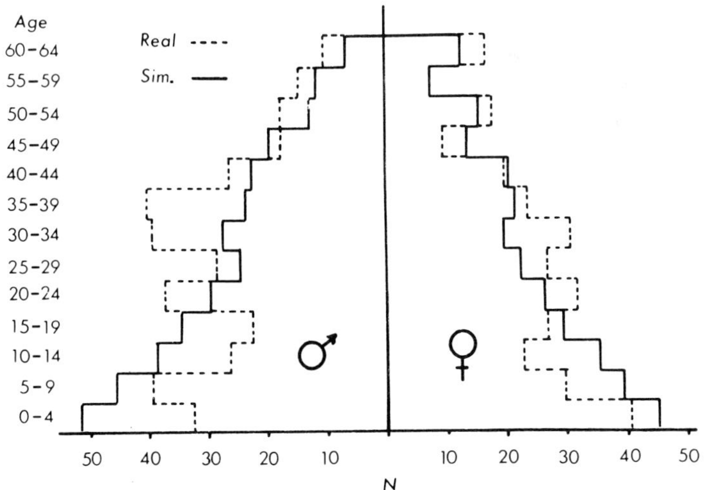

Figure 2. AGE STRUCTURE OF THE REAL POPULATION, AND THE MEAN FOR SIMULATED POPULATIONS WITH CONSTANT FERTILITY RATES. Reprinted from *Demography* Vol. 10, No. 3, August 1973 with permission of the publisher.

of age of married females.

(6) Probabilities of reproducing as a function of interval since previous birth.

(7) Sex ratio at birth.

Yearly decisions were made for each individual on the basis of probabilities specified in these parameters. Preliminary estimates for the last five parameters were made directly from the data. A series of five-replicate runs was made with input probabilities held constant within each set. The results of each set were averaged and compared with the real population; on the basis of this comparison input parameters of the next set were changed as needed to produce successively closer matching of selected demographic criteria used for validation. This process was continued until the pooled results of five replicates were judged to be sufficiently like the real population, at which point 20 additional replicates were made with the same input parameters. Ten criteria by which the real population and the averaged results of these 25 simulation runs were compared are shown in the first two columns of Table 1.

Although the match between the real and simulated populations is remarkably close according to these criteria, Figure 2 shows considerable discrepancy between real and simulated populations with respect to age structure. Comparison of Figures 1 and 2 indicates that the primary source of this discrepancy lay in the assumption of constant fertility.

ESTIMATION OF CHANGING FERTILITY

A relatively simple change in the computer program permitted changing input fertility rates for married women at specified intervals during the simulation. As before, five-replicate sets were made, their results averaged and compared with the real population. Input parameters, except for input fertility rates, were held constant at levels which gave the results shown above. Fertility rates were adjusted at five-year intervals in order that numbers of births simulated would match

		Real Population	Simulation Constant Fertility	Simulation Changing Fertility
Size of population in 1966	Males	349	354.6	341.9
	Females	308	302.2	304.9
	Total	657	656.8	646.8
Births	Males	330	338.3	329.0
	Females	300	295.6	301.9
	Total	630	633.9	630.8
Deaths	Males	105	106.7	110.1
	Females	88	89.4	93.0
	Total	193	196.1	203.1
Marriages		141	141.5	147.5
Age at paternity	Mean	33.09	33.39	33.35
	Variance	57.68	60.82	60.01
Age at maternity	Mean	28.13	28.10	27.98
	Variance	50.78	48.09	47.77
Birth interval	Mean	2.39	2.37	2.29
	Variance	3.23	3.49	3.15
Male age at first marriage	Mean	25.40	25.42	25.39
	Variance	22.24	24.16	23.27
Female age at first marriage	Mean	20.17	20.37	20.40
	Variance	17.22	16.62	16.79
Age difference of spouses (M-F)	Mean	5.16	5.20	5.21
	Variance	19.84	17.28	16.47

Table 1. COMPARISON OF DEMOGRAPHIC CHARACTERISTICS OF REAL AND SIMULATED POPULATIONS

numbers of births recorded for the corresponding five-year periods in the real population. These adjustments were accomplished by multiplying each probability in the input fertility schedule by a constant. Various constants were tried until one was found which adjusted fertility rates so that numbers of births simulated approached those of the real population in each period. This done, fertility for the first five years was held constant, and births simulated in the second five-year interval (1922-1926) were adjusted in the same manner. This was continued until births simulated matched the real population in all ten intervals (through 1966).

Validation criteria were monitored throughout this process. It became evident early that numbers of marriages were increasing beyond the 141 recorded in the real population. To correct for this excess it was necessary to reduce age-specific probabilities of males searching for mates by about 13 per cent. All other validation criteria remained stable throughout the experimentation, and adjustments to other input parameters were not required. As before, 25 final replicates were made using the same input probabilities, and the results averaged. In this case, of course, input fertilities differed from one five-year interval to the next as indicated by Figure 3, which shows probability of reproducing for 20-year-old married women over the 50-year period simulated. Also shown in the figure (broken line) is the input fertility rate for 20-year-old married women in the previous simulation series where fertility was held constant through time.

The last column in Table 1 gives validation criteria from the 25 replicates incorporating changing fertility, and Figure 4 shows the age structure of the real population in 1966 superimposed on that taken from the average of these 25 replicates. Having matched the real population to this extent, it was possible to estimate age-specific fertilities for all women as these rates changed through time. These are shown in Figure 5.

Figure 3. CHANGE IN PROBABILITIES OF REPRODUCING FOR 20 YEAR OLD MARRIED WOMEN REQUIRED TO PRODUCE AGE-STRUCTURE MATCH SHOWN*

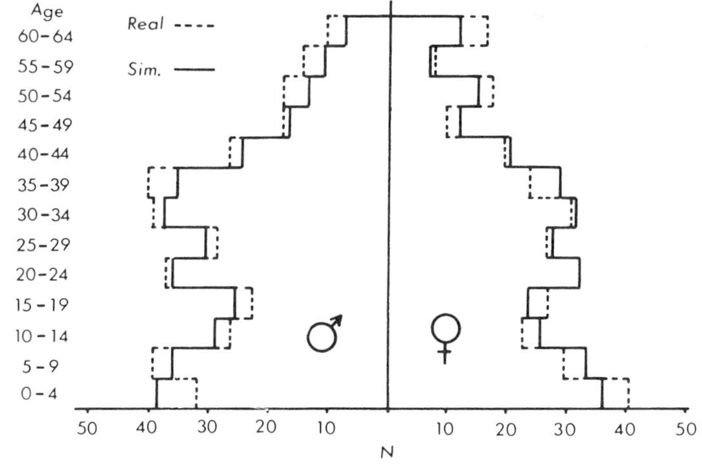

Figure 4. AGE STRUCTURE OF THE REAL POPULATION, AND THE MEAN FOR SIMULATED POPULATIONS WITH CHANGING FERTILITY RATES*

*Reprinted from *Demography* Vol. 10, No. 3, August 1973 with permission of the publisher.

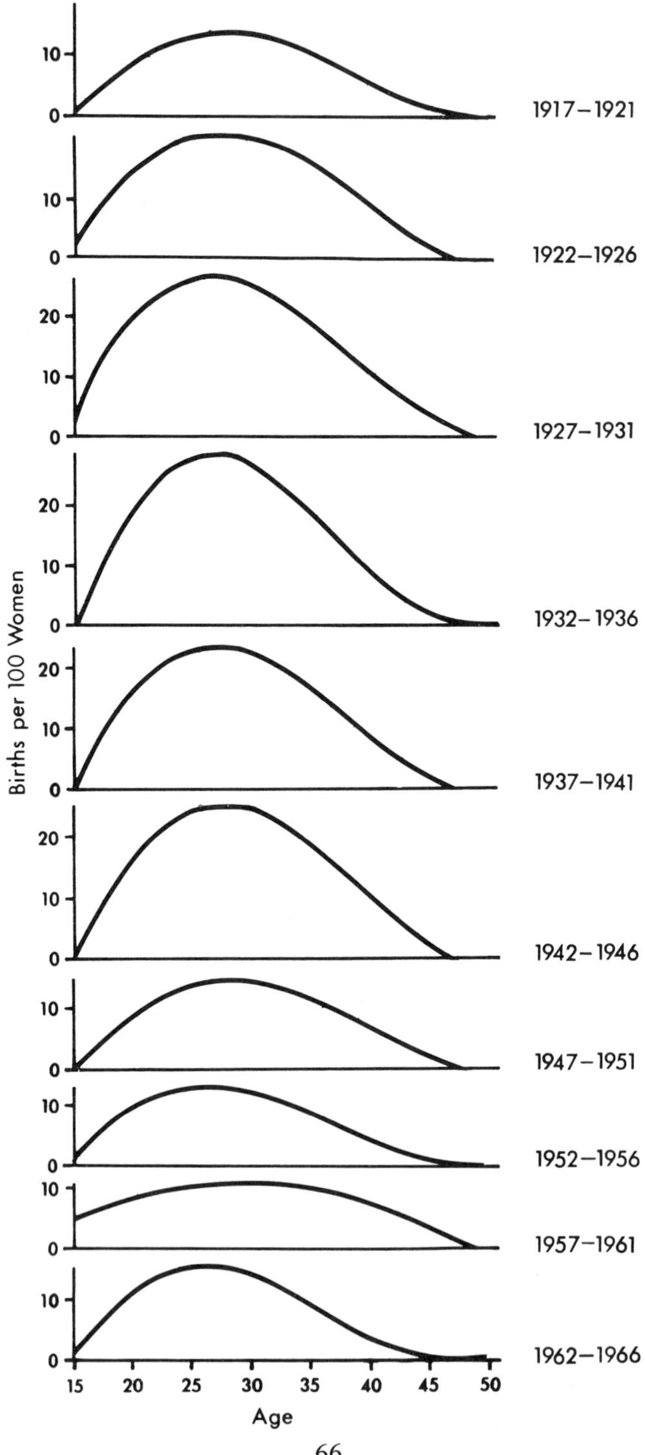

Births per 100 Women
1917–1921
1922–1926
1927–1931
1932–1936
1937–1941
1942–1946
1947–1951
1952–1956
1957–1961
1962–1966
Age

DISCUSSION

Close examination of Table 1 shows that the match between real and simulated populations is not exact for many of the validation criteria, especially in the case of simulating with changing fertility (last column). The largest discrepancies are in numbers of marriages and deaths simulated. The excess of marriages might quite simply have been reduced by further reducing input probabilities of males searching for mates. Since a large proportion of marriages occur in recent years, the effect of reducing their numbers from 147.5 to 141 would have had little detectable effect on population growth and structure, and consequently the effort to make such a correction was not made.

Because model mortality schedules were used, and because the assumption of constant mortality produced reasonably good results (as shown in Figure 1) as a first approximation, no attempt was made to change mortality rates through time in the same manner as was done with fertility. However, the excess of deaths and the precision with which numbers of births were matched in each five-year period suggest that changes in mortality over the 50-year period could be estimated without great difficulty. The effect of such changes on final population structure in the simulation would be small, and again for this reason, no attempt was made to improve the estimates already made.

Additional improvements suggest themselves in the form of closer matching of validation criteria, or making more realistic some of the assumptions which appear overly simplified (for example, constancy of nuptiality rates). The aims here have been limited to 1) showing that fairly detailed demographic behavior of a population can be imitated realistically with the simplification and abstraction inherent in computer simulation; 2) demonstrating the use of simulation as a tool in small population demography; and 3) estimating an approximate set of vital rates for the St. Thomas population.

Figure 5. AGE-SPECIFIC FERTILITY RATES FOR ALL WOMEN, THROUGH TIME

More refined measurements are quite possible using the techniques described here although they are likely to involve considerable expenditure of time and money.

REFERENCES

Coale, A. J. and P. Demeny 1966. Regional Model Life Tables and Stable Populations. Princeton: Princeton Univ. Press.

Dyke, B. 1970. La population de Northside dans l'île Saint-Thomas, un isolat français dans les Antilles, Population 25: 1197-1204.

Dyke, B. 1971. Potential mates in a small human population, Social Biology 18: 28-39.

Dyke, B. and J. W. MacCluer 1973. Estimation of vital rates by means of Monte Carlo simulation, Demography 10, In press.

MacCluer, J. W. 1967. Monte Carlo methods in human population genetics: a computer model incorporating age-specific birth and death rates, American Journal of Human Genetics 19: 303-312.

MacCluer, J. W. 1973. Monte Carlo simulation: the effects of migration on some measures of genetic distance, In Genetic Distance, J. F. Crow, C. Denniston and P. O'Shea (eds.) New York: Plenum Press.

MacCluer, J. W. and W. J. Schull 1970a. Frequencies of consanguineous marriage and accumulation of inbreeding in an artificial population, American Journal of Human Genetics 22: 160-175.

MacCluer, J. W. and W. J. Schull 1970b. Estimating the effective size of human populations, American Journal of Human Genetics 22: 176-183.

MacCluer, J. W., J. V. Neel and N. A. Chagnon 1971. Demographic structure of a primitive population: a simulation, American Journal of Physical Anthropology 35: 193-208.

Morrill, W. T. and B. Dyke 1966. A French community on St. Thomas, Caribbean Studies 5: 3-11.

ACKNOWLEDGMENTS

This research was supported by NSF Grant No. GS-27382.

SIMULATION OVER SPACE

ANTHONY WILLIAMS
JOHN LONGFELLOW
and
CHARLES MONROE

INTRODUCTION

Geographers use simulation modeling for the same sorts of reasons as other investigators (Dutton and Starbuck 1971). Among other things, the approach allows us to explore the implications of hypotheses using real or idealized data, to forecast effects of anticipated or possible system changes on performance, and generally, to approach the power and precision of the laboratory situation. By far the largest amount of work utilizing simulation ideas has focused on the diffusion of innovations (Hägerstrand 1953, Brown 1968a and 1968b) although a trend towards examining other phenomena such as urban growth and ghetto formation (Garrison 1962, Wärneryd 1968, Kibel 1972, Rose 1972), migration (Morrill 1965), and locational efficiency of facilities (Symons 1969, Monroe 1972) seems to be gaining strength.

A central concern for the spatial or distributional aspects of processes tends to differentiate geographic work on simulation from work in other social science disciplines. Thus, the basic component in many geographic simulation models is the *place* with its associated attributes (Williams 1968) rather than the individual or social group. Equally important, places are tied together by some kind of communications network which specifies permissible interactions and their intensities. Explicitly or otherwise, the construction of an attribute space and an associated connectivity space are basic to most geographic simulations. There are, of course, analogues to this in other disciplines, notably meteorology and geology. In the social sciences, the modeling of small group interaction by sociologists who use personal attribute spaces and a sociometric matrix of relationships is similar to the geographic approach (Gullahorn and Gullahorn 1964). We should also note a strong tendency of geographers to present results of simulation experiments in the form of maps.

In this paper, we examine quite briefly three fairly representative examples of geographic simulation models. All use Monte Carlo techniques, but one is meant for hand simulation while the other two are realized on digital computers. First is a very simple model of innovation diffusion which has been used for teaching purposes at Penn State for several years in undergraduate courses. Next is a recently developed simulation of the ambulance service of Madison, Wisconsin which was designed to help explore questions of locational efficiency in emergency services. Finally, we discuss a model currently under development which is designed to explore the spatial consequences of various assumptions about the development process in a new environment. We should note that while these cover the major types of work going on, they do leave out two important areas: work in physical geography (see Werrity 1969) and simulation models operationalized on analog and hybrid computers (Nunley 1971).

INNOVATION DIFFUSION

The diffusion process is of great significance in explaining, describing and predicting the movement of various phenomena through space over time. The processes one can examine include the spread of innovations, of plant species, of languages, religions and so on. Because of its importance, a consideration of diffusion processes is part of almost all introductory human geography courses. Students are expected to gain an understanding of them by focusing on such factors as: the nature of the innovation itself, including the ease with which it can be transferred over space; the nature of the originating area or person which affects the energy of spread; the nature of potential receiving areas in terms of resistance to the innovation; the presence of competing innovations which may affect diffusion rates and directions; and the existence and character of physical and cultural barriers.

One of the several laboratory exercises used to demonstrate principles of diffusion makes use of ideas suggested by Hägerstrand (1953) and Karlsson (1958). Its focus is on the diffusion of an innovation through a small village peopled by two social classes after the idea has been developed or adopted by a single innovator located somewhere in the village. Rules governing the operation of the model are simple. The innovation can only be accepted through contact with a previous acceptor. That contact depends on physical distance from previous acceptors (an inverse relationship) and on social distance; since there are two classes, it is assumed that communication within a class occurs with greater facility than between classes. Acceptance itself, given a contact, depends on an interplay between the trustworthiness or credibility of the innovator and the attitude of the potential acceptor toward new ideas. The process occurs over discrete time periods (generations). Within each generation, each knower attempts to "convert" his fellow villagers. This transmissive activity of the knower ceases after three generations as a "boredom" effect sets in.

The students are each given a "scenario" describing the above situation, a "map" which gives the location of each individual in the village along with his characteristics (social class, credibility, attitude towards new ideas), and probabilities for contact over space and social class and for acceptance of the innovation under the four possible combinations of teller: receiver interaction (credible teller: willing receiver; credible teller: conservative receiver, etc.). They are asked to simulate the diffusion process through ten time periods and to color in the map cells in order of acceptance. Thus, cells (individuals) accepting the innovation in the first time period might be colored red, those accepting in the second period orange, and so on. Since the diffusion process is governed by probability rules and events are determined by a Monte Carlo process, results are usually different. Students are then placed in teams which exchange results and write a short paper describing the variation in the spatial pattern of acceptance. For greater verisimilitude and more insight into geographic aspects of diffusion, different locations for the original knower are often assigned, or the simulation may be started with several knowers located at different points on the village "surface."

While the exercise is simple, it does give insights into the often apparently chaotic pattern of innovation diffusion and the role of chance mechanisms in social processes. Its major limitation is the length of time it takes the student to perform the simulation and the amount of "busywork" involved in looking up random numbers and coloring in the "map." As soon as an efficient interactive computer system is available for student use at Penn State, the model will be computerized to enable each student to perform more experiments with this and probably somewhat more elaborate diffusion models which allow for physical barriers, more spatial variation, and good graphic output.

SIMULATION OF A MUNICIPAL SERVICE

Municipalities offer services that may be classed as either improvements or protection. Examples of the first class include education, welfare, street maintenance; the second includes fire and police services and other emergency service activities. Demand for this second set of services is less predictable than the first because time and place of specific emergencies are not known in advance in any deterministic sense. Yet performance of protection services has an important effect on the overall level of satisfaction of a city's inhabitants. One important aspect of such performance, response time for emergencies, is strongly affected by geographic conditions, notably the location of emergencies and the location of the nearest protection unit. To achieve optimal spatial efficiency, peaks in the emergency surface should correspond to peaks in the protection availability surface. This leads to questions as to the modeling of the emergency surface, the protective surface, the coordination of the two, and effects of changes in either on system efficiency.

Here, we report on the simulation of one particular emergency service, the municipal ambulance service of Madison, Wisconsin. Our discussion is a much condensed version of a longer work (Monroe 1972) but should serve to illustrate the basic characteristics of efficiency-seeking simulation models. It should be noted at the outset that simulation is only one possible means of attacking such spatial allocation situations. Both queuing theory and various programming algorithms are well known alternatives and should be used if their assumptions can be satisfied. But in this and many other cases, such assumptions (linear response times, exponential service times, etc.) are poor approximations of reality and a Monte Carlo approach seems more reasonable, as well as more flexible.

The basic data for the simulation model consists of information collected for over 3000 emergency ambulance calls in Madison in 1970. The five city ambulances are presently based at three of ten fire stations (Figure 1) with the East and Central facilities each having one backup. The protection surface, then, has peaks at three locations. Although ambulances can provide services outside their respective districts in emergencies they are each supposed to cover only their own area of the city. The backup ambulances in the East and Central sections reflect the larger populations and greater accident potentials of these areas.

The emergency surface is generated from data

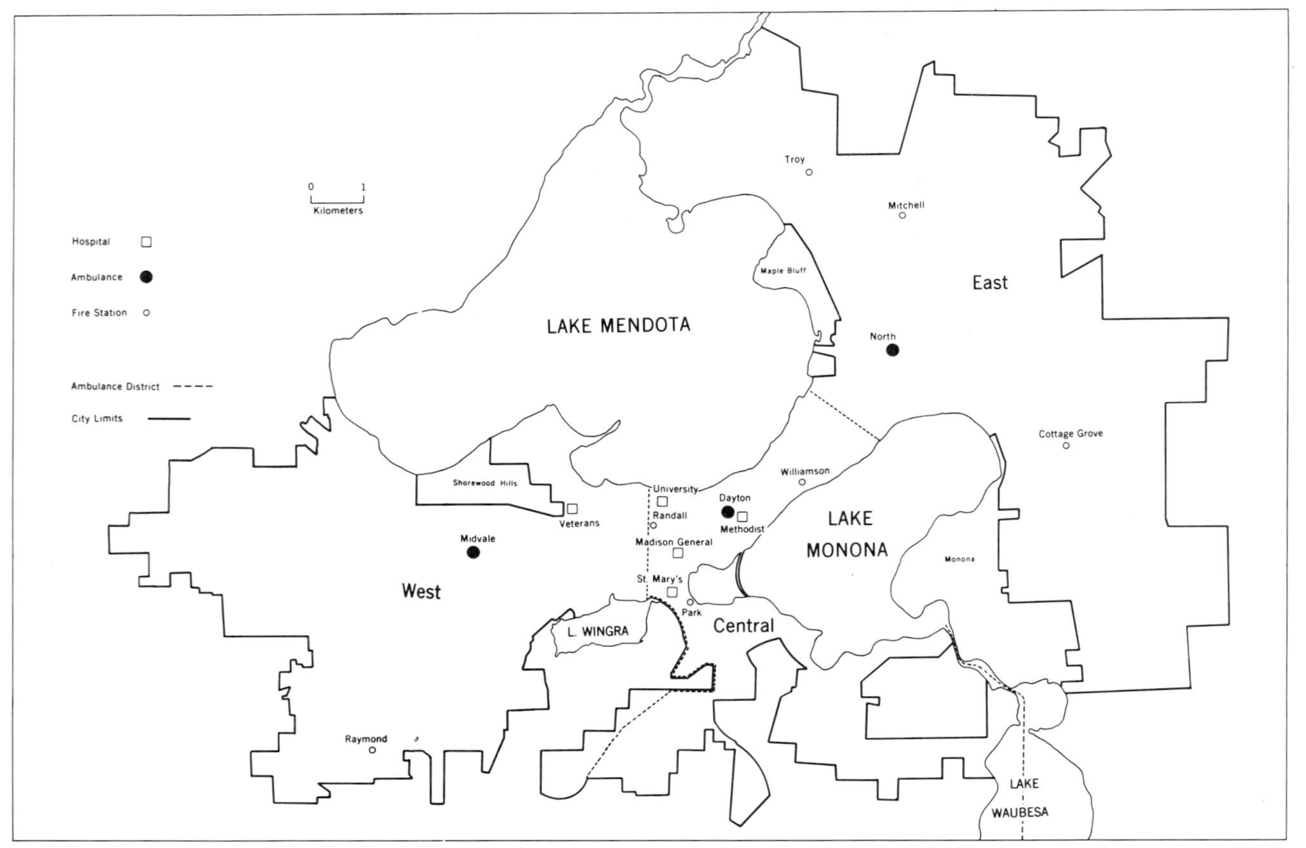

Figure 1. REFERENCE MAP FOR THE MADISON AMBULANCE SYSTEM

collected by the fire department for each call, which indicates the time and location of the emergency, the ambulance responding, time to reach the scene, mileage and so on. Process rules reflecting emergency frequency (which differs depending on time of day) are also derived from these data. The flow of the simulation model (Figure 2) encapsulates the progression of events in the model: occurrence of emergency; allocation of location of emergency; selection of responding ambulance; action taken by ambulance; computation of time taken and distance traveled; and generation of the next emergency followed by repetition of the above steps the number of times specified by the analyst.

Each location in the city has some probability of being the scene of an emergency. Since it was not deemed practical to describe each address, the city was divided into 537 grid cells, approximately 1500 feet to a side. Using the 1970 data it was possible to prepare an isarithmic map of accident calls (Figure 3) and to assign to each cell a probability of being the location of an emergency call. Each cell was given some probability, no matter how small, of being the scene of a particular emergency event although some had to be collected in classes (in the more remote and less peopled areas) and given an arbitrarily small probability (Table 1).

Operationally, emergencies were generated from one of four exponential distributions corresponding to different times of the day. The location of each emergency in one of the 537 cells followed. Associated with each cell in order are the numbers of the ambulances that would respond to a call. For instance, a call in the central district would be answered by ambulance 2 if possible; if that ambulance were busy, ambulance 4 (the backup ambulance for the central district) would respond; if that were busy, ambulance 3 or 5 would respond and if these were busy, ambulance 1 from the Western district would answer the call. After the location of the accident is generated, one of these ambulances is selected according to the priority rules established for the cell in which the

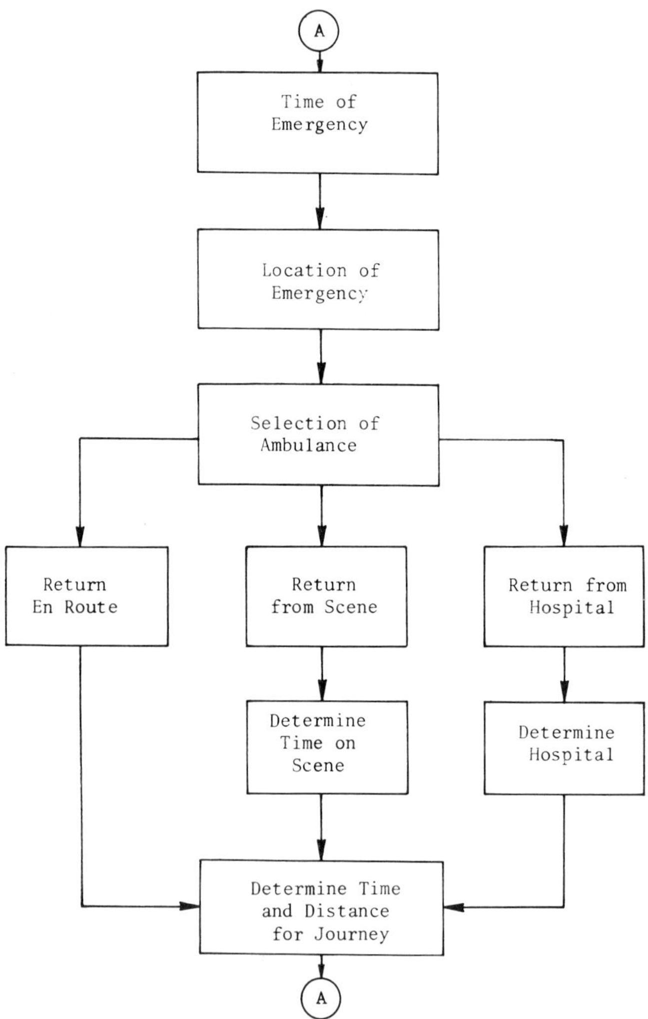

Figure 2. GENERALIZED FLOW CHART OF THE SIMULATION MODEL

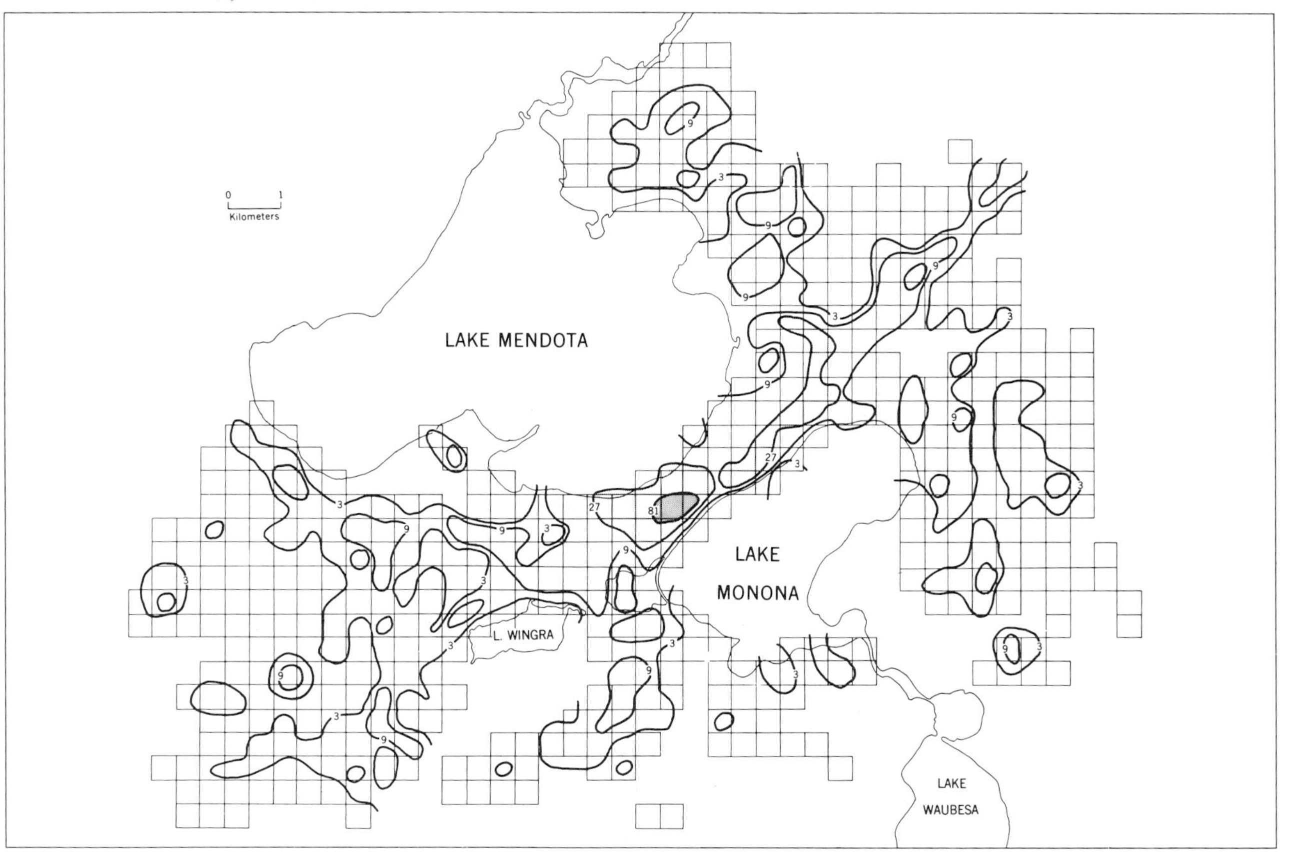

Figure 3. SPATIAL DISTRIBUTION OF AMBULANCE CALLS IN MADISON, 1970, REPRESENTED BY A GEOMETRIC PROGRESSION OF ISOCLINES

Original Cell Classes (by number of accidents observed)	Number of Cells per Class	Secondary Classes	Number of Cells per Secondary Class	Assigned Percentage of all Accidents Occurring in each Secondary Class	Accident Probabilities in each Cell
0*	68	1	68	.01	.000002
0*	76				
1	66	2	195	5.12	.000262
2	53				
3	41				
4	37	3	103	11.79	.001145
5	25				
6	31				
7	14	4	58	11.55	.001992
8	13				
9	11				
10	12	5	33	9.80	.002969
11	10				
12	6				
13	8	6	20	7.74	.00387
14	6				
15	5				
16	8	7	15	7.06	.00470
17	2				
18	3				
19	0	8	7	3.99	.00570
20	4				
21	2				
22	4	9	8	5.24	.00655
23	2				
24	4				
25	2	10	11	8.22	.00747
26	5				
27	0				
28	2	11	4	3.39	.00848
29	2				
30	2	12	2	1.78	.00893
31	1	13	1	.92	.00923
32	1	14	1	.95	.00953
34	1	15	1	1.01	.01016
35	1	16	1	1.04	.01043
42	1	17	1	1.25	.01251
46	1	18	1	1.37	.01370
47	1	19	1	1.40	.01400
53	1	20	1	1.57	.01578
60	1	21	1	1.78	.01787
71	1	22	1	2.11	.02114
78	1	23	1	2.32	.02323
80	1	24	1	2.38	.02383
84	1	25	1	2.50	.02502
122	1	26	1	3.63	.03634

*Unpopulated cells

Table 1. FORMATION OF EMERGENCY PROBABILITIES FOR LOCATIONS IN MADISON

emergency occurred.

At this point, the model generates one of three possible outcomes to the call (Figure 2) and computes the response time, service time, and distance traveled. A simple Euclidean distance function is obviously a poor surrogate for actual distance traveled between the home base of the ambulance and the emergency because of variations in street patterns, presence of natural barriers, and the location of high speed and low speed transport linkages. A generalized connectivity map of the city (Figure 4) was, therefore, generated to allow computation of distance and time measures in zones. Each zone k is characterized by a different Minkowski metric for measuring distance according to the formula

$$D_{i_j} = ((x_i - x_j)^k + (y_i - y_j)^k)^{1/k}$$

and travel time is computed by dividing distance by one of several speeds attainable in each district under emergency and nonemergency conditions.

The reliability of the model was examined using a sample of 100 ambulance calls for each district in 1970. The average response time (time elapsed between notification and arrival of ambulance on the scene of the emergency), average service time (time elapsed between the ambulance's departure from the station to its return), and the total distance traveled were computed for these. Then twelve simulations, each generating 125 emergency calls, were run for each district. Results comparing the actual and modeled system show that only three out of nine results are more than 10 per cent different from the actual data (Table 2). It was concluded that the simulation model represented the real system sufficiently well to run some sensitivity tests exploring effects on the system of increases in emergency frequency and changes in the location of the two backup ambulances.

Increasing the "workload" of the system by severalfold is an attempt to see the effect of this

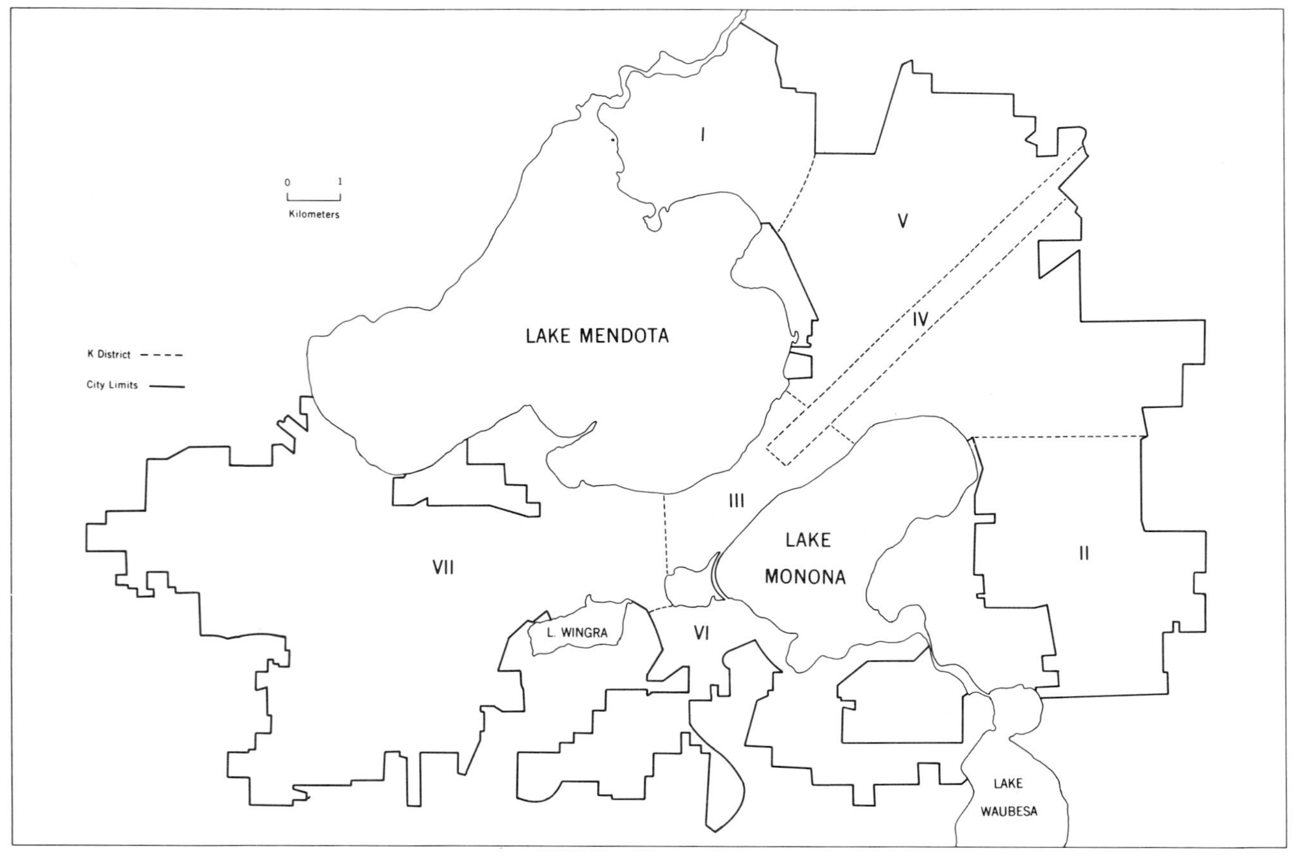

Figure 4. K DISTRICTS IN MADISON AS DEFINED FOR THE SIMULATION MODEL

	Actual System	West Model	% Difference
Response time	3.72	3.42	8.0
Service time	21.28	20.30	4.6
Mileage	8.18	6.56	19.8

	Actual System	Central Model	% Difference
Response time	2.98	3.06	2.7
Service time	16.98	14.46	14.8
Mileage	3.50	3.69	5.4

	Actual System	East Model	% Difference
Response time	3.56	3.43	3.6
Service time	22.74	26.35	15.8
Mileage	10.10	9.30	7.9

Table 2. SUMMARY STATISTICS FOR MADISON AMBULANCE DISTRICTS, 1970 (Response Time and Service Time in Minutes)

parameter on service response. As indicated below (Table 3) the major effect of such changes, which probably represent the upper bounds to be expected during the 1970's, is to increase the utilization of the two backup ambulances. This perhaps indicates that the city could manage reasonably well with one fewer ambulance and still have sufficient reserve capacity to provide adequate service.

1970 Arrival Rate (179 days)

Ambulance	Hours in Service	Percentage of Time in Service
1 (West)	6838	2.65
2 (Central)	7660	2.97
3 (East)	14460	5.60
4 (C. Backup)	193	0.07
5 (E. Backup)	878	0.34

Arrival Rate Increased by 50% (116 days)

Ambulance	Hours in Service	Percentage of Time in Service
1	6752	4.04
2	7626	4.56
3	14218	8.51
4	325	0.19
5	1117	0.66

Arrival Rate Doubled (86 days)

Ambulance	Hours in Service	Percentage of Time in Service
1	6621	5.34
2	7638	6.16
3	13671	11.03
4	490	0.39
5	1590	1.28

Arrival Rate Tripled (57 days)

Ambulance	Hours in Service	Percentage of Time in Service
1	6428	7.83
2	7607	9.26
3	12986	15.82
4	768	0.93
5	2246	2.73

Table 3. WORKLOAD FOR MADISON'S AMBULANCES AT VARIOUS ARRIVAL RATES (1500 CALLS GENERATED FOR EACH SIMULATION)

In an initial attempt to explore the consequences of changing the emergency protection surface (i.e., the location of the ambulances), the two backup ambulances were allowed to locate at any of the seven fire stations not currently providing ambulance service. The number of possible arrangements is

$$\binom{7}{2} = 21$$

The model was used to generate 1500 emergency calls for each of the 21 possible ambulance arrangements and for the set of present locations. All characteristics of emergency calls such as the time, location of hospital, and location of the emergency remained identical so that the effects of locational shifts could be directly examined. To determine the ambulance to be called, the model selected the one nearest the emergency if it was available for service.

Of the 21 alternate arrangements, eight allowed a smaller total service time than the current distribution and fourteen resulted in decreased mileage. Because of the dispersed positioning of the ambulances, all 21 arrangements had a shorter total response time than the present pattern. The optimal arrangements for the two backup ambulances (keeping the other three in their present locations) are at the Williamson and Randall street stations (Figure 1). This arrangement reduced average response time by .43 minutes per call. On a single call basis, this is rather insignificant. Expanded to a yearly basis, however, the summary statistics show that the fire department would experience an expected 21.5 hour reduction in system response time by relocating two vehicles. Further, the relocation would cut total distance traveled by the city's ambulances over 16 per cent or 620 miles a year. So in addition to an increase in human benefits attributable to a shorter response time, the reduction in mileage would also offer a savings in economic costs.

While this model does appear to replicate the real system quite well and allows the user to experiment with several parameters, it is still quite primitive. In particular, it needs a more theoretically justifiable basis for generating the accident/emergency surface. Further, that surface should be capable of being described in terms of fluctuations in the likelihood of emergency generation over time (weekday versus weekend, winter versus summer) more realistically than at present. More importantly, it would be highly desirable to couple this model or an improvement of it to a growth model generating changes in the land use and population surfaces of Madison to better predict and understand the response of the system to present and prospective emergency surfaces. Work toward these goals, in the context of a more general emergency service model, has just started.

SPATIAL DEVELOPMENT

The geographic aspects of development have long held a fascination for geographers as well as planners and some regional economists. A number of descriptive as well as analytical models have been developed to account for and predict the response of an area to variations in natural endowment, intensity of exploitation, changes in technology and other factors (Taafe *et al.* 1963, Morrill 1965). As our final example of geographic uses of simulation, we briefly report on an ongoing experiment (Longfellow 1972) in constructing a simulation model that mirrors the development process over space.

We start with a hypothetical country, Wasperantu. Its area is first divided into cells which are then described in terms of such natural characteristics as soils, topography, mineral resources and so on. An existing settlement pattern can also be described as one of the initial "endowments." Into this environment we introduce several "searchers" whose task it is to investigate the territory and generate settlement in promising areas. In a real world sense, the searchers could be colonial explorers, scouts for a migrating group, or even real estate developers. They are modeled so as to respond to environmental variation and move over space in a quasi-random fashion affected by the quality of the environment. They are each possessed of a memory and may have "public" knowledge of areas as well as self-generated information. The general behavior pattern of these instigators of development is one involving a random start process coupled with a search mentality that has its analogue in the method of steepest ascent - that is, a tendency to continue in directions that result in favorable discoveries and to eliminate searches in areas that give initially unfavorable results or that are difficult to penetrate.

Development follows search and involves the "generation" of a rural population in the initial stages. Favorable areas increase in population, and after a threshold population size is reached, generate an urban settlement. The density of rural settlement and the speed with which the transition to an urban dominated pattern occurs depend on the character of the environment and the closeness to existing settlement. Other things equal, the settlement pattern will thrust out from existing communities in a channeled wave-like fashion into areas that are most favorable to development. While urban centers are generated as a function of the density and size of rural population in cells and the presence of mineral resources, their size is also a function of the location of existing urban settlements. The model in effect postulates a competitive process of town growth where earlier settlements exert a "shadow" effect that prevents the establishment of nearby towns that might offer competition. This accords with theoretical postulates of central place theory (Christaller 1933). The process of urban growth and development also has associated with it the growth of a differentiated transportation network which also responds to environmental attributes, particularly in route selection.

While this model is still under development, it is already producing results that are interesting and roughly parallel to known patterns of development in

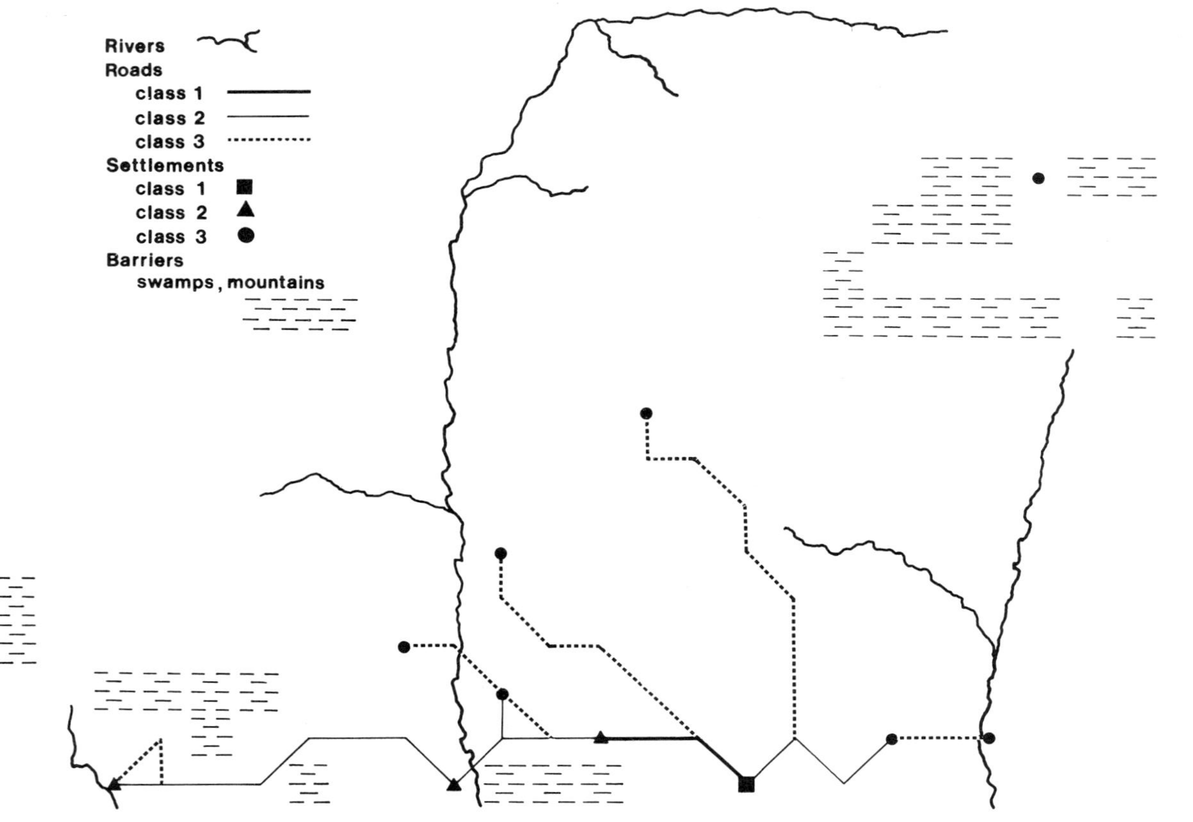

Figure 5. DEVELOPMENT OF URBAN CENTERS AND TRANSPORTATION IN WASPERANTU AFTER 75 GENERATIONS

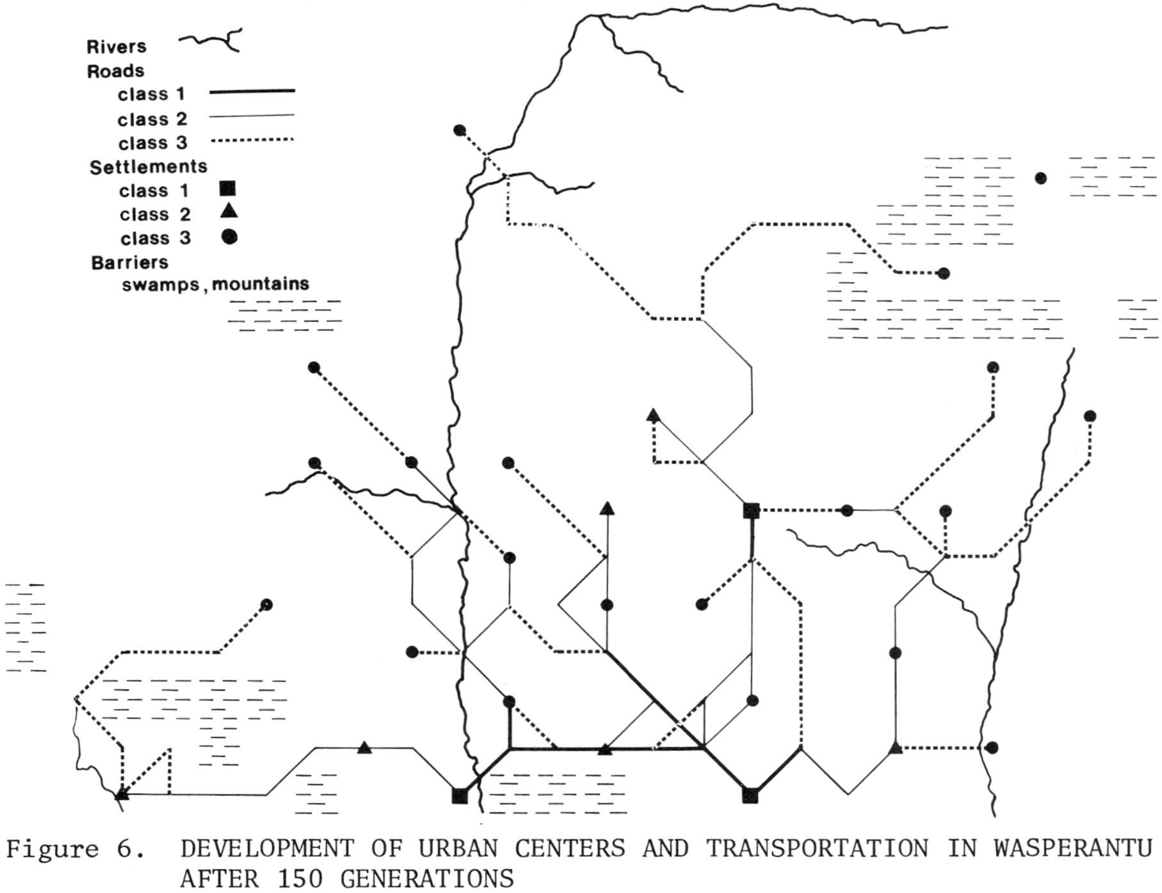

Figure 6. DEVELOPMENT OF URBAN CENTERS AND TRANSPORTATION IN WASPERANTU AFTER 150 GENERATIONS

colonial settings (Taafe *et al.* 1963). The preliminary results (Figures 5 and 6) seem to indicate some promise that the model may be capable of calibration with historical data and a possibility that it might also be useful in more current situations involving regional development. As an example of the construction of these types of models, we present in the Appendix a verbal description of the major subroutines. These are so constructed that they can be modified, replaced, or added to in the process of model building.

CONCLUSIONS

The three examples of geographic models using simulation approaches are obviously only indicative of the types of work done. Furthermore, all suffer from more or less serious conceptual or operational shortcomings which we can only hope are amenable to improvement. The treatment of each is brief and the reader is encouraged to look at the more complete descriptions of each model available in the references, as well as at other examples of geographic models. Still, we hope the flavor of geographic simulation with some of its promises as well as problems has been fairly presented here.

REFERENCES

Brown, L. A. 1968a. Diffusion dynamics, Lund: Lund Studies in Geography, B, 29.

Brown, L. A. 1968b. Diffusion Processes and Location. Philadelphia: Regional Science Research Institute.

Christaller, W. 1933. Die Zentralen Orte in Süddeutschland. Translated as, Central Places in Southern Germany, by C. Baskin 1966, Englewood Cliffs: Prentice-Hall.

Dutton, J. M. and W. Starbuck 1971. Computer Simulation of Human Behavior. New York: Wiley.

Garrison, W. L. 1962. Toward simulation models of urban growth and development, Proceedings of the IGU Symposium in Urban Geography, Lund Studies in Geography, B, 24: 91-108.

Gullahorn, J. T. and J. E. Gullahorn 1964. Computer simulation of human interaction in small groups, Proceedings, Spring Joint Computer Conference 25: 103-113.

Hägerstrand, T. 1953. Innovations för loppet ur Korologisk Synpunkt. Lund, Avh. 25.

Hägerstrand, T. 1957. Migration and area. Survey of a sample of Swedish migration fields and hypothetical considerations on their genesis, Lund: Lund Studies in Geography, B, 13.

Karlsson, G. 1958. Social Mechanisms. Glencoe, Illinois: The Free Press.

Kibel, B. M. 1972. Simulation of the urban environment, Commission on College Geography, Technical Paper No. 5, Washington: Association of American Geographers.

Longfellow, J. 1972. Wasperantu: simulation of a development process, Unpublished M.S. thesis, in preparation, Department of Geography, The Pennsylvania State Univ.

Monroe, C. 1972. A spatial simulation of ambulance service in Madison, Wisconsin, Unpublished M.S. paper, Department of Geography, The Pennsylvania State Univ.

Morrill, R. 1965. Migration and the spread and growth of urban settlement, Lund: Lund Studies in Geography, B, 26.

Nunley, R. 1971. Living maps of the field plotter. Analog simulation of selected geographic phenomena, Commission on College Geography, Technical Paper No. 4, Washington: Association of American Geographers.

Rose, H. 1972. The spatial development of black residential subsystems, Economic Geography 48: 43-65.

Symons, J. 1969. Locating emergency medical service vehicle dispatch centers in a metropolitan area, Unpublished M.S. thesis, Department of Geography, The Univ. of Washington.

Taafe, E. J., R. L. Morrill and P. R. Gould 1963. Transport expansion in underdeveloped countries: a comparative analysis, Geographical Review 53: 503-529.

Wärneryd, O. 1968. Interdependence in Urban Systems. Göteborg: Regionkonsult Aktiebolag.

Werrity, A. 1969. On the form of drainage basins, Unpublished M.S. thesis, Department of Geography, The Pennsylvania State Univ.

Williams, A. 1968. On some aspects of models for the analysis of spatial processes, Ph.D. dissertation, Department of Geography, Michigan State Univ.

APPENDIX

OUTLINE OF THE MAJOR SEGMENTS OF THE SPATIAL DEVELOPMENT MODEL

Initial Conditions

Input of potential surfaces for agriculture, transportation, mineral resources, and the initial settlement pattern.

Major Subroutines

1. The Search
   a. Place searchers at a selected number of the existing settlements.
   b. Determine whether the searchers have personal or public knowledge of the potential of the immediately surrounding environment.
   c. Let each searcher in turn evaluate the surrounding area based on knowledge and past experience and the actual potential surfaces.
   d. Maintain a continuing count of the number of searcher visitations in each cell. This will be used later as a surrogate for the interaction potential of the area.
2. Distribution of Population and Location of Settlements
   a. Using the results of searches, produce rural population surfaces in each grid cell.
   b. Locate and define the type of settlements based on the population surrounding a possible settlement site: determine whether a threshold population is available and whether there is a nearby competing settlement established in the potential service area.
   c. Define an urban population surface based on the number of searcher visitations, the type of settlements already existing, and the presence of surplus rural population.

3. Examination of the Level of Requirements for Connecting Transportation Links
   a. Using a list of the locations and types of settlements in existence, find the distance from each settlement to all others. Maintain this set of distances in a list.
   b. Decide what settlements the one currently being examined should be connected to. Use the rule that a settlement of one order will be connected to the nearest settlement of a higher order.
   c. Evaluate the stage of development. Initially, there will be constraints on connections among settlements. As development proceeds, these constraints should be successively relaxed.
4. Road Building
   a. Evaluate settlements to find out which ones should be connected.
   b. Generate actual connection routes based on:
      1. Existing road network: always link up to existing roads if possible.
      2. Density of settlement: route transportation through richest environment possible to generate traffic, subject to topographic constraints.
      3. Shortest distance path: route links so as to achieve shortest distance paths subject to (1) and (2).
5. Modification of Potential Surfaces
   a. Modify the surfaces to reflect the existence and amount of human interaction as measured by the settlement pattern and the number of searchers who have contacted each cell. Use the following criteria:
      1. For dispersed activities, larger urban populations will initially increase potential, then later decrease it as growth shifts to larger settlements and agglomeration becomes more important.
      2. For agglomerated activities, larger urban populations will increase potential.

    3. The presence of roads will increase potential.

6. Display of Development Maps
   a. Use the Calcomp plotter to show the locations of transportation links and presence and size of settlements at selected points in the simulation.

SIMULATING INFORMATION AND INNOVATION DIFFUSION PROCESSES*

GERHARD J. HANNEMAN

This paper discusses a phenomenon of considerable importance in the study of human populations, that of the distribution of information or innovation among the components of a social system. Modeling diffusion phenomena seems to make considerable heuristic sense for those concerned with human populations in that the distribution of people and information share similar underlying mathematical functions; the works of diffusion researchers, especially quantitative geographers, in their focus upon the spatial distribution of populations, may have modeling utility for others in the population field; and of course, the distribution of innovation or information in a social system may provide clues to population viability when a bit of information or an innovation has survival value (e.g., family planning information).

This paper not only examines the area of diffusion simulation, but also presents a validated stochastic model (SINDI 1) of innovation/information diffusion, and discusses new applications of diffusion simulation currently being tested.

INNOVATION DIFFUSION OR INFORMATION DIFFUSION?

There are basically two areas of diffusion simulation modeling. There are those models that deal with the spread of something innovative - a fact, a practice, an object - through a social system, with an implied encumbrance of some form of eventual

*Portions of this paper are reprinted from *Simulation and Games*, Vol. II., No. 4 (Dec. 1971), pp. 387-404 by permission of the Publisher, Sage Publications, Inc.

adoption behavior. Then there are other diffusion models dealing solely with the spread of information - messages about voting behavior, controversy, news - through a social system, without the encumbrance of eventual behavior consequent to learning the information. In a sense, however, both models do deal with information.

In innovation models, information about the new practice or object mediates what is called by Rogers and Shoemaker (1971) "the innovation decision process" - the steps an individual goes through from first knowledge to eventual adoption or rejection of an innovation. In essence then, the idea component and object component of an innovation are diffused separately; while the former may diffuse easily throughout a social system, the latter may meet normative, psychological, or practical resistance halting complete diffusion.

Thus, while the encumbrance factor distinguishes the diffusion models, seemingly identical models of information diffusion nevertheless operate on different parameters depending on whether information is being diffused about an innovation or solely for consumption. In the former case, information spreads on the basis of relationship, proximity and demography. Resistance to information spread is not considered in such models. Katz and Lazarsfeld (1955) and Troldahl and Van Dam (1965) discuss the theoretical aspects of information dissemination; such simulation models are reviewed in Abelson (1968) and Gullahorn and Gullahorn (1971). In innovation models (whether dealing with the idea component, the object component, or both), information may spread on the basis of proximity (the central assumption in the spatial diffusion models of quantitative geographers - see Brown 1965), but is also contingent upon system norms, friendship factors, characteristics of the innovation, and system demographics. Such models are reviewed in Stanfield, Lin and Rogers (1965), Brown and Moore (1968), Hanneman *et al.* (1969), and Gullahorn and Gullahorn (1971). It should be pointed out that both types of models generally have one concept in common: that of opinion leaders - the key individuals responsible for spreading information from specialized sources to groups of individuals. We will continue our discussion - with reference only to the diffusion of innovations - by briefly examining the elements of diffusion theory.

THE DIFFUSION OF INNOVATIONS

The diffusion of innovations is the communication of an innovation through certain channels among members of a social system over time (Rogers and Shoemaker 1971). Potential adopters are linked to specific interpersonal and/or mass communication channels, access to which is determined by various demographic factors and the mediation of opinion leaders.

Thus, diffusion can be viewed as a sequential process in which new ideas are first created and developed, then transmitted among members of a social system, and finally the consequences occur as the result of the introduction of the innovation in the social system.

In the diffusion process, Rogers hypothesizes that individuals go through four stages in deciding whether or not to adopt: (1) knowledge - first awareness and information about the new idea; (2) persuasion - attitude formation and change as a result of the information; (3) the decision - actual adoption or rejection of the new idea on the basis of the newly formed attitude; (4) confirmation - justification of the decision made by the individual. Note that information about the innovation is crucial during the first two stages and in the confirmation stage, and for that reason innovation diffusion theorists often talk interchangeably about diffusion of information (about an innovation - or as the idea) or diffusion of innovations.

Innovation diffusion theory is well formalized and has two main approaches. The first approach is that of spatial diffusion theory and accounts for the majority of diffusion simulation work; it is performed by quantitative geographers and is exemplified by the work of Hägerstrand (1953, 1967). The other approach is that of sociological communication diffusion theory characteristic of Coleman, Katz and Menzel (1966), and especially Rogers (1962, 1971). While the researcher in the first approach studies spatial variables (i.e., those dealing with relationships based on proximity) in the diffusion process, the researchers in the second approach study communication and social system variables (e.g. message channels, norms, roles, etc.). Both, however, are interested in the process by which new ideas diffuse or spread to individuals; they deal with variables representing characteristics of the individual and of the communication process. It is the assumption that change is virtually impossible to effect without communication which underlies and provides common grounds for the two diffusion approaches.

Researchers working in each of the approaches, then, manipulate many different independent variables in order to measure and/or predict the dependent variables of the rate of adoption of an innovation by an individual, and/or the rate of diffusion of an innovation in a social system (such as a peasant village) or in a geographical area.

FROM SPATIAL TO SOCIAL DIFFUSION

Diffusion simulation has been notably influenced by the work of Swedish geographer Torsten Hägerstrand (1953) in spatial diffusion. His major contributions - the "neighborhood effect" and the use of Monte Carlo (stochastic) simulation - have spawned a number of simulation models (for example, Deutschmann 1962; Pitts 1963; Wolpert 1967).

Hägerstrand's models generally start with one adopter of a hypothetical innovation. Individuals adopt when contacted. Although acceptance of the information occurs randomly, and more and more acceptance "outposts" arise, the center of the distribution of information becomes increasingly concentrated around the first knowers. In other words, there exists spatial continuity; this is what Hägerstrand calls the "neighborhood effect." The effect is influenced by the mean information field (MIF), which may be either private or public. Only private information fields are included in Hägerstrand's models since he assumes some information has already spread via the public field. The MIF is expressed in a matrix as the (conditional) probabilities of an individual in any cell being contacted by an individual in the central cell (the teller). The matrix expresses the idea that frequency of contact decreases with increasing distance.

Contact operates by means of a Monte Carlo process: a uniformly distributed random number is generated which falls somewhere within the matrix of the mean information field. The MIF is matched against another matrix (or map) and the location of the new knower-adopter is identified. In subsequent models this effect is mediated by the individual's resistance level - the higher the level, the more information "hits" are required.

Karlsson (1958) proposes an interpersonal communication model of diffusion in which the probability of some individual with social distance s and geographical distance g from the communicator, receiving certain information is denoted by p_{gs}. He uses a technique much like that of Hägerstrand's MIF, so that p_{gs} is also influenced by the number of individuals in the cell. The concept of social distance, however, he derives from communication research (see Karlsson 1958: 33-45). It includes such factors as perception and selectivity processes, reference groups, message characteristics, and source credibility determinants. He also considers messages being perceived as rumor, listing consequent effects derived from research on rumor communication: assimilation, sharpening and leveling. Karlsson neglects to describe the idea of opinion leadership *per se*.

Deutschmann (1962) outlined a Monte Carlo

simulation utilizing the social distance concept formulated by Karlsson, but dropping the reliance on spatial variables. Instead his model emphasized clique structure and selective exposure to communication channels.

What is interesting to recognize is the gradual transition from the spatial to the social simulation approach. Hägerstrand's model was almost exclusively spatial. Karlsson depended on spatial characteristics for information transmission but this was coupled with an equal emphasis on social characteristics. Finally, Deutschmann neglected spatial variables almost entirely - except in the assumption that message transmission is more probable within cliques than without.

Deutschmann never programmed his model on a computer, but he ran the simulation by "hand" to approximate the effects. However, Stanfield, Clark, Lin and Rogers (1965) built a model using Deutschmann's ideas which was the forerunner to the SINDI model.

MODELING DIFFUSION PROCESSES

There are of course a wide variety of modeling types available to diffusion researchers. Verbal models constitute the most widely used type (cf. Katz and Lazarsfeld 1955; Rogers 1971). Statistical models, such as linear regression (reported in Rogers 1969), represent a small subset of available diffusion modeling attempts. Other multivariate and mathematical models have been used to a considerable extent, and frequently the mathematical models are computerized in order to obtain solutions over time. For example, Griliches (1957) fitted logistic curves to diffusion data, while Brown (1963) attempted a Markov chain model of spatial diffusion. Coleman, Katz and Menzel (1966) fitted diffusion data about the adoption of new drugs by physicians to certain deterministic mathematical models described in Coleman (1964). Rapaport and his colleagues (see, for example, 1958) have developed random and biased net models, stochastic models bearing some resemblance to spatial diffusion models. Funkhouser (1970) predicted news diffusion within sampling error using a simple deterministic model (Coleman's third model, below).

A thorough review of all types of diffusion models may be found in Carroll (1969), while Funkhouser (1968) and Brown and Moore (1968) review mathematical models. However, the best single source on mathematical modeling of diffusion is Coleman (1964).

In the computer simulation of innovation diffusion, models are generally one of two types: either deterministic or stochastic, depending on whether simulated relationships are expressed as certainties or probabilities. Coleman (1964: 42-54) describes three simple deterministic models of diffusion: (1) the exponential law of population growth ($x=e^{kt}$), which assumes an infinite population and where the rate of diffusion is dependent only on the number of people who know the information; (2) the logistic curve of population growth, where diffusion occurs in a limited population and is dependent on those who possess the information and those who have yet to receive it; (3) a model ($x=N[1-e^{-kt}]$) for a limited population in which diffusion occurs from a constant external source and is proportional to the total number of non-knowers.

As Coleman (1964: 42) states, "in general, the stochastic models show a greater structural isomorphism with behavior than do deterministic ones." Indeed, the logistic curve model as applied by E. N. Griliches (1957) assumes that interactions are completely random, an assumption not consonant with reality. Coleman himself (Coleman, Katz and Menzel 1966) has applied his deterministic models to diffusion processes, but has expressed interactions among individuals probabilistically.

A working example of a hybrid (deterministic and stochastic) diffusion simulation is SINDI 2 (Carroll 1969). SINDI 2 simulates the information and innovation diffusion processes. It requires as input exposure probabilities, which are processed in a deterministic model to yield an expected-value solution. Thus, the model maintains the real-world analog, but requires only one run to yield a solution, rather than a series of runs necessary in pure stochastic models to calculate central tendencies.

But whatever the conformation of the model used, there are a number of weaknesses inherent in the creation of a diffusion simulation.

PROBLEMS OF SIMULATING DIFFUSION

Because diffusion is a macroprocess it can be subject to gross flaws in description at many levels - assigning group scores to individuals, for instance. Simulation models of diffusion may be vulnerable in at least three ways: parameter estimation, validity, and output. The degree of vulnerability depends on whether the purpose of the model is hypothesis testing, building a practicable predictive model, or merely exploratory construct manipulation. In a sense it is up to the simulation investigator to determine the level of susceptibility he is willing to tolerate.

When specific knowledge of mechanisms is desired, as in models designed for hypothesis testing, assumptions and analogs must be rigorous and precise; parameters whose sole purpose is to "tune" the model should not be used. On the other hand, simulation for practical projection may place more importance on adherence to certain pragmatic constraints: funds, computer time, and programming skills; in this case the model may be less detailed, wider confidence intervals may be tolerated, and the simulation may explain less variance of the diffusion process than might be the case were additional independent variables programmed. Of course the degree to which the simulation is validated will depend on the purpose of the model, too. In the applied case, real-world validation is important, but constrained; for hypothesis-testing models, however, it is crucial that extensive real-world validation be done. Hanneman (1971) discusses these points in more detail.

The most serious problems with diffusion simulation seem to occur in stochastic diffusion models. For example, contact probabilities are often assumed to be constant (cf. Hanneman and Carroll 1970, Rainio 1961). A more realistic model would contain provisions for a learning probability matrix, since the probability of an individual accepting information changes with the number of unsuccessful contacts. Likewise, the probability of remaining a nonknower changes in some relationship to the number of knowers in the system. These interactions are often unrealistically assumed to be random, as in the logistic curve diffusion models.

Assessing the output and validity of diffusion simulations also raises problems. At the present time the most commonly used technique is intuitive: visual comparison of plotted real data and simulation output, sometimes augmented by goodness of fit tests. Other methods are possible, however: Carroll (1969) in his SINDI 2 model employs an output subroutine which processes both the empirical and simulated data, providing correlational and goodness of fit tests, descriptive statistics and output plots. Thus the researcher is able to compare instantly the simulation output with the real data. The outcome of SINDI 1 (Hanneman and Carroll 1970) varies randomly since it is a stochastic model. The program computes mean and variance across runs for each adopter distribution. The model can then be tuned so that these means and variances are adjusted according to the experimenter's particular needs. Statistical comparisons of variances (F_{max}) might also be employed in order to make decisions about the acceptability of the model or its input parameters. Further discussion of techniques of evaluation can be found in Hanna (1970) and of simulation and validation in Starbuck (1961) and Pitts (1963).

Some of the problems just discussed derive from the acceptance of certain theoretical notions and their embodiment in computer statements. An example of how specific theoretical statements about spatial diffusion become operationalized into a working simulation is illustrated by SINDI 1.

SINDI 1

SINDI 1 (Simulation of INnovation DIffusion) is a stochastic simulation model of diffusion of innovation information to cliques in any small, relatively closed social system. It is programmed in USASI FORTRAN, level IV and has versions adaptable to either CDC FORTRAN compilers or IBM 360 FORTRAN G compilers. The model is fully described in the Appendix. Earlier runs are completely discussed in Hanneman *et al.* (1969) and Hanneman and Carroll (1970).

SINDI 1 incorporates the following assumptions:

(1) Message reception is selective. This assumption is operationalized as a comparison of an external channel contact probability with a random variable. The procedure says, in effect, that people have selective probabilities of receiving information from a particular channel or teller and for each message from that channel there is a selective probability that the message will be accepted.

(2) Initial contacts between individuals and communication channels are random.

(3) The probability of information transfer from a channel or teller to a nonknower depends on the nature of the relationship. Thus, the greater the social distance between clique members (as indicated by clique membership) the less the probability of imparting information.

(4) External channels will initiate local face-to-face communication if the person contacted is an opinion leader. This assumption is based on diffusion theory and is operationalized by a routine prohibiting non-opinion leader knowers from contacting

nonknowers.

(5) Only tellers are allowed intra- and inter-clique contacts; all other individuals are restricted.

(6) Face-to-face communication flows more frequently within than between cliques. This assumption is operationalized by setting within-clique contact probabilities higher than between-clique contact probabilities in the message matrices.

The following parameters are defined as input to SINDI 1: (1) the number of cliques, the number of members in each clique, and the number of potential tellers in each clique; (2) the number of contacts allowed to each external channel source per time period; (3) the number of contacts allowed to a teller once he becomes a knower; (4) the probability of a nonknower becoming a knower through any external channel source; (5) the probability of a member of a clique becoming a knower through contact with a teller from any clique.

Original runs were made to simulate the diffusion of information about 2,4D weed spray in a Colombian peasant village. External mass media channels were not simulated because they were not relevant for the particular setting. The simulation output approximated the empirical distribution after about 50 per cent of the simulated population were knowers. However, it failed to simulate the slow initial rise of the real curve. Figure 1 shows the diffusion curves for a peasant population of 56, divided into four interacting cliques and one group of 11 isolates. The data appear to behave more like Coleman's constant source model already discussed. The Colombian data were based on respondents' recall and thus dates covering exposure to first information (some 20 years prior to survey) may have been unreliable - perhaps explaining the disparity among the initial rise of the curves.

The formulation of SINDI 1 presents examples of several factors already discussed. First, the validation data were poor, based on a secondary analysis of

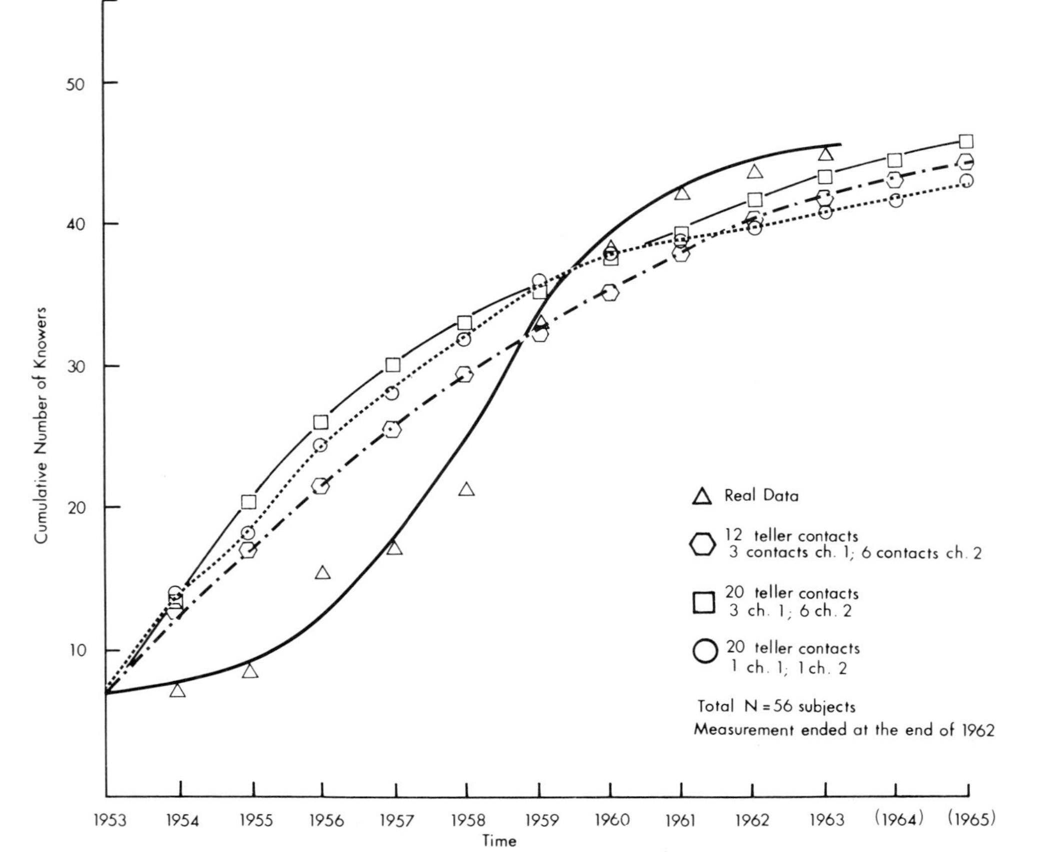

Figure 1. RESULTS OF THREE SERIES OF SIMULATION RUNS COMPARED TO REALITY CURVE

data collected without reference to the specific predictor variables (clique activity, opinion leadership, channel structure, and amount of knowledge). Second, the model assumes random interaction patterns - a structure unrelated to real life diffusion processes and the data collected. Third, exposure to information channels is rigidly constrained. Fourth, opinion leadership is considered to be a dichotomous trait.

APPLICATIONS OF DIFFUSION SIMULATION

Generally, diffusion simulators have restricted themselves to modeling innovation diffusion processes. Thus, there exist models simulating the spread of hybrid seed corn, cooperatives, television sets, dairy innovations, and blister rust in white pines (Hanneman and Carroll 1970). The utility of valid simulation studies of such processes is self-evident. But there are critical social applications of diffusion simulation often not considered by traditional diffusion theorists. In such applications the simplifying assumptions found in diffusion models of relatively closed systems (e.g. peasant villages) may still have general validity. One obvious application of diffusion simulation is to help planners in cross-cultural settings predict the success of large scale information campaigns, for example, the dissemination of family planning information. Another area in which diffusion modeling may have great utility is drug abuse: simulating the spread of drug use as well as the spread of drug abuse information.

Current efforts at the University of Connecticut are directed toward adapting SINDI 1 to simulate the dissemination of drug related information. Concurrently, validation data have been obtained about information networks providing drug abuse and drug use information to dealers, users, and nonusers (Hanneman 1972; Atkyns and Hanneman 1972). These data indicate that (1) friends are the primary sources of both drugs and drug abuse information; (2) the news media provide very little useful drug abuse information, except that they do create awareness among parents about the problems of drug abuse; (3) the naive nonuser is susceptible to media drug abuse information if it is presented in a two-sided appeal alluding to the social consequences of drug use; (4) drug users are relatively immune to influence about drug abuse; (5) users tend to "convert" an average of 1.4 persons per year to use (although this figure varies with the type of drug), and this conversion takes place with friends they have known an average of a year or more; (6) generally there appears to be an absence of opinion leadership relative to drug abuse; and, finally, (7) "drug help" telephone lines and doctors are the secondary sources of drug abuse information (after friends) about treatment and effects, although, as one moves up the scale of drug type - from marijuana to heroin - professional sources tend to be preferred over friends and nonprofessional sources.

From a brief summary of these findings, then, it becomes evident that some of the traditional diffusion notions, especially those ascribing considerable influence to both the media and opinion leadership, have minimal validity in the case of drug abuse. Although data are not available, it seems conceivable that these notions may not apply to the spread of family planning information either since such information seemingly shares with drug abuse information a reliance on private, rather than public sources.

In light of these findings a number of notions in the "old" SINDI 1 are being revised. For instance, since very little drug abuse information is disseminated from external channels, the EXTMES subroutine (see Appendix) is being revamped to be applicable only in the case of parents, or sometimes for the naive nonuser. Clearly the external channels will behave differently depending upon the population being modeled. Also, if the population is heterogeneous then demographic predictors of information seeking must be accounted for. New procedures are being considered which will take into account this kind of heterogeneity.

The SINDI 1 revisions, in addition to those already described, include a Hägerstrand type resistance factor based on a peer pressure formulation, including prior learning. The simulation will also have double utility in that (at separate times, or in alternating runs) it will be able to simulate the adoption of illicit drugs as well as the spread of drug abuse information, thus allowing projections about the spread of drug abuse information and its affect on drug use. Such a projection necessitates the inclusion of a "critical point" analysis of the adopter distribution for specified parameters in the output routine. Analyses of this type will be able to provide data as to the point in time when drug abuse information is sufficiently disseminated to affect drug use; the point at which drug treatment activities will be able to offset drug use; or the point at which costs for methadone maintenance equal estimated costs attributable to the illegal activities of addicts.

The application of diffusion simulation to social problems rather than to neat hypothetical exercises, seems a viable way to generate interest in simulation. It also provides the simulation researcher with an outlet for combining his talents as a social scientist and diffusion investigator with those required in simulation methodology. In effect, the applications discussed might move the social simulation field beyond what appears to be a somewhat stagnant, purely academic approach.

REFERENCES

Abelson, R. P. 1968. Simulation of social behavior, In The Handbook of Social Psychology, Vol. II, pp. 274-356, G. Lindzey and E. Aronson (eds.) Reading, Mass.: Addison Wesley.

Atkyns, R. L. and G. Hanneman 1972. Interaction patterns among drug dealers, DAIR Report No. 5, Project on Drug Abuse Information Research, Storrs: Univ. of Connecticut.

Brown, L. A. 1963. The diffusion of innovation: a Markov chain approach, Discussion Paper Series No. 3, Evanston: Northwestern Univ.

Brown, L. A. 1965. Models for spatial diffusion research - a review, Technical Report No. 3, Evanston: Department of Geography, Northwestern Univ.

Brown, L. A. and E. G. Moore 1968. Diffusion research in geography: a perspective, Discussion Paper No. 9, Iowa City: Univ. of Iowa.

Carroll, T. W. 1969. SINDI 2: simulation of dairy innovation diffusion in a Brazilian rural township, Technical Report No. 8, Project of Diffusion of Innovations in Rural Societies, East Lansing: Michigan State Univ.

Coleman, J. S. 1964. Introduction to Mathematical Sociology. New York: Free Press.

Coleman, J. S., E. Katz and H. Menzel 1966. Medical Innovation: A Diffusion Study. Indianapolis: Bobbs Merrill.

Deutschmann, P. J. 1962. A machine simulation of information diffusion in a small community, San Jose, Costa Rica: Programma Interamericano de Informacion Popular.

Funkhouser, G. R. 1968. A general mathematical model of information diffusion, Report. Stanford: Institute for Communication Research, Stanford Univ.

Funkhouser, G. R. 1970. A probabilistic model for predicting news diffusion, Journalism Quarterly 47, No. 1, 41-45.

Griliches, E. N. 1957. Hybrid corn: an exploration

in the economics of technological change, Econometrica 25: 501-522.

Gullahorn, J. T. and J. E. Gullahorn 1971. Social and cultural system simulations, In Simulation in Social and Administrative Science, H. Guetzkow and P. Kotier (eds.) Englewood Cliffs: Prentice-Hall.

Hägerstrand, T. 1953. Innovations for loppet ur Korologisk Synpunkt, Lund, Sweden: gleerup, Translated by A. Perd (1967) Innovation Diffusion as a Spatial Process, Chicago: Univ. of Chicago Press.

Hägerstrand, T. 1967. On the Monte Carlo simulation of diffusion, In Quantitative Geography, Part I, Economic and Cultural Topics, W. L. Garrison and D. F. Marbles (eds.) Evanston, Illinois: Northwestern Univ.

Hanna, J. 1970. Information-theoretic techniques for evaluating simulation models, In Computer Simulation in Human Behavior, W. A. Starbuck and J. M. Dutton (eds.) New York: Wiley.

Hanneman, G. 1971. Simulating diffusion processes, Simulation and Games 2: 387-404.

Hanneman, G. 1972. Dissemination of drug related information, DAIR Report No. 3, Project on Drug Abuse Information Research, Storrs: Univ. of Connecticut.

Hanneman, G. and T. W. Carroll 1970. SINDI 1: simulation of information diffusion in a peasant community, Technical Report No. 7 of the Project on Diffusion of Innovations in Rural Societies, East Lansing, Mich.: Department of Communication, Michigan State Univ.

Hanneman, G., T. W. Carroll, E. Rogers, J. D. Stanfield and N. Lin 1969. Computer simulation of innovation diffusion in a peasant village, American Behavioral Scientist 12: 36-45.

Karlsson, G. 1958. Social Mechanisms. Glencoe, Illinois: Free Press.

Katz, E. and P. F. Lazarsfeld 1955. Personal Influence. New York: Free Press.

Naylor, T. H., J. L. Balintfy, D. S. Burdick and K. Chu 1966. Computer Simulation Techniques. New York: Wiley.

Pitts, F. R. 1963. Problems in computer simulation of diffusion, Papers of the Regional Science Association II: 111-122.

Pitts, F. R. 1965. Hager III and Hager IV: two Monte Carlo computer programs for the study of spatial diffusion programs, Spatial Diffusion Study, Technical Report No. 4, Evanston, Illinois: Northwestern Univ.

Rainio, K. 1961. A stochastic model of social interaction, Transactions of the Westermarck Society, Volume 7, Copenhagen, Denmark: Munksgaard.

Rapaport, A. 1958. Nets with reciprocity bias, Bulletin of Mathematical Biophysics 20: 191-203.

Rogers, E. M. 1962. Diffusion of Innovations. New York: Free Press.

Rogers, E. M. 1969. Modernization Among Peasants: The Impact of Communication. New York: Holt, Rinehart, Winston.

Rogers, E. M. and F. Shoemaker 1971. Communication of Innovations: A Cross-Cultural Diffusion Approach. New York: Free Press.

Stanfield, D. J., N. Lin and E. M. Rogers 1965. Simulation of innovation diffusion, Project of Diffusion of Innovations in Rural Societies Working Paper No. 7, East Lansing: Michigan State Univ.

Starbuck, W. H. 1961. Testing case-descriptive models, Behavioral Science 6: 191-199.

Troldahl, V. C. and R. VanDam 1965. Face-to-face communication about major topics in the news, Public Opinion Quarterly 29: 626-634.

Wolpert, J. 1967. A regional simulation model of information diffusion, Public Opinion Quarterly 30: 597-608.

APPENDIX

SINDI 1 GENERAL DESCRIPTION

System Definition Parameters

1. NCLIQS is the maximum number of cliques in the population, and NMEMCQ(ICQ) is the number of members of each clique ($1 \leq ICQ \leq NCLIQS$). These are read in at the beginning of subroutine INPUT, and are used throughout the simulation in determining values of variables contingent on specific clique membership, e.g., information transfer probability. TOTIND, the sum of all NMEMCQ(ICQ) is computed in this subroutine, and is frequently used as a limiting value in various iterations.
2. NXCHAN is the number of external message channels; it is also defined in INPUT. The parameter controls the number of cycles through the external message contact routine. The program allows for up to five external channels.
3. CHANOR(IN) is the individual's channel orientation. It is defined in INPUT from the data card matrix of channel orientation for each clique member. It is used in the EXTMES routine to check the individual's orientation with the channel being used.
4. NXCCON(ICH) is the number of contacts allowed each external channel source, and is related to the number of external channels. That is, for each external channel, there is an associate NXCCON(ICH) value which determines the "activity" of the external channels in contacting individuals. The total number of contacts allowed two external channels per time period is equivalent to the sum of all the values of NXCCON(ICH).
5. PKWXCH(INCHNL,ICH) is the probability of a nonknower becoming a knower through contact with any external contact source: this is the dyad's information transfer probability based on the receiver's channel orientation and the particular

channel he is in contact with, and is determined by the matrix location of the intersection of the individual's channel orientation with the contacting channel's number. It is used as a comparison with a randomly generated decimal in the EXTMES routine.

6. NTELRS is the number of tellers in the simulation. This is determined from the total number of individuals listed in the teller orientation matrix in the data. The data defining the parameters are arranged so that the first individuals read in are the tellers. This parameter controls contact cycling in the TELCON routine.
7. NTLCON is the number of contacts allowed a teller once he becomes a knower. This parameter is defined in INPUT and determines the number of contacts each of the NTELRS can make during a time period.
8. PKWTLR(ICQ,ITELCQ) is the probability of a clique member becoming a knower through contact with a teller from any clique. This is a dyad's information transfer probability based on clique membership of the receiver and the clique membership of the contacting teller. It is compared with a randomly generated decimal to determine acceptance of information through local word-of-mouth channels in the TELCON routine.

Processing Parameters

In addition to the above values, there are certain parameters which control the processing of the program; they are as follows:

1. NPROBS, the number of problems, is read in from a data card in INPUT. It allows the program to be used with varying sets of data, simulating different situations, without the submission of new cards. Or, the same data may be run for a number of consecutive problems, with a variation in parameter settings for each problem in order to test the sensitivity of the parameters.

2. NRUNS is the number of runs. This parameter allows for replication of simulation without reinitializing the system definition parameters (which must be reinitialized for each problem). As has been suggested elsewhere (Stanfield, Lin and Rogers 1967, p. 17):

   > An important feature of the SINDI 1 model is that multiple runs or iterations of the simulation are facilitated. If we regard a complete run of SINDI 1 from generation (time period) 1 to n as a random sampling of one diffusion process from the many possible diffusions of an innovation in the village, we certainly would wish for a number of such elements in our total sample so as to be able to estimate sampling error and the true parameters. SINDI 1 can easily replicate the complete simulation periods as many times as specified, so that a sampling distribution of diffusions is obtained and estimates about the true parameters are made.

3. NTIMPS specifies the number of time periods. Each time period unit is equivalent to one year of real-world time; the parameter is defined at the beginning of the INPUT routine (see Figure 1A) from a value on a data card. This parameter controls the number of iterations through the EXTMES and TELCON routines, i.e., the number of *times* the channels are allowed to make contacts.
4. NPRINT controls the number of detailed printouts of the simulation. This parameter is also determined in INPUT and is used throughout the simulation as a check value of the number of runs completed and printed, with the number of runs yet to do.
5. LUNI, LUNO, and LUNP specify the logical units the user wishes for input, print or punch, respectively. These are set in the program deck.

There are also various internal indexes and keys used as programming aids.

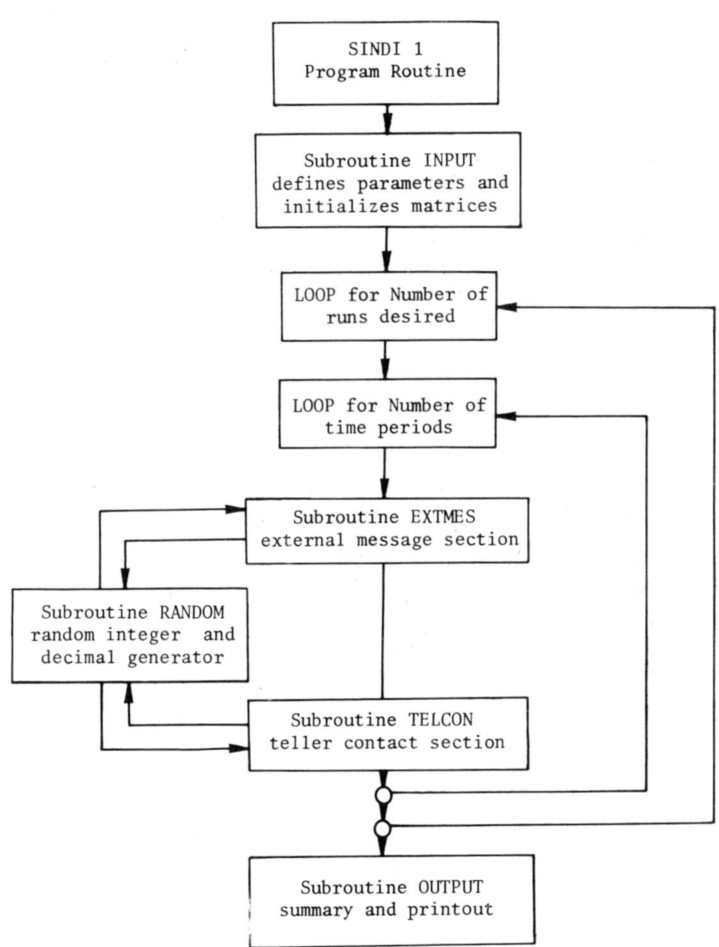

Figure 1A. GENERAL FLOWCHART FOR SINDI 1

STATE VARIABLES

If we imagine the system definition parameters as being input values to the simulation, we should then determine what they operate on to produce the output variables. The variables operated on may be thought of as state variables in that they take on different states (i.e., different values) during the course of the simulation run.

Individuals may then be thought of as having lists of attributes, or variables. As an analogy, we might imagine the parameters being the innate characteristics of a person, while the state variables are values which a person learns during life and which constantly change and affect his behavior, depending on the experiences he encounters. State variables in the simulation are as follows (each of the variables below takes on a different value for each individual in the simulation):

1. CHNSOR(IN) is the individual's "memory" of the channel source which informed him (if it has). This can take on a value of 0, 1, or 2 - depending on whether a local channel contacted him, or whether external channel 1 or 2 contacted him. It is primarily used as a memory trace for analysis of the output.
2. TLRKWR(IN) is a variable name which describes whether a new knower is also a teller; if he is, then he is activated one time period later as a contacting agent in the TELCON routine; if not he remains inactive. This variable is set to zero or one representing a "no" or "yes" that the teller is a knower.
3. KNOWER(IN) is a variable which tells whether the individual is a knower; the setting of this variable tells the routines that if he has been informed, he should not be counted again as a new knower. This also takes on a value of zero or one.
4. TELSOR(IN) is the individual's memory of the teller who informed him (if he has). It is the

actual individual identification number, and is primarily used as a memory trace in output. (Note, SINDI 1 is set up to simulate up to 100 individuals. If the simulation exceeds this amount, the array dimensions must be changed.)

DESCRIPTION OF SINDI 1

The SINDI 1 program consists of an executive routine and five subroutines (see Figure 1A). The main program routine handles monitoring tasks for the simulation. It executes the main DO loops (one for the problem cycle; one for the run cycle; one for the time period cycle) and calls the other subroutines. The first subroutine, INPUT, inputs parameters and initializes arrays for the beginning of a run and a particular time period. (One run ends after all the specified time periods have been completed.) This routine also prints parameter list headings in the output and handles other data input chores. The next routine, EXTMES, is the external message section. Here the theory about the external interpersonal channels is manifested: this routine simulates individual contacts by channel sources leading to either message acceptance (the person becomes a knower) or non-acceptance (the person remains a nonknower). Subroutine TELCON is the teller contact section, which includes the theory of local face-to-face contacts between tellers and nonknowers. Subroutine OUTPUT controls most output functions for the simulation program. It can be keyed to print out either detailed individual-by-individual contact traces, or statistical summary data, for each time period and for the entire simulation period (i.e., one run). Subroutine RANDOM is a random number generator which provides random integer numbers within a specified range, and associated random decimal numbers. The generator functions with or without replacement and is based on an extension of Lehmer's rule (Naylor *et al.* 1966).

The program begins by calling subroutine INPUT. Input reads in data from the data cards to determine the number of problems, runs and time periods, and the composition of the cliques. It creates a matrix of the clique composition of the social system which indicates the total number of individuals included in the simulation, their channel orientation, and whether or not they are tellers. This part of the model also arranges the information transfer probability matrix. The input parameters are printed out as an "Input Section" following the program listing to assure that all data are properly read in and ordered. Some of the statistical variables (e.g., means) are also initialized in this section. When all of the data have been processed, the input section and the individual identification list printed out, control returns to the executive routine. Then the program enters the run DO loop, cycling through attribute list initialization, followed by entrance to the simulation time period DO loop. If the print setting (NPRINT) is at least 1, headings are printed out for the output section.

The executive routine next calls the EXTMES routine (see the flowchart in Figure 2A). Here the simulation enters the external channel DO loop, cycling through the statements in the routine as many times as the NXCHAN setting allows. Subroutine RANDOM is called to supply as many random individual numbers as is dictated by the number of contacts for that channel (NXCCON). For each random individual generated (called RANIND) an associated random fraction in decimal form (RANDF) is also generated to compare with the listed information transfer probability. When the random generator is called, the arguments specify the type of desired sampling, the upper and lower limits of the random numbers (i.e., from one to the total number of individuals in the simulation), and the total number of random individual numbers desired. (While we could generate as many random numbers as the total number of individuals in the simulation, this would be wasteful of space in the computer's core memory - therefore their generation is limited to the number of contacts allowed each time period.)

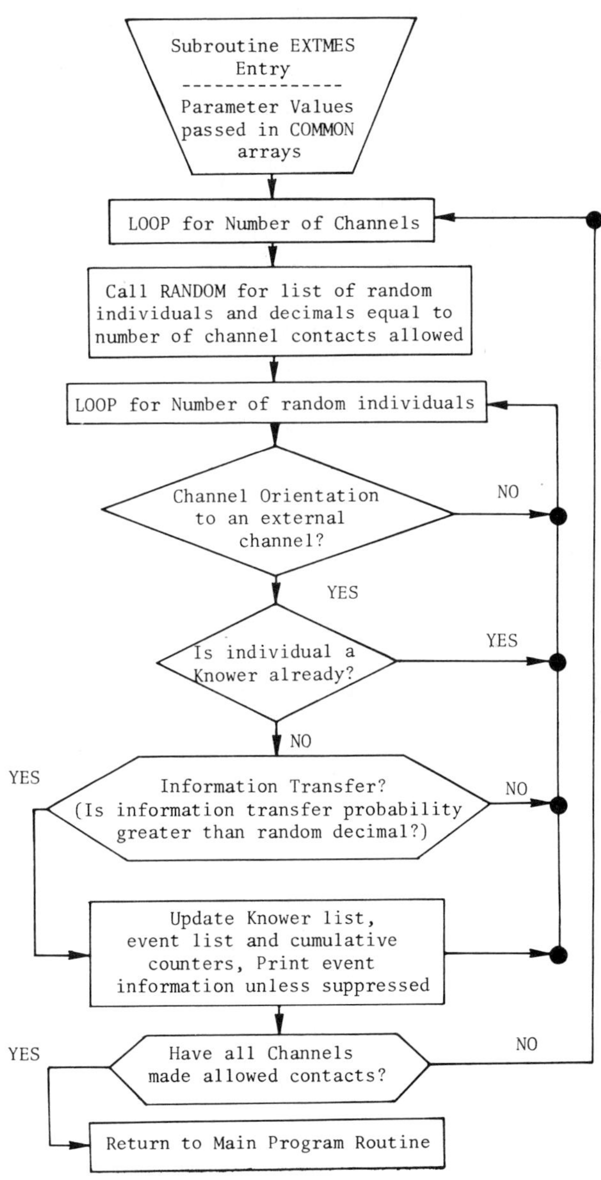

Figure 2A. FLOWCHART OF EXTMES ROUTINE

Control returns to the external message section and the random individual is located on the identification list to determine his channel orientation, and if he is already a knower. A random decimal is compared with the information transfer probability to represent the process of the individual's receiving information about the innovation from an external channel message contact. If the random decimal is less than his information transfer probability, then the individual becomes a knower; otherwise, he remains a nonknower.

If he does become a knower, the single event and cumulative event counters are incremented, and the knower tallies for each clique incremented. Also, the individual's attribute matrix is updated with the information that he is a knower and which channel contacted him. If the individual also happens to be a teller, the teller activation tally is incremented. To conclude the routine, the information just tallied is printed out (unless suppressed) for each individual in the output section. The external message section continues cycling until a channel has made all of its allowed contacts. Then, another channel is activated and the process is repeated for the number of contacts it is allowed. After all channels have made all of their message contacts, the TELCON subroutine is called.

The TELCON routine (see Figure 3A) does not process a knower-teller until one time period after his activation. This routine first checks the list of potential tellers to see if any are knowers from previous time periods. If not, the routine returns control to the main routine, checks to see if any of the new knowers from the external channel contacts are also tellers, sets the attribute matrices appropriately and returns control to the main routine, which then begins another time period.

But let's presume we have at least one activated teller from a previous time period. The teller contact routine would then call for RANDOM to return a list of randomly chosen individuals which the teller

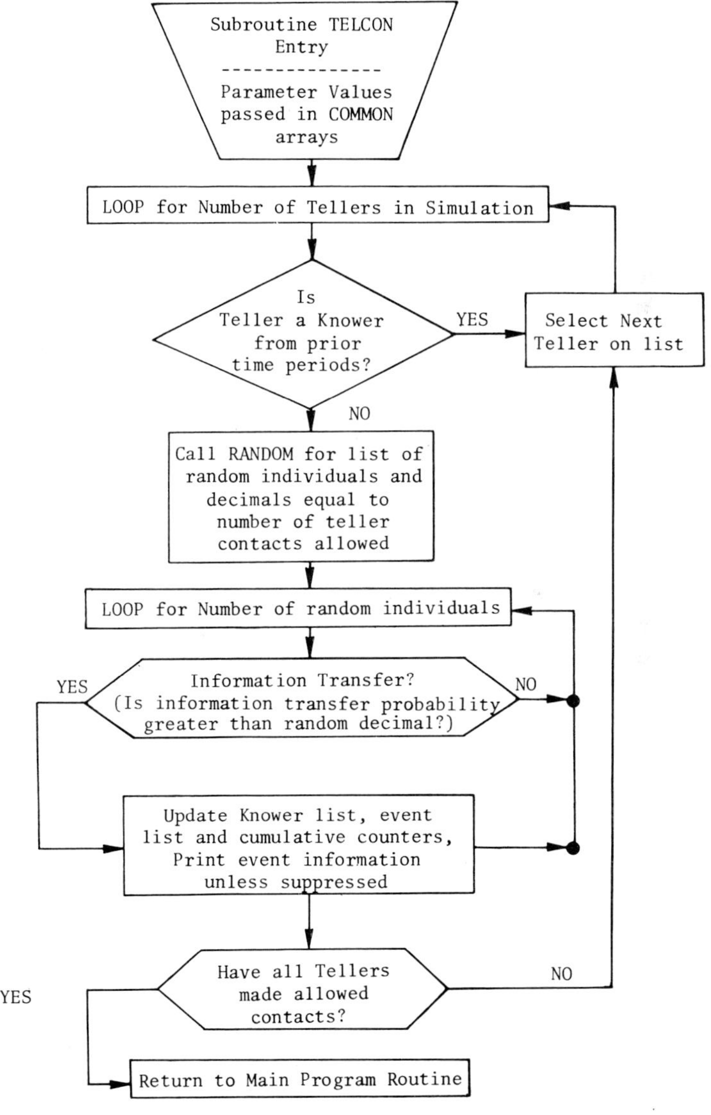

Figure 3A. FLOWCHART OF TELCON ROUTINE

will contact during the current time period. The number of individuals on this list is equal to the number of message contacts, NTLCON, allowed each teller during a time period. Each random individual is checked to see if he is a knower already - if he is, the teller has "wasted" one contact and goes on to the next individual. If the person is not a knower, the information transfer probability - based on his clique membership and the clique membership of the teller - is compared to the random decimal in the same manner as in the external channel routine. If the person becomes a knower, the attribute matrices and counters are changed. The routine runs down the list of random individuals until the contacts for that teller have been exhausted. When they are, a check is made to see if any tellers remain, and if so, the routine continues to cycle, repeating the procedure for each remaining teller and the number of contacts allowed during that time period. If no tellers remain control returns to the executive routine for updating of the teller-knower list. This process continues for the remaining number of runs and time periods. When all runs are completed, the OUTPUT subroutine is called to print a summary of contacts made, and descriptive statistics, if desired. OUTPUT can also be made to summarize data only after each run, if the detailed summary is not wanted.

The entire program cycle continues until there are no more problems left, at which time the simulation exits.

OUTPUT VARIABLES

Output variables are produced by the simulation on the basis of the parameters' effects on the state variables described above. For each time period the simulation outputs five items of information:

1. NEVENT is the number of events during a time period. It is the number of clique members who became knowers as a result of being informed by one of the three channels, i.e., each time someone

becomes a knower a diffusion event occurs.

2. NCUMEV is the number of cumulative events to date. This is used in determining the cumulative frequency curve of knowers over time.
3. NTELAC is the cumulative number of tellers activated during a time period. This is incremented only when the teller is actually active in the simulation, not during the time period that he becomes a knower.
4. KNOTLY is the number of new knowers in each clique this time period. This is used for purposes of analysis in the detailed output.
5. KNOSUM is the number of total new knowers to this time. This variable is also used for purposes of analysis in the detailed output.

In addition to the output variables, the simulation is able to print detailed summaries for each time period: (a) which channel-source contacted which individual, and (b) whether information was accepted during the contact. The comparisons of the information transfer probability with a random decimal are also listed for each contact, unless this type of output data is intentionally suppressed.

A listing of the CDC version of SINDI 1.5 is available from the author.

MODELS APPLICABLE TO GEOGRAPHIC VARIATION IN MAN

ALICE M. BRUES

The simulations presented in this paper have been developed to quantify old explanations and provide new ones, for the regional diversity of physical characteristics which we find in all widespread species, including man. We believe these regional differences to be due in considerable part at least to natural selection acting differently in different environments. Since, within the human species, genetic isolation of populations has never attained a physiological basis, it has remained incomplete, circumstantial and subject to change over time. A useful model of the development and maintenance of regional genetic differences, whether we refer to them as races, subspecies or system of clines, will be based to a great extent on differential local selection with varying amounts of gene flow between areas.

As Sakoda has pointed out in this volume, in many cases Monte Carlo simulation could usefully be replaced by "expected value" or deterministic programs. The program described here is a deterministic one originally developed in order to check the operation of a much more complicated Monte Carlo program, and subsequently to rough out problems in order that expensive chunks of computer time would not be spent on stochastic runs with ill-chosen parameters and inconsequential results. The potentialities of the deterministic program proved to be so interesting that it has been used independently for many problems. Of course these deterministic simulations are properly applicable only to large-scale phenomena in which chance factors are of minor importance, and thus may fail to display some critical types of event.

The basic assumption in the program here described is that the total population of an extended area may be divided into discrete sub-units which are randomly mating within themselves. (Very few real situations, of course, are that simple.) Each such sub-unit may be subject to specified selection pressures which may or may not be the same as those of their neighbors, and each sub-unit may receive specified amounts of migration or gene flow (for our purposes the terms are synonymous) in each generation from certain other population units. Since the calculations are deterministic, population size need not be specified. The principal data input to a run of this particular program consists of:

(1) Starting gene frequency, in each population, for each of three separate two-allelic loci.

(2) Selection, which can be defined independently for different populations, based, if desired, on combined effects of alleles at the three loci. Unique selection coefficients can be assigned to each of the 27 possible genotypes defined by the three loci. In a simpler run selection may be defined in terms of a single locus or combined effects of two loci. At present the program accepts 10 different selection schedules. Even this number is probably in excess of what can be conceptually useful.

(3) A matrix (up to 50 x 50 in dimensions) which specifies what decimal fraction of a parental generation in any population is derived from the previous generation of any other population. This "migration" across inter-population boundaries need not represent numerically reciprocal exchanges across boundaries, though that has been the scheme used in the runs later discussed in this paper.

Provision is made for amounts of mutation and back-mutation. In most problems this is only a minor disturbing factor and has generally been ignored.

The simulations developed from this program have added numerous options to conventional explanations of the distribution of physical traits in man. It is often assumed, in the absence of specific historical information, that large scale population movements and displacements in the past have played a considerable role in "distributing" traits. It is more conservative to assume that this sort of activity, which peaked in the 18th and 19th centuries, after being foreshadowed to some extent in the two or three millenia preceding that time, was negligible in Neolithic time and before - just as it is negligible in the many non-human species which exhibit regional variations over an extended range. Therefore the options which we have developed are ones by which non-uniformities of gene frequencies can be interpreted in terms of localized selection and interchange of genes between adjacent populations, without increase in size or territorial expansion of any population at the expense of any other, or even extended travel of any individuals. In effect, we are suggesting that "non-invasion" was the norm before recent times.

The simplest scheme to which this program is adapted is the simulation of a linear series of populations, some of which are subject to selection pressures different from others, and which are genetically related by small but constant amounts of gene flow across inter-population boundaries. Such a series of populations can represent a section across a two-dimensional area, and show in simplified form the same phenomena as a more realistic two-dimensional model. All the simulations shown here are based on a linear series of 10 populations, with a reciprocal gene flow of 2 per cent in either direction across each of the 9 inter-population boundaries, except, in some instances, with a lesser flow - ½ per cent in either direction - across the boundary in the center of the model. This provides a standard common base to judge the effects of differences in intensity and direction of selection, and of the relation of points of active selection to the extremities of the model and to the partial barrier, if present. Since population size is in no way specified by this type of program, some comments should be made about how the models can be interpreted in terms of specific sizes. The same gene flow model may represent either a group of small populations with small individual mobility on the part of individuals, or a group of large populations with large individual mobility. Two per cent gene flow between villages would imply very small individual mobility: Two per cent gene flow between states implies much larger individual mobility; yet the same model could describe both. If we imagine such a model to represent large population units, the problem arises that randomness of mating will not be fully realized within single populations, since they are themselves somewhat subdivided genetically. It can be seen, however, that for comparing major variations in the effects of the selection and migration, that is not a serious problem, though it might be if exact fit to some empirical data were attempted.

Other considerations based on some trial runs not presented here are of interest. Increasing intensity of selection, while holding constant the magnitude of gene flow, will result in more marked regional differentiation in gene frequencies, whereas increasing gene flow, with selection intensity remaining the same, results in less differentiation. This is not surprising. If both selection intensity and gene flow are increased, an equilibrium condition will be reached rapidly; a slower approach to equilibrium will take place if both selection and gene flow are decreased.

A basic paradigm to demonstrate the development of regional gene frequencies in partially isolated populations is shown in Figure 1. Here it is assumed that the series of populations (numbered 1 to 10) is divided into two equal portions, half characterized by selection *for* an allele, the other half by selection *against* it. In this case the positive selection (+.04 when the allele was in homozygous, and +.02 in heterozygous form) was twice the negative selection (-.02 for homozygotes and -.01 for heterozygotes).

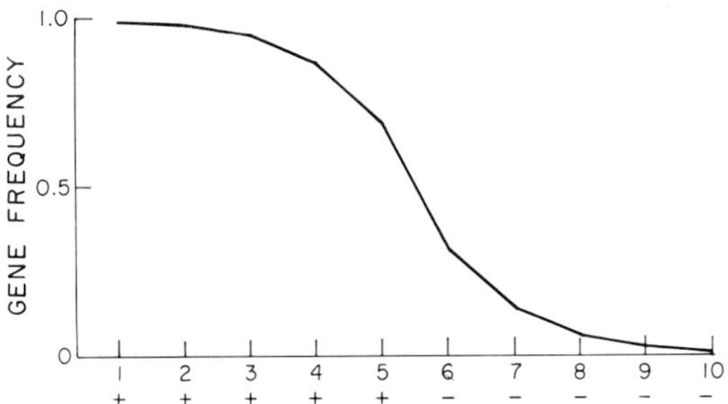

Figure 1. DISTRIBUTION OF GENE FREQUENCIES IN TEN ADJACENT POPULATIONS, OBTAINED AFTER 500 GENERATIONS OF POSITIVE AND NEGATIVE SELECTION LOCALIZED AS INDICATED BY PLUS AND MINUS SIGNS; SMALL UNIFORM GENE FLOW BETWEEN ALL ADJACENT POPULATIONS; AND INITIAL GENE FREQUENCIES IDENTICAL

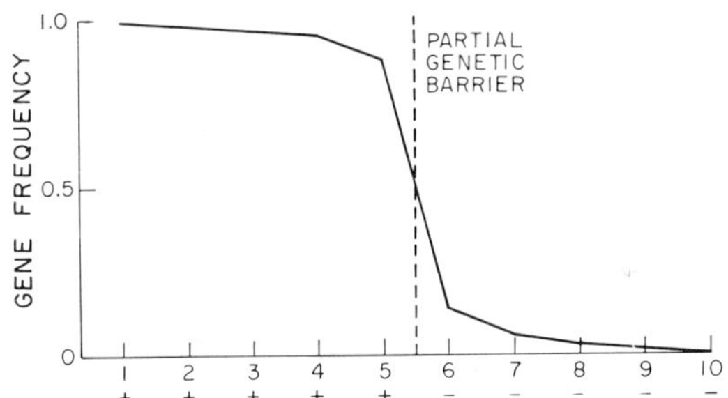

Figure 2. THE MODEL OF FIGURE 1, MODIFIED ONLY BY THE INTRODUCTION OF ONE POINT OF REDUCED GENE FLOW IN THE CENTER OF THE MODEL

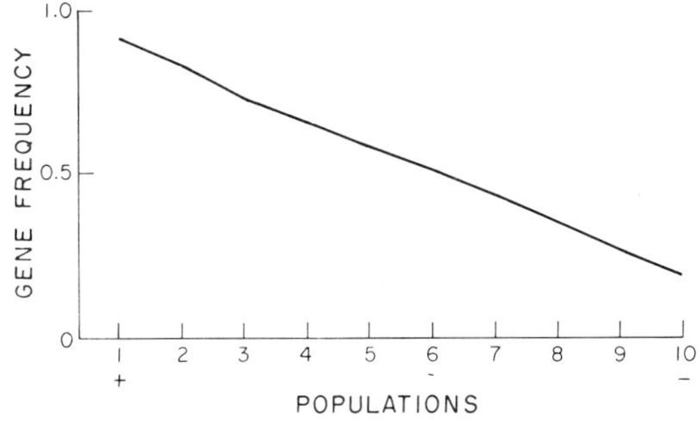

Figure 3. THE GENE FREQUENCY GRADIENT OBTAINED AFTER 500 GENERATIONS, WITH CONDITIONS AS IN FIGURE 1, EXCEPT THAT SELECTION IS LIMITED TO THE POPULATIONS AT THE TWO ENDS OF THE MODEL

Selection was applied uniformly within each five-population section, so that the transition between positive and negative selection at the central boundary is abrupt. Since in this example there is a uniform 2 per cent exchange of genes in every generation between all adjacent populations, differentiation of gene frequencies across the central boundary remains less after 500 generations than that between populations at the "geographical" extremes. The peripheral populations are well buffered against the effects of gene flow by the intervening presence of populations undergoing the same selection pressures as themselves. Fixation of alleles in the end populations is nearly complete in spite of the difference in intensity of selection. Figure 2 shows the equilibrium results when gene flow is reduced to ½ of one per cent at the point where selection coefficients change. The contrast between the two sections is enhanced, and gene frequencies within them are more uniform. Such a pattern would result in nature when an ecological boundary resulting in differences in selection coefficients was also a deterrent to migration of individuals. This situation is one which is particularly likely in man (except for the very modern variety) due to rather precise adaptations of culture to ecology.

Consideration of gene frequency variation in human populations suggests still another variation in model-building. In man certain major racial variations are peculiar to areas of continental or subcontinental size, within which there exist climatic and ecological differences far greater than any "average" difference between one continent and another. This has confused interpretations of racial differences in terms of selection. Therefore we have constructed some models in which active selection is limited to small areas, and a great part of the total area left selectively neutral. Some early tests had demonstrated the degree to which selectively neutral populations can be affected by the nearby presence of an area of selection with which it exchanges genes at a low rate. In fact, if an area of selective advantage for a particular allele is present among a group of populations, the rest of which are neutral in respect to selection for that allele, differences in gene frequency within the group eventually disappear. The gene involved continually increases in the population in which it is selectively favored, and gradually diffuses outward into the "neutral" areas. At first a gene frequency gradient exists, but eventually the frequency approaches 100 per cent in the entire area. In order to maintain gene frequency gradients on a permanent basis, there must be both positive and negative selection within the model.

The patterns of gene frequency distribution which appear when active selection is limited to parts of areas are extremely varied, since a new factor is introduced - differences in location of active selection with reference to the total area and to the location of gene flow restrictions, if any. Figures 3 - 6 show some of these patterns for the one-dimensional case. Figure 3 represents the equilibrium gene frequencies attained when positive and negative selection for an allele are limited to populations at the extremities, all those in between being neutral in selection. A smooth gradient in gene frequency is established when gene flow is uniform across all inter-population boundaries. When a partial barrier is placed in the center (Figure 4), a slight steepening of gradient occurs at this point. In Figure 5 the focus of active selection on one side is placed near the central boundary (in population 6), and on the other side near the extreme (population 2). The smooth gradient now disappears on this side, and is replaced by a "hinterland effect" in which the neutrally selected peripheral populations take on passively the selective bias of the population which separates them from any area of selection in the reverse direction. A total equilibrium condition in this situation would see gene frequencies in the peripheral populations identical to that of the

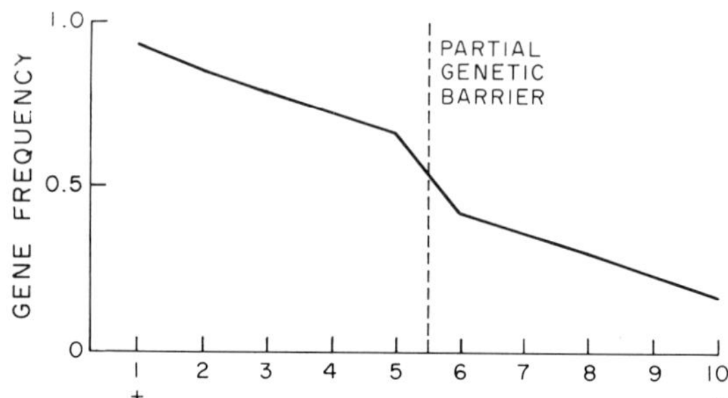

Figure 4. THE MODEL OF FIGURE 3, MODIFIED ONLY BY THE INTRODUCTION OF ONE POINT OF REDUCED GENE FLOW IN THE CENTER OF THE MODEL*

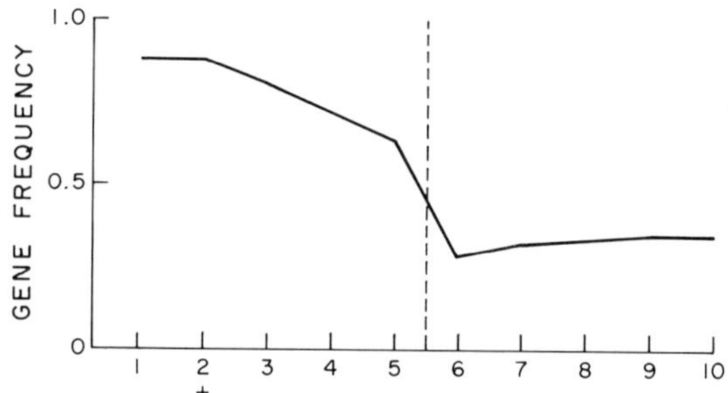

Figure 5. THE MODEL OF FIGURE 4, WITH THE FOCI OF SELECTION MOVED AS INDICATED*

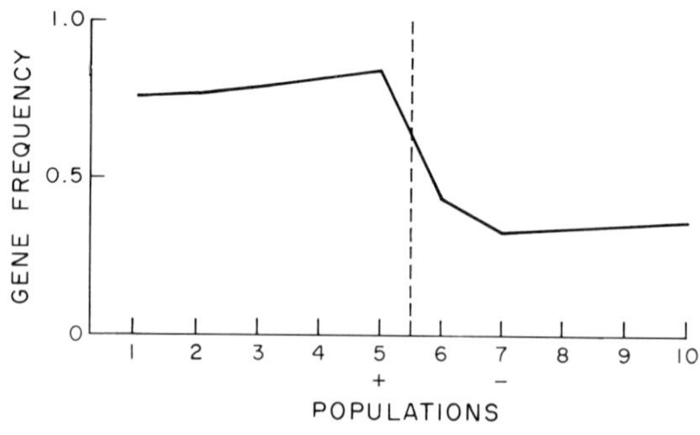

Figure 6. ANOTHER VARIANT, DIFFERING FROM FIGURES 4 AND 5 BY THE LOCATION OF FOCI OF SELECTION*

*Reprinted with permission of Wistar Institute Press

population subject to selection. This was not yet attained in the 1,000 generation run shown here. In Figure 6 both the positive and negative selection points are near the center of the model, and a hinterland effect appears on both sides.

The usefulness of these models lies in their relation to erroneous interpretations which might be intuitively made of empirical gene frequency distributions of this kind. Figures 3 and 4 could be interpreted as indicating a smooth gradient of selective effect across an area, though in fact the model is based on discrete and very localized foci of selection. Figures 5 and 6 might be taken to indicate that equal selection pressures existed in the groups of populations which had attained similar high or low gene frequencies, or that some one population selected in a particular way had "invaded" a larger area.

An example of different hypotheses applied to the same data may be given from the known gradient of skin color, apparently involving several loci subject to consistent selection, which exists across Europe and Africa from north to south. From northern Europe to North Africa, across a genetically contiguous area (the Mediterranean Sea being virtually no population barrier) there is a continuous gradient of darkening average skin color from north to south. South of the Sahara Desert, which is the real genetic barrier in this geographic continuum, skin color becomes maximally dark, and with few exceptions is much the same throughout sub-Saharan Africa. On the assumption that the skin color closely reflected local selection pressure, we would assume that from northern Europe to North Africa there was a gradual increase of selective pressure for darker skin, and that south of the Sahara selective pressure for darker skin was strong and uniform, despite the environmental variety within this area, ranging from tropical rain-forest to very dry temperate climate. We might invoke migration to account for the uniformity of sub-Saharan skin color, assuming that some group strongly selected in the equatorial belt had spread and displaced older populations in the southern part of the continent (I am not saying that this may not be a factor). But the gradient observed might also be explained in terms of a relation of foci of selection to genetic barriers similar to that shown in Figure 5. If positive selection for light skin were concentrated in the northern-most parts of Europe, with the rest of Europe and North Africa neutrally selected in this respect, and positive selection for darker skin principally effective in the equatorial belt just south of the Sahara, with the southern part of that continent relatively neutral with respect to selection for skin color, a distribution pattern similar to that of Figure 5 would result without any massive migrations or population displacements.

The last models represent a very generalized test of an evolutionary hypothesis concerning man. In recent years many students have leaned towards the assumption that man and his immediate ancestors have for a very long time comprised a widespread species with various local races, and that gene exchange between widely separated populations has made possible the spread through the entire species of mutations which control traits of universally advantageous effect, at the same time that local or racial differences developed and were maintained in response to selection of a local nature (Dobzhansky 1944, Coon 1962). This is in contrast to older hypotheses, which assumed that there must be a closely localized "cradle of man" in which the lineage of modern man became specifically distinct, later spreading out over the world and secondarily developing local variations. The test made, a very simple one, using some of the parameters of the other models described in this paper, was to determine whether one and the same genetic filter, given modest selective coefficients, could permit simultaneously, wide distribution of species characters, and localized development of racial characters. This was done without attempting to simulate any particular time or space scale.

Figures 7 - 9 use one of the 10-population gene

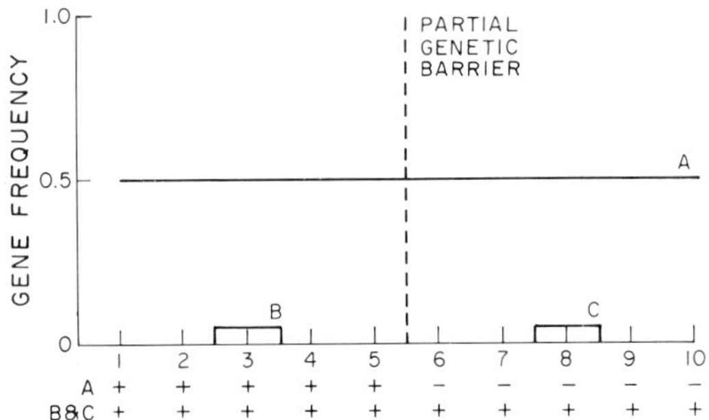

Figure 7. THE INITIAL CONDITIONS FROM WHICH THE MODELS OF FIGURES 8 AND 9 WILL BE DERIVED. GENE A HAS A FREQUENCY OF .5 THROUGHOUT: GENES B AND C START AT FREQUENCY .05 IN TWO SINGLE POPULATIONS. A WILL BE DIFFERENTIALLY SELECTED IN THE TWO HALVES OF THE MODEL: B AND C WILL BE POSITIVELY SELECTED THROUGHOUT

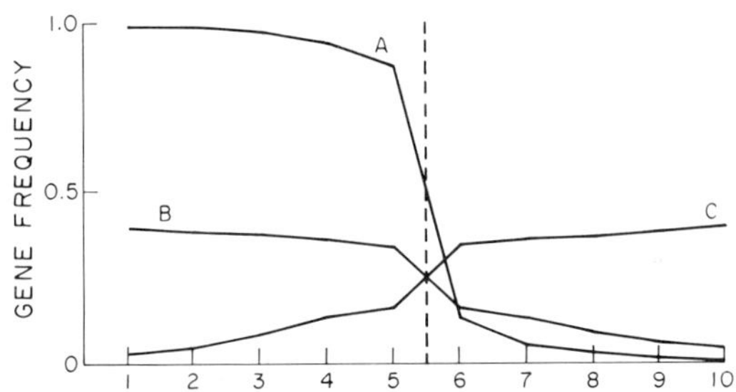

Figure 8. 250-GENERATION DEVELOPMENT FROM FIGURE 7. THE FREQUENCY OF GENE A HAS DEVELOPED A STRONG LOCAL DIFFERENTIATION. GENES B AND C ARE SPREADING AND INCREASING

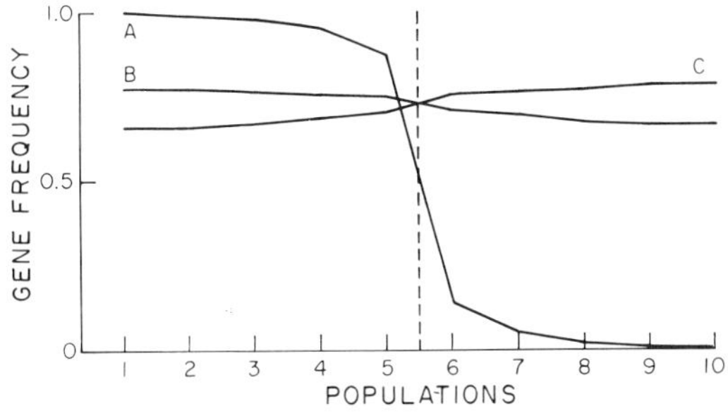

Figure 9. 500-GENERATION DEVELOPMENT FROM FIGURE 7. GENE A IS MAINTAINING ITS LOCAL DIFFERENCE IN FREQUENCY AND B AND C HAVE LARGELY DISPLACED THEIR ALLELES THROUGHOUT

flow systems of the previous tests, with a special set of selection coefficients and pattern of initial gene frequencies. "Gene A" is in fact the allele of Figure 2 with positive selection in five contiguous populations and negative selection in the other five, the areas of different selection being separated by partial barrier. For reasons which will appear, a 250-generation development as well as a 500-generation one are presented. The process starts with a uniform 50 per cent frequency of the allele A across the board. As shown previously, differential selection (for magnitude of selection see description of Figure 2) produces markedly different levels of frequency of gene A in the two halves of the model, and approaches an equilibrium condition, which in fact is essentially reached during the first half of the time period (Figure 8). Genes B and C are given positive selection *everywhere*, at a rate of +.02 for heterozygotes and +.04 for homozygotes, and start at 5 per cent levels in two single populations, one in the right half of the model and one in the left half. We have described above the effect of one-way selection, in which positive selection in one part of a model is not balanced out by negative selection in another part. Genes B and C are subject to only positive selection in this model and therefore do not approach stabilized differential frequencies as does gene A. Instead, each increases in its initial location, diffuses to and increases in adjacent populations, then with a visible retardation at the partial barrier, seeps into the other half of the model and increases there. After an initial state of differential frequency between the two halves of the model, controlled by the locality of first appearance of B and C, the frequencies of the two genes across the entire area become more similar as they increase throughout. The clear eventuality is a 100 per cent level for both B and C across the board. If local selection and gene flow remain the same, the regional differential in frequency of gene A therefore can be maintained indefinitely while numerous mutations similar to B and

C in their selective advantage are exchanged between the two areas, and eventually attain high and indistinguishable levels in both. No problem exists, therefore, in assuming that local differences in some gene frequencies can develop and be maintained while other genes are traded back and forth and their advantages exploited by all segments of a species.

This is a very simple program compared to many others which are presented in this volume. Nevertheless, it has been very effective in constructing and testing hypotheses of interest to physical anthropology.

REFERENCES

Brues, A. M. 1972. Models of clines and races, American Journal of Physical Anthropology 37: 389-399.

Coon, C. S. 1962. The Origin of Races. New York: Knopf.

Dobzhansky, T. 1944. On species and races of living and fossil men, American Journal of Physical Anthropology 2: 251-265.

RECESSIVE LETHALS AND THE BIRTH INTERVAL

DAVID L. ROSSMANN
and
WILLIAM J. SCHULL

If the increased risk of homozygosity for deleterious recessive mutants that occurs among the offspring of consanguineous marriages results in an increased likelihood of abortion, stillbirth or neonatal death, as genetic theory predicts, then in the absence of family planning and limitation, the mean interval between the termination of successive pregnancies of a couple may be a function of their biological relationship. This mean interval which we shall term the "birth" interval, may be affected by the consanguinity of the couple in one of two ways. First, if the interval is taken to be between successive live births or from the beginning of cohabitation to the first live birth, the mean interval will be longer among consanguineous than non-consanguineous matings. This follows because the risk of abortion and stillbirth rises with consanguinity with a resultant lengthening of the time to a live born infant. Second, the mean interval between successive pregnancies without regard to type of termination, will be decreased among consanguineous matings, for the birth interval following a termination which results in an abortion or stillbirth is shorter on the average than that which follows a live birth and consanguineous couples have an increased risk of abortion and stillbirth.

Prompted by the argument just set forth, Slatis *et al.* (1958) investigated the birth interval among consanguineous couples in Chicago as did Schull (1958) for the cities of Hiroshima, Nagasaki and Kure in Japan. Neither study, however, was able to demonstrate that a change actually took place. It was not clear whether this inability to discern a difference was due to the smallness of the consanguinity effect or to concomitant extraneous variation. The optimal conditions for detecting a consanguinity effect on the birth interval would occur presumably when the action of the mutant gene involved complete penetrance and 100 per cent lethality. This type of allele should produce the greatest difference between mean birth intervals from randomly mating and consanguineously mating couples.

There are, of course, a number of ways by which the magnitude of this difference might be estimated. If the distributions were indeed known or could be sensibly inferred, estimation becomes an exercise in the calculus, at least in the large sample case. For example, if we assume that $f(x_c)$, $f(y_c)$, $f(z_c)$, $f(x_r)$, $f(y_r)$, and $f(z_r)$ are the distributions of birth intervals following a live birth, neonatal death and stillbirth among consanguineously and randomly mating couples respectively and that $p(x_c)$, $p(y_c)$, $p(z_c)$, $p(x_r)$, $p(y_r)$, and $p(z_r)$ are the frequencies with which these events occur, where

$$p(x_c) + p(y_c) + p(z_c) = 1$$

and

$$p(x_r) + p(y_r) + p(z_r) = 1$$

then the means of the birth intervals from consanguineously and randomly mating couples are just the weighted expectations of the above birth interval distributions,

$$m_c = p(x_c) \int x_c \, f(x_c) \, dx + p(y_c) \int y_c \, f(y_c) \, dy + p(z_c) \int z_c \, f(z_c) \, dz$$

and

$$m_r = p(x_r) \int x_r f(x_r)\,dx + p(y_r) \int y_r f(y_r)\,dy + p(z_r) \int z_r f(z_r)\,dz$$

Or, if one had available empirical distributions of birth intervals by type of termination from a group of randomly mating couples and similar distributions from consanguineously mating couples, it should be possible to determine the density of these distributions. Contrasting the densities from randomly mating and consanguineously mating couples would then result in an analytic solution to the problem. While this might be the most satisfying approach intellectually, there are some difficulties in its implementation. First, distributions of termination interval by type of termination from randomly mating and consanguineously mating couples from the same population are hard to come by. These data are not easy to collect, and as a result there is little empirical information available. Second, even if these data were available, it is often difficult and time consuming to approximate accurately the density of the empirical distributions if they are not normal.

Monte Carlo simulation is another approach which while not as accurate as the analytic one does produce a good first approximation while avoiding some of the problems encountered in the analytic solution. Modeling the process of reproduction when one is primarily concerned only with the interval following a type of termination and not with all of the biological, demographic and socio-economic factors which affect the length of that interval is relatively straight-forward and requires little time. This approach also requires distributions of birth intervals by the type of termination, though these need not be further categorized as to the degree of consanguinity of the couples from which the data are collected. While still rare, these distributions are not quite as difficult to obtain as those which are categorized by degree of consanguinity. It is thus in an attempt to produce a quick, though not completely accurate result, and as an exercise in methodology that we approach this problem through Monte Carlo simulation. This may be a useful approach for a number of problems with relatively intractable analytic solutions. The simulation can be done rather quickly and from the results of the simulation one is in a better position to decide if it will be fruitful to pursue the analytic solution. It is also worth noting that if the empirical distributions are based upon reasonably large samples, this approach is essentially "non-parametric" in the sense that no assumptions are made about the nature of the distributions nor the number of parameters required to represent these distributions accurately; thus it can serve to test the "robustness" of the parametric approaches with their assumptions about functional forms. Parenthetically, this approach also serves another interest of ours, namely, an evaluation of the effect upon the distribution of birth intervals of the application of various "stopping rules" associated with family planning practices.

The simulation was conducted under the optimum conditions set forth above in order to produce the "best" discrimination one could obtain between random and consanguineous birth intervals. It involved constructing a set of files of simulated families from which were computed the mean pregnancy termination intervals. The simulation proceeded as follows (see Figure 1):

(1) an age at marriage was selected for each woman at random from a distribution of ages at marriage;

(2) a genotype was then selected randomly for the woman from a distribution of parental genotypes. In the instance of only one locus with two alleles, there are three possible genotypes, of course, but since the recessive homozygote is defined to be lethal, only two genotypes are actually represented among the reproducing population;

(3) a genotype was randomly selected for the woman's mate from the same distribution of

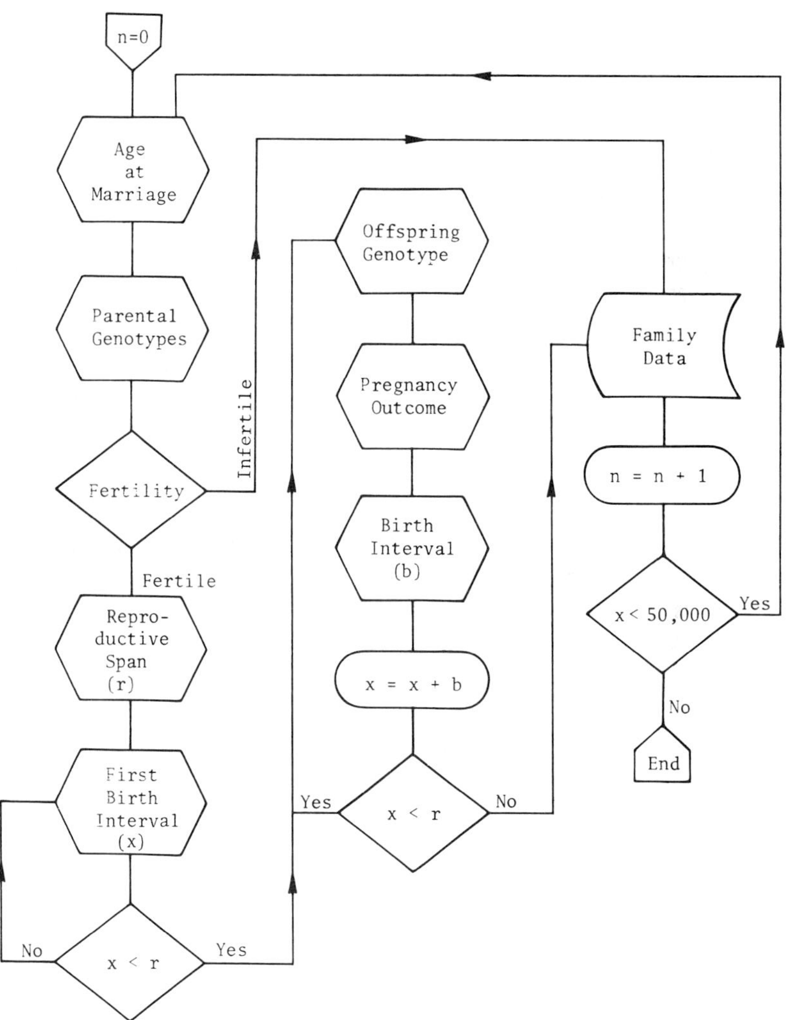

Figure 1. FLOW CHART OF FAMILY SIMULATION

parental genotypes;

(4) the sterility or non-sterility of the mating was then determined from a distribution of the frequency of infertile marriages given the age of the wife at marriage;

(5) if the marriage was sterile the wife's age at marriage, husband's and wife's genotypes and the observation that the marriage was sterile were written into a file and the simulation of another family was begun.

(6) if the marriage was fertile a reproductive span was randomly selected from a distribution of reproductive span lengths as a function of maternal age at marriage. In this context, reproductive span is the interval between the beginning of cohabitation and the termination of the last known pregnancy;

(7) a first birth interval was then randomly selected from a distribution of first birth intervals;

(8) this interval was compared to the length of the reproductive span for that mating;

(9) if the interval was longer than the reproductive span another interval was selected, since there must be at least one pregnancy in a fertile marriage;

(10) if the interval was smaller than the reproductive span a genotype was randomly selected for the offspring from a distribution of offspring genotypes given the parental genotypes;

(11) the outcome of this pregnancy, a live birth, neonatal death, or stillbirth was then randomly determined from a distribution of pregnancy outcomes given the offspring's genotype and a non-genotype dependent probability of each pregnancy outcome.

(12) The subsequent birth interval was then randomly selected from a distribution of intervals as a function of the previous

pregnancy outcome;

(13) this interval was added to the previous interval and their sum was compared with the length of the reproductive span;

(14) if this sum was less than the reproductive span a genotype, pregnancy outcome, and subsequent birth interval were generated.

(15) if the sum was greater than the reproductive span, 20 months were added to the reproductive span and the sum checked against this value. This was necessary since the probability is much greater that not all of the reproductive span will be filled with pregnancies, than is the probability that the reproductive span will be completely filled. If this were the case then the simulated distribution of reproductive spans would have a smaller mean value than the empirical distribution. The addition of 20 months to the span in which only one more termination is allowed takes care of this problem. (It should be noted, however, that while the mean values of the simulated and empirical distributions are nearly the same, the variance of the simulated distribution will be larger as a result of this correction.) If the birth interval sum was smaller than this adjusted span, then a final genotype and pregnancy outcome were generated and the following information on the family was written into a file. If the sum was still larger than the adjusted reproductive span, the following information was immediately written into a file:

(a) age at marriage of the mother,
(b) the maternal genotype,
(c) the paternal genotype, and
(d) the length of the reproductive span;

then for each pregnancy termination was recorded:

(a) the time into the reproductive span

when this termination occurred,
(b) the genotype of the offspring, and
(c) the outcome of the pregnancy.

This process was repeated until 50,000 families had been simulated.

The input necessary for this simulation are distributions of:

(1) maternal age at marriage
(2) parental genotypes
(3) sterility by age at marriage
(4) reproductive span by age at marriage
(5) length of the first birth interval
(6) length of the birth interval following a live birth surviving
(7) length of the birth interval following a neonatal death
(8) length of the birth interval following a stillbirth
(9) offspring genotype given parental genotypes
(10) pregnancy outcome given offspring genotype.

The distributions of parental and offspring genotypes are Hardy-Weinberg expected proportions for various frequencies of the recessive allele. The distributions of maternal age at marriage, length of the reproductive span and length of the four types of birth intervals were derived from a joint census conducted by the University of Michigan and a number of Japanese institutions on the island of Hirado in Japan. This census encompassed approximately 10,000 marriages and 40,000 pregnancies. These data are excellent for use in the simulation since there appears to have been little family limitation practiced among the families of completed reproductive performance censused, which results in simulated families with approximately "natural" reproductive histories. The number of parities per family is about five so that in the simulation of 50,000 families about 250,000 pregnancies have been generated.

The output of the simulation, then, is a file of simulated families. From this file the average interval and its variance were computed for each parity by the size of the family and the order of the parity. These birth intervals were computed from those simulated matings which were potentially segregating for the lethal allele and separately for those which were not. Ascertainment of potentially segregating families was through the mating type of the parents. The gene frequencies used to construct this file were chosen so that an approximately equal number of potentially segregating and non-segregating matings would be generated. The expected proportions of potentially segregating and non-segregating matings were then calculated, assuming random mating and first cousin mating for a number of frequencies of the lethal allele (Li 1961: 175). Using these proportions, mean birth intervals were derived for random matings and for first cousin matings from the array of birth intervals computed from potentially segregating and non-segregating simulated families. This procedure was carried out twice. In the first simulation the lethal homozygous recessive was assumed to act as a stillbirth and in the second, as a neonatal death. The mean and variance of birth intervals from random and first cousin mating for lethality by stillbirth and neonatal death were then calculated. In all cases the difference in birth intervals was very small, being at most no greater than about 0.05 months. The difference in the time to last pregnancy termination did not rise above 0.3 months. At all frequencies of the lethal allele the difference between random and consanguineous matings was larger for lethality by stillbirth than lethality by neonatal death, as was to be expected. This is because the average birth interval following a neonatal death is slightly longer than the average interval following a stillbirth. While the size of the difference between random and consanguineous matings in birth interval was very small, as stated, the direction was as we would have expected. The first cousin matings, being at greater risk of homozygosity and, therefore, of a pregnancy terminating in a stillbirth or neonatal death displayed a shorter birth interval. To recapitulate briefly, for this test of the recessive lethal effect on the birth interval the direction of the effect is consistent with the theory, but the size of the effect is quite small.

In an attempt to increase the size of this difference we next approached the mating, with respect to segregation, through the children rather than through the mating type of the parents. In this way instead of the segregating class consisting of all those matings which were potentially segregating it contained only those matings in which segregation did in fact occur, plus those matings in which a stillbirth (or neonatal death) occurred at random from causes other than the recessive lethal under study. In this test two files of families were generated with the recessive lethal acting through stillbirth. The first file was a simulation of 50,000 randomly mating families, with the frequency of the recessive allele of 0.15. This frequency was chosen because in the previous work it was shown to be the optimum gene frequency for obtaining the maximum difference in the number of potentially segregating matings between random and first cousin matings. The second file was a simulation of 50,000 first cousin matings with the same frequency for the recessive allele. The mean intervals between terminations for all those families which contained a stillbirth were computed by family size and order of the parity from both files. These data appear in Tables 1 - 6. In all six tables, homozygosity for the mutant allele results in a stillbirth; the frequency of the mutant allele is 0.15; and ascertainment is through affected offspring. Notice that the mean of the termination interval is around 30 months and the variance near 180 months, which is consistent with the distribution reported by Jacquard and Léridon in this volume, for families not practicing birth control. This procedure was carried out again for lethality acting through neonatal death. The differences in the termination intervals are larger here than in the previous study, ranging from about 0.3 to 0.9 months. For the time to last pregnancy termination

Family Size	N		Rank of Birth 1	2	3	4	5	6	7	8	9	10+
1	45	$\bar{X}$	19.16									
		$\hat{\sigma}^2$	233.36									
2	339		22.06	28.08								
			493.55	296.56								
3	454		22.36	31.63	31.50							
			394.66	316.22	300.03							
4	703		22.63	31.11	32.16	33.41						
			350.49	249.66	283.83	309.23						
5	1096		21.58	31.42	32.14	31.82	32.03					
			297.11	234.00	231.85	225.35	237.73					
6	1238		19.89	31.01	31.51	31.21	31.82	32.03				
			239.04	218.42	222.79	216.35	234.93	214.78				
7	1396		19.69	30.81	30.04	31.25	30.59	31.34	31.37			
			211.69	188.72	171.97	221.20	174.71	205.95	193.19			
8	1201		18.13	30.35	29.66	30.65	30.97	30.34	30.18	30.49		
			150.73	172.20	157.68	192.92	180.79	176.72	172.42	154.88		
9	1015		17.96	28.35	29.52	29.39	29.66	29.40	29.12	29.01	29.13	
			133.52	134.46	143.42	140.09	152.28	130.55	140.70	130.11	113.67	
10+	923		15.77	27.17	27.27	27.21	27.89	27.40	28.44	27.49	27.61	28.05
			99.63	117.95	107.49	108.73	117.43	106.77	111.39	112.00	109.14	116.51
TOT	8410		19.59	30.11	30.38	30.69	30.61	30.31	29.95	29.13	28.41	28.05
			233.27	200.63	193.95	202.63	187.28	174.93	160.44	135.68	112.04	116.51
		N	8410	8365	8026	7572	6869	5773	4535	3139	1938	1427

Table 1. BIRTH INTERVALS FOR RANDOMLY MATING FAMILIES SEGREGATING FOR THE MUTANT ALLELE

Family Size	N		Rank of Birth 1	2	3	4	5	6	7	8	9	10+
1	45	$\bar{X}$	18.71									
		$\hat{\sigma}^2$	252.03									
2	326		22.12	27.96								
			505.20	310.90								
3	433		22.57	31.35	31.41							
			396.50	303.19	280.28							
4	676		22.64	31.40	31.79	33.55						
			353.93	264.82	273.82	313.32						
5	1079		21.69	31.63	32.20	31.79	31.80					
			287.44	237.79	231.97	227.73	232.70					
6	1200		20.03	30.98	31.40	31.25	32.11	31.85				
			247.38	222.35	226.63	217.23	241.42	205.38				
7	1369		19.51	30.81	30.13	31.64	30.54	31.36	31.49			
			205.16	192.70	178.03	224.91	174.75	201.50	200.01			
8	1171		18.13	30.40	29.49	30.75	31.32	30.08	30.31	30.59		
			153.18	177.14	149.59	195.44	186.56	170.30	175.30	155.50		
9	997		17.93	28.53	29.47	29.49	29.68	29.49	28.99	29.01	29.18	
			135.49	138.57	141.36	137.82	149.79	135.27	133.00	127.12	110.39	
10+	903		15.98	27.15	27.29	27.19	27.84	27.44	28.47	27.56	27.81	28.03
			101.48	118.35	108.36	107.05	116.42	105.42	115.24	113.79	107.23	113.20
TOT	8199		19.62	30.16	30.32	30.80	30.67	30.24	30.00	29.18	28.53	28.03
			233.29	204.49	191.88	204.01	188.22	170.86	162.52	135.47	109.30	113.20
		N	8199	8154	7828	7395	6719	5640	4440	3071	1900	1376

Table 2. BIRTH INTERVALS FOR CONSANGUINEOUSLY (FIRST COUSIN) MATING FAMILIES SEGREGATING FOR THE MUTANT ALLELE

Family Size		Rank of Birth 1	2	3	4	5	6	7	8	9	10+
1	$\bar{X}$	0.22									
	$\hat{\sigma}^2$	2.70									
2		0.41	0.61								
		0.75	0.46								
3		0.43	0.89	0.79							
		0.45	0.35	0.33							
4		0.44	0.47	0.81	0.59						
		0.26	0.19	0.20	0.23						
5		0.12	0.14	0.22	0.26	0.37					
		0.13	0.11	0.11	0.10	0.11					
6		0.24	0.50	0.54	0.47	0.35	0.59				
		0.10	0.09	0.09	0.09	0.10	0.09				
7		0.28	0.30	0.25	0.11	0.32	0.29	0.25			
		0.08	0.07	0.06	0.08	0.06	0.07	0.07			
8		0.23	0.36	0.46	0.34	0.22	0.51	0.32	0.34		
		0.06	0.07	0.06	0.08	0.08	0.07	0.07	0.07		
9		0.17	0.17	0.29	0.21	0.25	0.22	0.32	0.26	0.24	
		0.07	0.07	0.07	0.07	0.08	0.07	0.07	0.06	0.06	
10+		0.07	0.31	0.29	0.31	0.33	0.28	0.30	0.27	0.20	0.52
		0.06	0.06	0.06	0.06	0.06	0.06	0.06	0.06	0.06	0.04
TOT		0.23	0.36	0.41	0.31	0.31	0.39	0.29	0.29	0.22	0.52
		0.01	0.01	0.01	0.01	0.01	0.02	0.02	0.02	0.03	0.04

Table 3. DIFFERENCE BETWEEN THE BIRTH INTERVALS OF RANDOMLY MATING AND CONSANGUINEOUSLY MATING FAMILIES (RANDOM-FIRST COUSIN) SEGREGATING FOR THE MUTANT ALLELE

Family Size	Mean	Variance	Number
1	19.16	233.36	45
2	50.15	832.42	339
3	85.50	978.66	454
4	119.31	1062.32	703
5	148.99	1069.38	1096
6	177.47	1115.70	1238
7	205.08	1053.70	1396
8	230.76	996.22	1201
9	251.54	844.35	1015
10+	279.62	844.96	923

Table 4. REPRODUCTIVE SPANS FOR RANDOMLY MATING FAMILIES SEGREGATING FOR THE MUTANT ALLELE

Family Size	Mean	Variance	Number
1	18.71	252.03	45
2	50.07	866.19	326
3	85.33	958.19	433
4	119.38	1084.86	676
5	149.12	1050.85	1079
6	177.62	1119.39	1200
7	205.48	1056.74	1369
8	231.07	997.05	1171
9	251.78	844.90	997
10+	279.44	845.03	903

Table 5. REPRODUCTIVE SPANS FOR CONSANGUINEOUSLY (FIRST COUSIN) MATING FAMILIES SEGREGATING FOR THE MUTANT ALLELE

Family Size	Mean	Variance
1	0.22	2.70
2	1.02	1.28
3	2.11	1.09
4	2.30	0.78
5	1.10	0.49
6	2.70	0.46
7	1.80	0.38
8	2.77	0.42
9	2.13	0.42
10+	3.15	0.46

Table 6. DIFFERENCE BETWEEN THE REPRODUCTIVE SPANS OF RANDOMLY MATING AND CONSANGUINEOUSLY MATING FAMILIES (RANDOM-FIRST COUSIN) SEGREGATING FOR THE MUTANT ALLELE

the differences range to over three months. Again, the interval differences are in the proper direction with all first cousin matings giving birth intervals shorter than the random mating intervals.

From this study it could be concluded that there is a recessive lethal effect on the intervals between pregnancy terminations, though this effect is small. It is even smaller when one considers that this study dealt with optimal circumstances for detecting that difference, namely 100 per cent lethality and complete penetrance. Any allele which was a semi-lethal would produce a smaller effect. Also the consanguinity of the marriages used here is high (first cousins); any lesser degree of relationship would also result in a smaller difference. So it would seem that the chance of measuring this recessive lethal effect in real populations is small, since the sample size needed to detect these differences would be impracticably large. But there are other factors this study did not take into account, some due to the nature of the Hirado data, which might increase the size of the difference. First, the first birth interval was drawn from the same distribution for random and first cousin matings. If this interval could have been calculated separately for each type of mating, there might have been a larger difference in the first birth intervals between random and first cousin matings. Secondly, all pregnancy terminations before the 28th week were ignored, since quite a large number of these probably went unrecorded, due to the failure of informants to recall them completely. These were subsumed in the next birth interval for that individual. Thus, any recessive lethal effects that result in early abortions were not simulated in this study. In the simulation itself some of the stillbirths or neonatal deaths were caused by factors other than the lethal locus studied. There was a probability that 2.8 per cent of all terminations ended in stillbirth from environmental and other genetic causes. For neonatal deaths this probability was 5.6 per cent. Thus, of the approximately 13,500 stillbirths simulated, only approximately

45 per cent were due to the lethal allele. Part of the reason for the small difference may be due then to the large number of families who were incorrectly included as segregating for the lethal allele on the basis of the occurrence of a stillbirth. In this simulation only one lethal allele was studied, although, of course, there are probably many potentially lethal alleles segregating in real populations. If the effect of these alleles is approximately additive, the difference in the birth interval should go up as the number of segregating loci increases. This would also dampen the effect of the non-genetic stillbirth component. Thus, with an increase in the complexity of the genetic constitutions simulated and some improvement in the input data, it may be possible to contrast birth interval differences collected in the field with theoretical ones generated by this simulation, or eventually analytically, in order to approximate the number of lethal equivalents segregating in a population.

REFERENCES

Li, C. C. 1961. Human Genetics, Principles and Methods. New York: McGraw-Hill.

Schull, W. J. 1958. Empirical risks in consanguineous marriages: Sex ratio, malformation, and viability, American Journal of Human Genetics 10: 294-343.

Slatis, H. M., R. H. Reis and R. E. Hoene 1958. Consanguineous marriages in the Chicago region, American Journal of Human Genetics 10: 446-64.

ACKNOWLEDGMENTS

The support of U.S. Atomic Energy Commission Grant AT(11-1) -1552 and the National Institutes of Health, through grant GM 19513, is gratefully acknowledged.

A BRIEF DISCUSSION OF THE ROLE OF CO-ADAPTED SETS IN THE PROCESS OF ADAPTATION

JOHN H. HOLLAND

Theses:

(Suggested by theoretical and simulation studies, but requiring experimental verification)

1. The adaptive process works largely in terms of pools of co-adapted sets of alleles (rather than gene pools).
2. The genetic operators *crossover*, *inversion*, and *dominance change* are crucial to this process and new adaptations frequently arise from their action.
3. Mutation often serves as a "background" process, generating new alleles but being secondary to the other operators in generating "deeper" adaptations.
4. To understand current (or recent) genetic patterns the action of genetic operators on co-adapted sets must be taken into account (or be explicitly discounted).

Theoretical Basis:

(There is a close relation between the processes discussed here and the models discussed by Alice Brues in this volume).

Let $\mathcal{A}$ be the set of genotypes of interest and let $\delta_i: \mathcal{A} \to V_i$ designate for each genotype $A \in \mathcal{A}$ the allele occurring at the ith locus. That is, for genotypes involving ℓ genes, $(\delta_1(A), \delta_2(A), \ldots, \delta_\ell(A))$ gives the set of alleles belonging to A. Our objective is to designate subsets of $\mathscr{A}$ which have specified sets of alleles in common. To do this let the symbol "□" indicate that we "don't care" what allele occurs at a given locus. Thus $(v_{13},\square,\square,\ldots,\square)$ designates the subset of all elements in $\mathscr{A}$ having the allele $v_{13} \varepsilon V_1$ at locus 1. (Equivalently, $(v_{13},\square,\ldots,\square)$ designates the set of all ℓ-tuples in $\mathscr{A}$ beginning with the symbol v_{13}; hence, for $\ell = 3$, (v_{13},v_{22},v_{32}) and (v_{13},v_{21},v_{31}) belong to $(v_{13},\square,\square)$, but (v_{12},v_{22},v_{32}) does not). The set of all ℓ-tuples involving combinations of "don't cares" and alleles is given by the augmented product set $\Xi = \Pi_{i=1}^{\ell}\{V_i \cup \{\square\}\}$. Then any ℓ-tuple $\xi = (\Delta_{i_1},\Delta_{i_2},\ldots,\Delta_{i_\ell}) \varepsilon \Xi$ designates a subset of $\mathscr{A}$ as follows: $A \varepsilon \mathscr{A}$ belongs to the subset if and only if (i) whenever $\Delta_{i_j} = \square$, any allele from V_j may occur at the jth locus of A, and (ii) whenever $\Delta_{i_j} \varepsilon V_j$, the allele Δ_{i_j} must occur at the jth position of A. (For example, $(v_{11},v_{21},v_{31},v_{43})$ and $(v_{13},v_{21},v_{32},v_{43})$ belong to $(\square,v_{21},\square,v_{43})$ but $(v_{11},v_{21},v_{31},v_{42})$ does not). The set of ℓ-tuples belonging to Ξ will be called the set of *schemata*; Ξ amounts to a decomposition of $\mathscr{A}$ into a large number of subsets based on the occurrence of specified combinations of alleles.

A schema will be said to be *defined on* the set of loci $\{i_1,\ldots,i_h\}$ at which $\Delta_{i_j} \neq \square$. A given genotype $A \varepsilon \mathscr{A}$ is an *instance* of schema $\xi \varepsilon \Xi$ just in case it is a carrier for the alleles which define ξ. Each genotype $A \varepsilon \mathscr{A}$ is an instance of 2^ℓ distinct schemata, as can be easily affirmed by noting that A is an instance of any schema ξ defined by substituting "□"s for one or more of the ℓ alleles defining A's genotype. Thus a single genotype A constitutes a trial of 2^{ℓ} distinct schemata. (If ℓ is only 20 this is still information about a million schemata!)

Consider a population $\mathcal{A}(t) = \{A_j(t), j = 1,\ldots,N(t)\}$ of $N(t)$ individuals at time t, where each individual $A_j(t)$ has fitness $\mu_j(t)$ at that time. Let $\delta_\xi(A) = 1$ if $A \varepsilon \xi$ (that is, if A carries the set of alleles defining ξ), otherwise $\delta_\xi(A) = 0$. Then the average fitness $\hat{\mu}_\xi(t)$ observed for the carriers of ξ at time t is given by

$$\hat{\mu}_\xi(t) = \frac{\Sigma_{j \text{ such that } A_j \text{ carries } \xi}\, \mu_j(t)}{N_\xi(t)}$$

$$= \frac{\Sigma_{j=1}^{N(t)} \delta_\xi(A_j(t))\mu_j(t)}{N_\xi(t)} ,$$

and by the definition of fitness

$$N_\xi(t+1) = \Sigma_{j=1}^{N(t)} \delta_\xi(A_j(t))\mu_j(t)$$

gives the number of offspring carrying ξ. Whence

$$N_\xi(t+1) = (\Sigma_{j=1}^{N(t)} \delta_\xi(A_j(t))\mu_j(t))N_\xi(t)/N_\xi(t)$$

$$= \hat{\mu}_\xi(t)N_\xi(t)$$

From this we see that the rate of increase of *each* schema (i.e., the number of its carriers) is equal to the average fitness of *its* instances. In effect, then, we can assign a fitness (at each instant) to *each* schema which has one or more instances in the population. The number of distinct schemata present in $\mathcal{A}(t)$ is astronomically larger than the number of alleles, giving selection a much broader scope and allowing it to act much, much more rapidly. (With 2 alleles per locus and ℓ loci, a population of 100 individuals would typically exhibit $\sim 2\ell$ alleles, but some multiple of 2^{ℓ} schemata. For $\ell = 100$ this is 200 vs. 10^{30}!)

From the foregoing it should be clear that the average fitness of the population (its "adaptedness"), $\overline{\mu}(t)$, increases mainly in terms of increases in the number of carriers of co-adapted sets of alleles (schemata for which $\hat{\mu}_{\xi}(t) > \overline{\mu}(t)$) rather than of individual alleles alone.

Now let us look at crossover and inversion in this context:

Crossover affects the pool of schemata by:
(i) generating *new instances* of schemata in the pool, thus increasing confidence in the observed averages (cf. ξ in the diagram);

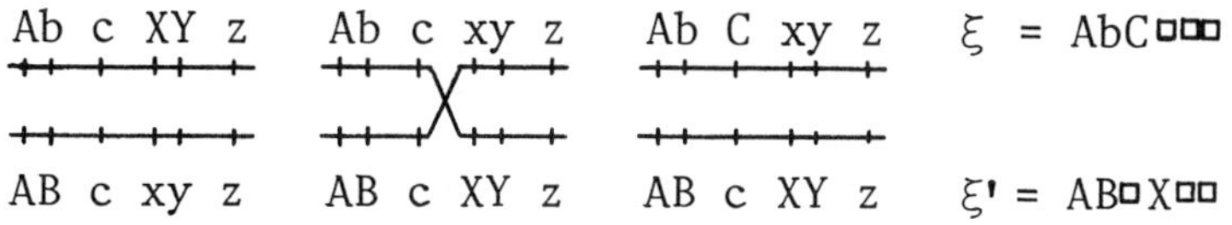

Ab c XY z   Ab c xy z   Ab C xy z ξ = AbC□□□

AB c xy z   AB c XY z   AB c XY z ξ' = AB□X□□

(ii) generating *new* (potentially co-adapted) *schemata* to add to the pool (cf. ξ' in the diagram).

Inversion affects the pool of schemata by changing the linkage (separation of alleles defining a schema) of schemata. In combination with reproduction, the net effect is to increase the linkage of *co-adapted* schemata.

Overall: Selection in terms of fitness combined with the genetic operators acts to continually test very large numbers of schemata for *new* adaptations (co-adapted schemata) while simultaneously exploiting and spreading adaptations (co-adapted schemata) already tested.

REFERENCES

Frantz, D. R. 1972. Non-linearities in genetic adaptive search. The Univ. of Michigan Ph.D. Dissertation.

Holland, J. H. 1971. Processing and processors for schemata, In Associative Information Techniques, E. L. Jacks (ed.) New York: American Elsevier.

Holland, J. H. Genetic algorithms and the optimal allocation of trials. In press.

SIMULATION OF SMALL HUMAN POPULATIONS

M. H. SKOLNICK
and
C. CANNINGS

INTRODUCTION

Our purpose here is twofold. First we shall describe a simulation program for the study of human populations (Cannings and Skolnick 1971), comparing and contrasting its various facets with other programs having similar objectives. Second, we shall present some of the results of our simulations, together with a theoretical discussion of their importance.

THE PROGRAM

Cavalli-Sforza and Zei (1966) (see also Barrai and Barbieri 1964), MacCluer (1967) and others (see MacCluer 1973) have developed simulation programs incorporating age and sex-specific fertilities and mortalities, marriage rules and a variety of other features. Our program incorporates the same basic elements, but has a different structure with, in our opinion, vital differences. We should emphasize here that we are concerned only with simulations which attempt to study the complete population process. There are many other programs referred to in this volume which concentrate on a portion of the life-cycle.

The populations in the programs of Cavalli-Sforza and Zei, and MacCluer develop in a similar way to a demographic projection (see for example Keyfitz 1968). Thus at equally spaced points in time one examines each individual in the population, asking a variety of simple questions: (i) does he (or she) die? (ii) if single, does he (or she) marry? (iii) if married, does he (or she) have a child? Each question is answered using the appropriate probability from the mortality and fertility tables which are being used. There are three important points to emphasize here: (i) a large number of questions are asked about each individual during his lifetime, (ii) a considerable amount of information has to be stored about each and every individual and (iii) considerable computer time is spent changing back and forth from person to person.

Our program poses essentially different types of questions at two points in the lifetime of each individual. Thus at the birth of an individual we immediately determine the age of death, and for a female also the age at marriage. At marriage we immediately determine the whole reproductive performance of the couple with a series of questions (as described in detail below). Thus in contrast to the programs above we need to store only information about individuals who are unmarried, and about the most recently married couple while carrying out their reproduction. Secondly, fewer questions are asked about each individual during his lifetime. These two facts result in economy of both time and space but, as we shall see below, there are other more important effects.

Overall Structure

The basic structure has been outlined above. We can best describe it by referring to a flow chart of an individual's life (see Figure 1).

I. Age of Death

At conception an age at death is assigned according to input mortality tables (sex-specific). We have extrapolated these tables to cover the foetal period, though little information is actually available on mortality at this stage. We have considered this extrapolation worthwhile since we believe that in primitive societies the high frequency of abortions will be

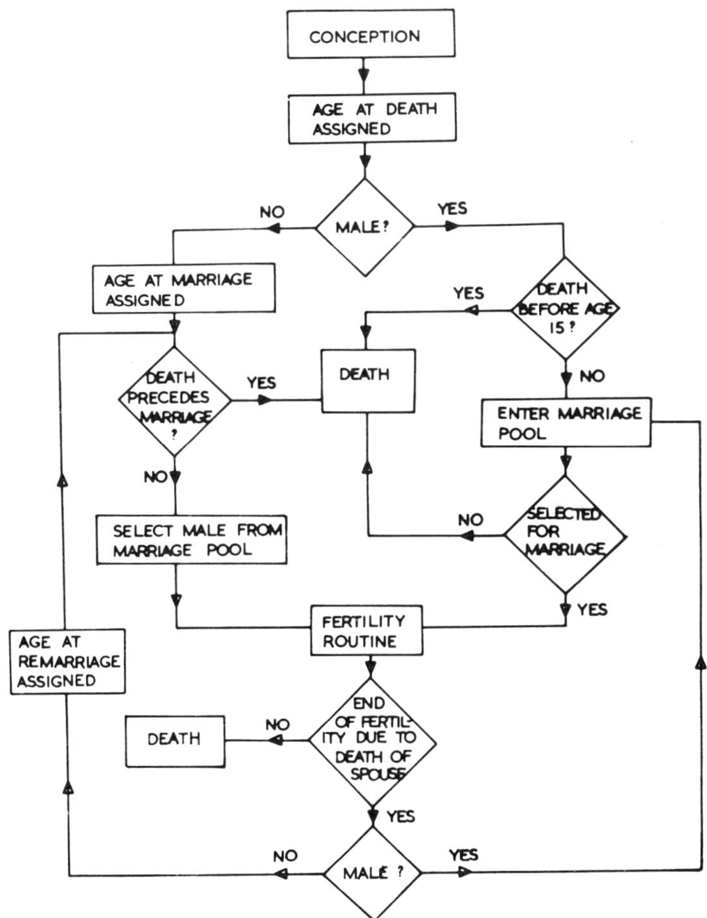

Figure 1. FLOW DIAGRAM OF INDIVIDUAL'S LIFE

important in determining the distribution of family size.

An individual who dies before the age of 15 years (or any other preferred age) is removed immediately; others will enter the marriage pool.

II. Marriage System

Assuming that a female does not die early, an age at marriage is assigned (Figure 2). This is the age at which a female will attempt to pick a mate from the available males.

For convenience we work in one year periods when determining the marriages. Each year all the females who are to pick mates during that year are identified. They are randomly ordered to prevent any systematic effects. The women are then taken one at a time, and a weight is assigned to every male in the pool (available males) dependent on age of male, age of female, clan membership, incest taboos, social class and any other desired criteria. A male is then drawn at random with probability proportional to the weighting. The possibility of a female failing to find a mate is incorporated, and is dependent on the suitability of the males available. An individual may also enter the pool upon divorce, or on the death of his or her spouse

Our model was formulated as an attempt to permit mate selection to be made according to multiple criteria considered simultaneously. We hope to further improve our model in the future by attempting to incorporate a system which involves all the men and women, rather than one woman and all the men, then another woman and all the men and so on.

III. Reproduction

Upon marriage, the couple enter the family building routine which is illustrated in Figure 3. The structure is basically the same as that of Ridley and Sheps (1966). The process is intended to mimic the reproductive process of a human couple. There is a

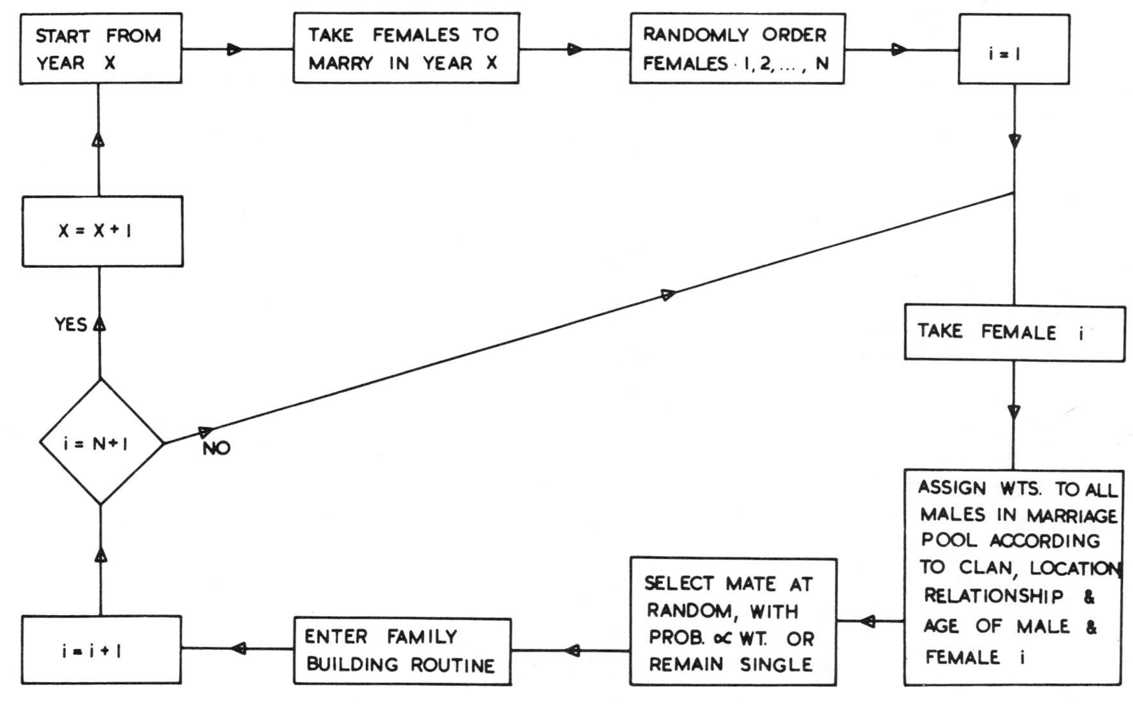

Figure 2. FLOW DIAGRAM OF MARRIAGE MARKET

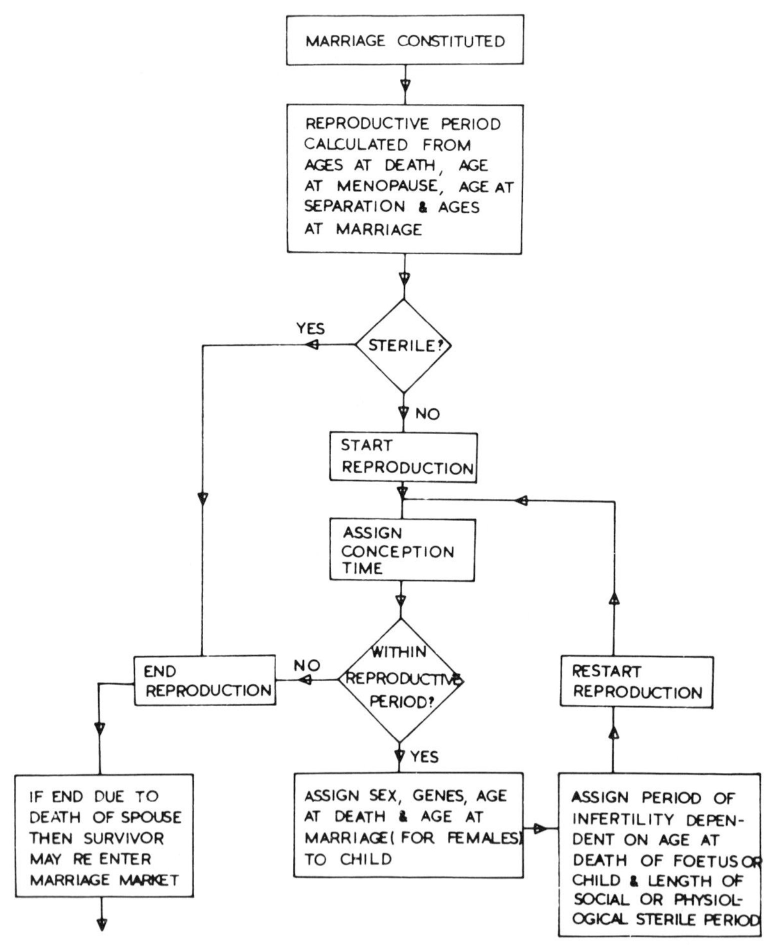

Figure 3. FLOW DIAGRAM FOR FERTILITY ROUTINE

waiting time to conception due to chance (see for example Singh and Bhattacharya 1970, for a discussion of fertility of couples), and due to fertility dependent on age and/or parity, and to individual variation. Abortion or birth is followed by a period of infertility which may result from taboos or physiological factors. The process then repeats itself until death, menopause or divorce terminates reproduction. Each child will have been assigned an age of death, and for females an age at marriage. If the reproduction is terminated by the death of one of the couple the survivor is allowed to re-enter the marriage routine.

In order to appreciate the effect of this routine vis-a-vis the reproductive process implicit in simulations which do not consider birth intervals, we consider a reproductive period of fixed length. Given the age at marriage of both male and female these latter programs can then assign a set of probabilities $p_i (i = 1, 2, ..., N)$, which correspond to the probabilities of there being a birth in the ith year of marriage. The distribution of family size for this couple is then Poisson-Binomial (Aitken 1957), and births occur independently of each other. Available evidence suggests that childspacing is practiced by many groups (e.g. Turnbull 1970, Neel 1970) which will have the effect of increasing the variance of the distribution of family size, and of course invalidating the assumption of independence of births within different intervals. The above model will thus be likely to underestimate the variance in family size (as occurs in MacCluer and Schull 1970b), and to produce child spacing distributions which are quite different from those observed in primitive populations.

In order to overcome the above strictures one can attempt to adjust p_i according to parity, or any other factor considered relevant. However, since the whole of the married population is stored at each point in time, a considerable increase in storage space will be needed, and additional computer time will be required.

Many of the problems which we wish to study are sensitive to family structure, and we believe that a simulation program must incorporate a structure of the type we have adopted.

We should point out here that there are various types of studies involving changing demographic parameters which can easily be made using our program. If the parameters are to change through time in some predetermined fashion, or if population structure is to affect marriages to be made in the near future these factors can easily be incorporated (Skolnick and Cannings 1972, Cannings and Skolnick 1971). On the other hand changes which are to occur instantaneously due to population size or structure, while not impossible to incorporate in our program, can more easily be encompassed in the other type.

It remains to be investigated how great are the effects of the various assumptions implicit in the two types of models. We believe however that they will be considerable, and that where doubt exists as to the effect of some factor in simulation it is best to attempt realism in one's adopted procedure.

Genetics

Each individual possesses genetic information which passes to his (or her) offspring according to the usual Mendelian rules (including sex-linkage and autosomal linkage).

There are two distinct categories of genetic problems which we wish to study. In the first the alleles are neutral, i.e., they have no effect on the survival or reproduction of an individual. In this case there is no need to give each individual genes during the population simulation, and there are advantages to be gained by not doing so. Our procedure is as follows. For each simulation run we output onto disk or tape the complete set of families with all demographic information. We then reconstruct pedigrees using a separate program. It might be noted that this reconstruction is facilitated by the fact that our families are generated in series rather than in parallel. We can then simulate the flow of genes through our pedigrees following an idea of Edwards (1969). This enables us to run an arbitrary number of loci even for rather large pedigrees without exceeding available storage. We have for example run as many as 30 loci, each with multiple alleles for a pedigree of some 1800 years in length. This capacity to run many loci enables us to separate the effects of population structure, and the effect of random segregation.

The second category of problems are those in which the genome affects the mortality and/or fertility of the individual. In these problems one clearly must transmit the genetic material to each individual during the main simulation run.

INPUT FUNCTIONS

We have selected a set of input functions which we hope roughly accord with a primitive hunting and gathering population. The paucity of data on such populations naturally implies that we are to a large extent guessing, but, we hope, guessing intelligently.

(i) Age- and Sex-specific Mortalities

These have been taken from Coale and Demeny (1966), East level 5. Life expectancy at birth for a male is 27.4 years and for a female 30.0 years. We have added a probability of foetal mortality since this is important in determining childspacing. A birth crisis is also incorporated. The values adopted are given in Table 1.

(ii) Fertility

Eight per cent of couples are taken as sterile. In the present runs no differences in fertility are assumed for other couples, except those implied by differential age at marriage, age at menopause, and the adjustment in the post-conception sterile period

Months After Conception	0-1	1-2	2-3	3-4	4-5	5-6	6-7	7-8	8-9
Probability of Death	.08	.05	.03	.02	.01	.01	.01	.01	.08

Table 1. FOETAL MORTALITY. THE PROBABILITY OF DYING WITHIN EACH MONTH FOLLOWING CONCEPTION.

	Mean	Variance
Conceptions	6.46	14.52
Births	4.04	6.73
Children dying before age 5	4.08	9.18
Children surviving past age 5	2.38	2.37
Children surviving past age 15	2.16	2.17

Table 2. MEAN AND VARIANCE OF TOTAL CONCEPTIONS, BIRTHS, OFFSPRING DYING BEFORE THE AGE OF 5 INCLUDING FOETAL DEATHS, CHILDREN SURVIVING PAST THE AGE OF 5 YEARS, AND CHILDREN SURVIVING PAST THE AGE OF 15 YEARS.

(See text for details)

implicit in the population control mechanism used (Skolnick and Cannings 1972). Other causes of variance in fertility were held constant in these simulations to emphasize eventual differences caused by prescriptive marriage rules.

(iii) Menopause

This is taken as N(40,3) (i.e. normal with mean 40 and standard error 3). Burch and Gunz (1967) suggested that the normal distribution is reasonable though the evidence is not strong.

(iv) Age At Marriage For Females

This is taken as 15 years plus a lognormally distributed random variable; i.e. 15 + EXP[C*0.7+0.75] where C is N(0,1). Thus the age at marriage for females has mean approximately 17.7 years and variance approximately 4.63.

(v) Post Conception Sterile Period, Y

Y is 1 + X*EXP(C/2) where C is N(0,1). Thus the mean is 1 + X*1.13 and variance X^2*0.36.

(vi) Conception Time, Z

Z is X*EXP(C) where C is N(0,1). Here X was taken as 0.3 so the mean conception time was approximately six months, and the variance approximately four months.

(vii) Age-difference Between Mates

Suppose that when a woman is to marry her age is AF, and a male in the marriage pool is aged AM, then the weight assigned to that male is equal to the standard normal probability density for $\left\{\frac{(AM-AF)-5}{3}\right\}$. Thus the most favored age difference is five years.

(viii) Clan-preference

A weight of 10 is used for a preferred as opposed to a non-preferred clan.

OUTPUT FUNCTIONS

We present here a variety of output functions related to the reproduction of 7753 families. Table 2 gives the mean and variance in number per family of (1) conceptions, (2) births, (3) children dying before the age of five years, (4) children surviving past age of five years and (5) children surviving past age of 15 years. These figures include sterile couples. Figure 4 shows graphs of (1), (3) and (4).

Figure 5 shows the distribution of length of reproductive period, including reproductive periods of length zero for the eight per cent of couples assumed to be sterile.

CLAN SYSTEMS

We have already indicated that the choice of mate is determined, amongst other things, by clan membership and relationship. In many modern societies certain prohibitions exist on marriages between certain close relatives, and the concept of relative is defined in accordance with biological relationship. On the other hand Fox (1967) suggests, and we are inclined to accept his arguments, that primitive populations may base their marriage rules on classificatory rather than biological relationships. As an example of this consider a tribe subdivided into two subgroups, or clans, A and B. A person in clan A regards all members of clan A as "brother" or "sister," but does not regard members of B in a similar manner. Clan B similarly regards itself as consisting of "brothers" and "sisters." A simple rule of exogamy, i.e. marriage must be made between members of different clans, is then equivalent to a prohibition of marriage between classificatory sibs. Similarly Fox points out

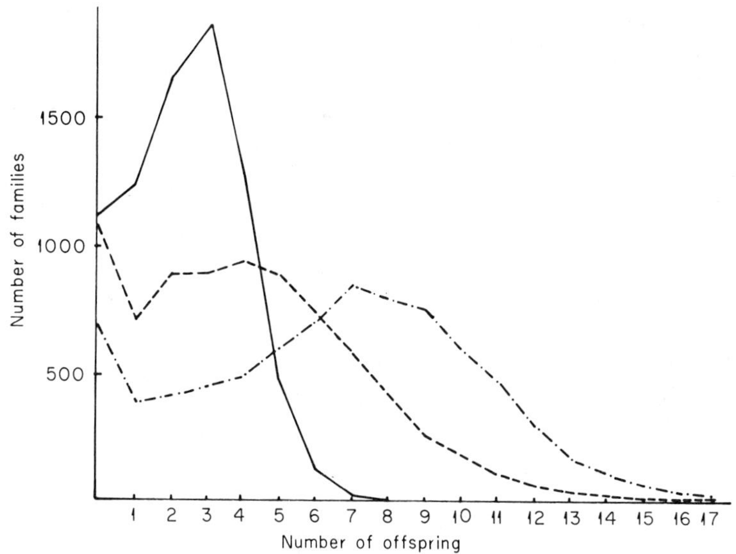

Figure 4. DISTRIBUTION OF NUMBERS OF CONCEPTIONS (———), CHILDREN DYING BEFORE AGE 5 (----) AND CHILDREN SURVIVING PAST AGE 5 (-·-·-·), FOR 7753 FAMILIES

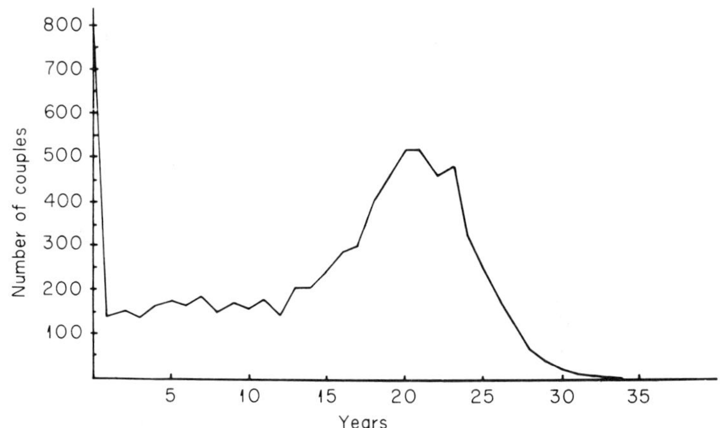

Figure 5. DISTRIBUTION OF LENGTH OF REPRODUCTIVE PERIOD

that a rule specifying a preference as well as prohibition may have a classificatory rather than a biological basis.

Since one of our main purposes is a study of the effect of clan structure on population dynamics we begin with a short discussion of some simple systems involving exogamy.

(i) 2-clans

The only possible system with two clans is represented in Figure 6, the arrow indicating the direction of movement of women at marriage. We shall assume that the children become members of their father's clan, i.e. the systems are patrilineal.

Such a system clearly excludes the possibility of sib-mating (assuming it to be strict) as does any exogamous system. Certain kinds of cousin marriages are, however, permitted. Individuals may be single first cousins in four ways, which we denote by (M*M), (M*F), (F*M) and (F*F). These brackets are to be interpreted in the following way: the symbol (or symbols) before the asterisk refer to the husband's ancestral line, those after to the wife's ancestral, M stands for a male ancester, F for a female ancestor and the asterisk denotes "is the sib of." Hence (M*M) should be read as "the husband's father is a sib of the wife's father." Other methods of writing relationships of this type have been discussed by Carnap (1958), Haldane and Jayakar (1962) and Kendall (1971). For the two clan exogamous system only two of the above four possibilities can occur, namely (M*F) and (F*M).

Similarly, of the two possible double first cousin marriages [(M*F) $\cup$ (F*M)] and [(M*M) $\cup$ (F*F)] (where "$\cup$" is read as "and") only the former is possible.

This illustrates a simple principle associated with 2-clan exogamous systems: relationship between spouses is through unlike sexed individuals.

(ii) 3-clan Systems and Cycling Systems

With three clans, five essentially different

Figure 6. TWO-CLAN MARRIAGE SYSTEM

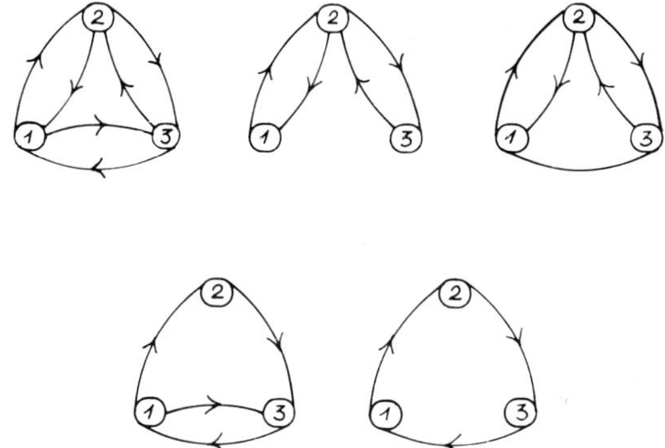

Figure 7. THREE-CLAN MARRIAGE SYSTEMS

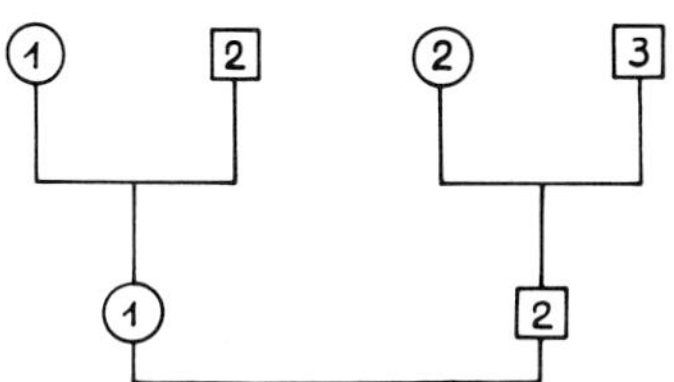

Figure 8. STANDARD TWO-GENERATION PEDIGREE FOR A MARRIED PAIR

systems arise (Figure 7).

There are essentially three distinct categories within these five possibilities. The first two contain only reciprocal arrangements, i.e., if a male of clan i may marry a female of clan j then a male of j may marry a female of i. The possible first cousin matings are the same as a 2-clan exogamous system. The third and fourth contain both reciprocal and non-reciprocal arrangements, and accordingly the types of cousin marriage allowed will depend on the clans in question. We shall not discuss this particular category here but concentrate instead on the third category of which the fifth system is the only case. In this case only non-reciprocal arrangements exist, and the system is cyclic. Here certain novel features of importance occur. As before, sib-mating is excluded. We may represent the standard two-generation pedigree for a married pair as in Figure 8. It is clear that the only possible single first cousin mating is (F*M), and no double first cousin matings are possible.

It should be noted that the one first cousin mating permitted is the demographically most favored one. In any system in which the male and female generation lengths differ, reflecting different ages at marriage, the most probable first cousin marriage is (F*M). The age at marriage of the husband plus the age at marriage of his mother then has the same expected value as the age at marriage of the wife plus the age at marriage of her father. Fox (1967) has pointed out this feature of indirect exchange systems, of which a cycling system is an example. A discussion of the frequency of consanguineous marriages of various types is given by Cavalli-Sforza *et al.* (1966), Barrai *et al.* (1962) and Hajnal (1963).

For an n-clan cycling system we can deduce a similarly simple rule specifying which m^{th} cousin $(m < n)$ marriages are possible. We call two individuals m^{th} cousins only if they are not k^{th} cousins for any $k < m$. We observe that the clan membership of any person in an ancestral line of an individual may be determined by counting the number of females in the ancestral line (if we arrange our labelling of clans sequentially around the cycle). Thus for an individual in clan i the ancestor specified by MMFF (i.e. his paternal grandfather's maternal grandmother) must be in clan (i+2), or more strictly clan (i+2) mod(n). If an ancestor of the husband is a sib of an ancestor of the wife, and hence is in the same clan, marriage can occur only if there is one more female in the husband's ancestral line than in the wife's ancestral line. Hence the possible first cousin marriages are (F*M), the possible second cousin marriages (FM*MM), (MF*MM), (FF*MF) and (FF*FM), and so on. Once again we see that only the demographically favored m^{th} cousin marriages occur, i.e. the expected time from the births of the common ancestors to the marriage of the descendants is the same for husband and wife.

As an indication of the effect of a cycling system on frequencies of cousin marriage we present Table 3 which records the number of possible types of mth cousin matings in n-clan cycling systems. The assumption $m < n$ has been removed so that situations are possible in which one of the ancestral lines contains a complete cycle of clan numbers, or in which the two ancestral lines together contain a complete cycle. These latter possibilities introduce some cousin matings which are not demographically *favored*. The total number of possible types of mth cousin matings is 2^{2m}. The last line contains the asymptotic value of the proportions of cousin matings permitted for various n.

(iii) Alternating Generation Systems

The above systems all permit some degree of first cousin marriage. Systems which are to exclude all first cousin marriages and which are to be both patrilineal and exogamous require some additional complexity.

m \ n	2	3	4	5	6	7	8	9	
1	2	1	1	1	1	1	1	1	
2	8	5	4	4	4	4	4	4	
3	32	21	16	15	15	15	15	15	
4	128	85	64	57	56	56	56	56	
5	512	341	256	220	211	210	210	210	
6	2048	1365	1024	859	804	793	792	792	
. . .									
∞	1/2	1/3	1/4	1/5	1/6	1/7	1/8	1/9	... 1/n

Table 3. THE NUMBER OF PERMISSIBLE TYPES OF mth-COUSIN MATINGS IN n-CLAN CYCLING SYSTEMS, WHERE 2^{2m} IS THE TOTAL NUMBER OF TYPES.

One way of achieving the elimination of first cousin marriage is to change the cycling rules from generation to generation, permitting matings of clans (1x2) and (3x4) in one generation and (1x3) and (2x4) in the next. This system would then permit the following four second cousin marriages of the sixteen possible types, (MM*MM), (MF*MF), (FM*FM) and (FF*FF).

Our purpose above has been to show how simple classificatory rules lead to somewhat complex prohibitions on marriages between biologically related individuals.

We should further note a facet of cycling systems, and indeed of some other systems; the system may break down completely if one clan becomes small. In contrast, the first four of the cases for 3-clan systems may degenerate, but not break down, if one of the clans disappears. This poses a problem in many simulations. One attempts to study the effect of some social system only to find that the system breaks down or degenerates during the simulation. We must therefore attempt to study ways in which systems maintain themselves, degenerate or evolve before we can move on with confidence to study their effects on population structure. This was one of our original objectives; and we have made a start on this aspect (Cannings and Skolnick, in preparation), and further work is in progress. We shall present in the next section, some results regarding rates of genetic drift in various systems.

Population Size

One of the problems we have encountered is control of population size. This is in general necessary if runs of a reasonable length are to be made. Accordingly we have effected a link between the period of post-conception sterility and population size.

We have discussed elsewhere (Skolnick and Cannings 1972) a tentative biological justification of our approach, suggesting prolonged lactation as a possible natural response to reduced food supply. Our attention has since been drawn to a possible direct connection between poor food intake and sterility (LeRoy Ladurie 1969 and references therein). These latter sources further validate our adopted method of control. We include here an example of population size control by this mechanism (Figure 9), others having appeared in Skolnick and Cannings (1972) and Cannings and Skolnick (in press).

One of our objectives in developing the present program was to study the evolution and natural selection of clan systems. Certain systems possess internal stability which should permit them to persist for long periods, while others break up rapidly, or require additional constraints. Figures 10 and 11 show how the Australian aborigine Kariera system incorporates a self-correcting factor which adjusts the clan sizes to approximate equality, whereas the cycling system, and others, rapidly lose one or more of the clans. Once a system loses a clan it may be impossible for some groups to find mates of the desired type. A brief discussion of this phenomenon is given in Cannings and Skolnick (in press) and further work is in progress.

Genetic Drift in Clan Systems

A variety of models have been developed for the study of the loss of variability of a population due to the sampling process which is implicit in Mendelian genetics. The results of these models are usually synthesized into a single measure called the rate of drift. This rate of drift corresponds to the largest non-unit latent root of the associated Markov matrix and specifies the asymptotic approach to fixation. It also corresponds to a multiplying factor for a certain function of the moments of the gene-frequency distribution (under fairly general conditions, Karlin and MacGregor 1965, Chia and Watterson 1969).

Thus for a non-overlapping two type haploid model with 2N individuals we may write

$$p_{t+1}(1-p_{t+1}) = \lambda p_t(1-p_t)$$

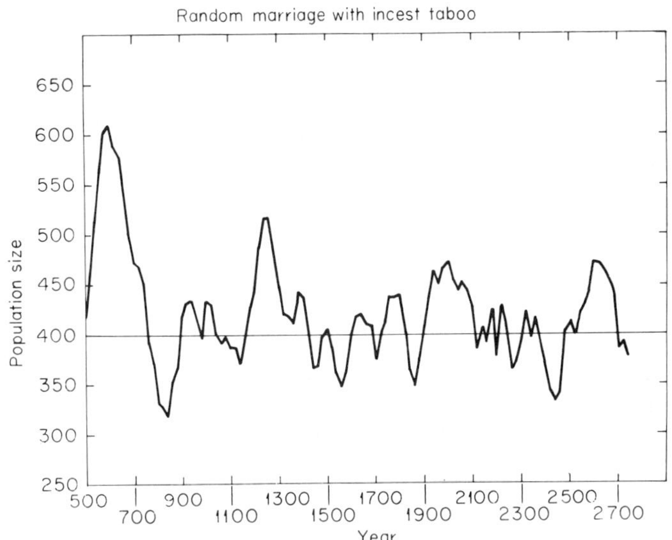

Figure 9. POPULATION SIZE CONTROLLED BY LENGTH OF POST-CONCEPTION STERILE PERIOD, IN A POPULATION WITH INCEST TABOO

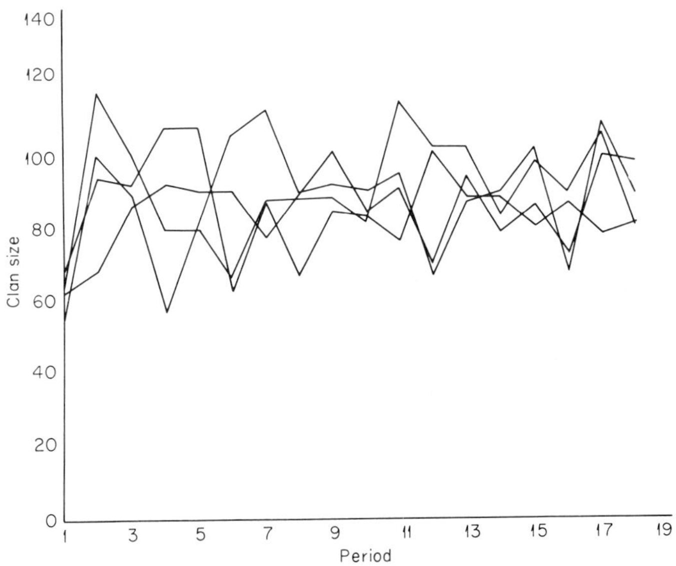

Figure 10. CLAN SIZES IN A SIMULATION OF THE AUSTRALIAN ABORIGINE KARIERA SYSTEM

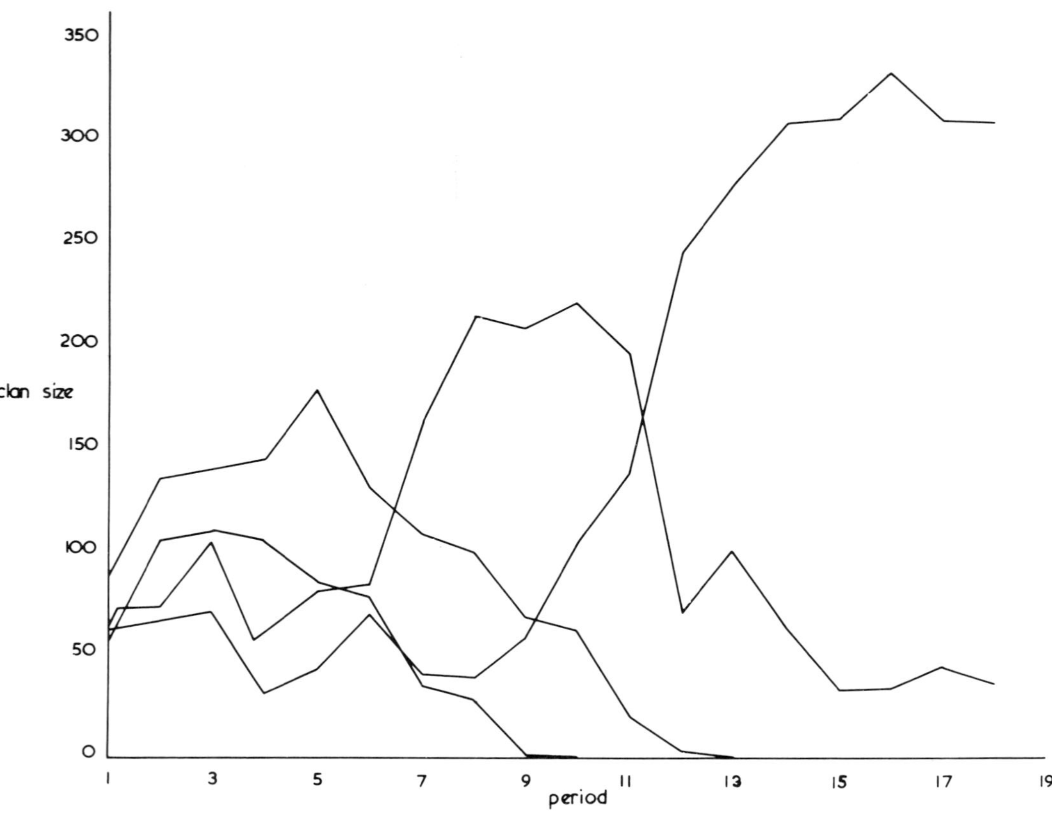

Figure 11. CLAN SIZES IN A SIMULATION OF A CYCLING SYSTEM

where p_t is the frequency of one of the types, and $\lambda = (1-\frac{1}{2N})$ (Wright 1931). This can be generalized to include m types and overlapping generations to give

$$H_{t+1} = \lambda H_t$$

where

$$H_t = \sum_{i \neq j} p_{it}\, p_{jt},$$

p_{it} is the frequency of the ith type in the tth generation. H_t is of course equal to (1 - probability of identity by descent) if we initiate the process with 2N different types.

The same situation arises when overlapping generations occur, as in the models of Moran (1958) and Chia and Watterson (1969).

Thus for a wide class of models (see Cannings 1973 for a discussion of some necessary conditions) we may deduce λ by considering the function H_t through time. Moreover if λ is close to unity H_t is approximately linear in t, i.e.

$$H_t = \lambda^t H_o = (1-\frac{1}{2N_e})^t H_o$$

$$\doteq H_o \left[1-\frac{t}{2N_e}\right]$$

where N_e is the effective population size (see for example Crow and Kimura 1972). This approximation provides a useful method of estimating N_e when H_t and H_o have been observed (possibly from a simulation). This is the method employed by MacCluer and Schull (1970a) for their simulations.

However the underlying model for our simulation is very far from the mathematical models mentioned above. We have incorporated different sexes, a clan structure, an age structure etc. all of which require the consideration of additional functions. These functions will be of a similar type to H_t but will relate to genes selected from various subpopulations (e.g. females of clan 1 with males of clan 2 etc.). The function H_t taken for the whole population will not satisfy an equation of the above type, and estimating N_e from H_t alone may give one a misleading value. Kimura and Crow (1963) have treated some systems involving subdivision of the population and have plotted H_t for some of these. It will readily be seen what the effect on our estimates of N_e might be if only H_t were considered.

Unfortunately, the exact functions which should be considered have not yet been found. Accordingly we will present graphs of H_t for the various systems without implying that λ can be calculated from these graphs. These plots are shown in Figures 12 and 13. The most surprising aspect of these graphs is that, notwithstanding the points mentioned above, H_t is approximately linear in t. The theoretical work on genetic drift is not yet adequate to provide an answer to this problem, but certain discrete generation models incorporating clan systems also show linearity in H_t (Cannings and Skolnick, in preparation).

For the moment we ignore this problem, and assume that the approximate linearity of a function through time allows us to obtain an approximation to λ (the dominant latent root). With this assumption we obtain $N_e = 250$ for a random mating population with a harmonic mean of $N = 420$.

The rate of genetic drift in the other systems simulated is approximately the same as the random mating system. However since the systems involved degenerate, with the exception of the Kariera, no valid comparison is at the moment possible. Theoretical work on the rates of drift in various clan systems

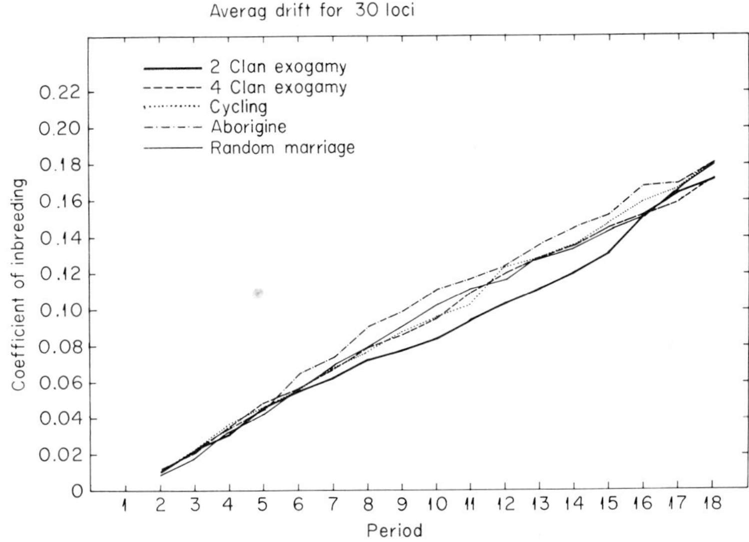

Figure 12. AVERAGE DRIFT FOR 30 LOCI

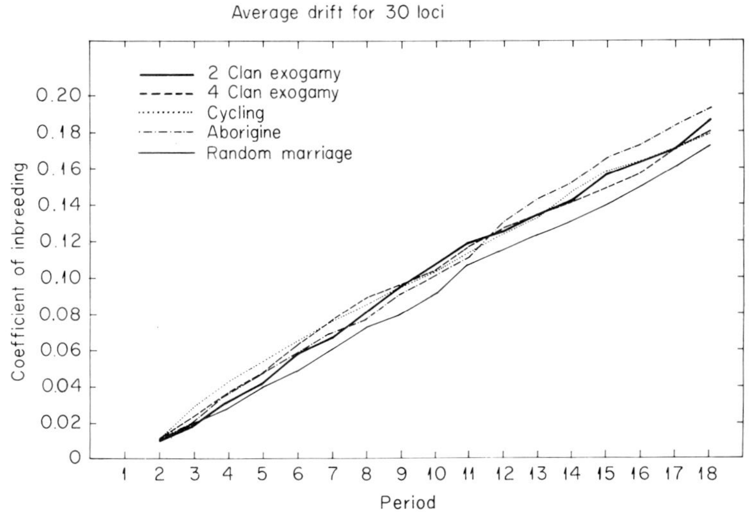

Figure 13. AVERAGE DRIFT FOR 30 LOCI

is in preparation.

DISCUSSION

We have described a model for simulating small human populations. The model has been implemented and we have attempted to investigate the effect of marriage systems on drift. As shown earlier, different marriage systems imply different levels of consanguineous marriage, and this might be expected to have an effect on drift. Nonetheless, we have found no evidence of significant differences in rates of drift. This may be due to the degeneration and breakdown of some systems, and to the relatively low preference for marrying according to the prescribed rules. However, the preliminary results from further simulations incorporating lower probabilities of violating the system (including zero probability) have shown similarly small differences in genetic drift. The investigation of the effect of degeneracy of the marriage systems on drift is more difficult. Increasing population size and decreasing the probability of violating the marriage system reduces the probability of systems degenerating, and again such simulations showed only small differences in rates of drift. However, it will be necessary to run more replicates in order to separate the effects of each factor before we can determine their relative roles.

REFERENCES

Aitken, A. C. 1957. Statistical Mathematics. Eighth Edition. Edinburgh: Oliver and Boyd.

Barrai, I. and D. Barbieri 1964. Drift in una popolazione simulata, Atti. Ass. Genet. 9: 233-245.

Barrai, I., L. L. Cavalli-Sforza and A. Moroni 1962. Frequencies of pedigrees of consanguineous marriages and mating structure of the population, Annals of Human Genetics 25: 347-376.

Burch, P. R. J. and F. W. Gunz 1967. The distribution of the menopausal age in New Zealand: an exploratory study, New Zealand Medical Journal 66: 6-10.

Cannings, C. 1973. The equivalence of some overlapping and non-overlapping models for the study of genetic drift, Journal of Applied Probability, In press.

Cannings, C. and M. H. Skolnick 1971. A study of human evolution by computer simulation, Paris: Fourth International Congress of Human Genetics.

Cannings, C. and M. H. Skolnick. Homeostatic mechanisms in human populations: a computer study, Oxford: International Congress of Cybernetics and Systems, In press.

Cannings, C. and M. H. Skolnick. Genetic drift in prescriptive marriage systems, In preparation.

Carnap, R. 1958. Introduction to Symbolic Logic and its Applications. New York: Dover.

Cavalli-Sforza, L. L., M. Kimura and I. Barrai 1966. The probability of consanguineous marriages, Genetics: 54: 37-60.

Cavalli-Sforza, L. L. and G. Zei 1966. Experiments with an artificial population, Chicago: Proceedings of the Third International Congress of Human Genetics.

Chia, A. B. and G. A. Watterson 1969. Demographic effects on the rate of genetic evolution 1: constant size populations with two genotypes, Journal of Applied Probability 6: 231-249.

Coale, A. and P. Demeny 1966. Regional Model Life Tables and Stable Populations. Princeton: Princeton Univ. Press.

Crow, J. F. and M. Kimura 1970. An Introduction to Population Genetics Theory. New York: Harper and Row.

Crow, J. F. and M. Kimura 1972. The effective number of a population with overlapping generations: a correction and further discussion, American Journal of Human Genetics 24: 1-10.

Edwards, A. W. F. 1969. Discussion to paper by A. P. Mange: Computer Applications in Genetics. N. E. Morton (ed.) Honolulu: Univ. of Hawaii Press.

Felsenstein, J. 1971. Inbreeding and variance effective numbers in populations with overlapping generations, Genetics 68: 581-597.

Fox, R. 1967. Kinship and Marriage. London: Penguin.

Hajnal, J. 1963. Concepts of random mating and the frequency of consanguineous marriages, Proceedings of the Royal Society B, 150: 125-174.

Haldane, J. B. S. and S. D. Jayakar 1962. An enumeration of some human relationships, Journal of Genetics 58: 81-107.

Karlin, S. and J. McGregor 1965. Direct Product Branching Processes and Related Induced Markoff Chains. I. Calculations of Rates of Approach to Homozygosity. Bernoulli, Bayes, Laplace Anniversary Volume. Berlin: Springer-Verlag.

Kendall, D. G. 1971. The algebra of genealogy, Mathematical Sprectrum 4: 7-9.

Keyfitz, N. 1968. Introduction to the Mathematics of Population. Reading, Mass.: Addison-Wesley.

Kimura, M. and J. Crow 1963. On the maximum avoidance

of inbreeding, Genetical Research 4: 399-415.

Le Roy Ladurie, E. 1969. L'aménorrhée de famine, Annales Economies, Sociétés, Civilisations 24: 1589-1601.

MacCluer, J. W. 1967. Monte Carlo methods in human population genetics: a computer model incorporating age-specific birth and death rates, American Journal of Human Genetics 19: 303-312.

MacCluer, J. W. 1973. Computer simulation in anthropology and human genetics, In Methods and Theories in Anthropological Genetics, M. H. Crawford and P. L. Workman (eds.) Albuquerque: Univ. of New Mexico Press.

MacCluer, J. W. and W. J. Schull 1970a. Estimating the effective size of human populations, American Journal of Human Genetics 22: 176-183.

MacCluer, J. W. and W. J. Schull 1970b. Frequencies of consanguineous marriages and accumulation of inbreeding in an artificial population, American Journal of Human Genetics 22: 160-175.

Moran, P. A. P. 1958. A general theory of the distribution of gene frequencies, I. Overlapping generations, Proceedings of the Royal Society B 149: 102-112.

Neel, J. V. 1970. Lessons from a "primitive" people, Science 170: 815-822.

Nei, M. and Y. Imaizumi 1966. Genetic structure of human populations II: differentiation of blood group gene frequencies among isolated populations, Heredity 21: 183-190.

Ridley, J. C. and M. C. Sheps 1966. An analytic simulation model of human reproduction with demographic and biological components, Population Studies 19: 297-310.

Singh, S. and B. Bhattacharya 1970. A generalized probability distribution for couple fertility, Biometrics 26: 33-40.

Skolnick, M. H. and C. Cannings 1972. The natural regulation of population size for primitive man, Nature 239: 287-288.

Turnbull, C. M. 1970. The Forest People. New York: Simon and Shuster.

Wright, S. 1931. Evolution in Mendelian populations, Genetics 16: 97-159.

ACKNOWLEDGMENTS

We should like to thank Professor L. L. Cavalli-Sforza for making available funds for developing the simulation program and running some initial simulations at the University of Pavia Computer Center under AEC grant AT (30-1)-2280. We also thank the Social Science Research Council and the Directors of the Statistical Laboratory and the Computer Laboratory, University of Cambridge, for providing facilities for the later simulations.

AVOIDANCE OF INCEST: GENETIC AND DEMOGRAPHIC CONSEQUENCES

JEAN WALTERS MacCLUER

Demographic methods and data are occasionally used in genetics to study the relationships between the demographic characteristics of populations and their genetic structure. Geneticists are interested in the consequences for population structure of genetically determined differences in vital rates, in methods for detecting such differences, and in the possibility that systematic changes in genetic structure might arise as a secondary consequence of certain kinds of demographic or social stratification. For many problems of population genetics, however, existing demographic techniques are inadequate. Population projection methods have been developed for predicting changes in age structure through time, but predictions must be made separately for the two sexes. No allowance is made for the fact that rates of reproduction in one sex may be greatly influenced by the availability of members of the opposite sex. Considerable effort is being made to develop marriage models which take into account age preferences for spouses and allow for fluctuations in the number of marriages according to the numbers of single males and females in various age groups (see McFarland 1972 for a critical review). However none of the models suggested have received widespread acceptance, and of course none of them take into account genetic heterogeneity of populations. Ideally, what is required for genetic studies is a marriage model which allows for age-specific differences in probabilities of mating and in desired characteristics of mates; incorporates divorce, widowhood and remarriage; takes into account biological and/or cultural restrictions on mating; and considers limitations on mating and variations in marriage rates and characteristics of spouses as a result of small population size. In addition it should be possible to consider all of these variables as functions of the genotypes of the individuals involved and the Mendelian principle of segregation should be incorporated.

In the absence of a suitable mathematical model including all these features, we have developed a discrete-time, stochastic microsimulation model which has been used to simulate the genetic and demographic characteristics of a variety of human populations and to investigate a number of genetic-demographic problems. With this model it has been possible to examine 1) the genetic consequences of socially derived advantages in mating, for example as a function of membership in a powerful clan, family or village; 2) the effect on genetic differentiation between populations of various patterns of nonrandom migration; 3) the rates and types of consanguineous marriage to be expected in populations with various kinds of mating rules; and 4) the rate of gene frequency drift in small age-structured populations. The results of these studies are summarized in MacCluer (1973a). In addition the program is being used to estimate age-specific birth and death rates in populations which are too small for the use of standard estimation procedures (Dyke and MacCluer 1973; Dyke 1973). We present here a further application of this computer simulation model, to the problem of the genetic and demographic consequences of incest prohibition.

THE SIMULATION PROGRAM

The simulation program used in this study is a modification of earlier simulation models of 1) a rural Japanese island population (MacCluer 1967; MacCluer and Schull 1970a, b); 2) a tribe of primitive South American Indians (MacCluer *et al.* 1971; MacCluer and Neel, in preparation); 3) a small French-speaking isolate in the Caribbean (Dyke and MacCluer 1973; Dyke 1973); and 4) a set of hypothetical human populations which are subdivided to varying degrees, with migration between subdivisions (MacCluer 1973b). The program, written originally for the IBM 7090 computer and later modified for a much smaller machine, the IBM 1130, has now been adapted for use on the IBM 360/67 and IBM 370/165 systems and should be adaptable for use on any large computer with a FORTRAN IV compiler. Approximately two minutes of CPU time are required on the IBM 360/67 to simulate births, deaths, marriages and migrations for 200 years for a population of size 400 subdivided into four villages. The program can simulate a population as large as 2,000 individuals with virtually no limit on the number of years simulated. All simulation output is stored on magnetic tape in order to simplify analysis of simulation results and to facilitate comparisons of results with those of other investigators. A simplified flow chart of the program is shown in Figure 1.

Input for a simulation run consists basically of 1) a set of variables describing each member of an initial population; 2) age- and sex-specific probabilities of dying, reproducing, migrating and searching for a mate; 3) a set of control parameters defining, among other things, the length of the reproductive period, the sex ratio at birth, the maximum number of wives a male may have at a given time, the maximum age attained by members of the population and the number of years to be simulated; and 4) a random number which is changed for each simulation run and which specifies the beginning of the sequence of pseudo-random numbers to be used in decision making. The description of the initial population includes for each member his identifying number and those of his parents, grandparents and great-grandparents (if known); sex, birth date, death date if dead, genotype (for an actual or hypothetical genetic locus), marital status, patronym (or lineage, or clan) and residence; and for females, number of offspring and interval since last birth. Vital rates may be genotype-dependent and may be held constant or varied through time according to specified patterns. The composition of the initial population is updated on a

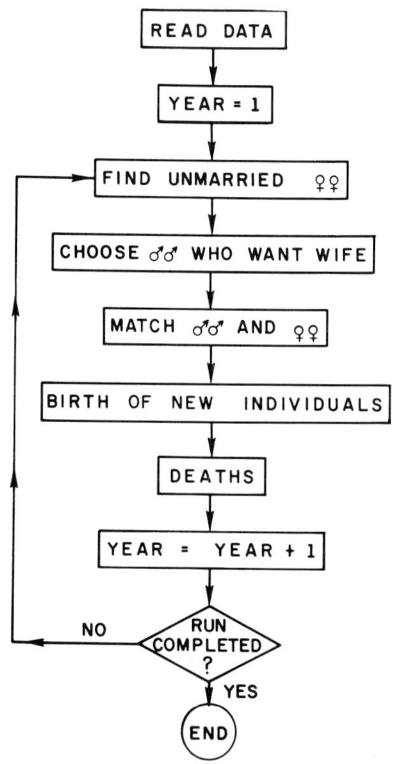

Figure 1. SIMPLIFIED FLOW CHART OF THE SIMULATION PROGRAM (Reprinted with permission of the Wistar Institute Press)

yearly basis with decisions being made for each individual with respect to marriage, reproduction, migration and survival.

The mating system may be either monogamous or polygynous. In either case males choose females, and the probability of searching for a mate is a function of the male's age and marital status (and genotype); his success in finding a mate may be allowed to vary according to clan or village affiliation. These variables, as well as age, may also be considered in determining the marriageability of a female or her appropriateness for a particular male. Although at present marriage may be terminated only by the death of a spouse, the model is being revised to allow for divorce. Individuals may remarry after they are widowed, according to age-specific probabilities of remarriage. Probabilities of reproduction may be a function not only of female age but also of interval since last birth. Although reproduction is limited mostly to married females, a frequency of nonpaternity may be specified. Migration is allowed not only between subdivisions of the population but outside as well, with migration rates varying according to residence, age, sex and marital status. In general, children migrate only with their parents and married women only with their husbands. In the version of the program now being developed, it is possible to specify a given rate of immigration from an infinite external population with predetermined characteristics (age and sex distribution, genotype frequencies, etc.). If desired these immigrants may share common ancestors with individuals in the artificial population. When an individual migrates the date of migration and the villages of origin and destination are recorded. At death the date of death is recorded and the information associated with the individual is retained for subsequent analysis.

In addition to the basic simulation program, a set of ancillary programs is used to store and reorder simulation output for subsequent analysis, to summarize simulation results across runs, to analyze fertility, mortality, mating and migration patterns in the artificial populations, to simulate gene segregation for any number of loci, to analyze genetic structure of artificial populations, to compute inbreeding coefficients and to perform simple simulations of demographic processes.

THE SIMULATION OF INCEST AVOIDANCE

In order to investigate the effects of incest avoidance on population structure, matched sets of simulation runs were done. For each set of simulations in which there was some degree of incest avoidance another set was run with the same initial conditions (population size and structure, probabilities of marrying, reproducing and dying) but with mating occurring at random with respect to the relationship of the potential spouses. Genetic and demographic analyses were done for each run and averages were computed for each set. By comparing the average performance of populations with and without incest, it was possible to draw certain conclusions about the consequences of incest avoidance. The initial populations were constructed on the basis of Coale and Demeny's *Regional Model Life Tables and Stable Populations* (1966). The age distribution for most sets of runs was that of a stable population subjected to mortality level 22 West (low mortality) with an intrinsic rate of increase of 0.5 per cent per year (exceptions will be pointed out later). Age-specific fertility rates were chosen according to the low fertility, broad peak pattern described in *Population Bulletin of the United Nations No. 7* (1965) and made to conform to the expected birth rates for the stable population. Probabilities of searching for wives for males, as well as the distribution of desired age of spouse for males of different ages, had to be determined on the basis of our experience with simulations of other low fertility, low mortality populations since there are no model nuptiality curves available.

In all sets of simulation runs the initial

population size was either 100 or 200 and run length was 200 years. Members of the population were assumed to live in one "village" with no migration either in or out. The limits of the reproductive period were assumed to be 15 to 50 for females and 15 to 65 for males. No individual lived beyond age 65. Marriage was monogamous, and there was no illegitimate birth. Unless otherwise stated, any mating closer than second cousins once removed was defined as incestuous. Thus, in runs in which incest was prohibited there were no matings between parent and child, siblings, uncle and niece, aunt and nephew, or first, first once removed, or second cousins. Certain other consanguineous marriages (e.g., grandparent-grandchild, first cousins twice removed) were also prohibited, but would be expected to be quite rare in any case because of the large age difference between the individuals involved.

EXPECTED CONSEQUENCES OF INCEST AVOIDANCE

Before turning to the results of the simulation experiments, it would be useful to consider on an intuitive level the expected effects of incest prohibitions on the genetic and demographic structure of populations. The most striking demographic consequence will be that when incest is prohibited, a certain proportion of females will be eliminated from the potential mate pool for each male and as a result it will be more difficult for males to find mates. It might therefore be expected that the mean age at marriage for both males and females would be elevated and that more individuals of both sexes would complete the reproductive period without marrying. In addition, the mean age difference between mates might be slightly increased, as would the variance in age difference. Later marriages will lead to longer generation times for both males and females, to smaller completed family sizes, and to longer average birth intervals (since fertility rates generally decline with age). Ultimately, the avoidance of incest should result in a reduced rate of population growth.

The expected genetic consequences of incest avoidance are perhaps less obvious. We will inquire first as to the effects of incest avoidance on the probability that a gene drawn at random from individual I is identical by descent to a gene drawn at random from individual J, simply as a result of sampling in a small population. The increase in this probability through time will be accompanied by a change in gene frequencies and may be considered as equivalent to genetic drift. We will next ask how genotype frequencies may be expected to deviate from Hardy-Weinberg proportions when there is (nonrandom) avoidance of mating between close relatives.

Change in Gene Frequencies

Consider an initial population of N individuals with 2N individually labeled genes at a single autosomal locus. As a consequence of random sampling, some of these genes will be represented more than once in subsequent generations and others will be eliminated. Avoidance of inbreeding in a monogamous population may be expressed in terms of avoidance of mating between individuals who have genes identical by descent. If one of the original genes g_i reaches a high enough frequency in some subsequent generation, individuals carrying the gene will have fewer potential mates, since they may not mate with individuals who carry g_i. Some of them may be unable to find a mate, thus reducing the frequency of g_i in the next generation. Thus, avoidance of inbreeding will tend to counteract drift in a monogamous population. Another way of viewing this effect is as a reduction in the variance in number of gametes produced by members of the population: The more gametes a parent contributes to the next generation, the less likely it will be that his offspring and more remote descendants will be able to find unrelated mates, therefore the fewer gametes these descendants will contribute. The effect of such a reduction in variance is to increase the effective size of the population and therefore to reduce the rate of gene frequency drift. This reduction will be cancelled out to some extent by the fact that populations avoiding incest also tend to grow more slowly than randomly mating populations.

Deviation from Hardy-Weinberg Proportions

It would be expected that avoidance of mating between close relatives would result in an increase in the frequency of heterozygotes, at least initially. (Kimura and Crow (1963) have shown, however, that maximum avoidance of mating between relatives does not necessarily minimize the ultimate rate of decrease in heterozygosity.) As an illustration, the magnitude of the increase in heterozygote frequency may be computed for avoidance of mating between first cousins. Using the ITO method (Li 1955), one can derive the matrix of conditional probabilities for the genotypes of first cousins in a random mating population:

$$\underline{C} = \begin{bmatrix} \frac{1}{4}p + \frac{3}{4}p^2 & \frac{1}{4}q + \frac{3}{4}2pq & \frac{3}{4}q^2 \\ \frac{1}{8}p + \frac{3}{4}p^2 & \frac{1}{8} + \frac{3}{4}2pq & \frac{1}{8}q + \frac{3}{4}q^2 \\ \frac{3}{4}p^2 & \frac{1}{4}p + \frac{3}{4}2pq & \frac{1}{4}q + \frac{3}{4}q^2 \end{bmatrix}$$

The corresponding matrix for members of the general population is

$$\underline{O} = \begin{bmatrix} p^2 & 2pq & q^2 \\ p^2 & 2pq & q^2 \\ p^2 & 2pq & q^2 \end{bmatrix}$$

Letting k equal the average proportion of the population who are first cousins of a given individual, the relationship between $\underline{C}$ and $\underline{O}$ may be expressed as

$$\underline{O} = k \cdot \underline{C} + (1 - k) \cdot \underline{D}$$

where D is the matrix of conditional probabilities for non-first cousins. Solving this expression for $\underline{D}$ and multiplying the first row of the $\underline{D}$ matrix by p^2, the second row by 2pq and the third row by q^2, we obtain the matrix of genotype frequencies for pairs of non-first cousins:

$$\begin{bmatrix} \dfrac{p^4-\frac{1}{4}kp^3(1+3p)}{1-k} & \dfrac{2p^3q-\frac{1}{4}kp^2q(1+6p)}{1-k} & \dfrac{p^2q^2-\frac{3}{4}kp^2q^2}{1-k} \\ \dfrac{2p^3q-\frac{1}{4}kp^2q(1+6p)}{1-k} & \dfrac{4p^2q^2-\frac{1}{4}kpq(1+12pq)}{1-k} & \dfrac{2pq^3-\frac{1}{4}kpq^2(1+6q)}{1-k} \\ \dfrac{p^2q^2-\frac{3}{4}kp^2q^2}{1-k} & \dfrac{2pq^3-\frac{1}{4}kpq^2(1+6q)}{1-k} & \dfrac{q^4-\frac{1}{4}kq^3(1+3q)}{1-k} \end{bmatrix}$$

This matrix also gives the frequencies of mating types in a population which avoids cousin mating, and therefore the resulting offspring genotype frequencies in such a population may be readily obtained:

$$\text{AA:} \quad p^2 - \frac{kpq}{16(1-k)}$$

$$\text{Aa:} \quad 2pq + \frac{2kpq}{16(1-k)}$$

$$\text{aa:} \quad q^2 - \frac{kpq}{16(1-k)}$$

It should be noted that with overlapping generations, k is best interpreted as the proportion of an individual's potential mates who are first cousins, and gene frequencies should be calculated for the mating population. For a population which avoids only sib mating, the genotype frequencies may be obtained in a similar fashion:

$$AA:\ p^2 - \frac{kpq}{4(1 - k)}$$

$$Aa:\ 2pq + \frac{2kpq}{4(1 - k)}$$

$$aa:\ q^2 - \frac{kpq}{4(1 - k)}$$

In this case, k is the average proportion of the population who are sibs of a given individual.

To summarize, the avoidance of incest may be expected to reduce the rate of gene frequency drift, that is, to increase the effective population number. As a secondary consequence, it would be expected that the rate of differentiation between populations will be reduced. The frequency of heterozygotes will be increased by a magnitude which is a function of 1) gene frequencies and 2) the size and structure of the population and degree of incest avoidance. The coefficient of inbreeding, as computed from pedigrees, will probably be reduced, as will the frequency of isonymy (marriages between individuals with the same surname).

SIMULATION RESULTS

Demographic Comparisons

Table 1 shows a comparison of average demographic characteristics for artificial populations generated in two sets of ten simulation runs, each begun with population size 100 and run for 200 years. In the first set of ten runs mating was random with respect to relationship of spouses, and in the second set matings of close relatives (second cousins or closer) were prohibited. As expected, population growth over

		Random Mating	No Close Consanguinity
N_{200}		173.1	150.4
Age at Paternity	μ	31.59	32.29
	σ^2	58.08	64.63
Age at Maternity	μ	27.54	27.53
	σ^2	38.54	37.57
Birth Interval	μ	4.74	4.90
	σ^2	14.98	15.69
Completed Family Size	μ	2.17	2.22
	σ^2	2.40	2.35
First Marriage			
Male Age	μ	20.11	21.20
	σ^2	41.94	52.18
Female Age	μ	16.11	16.41
	σ^2	16.65	18.28
Age Difference	μ	3.92	4.63
	σ^2	17.98	25.39
Proportion Who Never Marry			
Males		0.025	0.038
Females		0.066	0.050
Frequency of Isonymy		0.205	0.120

Table 1. COMPARISON OF DEMOGRAPHIC CHARACTERISTICS IN ARTIFICIAL POPULATIONS WHICH ARE 1) MATING RANDOMLY, OR 2) AVOIDING CLOSE CONSANGUINITY

(AVERAGES FOR 2 SETS OF 10 RUNS EACH, N_0 = 100)

the 200 year period was slower with avoidance of incest: the average population size was only 150.4 as compared to 173.1 with random mating. Also in accordance with expectation, the frequency of isonymy was decreased and means and variances in birth interval, age at first marriage for males and females, and age difference between spouses were elevated. Contrary to expectation, mean completed family size was actually slightly higher with avoidance of incest and mean age at maternity was unchanged. Furthermore, although the proportion of males who completed the reproductive period without marrying was higher with avoidance of incest, the proportion of never-married females was lower. It should be mentioned that in this and the following tables, the variances listed are average variances within runs, not variances between runs. Comparisons between runs of a given set revealed no striking heterogeneity except in final population size, a point which will be discussed in greater detail later.

In Table 2 is a summary of demographic characteristics for two sets of simulations run under conditions identical to those of the simulations described in Table 1, except that the initial population size was 200 instead of 100. In most respects the results presented in the two tables are consistent. The most striking difference is that in the runs with initial population size 200, the rate of population growth was higher when incest was prohibited, contrary to expectation and in marked contrast to the effect of incest avoidance in populations with initial size 100. It is not surprising that the effects of incest avoidance on population growth are more severe in a small population than in a larger one: In a small population, it is quite likely that a majority of an individual's potential mates will be close relatives. However it is difficult to imagine a mechanism whereby avoidance of inbreeding would result in an increased rate of population growth, in populations in which there is no selection or migration. In view of the great variability between runs in final population size (standard

		Random Mating	No Close Consanguinity
N_{200}		422.1	432.7
Age at Paternity	μ	31.05	31.55
	σ^2	55.12	57.62
Age at Maternity	μ	27.44	27.63
	σ^2	38.22	39.43
Birth Interval	μ	4.83	4.94
	σ^2	14.99	15.70
Completed Family Size	μ	2.32	2.36
	σ^2	2.26	2.31
First Marriage			
Male Age	μ	19.34	19.81
	σ^2	35.49	41.83
Female Age	μ	15.76	15.55
	σ^2	11.13	7.12
Age Difference	μ	3.37	3.75
	σ^2	13.39	14.74
Proportion Who Never Marry			
Males		0.013	0.014
Females		0.026	0.028
Frequency of Isonymy		0.153	0.120

Table 2. COMPARISON OF DEMOGRAPHIC CHARACTERISTICS IN ARTIFICIAL POPULATIONS WHICH ARE 1) MATING RANDOMLY, OR 2) AVOIDING CLOSE CONSANGUINITY

(AVERAGES FOR 2 SETS OF 10 RUNS EACH, $N_0 = 200$)

deviations between runs within the four sets ranged from 61.0 to 110.7), the observed differences in final size between populations which avoided consanguinity and those which did not are probably not significant. Additional differences between Tables 1 and 2 are that in Table 2, mean and variance in age at maternity increase with avoidance of incest (as expected) and mean and variance in female age at first marriage decrease (contrary to expectation).

It should be noted that variation in demographic structure can be expected simply as a consequence of differences in population size, even in populations which experience identical age-specific probabilities of reproducing, dying and searching for mates. Individuals in a small population have fewer potential mates than those in a large population, and might therefore have to search longer before finding an appropriate spouse. A higher proportion of them will remain unmarried and those who do marry will on the average bear children at a more advanced age. They will have smaller completed families than individuals in a large population, and the rate of population growth will be slower. These predictions are borne out by the results given in Tables 1 and 2.

Consanguineous Marriages

Consanguineous marriages in the randomly mating artificial populations were tabulated according to relationship of spouses (Table 3) in order to estimate how much consanguinity is avoided in small populations and to determine whether the numbers of consanguineous marriages of different types were in agreement with the predictions of a model developed by Hajnal (1963). For ease of comparison the numbers of marriages between first, first once removed, and second cousins are marked (*). The numbers of relationships of a given type are not expected to vary as a function of population size, and with the exception of second cousin marriages, the results of Table 3 are in agreement with expectation. The discrepancy in the case of second

	N_0 = 100		N_0 = 200	
	Number	Frequency	Number	Frequency
Sibs	123	.068	120	.029
FaDa	2	.001	2	.001
MoSo	0	.000	0	.000
U-N	23	.013	31	.007
A-N	6	.003	1	.000
1C: FaBroDa	98	.055	76	.018
MoBroDa	88	.049	99	.024
FaSisDa	79	.044	95	.023
MoSisDa	73	.041	96	.023
Total 1C	338 *	.188	366 *	.087
$1\frac{1}{2}$C: ♂ in Longer Line	50	.028	67	.016
♀ in Longer Line	215	.120	196	.047
Total $1\frac{1}{2}$C	265 *	.147	263 *	.063
2C	771 *	.429	1044 *	.249
Unrelated	271	.151	2362	.564
Total Marriages	1779	1.000	4189	1.000

Table 3. CONSANGUINEOUS MARRIAGES IN RANDOMLY MATING ARTIFICIAL POPULATIONS

(TOTAL NUMBERS FOR 2 SETS OF 10 RUNS EACH)

cousins is an artifact of the method by which cousin marriages were counted. If a couple were related as second cousins in more than one way (e.g., if they had two sets of great-grandparents in common) the marriage was counted only once. In a population as small as 100 there will be fewer individuals married to second cousins than would be the case in a larger population, but there will be more multiple relationships among these second cousins. As expected, the *proportion* of marriages in which spouses are related at least as closely as second cousins is much higher in the small populations (85 per cent) than in the larger ones (44 per cent). In view of the high frequencies of consanguineous marriages in these populations, it is perhaps surprising that prohibition of such marriages does not dampen the rate of population growth to a greater extent.

Table 4 gives numbers of marriages by relationship of spouses (averaged over each of two sets of ten runs) and the numbers predicted by the Hajnal model for artificial populations of initial sizes 100 and 200. The Hajnal predictions are based upon the following assumptions: 1) the probability that a newborn male and female will marry is a function only of the difference between their dates of birth; 2) the distributions of ages at maternity, paternity, and age differences between relatives of various kinds are normal; and 3) there are no correlations between relatives in vital rates. The data needed to compute the expectations are generally either obtainable from published demographic information or easily estimated. We have previously verified (MacCluer and Schull 1970a) that for a population varying in size between 400 and 800 the Hajnal predictions are quite accurate. It is encouraging to find that even in randomly mating populations as small as 100 (Table 4), the observed and expected numbers of marriages by consanguinity type are in remarkably close agreement.

A more detailed analysis of the relative numbers of various types of cousin marriages reveals some rather large discrepancies between observed and

	N_0 = 100		N_0 = 200	
	Observed	Expected	Observed	Expected
Sibs	12.3	11.4	12.0	11.2
FaDa	0.2	-	0.2	-
MoSo	0.0	-	0.0	-
U-N	2.3	2.7	3.1	2.4
A-N	0.6	0.6	0.1	0.7
1C: FaBroDa	9.8	10.3	7.6	10.0
MoBroDa	8.8	10.3	9.9	10.0
FaSisDa	7.9	8.8	9.5	8.8
MoSisDa	7.3	9.6	9.6	9.4
Total 1C	33.8	39.0	36.6	38.3
$1\frac{1}{2}$C: ♂ in Longer Line	5.0	7.0	6.7	7.1
♀ in Longer Line	21.5	17.0	19.6	15.5
Total $1\frac{1}{2}$C	26.5	24.0	26.3	22.6
2C	77.1	83.5	104.4	82.0
Unrelated	27.1	-	236.2	-
Total Marriages	177.9		418.9	

Table 4. COMPARISON OF OBSERVED NUMBERS OF CONSANGUINEOUS MARRIAGES AND NUMBERS PREDICTED BY THE HAJNAL MODEL, FOR RANDOMLY MATING ARTIFICIAL POPULATIONS

(AVERAGES FOR 2 SETS OF 10 RUNS EACH)

	$N_0 = 100$		$N_0 = 200$	
	Observed	Expected	Observed	Expected
1	338	365.5	366	448.4
$1\frac{1}{2}$	265	225.3	263	264.3
2	771	783.2	1044	960.3
	1374	1374	1673	1673
	$\chi^2_2 = 9.25$*		$\chi^2_2 = 32.99$*	

	$N_0 = 100$		$N_0 = 200$	
	Observed	Expected	Observed	Expected
FaBroDa	98	89.2	76	95.9
MoBroDa	88	89.2	99	95.5
FaSisDa	79	76.4	95	84.6
MoSisDa	73	83.2	96	90.0
	338	338	366	366
	$\chi^2_3 = 2.20$		$\chi^2_3 = 5.96$	

Table 5. RELATIVE NUMBERS OF COUSIN MARRIAGES

expected values (Table 5). In populations of initial sizes 100 and 200, there are significant deviations from expected proportions of first, first once removed, and second cousin marriages ($p < .01$). However in comparing observed and expected proportions of the four types of first cousin marriages in these populations, the difference is not significant ($p > .10$).

In order to examine the effects of incest avoidance on certain other measures of genetic structure, we used a group of artificial populations originally generated for another study. In each of six runs a population consisting of four isolated villages was simulated. Each village had initial size 100 and all had identical age and sex distributions. Simulations were done under conditions of high fertility and mortality with average village size nearly doubling during 200 years (Table 6). Since there was no migration between villages in any of the runs it was possible to consider each of the villages as a separate population for purposes of computing effective population size and deviation of genotype frequencies from Hardy-Weinberg proportions. However to evaluate the effect of incest avoidance on genetic differentiation between villages, the four villages of each run were grouped into a single subset. Random mating was specified in three of the six simulation runs (12 villages), and avoidance of nuclear family mating in the other three. The pedigree for each of the 24 villages was stored on tape. A comparison of the demographic characteristics for the two sets of 12 villages showed no great differences except for population size. However in view of the large variability in population growth between villages, it is doubtful that any importance should be attached to this difference in average final population size.

After all runs were completed a second program was used to simulate gene segregation for 60 loci in the pedigree of each village. A more detailed description of the procedure is given in MacCluer (1973b). The calculations summarized in Table 6 were based on the gene and genotype frequencies at these 60 loci at the end of 200 years: Effective population size (N_e) was computed from the variance in gene frequency between loci; F from the average deviation from Hardy-Weinberg proportions for the 60 loci; and F_{ST} (Wright

		Random Mating	No Nuclear Family Mating
N_{200}	Av	180.2	193.3
	Range	90 to 303	72 to 341
N_e / N	Av	.429	.460
	Range	.284 to .599	.318 to .739
F (60 loci)	Av	-.0128	-.0090
	Range	-.0313 to .0064	-.0497 to .0121
F_{ST}(60 loci)	Subset 1	.0357	.0300
	Subset 2	.0364	.0275
	Subset 3	.0260	.0212

Table 6. MEASURES OF GENETIC STRUCTURE IN ARTIFICIAL POPULATIONS WHICH ARE 1) RANDOMLY MATING, OR 2) AVOIDING NUCLEAR FAMILY MATING

(2 SETS OF 12 VILLAGES EACH)
$N_0 = 100$

1951) from $\sigma_q^2/\bar{p}\bar{q}$, where σ_q^2 is the variance in gene frequency between villages (in a four village subset) and $\bar{q}$ is the mean gene frequency ($\bar{p} = 1 - \bar{q}$).

As can be seen in Table 6, the ratio of effective to actual population size is somewhat higher in populations avoiding nuclear family mating than in randomly mating populations. As discussed in an earlier section this result is in agreement with expectation. It would be expected that in the randomly mating populations, the deviation from Hardy-Weinberg proportions as measured by F would be approximately zero, and that in the populations avoiding incest F would be negative. In these simulations, F was negative in both sets of populations and in fact it was slightly more negative in the randomly mating populations than in those avoiding close consanguinity. However the range in F values was so great that the difference between the two sets cannot be considered significant. The degree of genetic differentiation between villages as measured by F_{ST} is slightly less for the populations avoiding incest than for the randomly mating populations, as expected. The differences are consistent over all three subsets.

It is interesting to note that differences of the magnitude shown in Table 6 can arise simply as a result of prohibiting matings between sibs and between parent and child. It would be expected that the genetic consequences of more extensive incest prohibitions would be considerably greater.

CONCLUSION

Avoidance of incest, practiced in most societies, is shown to have an impact on both the demographic and genetic structures of small populations. However even in populations as small as 100 incest prohibitions do not appear to result in a greatly diminished rate of population growth, and most individuals are able to find mates. Perhaps the most important consequences for genetic structure are a decrease in the rate of gene frequency drift with avoidance of incest and a corresponding decrease in the rate of genetic differentiation between the subdivisions of a population.

REFERENCES

Coale, A. J. and P. Demeny 1966. Regional Model Life Tables and Stable Populations. Princeton: Princeton Univ. Press.

Dyke, B. 1973. Estimation of changing rates by simulation, In Computer Simulation in Human Population Studies, B. Dyke and J. W. MacCluer (eds.) New York: Seminar Press.

Dyke, B. and J. W. MacCluer 1973. Estimation of vital rates by means of Monte Carlo simulation, Demography 10, In press.

Hajnal, J. 1963. Concepts of random mating and the frequency of consanguineous marriages, Proceedings of the Royal Society, Part B 159: 125-177.

Kimura, M. and J. F. Crow 1963. On the maximum avoidance of inbreeding, Genetical Research 4: 399-415.

Li, C. C. 1955. Population Genetics. Chicago: Univ. of Chicago Press.

MacCluer, J. W. 1967. Monte Carlo methods in human population genetics: a computer model incorporating age-specific birth and death rates, American Journal of Human Genetics 19: 303-312.

MacCluer, J. W. 1973a. Computer simulation in anthropology and human genetics, In Methods and Theories in Anthropological Genetics, M. H. Crawford and P. L. Workman (eds.) Albuquerque: Univ. of New Mexico Press.

MacCluer, J. W. 1973b. Monte Carlo simulation: the effects of migration on some measures of genetic distance, In Genetic Distance, J. F. Crow, C. Denniston and P. O'Shea (eds.) New York: Plenum Press.

MacCluer, J. W. and J. V. Neel. Genetic structure of a primitive population: a simulation, In preparation.

MacCluer, J. W., J. V. Neel and N. A. Chagnon 1971.

Demographic structure of a primitive population: a simulation, American Journal of Physical Anthropology 35: 193-208.

MacCluer, J. W. and W. J. Schull 1970a. Frequencies of consanguineous marriage and accumulation of inbreeding in an artificial population, American Journal of Human Genetics 22: 160-175.

MacCluer, J. W. and W. J. Schull 1970b. Estimating the effective size of human populations, American Journal of Human Genetics 22: 176-183.

McFarland, D. D. 1972. Comparison of alternative marriage models, In Population Dynamics, T. N. E. Greville (ed.) New York: Academic Press.

United Nations 1965. Population Bulletin of the United Nations No. 7-1963, with special reference to conditions and trends of fertility in the world.

Wright, S. 1951. The genetical structure of populations, Annals of Eugenics 15: 323-354.

ACKNOWLEDGMENTS

This work was supported by National Science Foundation Grant No. GS-27382. The development of the computer model was begun at the Department of Human Genetics, University of Michigan and was supported by Atomic Energy Commission Grant AEC-AT(11-1)-1552.

A SIMULATION OF THE FATE OF A MUTANT GENE OF NEUTRAL SELECTIVE VALUE IN A PRIMITIVE POPULATION

FRANCIS H. F. LI
and
JAMES V. NEEL

INTRODUCTION

The probability of loss (or survival) of a newly-arisen mutant gene is a basic parameter of population genetics. Fisher in 1922 (see also 1930) derived the cumulative probability of mutant loss in any given generation following the mutation by the method of generating functions, for a mutant whose phenotypic effects do not alter its possessor's fitness (a so-called neutral mutation), on the assumptions of a large (infinite) and stable population amenable to a deterministic solution of the problem. The probabilities derived from this formulation for various generations have been widely quoted: For instance, the probability of extinction is 0.79 after 7 generations, and 0.99 after 127 generations. More recently, with the growing interest in populations of finite size, Kimura and Ohta (1969a, 1969b) have derived an explicit formula by diffusion equations for predicting the average extinction time of a single neutral mutant in a finite population, namely,

$$\bar{t}_o = 2\frac{N_e}{N}\log_e(2N) \qquad (1)$$

where $\bar{t}_o$ is the mean extinction time, N is the size of the population and N_e is "effective" population size. In an organism with overlapping generations, such as man, N must be based on the number of individuals in the "reproductive generation," in order to render the definition comparable with "annuals." "Effective" population size has been variously defined and calculated; for a randomly-mating population one definition is "the population size that would give the same amount of drift in a reproducing population as that in the ... model having N constant in time, non-overlapping generations, and all individuals and each sex expected to make equal contributions to the progeny" (Cavalli-Sforza and Bodmer 1971). This particular N_e is sometimes termed the "variance effective number," and it is this N_e which Kimura and Ohta (1969b) employ in the above formula. It is assumed that the mutant allele is represented only once at the moment of its appearance, with initial frequency $p = \frac{1}{2N}$; the $\bar{t}_o$ value, of course, excludes those mutants going to fixation. Now no generalization regarding survival can be made, since the rate of loss depends on N and N_e.

In this presentation we describe the survival of a mutant gene in a computer simulation of a specific tribal-type population, using the model based on four interbreeding villages of the Yanomama Indians developed by MacCluer, Neel and Chagnon (1971). The implication of this survival ($\bar{t}_o$) for an estimate of N_e will then be considered. It will be shown that despite 16.6 per cent intervillage migration of females each generation, the N_e predicted from the simulation $\bar{t}_o$ is substantially less than the N_e's derived from two estimation techniques which assume all four villages to constitute a single population. We are thus led to recognize a "mutant survival N_e" which, given this population structure, differs from the other types of N_e previously derived.

THE SIMULATION MODEL USED FOR THE PRESENT STUDY

The simulation model used in this study was constructed by MacCluer, Neel and Chagnon (1971) on the basis of the genetic and demographic composition of four Yanomama villages. The strategy of model formulation and testing has been to build a model which behaves as nearly as possible like the real population. Results from previous simulation runs with this model indicate it to be reasonably realistic and reliable (MacCluer, Neel and Chagnon 1971), although (see below) certain improvements now seem necessary.

A simulation begins with the files of men and women of each village in the initial population. For each person there is information on his age, marital status, lineage, village of birth, village in which he last resided, parents' identification numbers (I.D.), grandparents' I.D., great-grandparents' I.D. (if known), genotype, number of offspring (women), spouse's I.D. (women), or number of wives (men). Composition of the initial population changes yearly as birth and death occurs according to age- and sex-specific probabilities. Marriage has been simulated according to the conventions observed by the Indians, as determined by field observations. The initial population is eventually replaced by the artificial population; because of the storage capacity of the computer employed, the maximal duration of a simulation run has been 400 years, which is approximately equivalent to 15 generations, but the simulation may be recycled if indicated.

Despite a strong preference for village endogamy in the simulation, it was found that in the course of the entire simulation, on the average 16.6 per cent of males who married found a wife outside their village of birth (MacCluer, Neel and Chagnon 1971). Thus, there is an active exchange matrix between villages, leading us to explore initially the appropriateness of considering all four villages as the basis for computing N_e, as has been our custom in other simulations involving this population. The nature of the matrix is such that a man may acquire a wife from any one of the other three villages; intervillage migration is anisotropic.

In the study of mutant survival, a single mutant of neutral selective value was introduced into each of the four villages, in turn, in successive simulation runs. The sequence was repeated until 214 runs had been completed. Because of the loss of some runs for technical reasons, the number of successful runs varies slightly from village to village. Within each village, the mutant was assigned to the first new-born child produced by the simulation after the run began, by a random numbers procedure. Since the villages were of unequal size (86, 50, 71 and 244), the assignment of the mutation was not in proportion to village population size. The influence of village size on mutant loss will be considered below.

Because of the limited number of potential parents in some villages, the same couple might repeatedly serve as the parents of the child with the mutant allele. The distribution of mutants by couple is shown in Table 1. In the simulation input population of 451 persons, there were a total of 100 women of childbearing age. Of these, 73 bore at least one mutant child, the number of such children ranging from one to eight. It should be noted that because of provision in the simulation for adultery, these women might have children by more than one man, including males who were unmarried. It will be noted that 27 women in the childbearing age, 24 in the largest village, failed to bear a mutant child. This disproportionate representation of village 4 reflects the manner in which mutations were assigned by village, and must be corrected. Since the initial population framework is fixed, this means that in the strict sense the simulation runs are not entirely independent of one another. This introduces an element of approximation into the estimate of the standard error of $\bar{t}_o$ to be derived.

The simulation run continued only as long as the mutant gene persisted in the population. The composition of the simulated population was printed out on an

Distribution of mutants by couple	Village V_1	V_2	V_3	V_4	Σ
0	3	0	0	24	27
1	4	0	0	9	13
2	6	2	5	5	18
3	4	3	8	5	20
4	4	3	3	2	12
5	2	1	1	2	6
6		1	1		2
7		1			1
8		1			1
No. couples	23	12	18	47	100
Runs	54	51	57	52	214

Table 1. THE NUMBER OF "MUTANT CHILDREN" BORNE BY EACH COUPLE IN THE FOUR VILLAGES WHERE THE WIFE WAS OF CHILD-BEARING AGE

annual basis; information available for each individual includes those file items enumerated earlier. Thus it is possible to trace the exact history of any mutant, and to analyze the factors influencing mutant extinction.

RESULTS

A total of 214 simulation runs were performed. The results are summarized in Table 2. In 133 of these runs, the mutant allele became extinct after

Generation in which the mutant allele becomes extinct from the population	Number of observations
1	133
2	33
3	11
4	7
5	11
6	5
7	3
8	3
9	2
10	2
12	1
14	1
18	1
21	1

Mean = 2.30 generations

Table 2. DISTRIBUTION OF EXTINCTION TIMES OF THE NEUTRAL MUTANT ALLELE

the first generation. The causes of loss in the first generation were as follows: (a) in 92 cases the extinction of the mutant allele was due to the death of the carrier before reaching reproductive age, taken to be 15 years, (b) in 18 cases the carrier died between

15 and 30 years of age without having found a wife, or, if married, died before reproducing, and/or without having transmitted the mutant allele by adultery, (c) in seven cases even though the male carriers survived beyond age 40 they were unable to find a mate under the conditions imposed by the model, and (d) in the remaining 16 cases the loss of the mutant allele was due to failure to transmit the allele to any of the children resulting from the marriage of the carrier. The apparently high death rate results both from infanticide and natural causes. In 81 cases (38 per cent) the mutant allele was transmitted to the second generation, but in only 17 per cent of the 214 cases has the mutant allele survived beyond the third generation. The average extinction time observed in the simulated population is about 2.3 generations. Because of the highly skewed nature of the distribution of $\bar{t}_o$, a standard error of the mean calculated in the usual fashion is only approximate, but has a value of 0.5.

It is at this juncture appropriate to return to Fisher's formulation, for a consideration of $\bar{t}_o$. In the strict sense this is impossible, because a few mutations are expected to persist for a very, very long time. However, employing Fisher's formulations (1922, 1930) and disregarding all mutant alleles which were not extinct by generation 127 (the last generation treated in Fisher's table, with cumulative probability of loss 0.9847), $\bar{t}_o$ is found to be 6.6. If the series is extended to 100,000 generations (probability of loss of 0.999980), $\bar{t}_o$ becomes 19.8. Thus, in Fisher's formulation $\bar{t}_o$ is greatly influenced by a very few genes which persist for a very long time. The finite size of the type of population we are simulating renders such a disproportionate contribution by a very few surviving mutants highly unlikely. On the other hand, one can visualize that in another series of 214 runs, a few mutants might by chance have persisted much longer. Thus, we regard the present estimate as an approximation, but yet clearly the true value is far below the value yielded by the Fisher formulation and as we will see, also below the value predicted by the formulation of Kimura and Ohta.

There are differences in the life curves of males and females in this population, and because of polygyny the variance of male reproductive indices tends to be greater than that of the corresponding female indices. Because of these and other differences between males and females built into the model, we have calculated $\bar{t}_o$ separately for the 101 times the mutation was assigned to a male and the 113 times to a female. The $\bar{t}_{o_m}$ was 2.4 and the $\bar{t}_{o_f}$ 2.0.

There are at present five aspects of the simulation which we consider somewhat unsatisfactory for the present purposes, and which are being modified. Firstly, the initial population has a deficiency of both females and males in the age group 10 to 19 and/or excess in the interval 20-29 (see Neel and Chagnon 1968; MacCluer, Neel and Chagnon 1971). This deficiency undoubtedly has some influence on the growth of the population, and could introduce a specific perturbation (for this population) into its growth pattern, and hence into the likelihood of transmission of the mutant. Secondly, the present four villages form a closed system, with no migration matrix with the "outside world." Thirdly, in the present simulation 30 per cent of males fail to find wives. In our simulation, women once married become eligible for a second marriage only on death of the husband. In the real Yanomama world, married men not infrequently "discard" a wife (divorce is too kind a word) and such women almost immediately remarry. By this device, few men go without a wife at some time during their life. In our simulation, 3.5 per cent of all gene extinctions occurred because men failed to marry. This figure would be reduced by their marriage, but we will not now hazard a guess to what extent; the model is being modified. Fourthly, it seems better in retrospect to make the probability of occurrence of a mutant in a village correspond to village size (rather than assigning mutants sequentially to the four villages). Finally, the present simulation program does not allow for village fission when a critical size is exceeded, a limitation probably of little importance in the present context but of greater import to efforts to estimate inbreeding. It is very difficult to make allowance for the impact of these factors on the estimate of $\bar{t}_o$. Intuitively we doubt if correction of these imperfections in the model and the input data will add more than a generation to the average of $\bar{t}_o$, which would then become 3.3.

Fisher's treatment began with adult heterozygotes who then mated, whereas we introduced the mutation into a newborn. If we exclude all those cases, 110 in number, where the carrier of the mutation died before maturity or died between 15 and 30 without offspring, to render our situation more similar to Fisher's, $\bar{t}_o$ becomes 3.7 generations, or 4.7 if we add one generation as an intuitive allowance for the imperfections of the model. After the seventh generation of simulation, 95 per cent of the mutations have been extinguished (in contrast to 79 per cent in Fisher's treatment). It is of interest that Fisher recognized that if the mutant gene were introduced into newborn infants subject to a substantial risk of death (rather than in adults), $\bar{t}_o$ would be decreased. Thus we read (1922, p. 326): "...the arbitrary element thus introduced into the question of the survival of a mutant gene is due to the fact that...its survival depends on that of the individual in which it occurs...; once, however, it has reached...an adult individual capable of leaving many offspring, the conditions of its survival are similar in all cases...."

The mutation did not spread beyond the village of origin in 192 runs. In 18 cases it spread to a second village, in three cases to a third, and in two cases to the fourth village.

Having derived this estimate of $\bar{t}_o$, we can proceed in either of two directions. We can ask how well this $\bar{t}_o$ agrees with the $\bar{t}_o$ predicted from the Kimura formulation, N_e being estimated on the assumption that from the standpoint of mutant loss, the four interbreeding villages can be regarded as constituting a single breeding unit. Conversely, we can ask, given our knowledge of $\bar{t}_o$, and N, what value for N_e must be inserted to balance the equation.

In pursuit of the first question, we have computed N_e for the population of four villages by two approaches. The first approach, based on simulation, incorporates differential fertility and inbreeding, but suffers from the present defects in the simulation mentioned above. The second of the approaches must be regarded as approximate, in the sense that we make no allowance for a number of aspects of this population, such as marked differential fertility and inbreeding. However, as we shall see, the discrepancies between the simulated and predicted $\bar{t}_o$'s are of such a magnitude that it is very unlikely that adjustment for these factors would alter the point to be made.

(1) The first estimate of N_e is obtained from the variance of the gene frequency obtained in a series of simulations, namely, $N_e = \frac{pq}{2V_p}$, where V_p is the variance of gene frequency obtained by dropping a pair of alleles with initial frequencies p = q (= 0.5) 100 times through a pedigree constructed from a 400 year simulation of this population (MacCluer and Neel, unpublished). Two different pedigrees were used. During the course of the simulation the two populations increased in size from the initial value of 451 to 465 and 551 persons, respectively. The two estimates of

N_e were 180 and 210; we shall use the average of 195.

(2) The second of the estimates results from a formulation by Nei and Imaizumi (1966), as independently extended by Cavalli-Sforza and Bodmer (1971) and Crow and Kimura (1972). These formulations attempt to take into consideration the occurrence of overlapping generations in human populations but assume a stable age distribution and that age specific birth and mortality rates are constant. The formulations of Cavalli-Sforza and Bodmer (1971) and Crow and Kimura (1972) yield similar results in this population; we shall use the latters', namely

$$N_e = N_o \bar{\ell} \tau \qquad (2)$$

where N_o is the number of births in one census unit (say, 1 year), $\bar{\ell}$ is the weighted probability of surviving into the reproductive period, and τ is the average age at reproduction. Since $\bar{\ell}$ and τ are based on age-specific vital rates, they (and N_e) differ for males and females, and so we must compute N_e as twice the harmonic mean of male and female effective sizes, according to the formula

$$N_e = \frac{4N_{e_f} N_{e_m}}{N_{e_f} + N_{e_m}} \qquad (3)$$

As shown in Table 2, mutant loss may occur in almost any generation of the simulation. Rather than derive a weighted estimate of N_e based on all the simulation runs, we have for present purposes simply computed N_e on the basis of the population present at the completion of the simulation in the two 400-year simulations referred to earlier. This should result in satisfactory comparability between estimates (1) and (2). The two estimates are 204 and 213, and again we shall use the average, of 209. We note in passing that these two estimates of N_e are derived from the population at the completion of the simulation, whereas the estimate of N_e to be derived from $\bar{t}_o$ is based largely on the population towards the beginning of the simulation. Since for these two runs population size changed relatively little during the simulation, this cannot be an important source of discrepancy.

For the computation of $\bar{t}_o$, we will set N at 200, twice the number of women in the reproductive age. This is done to extract from this population containing representatives of four overlapping generations, an estimate of N comparable to that employed for an annual species. Because of polygyny and adultery, we cannot in the strict sense speak of couples, but the 100 women correspond roughly to 100 sets of reproductive partners, with some men having children by several wives, and vice-versa. In equating N to this value rather than the census value, we are, we believe, using N in the sense employed by Kimura and colleagues in the derivation of equation (1). We note how similar in this population N is to our estimates of N_e. The reader will recall that due to the way mutations were assigned to the villages, three women in village 1 and 24 women in village 4 failed to bear any mutant children (villages 1 and 4 are the largest villages). Nevertheless, the progeny of these women are available for marriage. Since in the computation of $\bar{t}_o$ the important ratio of $\frac{N_e}{N}$ would be changed relatively little by an attempt at correction which subtracted these couples from both numerator and denominator, we have elected to include these women and their spouses in the calculation, making this a point to be reexamined as the model is improved.

The values of $\bar{t}_o$ predicted from these two estimates of N_e are given in Table 3. They are 11.7 and 13.1 generations, as compared to an observed $\bar{t}_o$ of 2.3. It is not our purpose to belabor the point of which of the two values of N_e best represents the "variance effective number," as the term is usually employed, and so results in the "best" estimate of $\bar{t}_o$. We are satisfied to establish an approximate value for the predicted $\bar{t}_o$.

Following the converse procedure, we also give in Table 3 the N_e which can be inferred from the simulation $\bar{t}_o$ by the formulation

$$N_e = \frac{\bar{t}_o N}{2 \log_e 2N} \qquad (5)$$

This is 38. In this calculation, we have taken N as 200; this choice may be debated but we see no clear alternative. It is obvious that there is a dichotomy between the simulation results and the results predicted by an N_e based on all four villages, whichever of the two estimates of N_e is taken as reference point. To a first approximation, the $\bar{t}_o$ derived from simulation is approximately one quarter that predicted from the calculations of N_e.

DISCUSSION

The foregoing results must be regarded as preliminary. Complex though the present simulation is, there are several aspects which do not yet satisfy us. Given the implications of the present findings regarding the simulated $\bar{t}_o$, we feel it imperative that the model be improved. On the other hand, it seems

Average extinction time observed in simulated primitive populations	$\bar{t}_o$ = 2.3 generations	$N_e{}^*$ = 38
Average extinction time predicted by diffusion method using different estimates of effective population sizes	$\bar{t}_{o_1}$ = 11.7 generations	N_{e_1} = 195
	$\bar{t}_{o_2}$ = 13.1 generations	N_{e_2} = 209

Table 3. COMPARISON OF THE AVERAGE EXTINCTION TIME ($\bar{t}_o$) OF A SINGLE NEUTRAL GENE IN A PRIMITIVE POPULATION PREDICTED BY DIFFUSION METHOD AND OBSERVED FROM MONTE CARLO SIMULATION

$^*N_e$ = estimate from Kimura-Ohta formula by using simulated $\bar{t}_o$ and N = 200.

N_{e_1} = estimate from variances of gene frequency ($N_e = \frac{pq}{2V_p}$) where V_p is obtained by dropping a pair of alleles through a pedigree 100 times with initial frequencies p = q = 1/2 (MacCluer and Neel, unpublished).

N_{e_2} = twice the harmonic mean of the effective population size of each sex, computed after Crow and Kimura (1972), as described in text.

unlikely that the "amended" simulation value of $\bar{t}_o$ will be increased by more than one or two generations by whatever changes may be introduced later.

The principal point to emerge from this exercise is that the average extinction time is small, smaller than predicted when estimates of N_e derived for the total population by several independent methods are used to predict $\bar{t}_o$. Such a discrepancy can arise either from unusual features in the simulation, from departures from the assumptions of the Kimura-Ohta formulation, or from the fact that the N_e of reference should not be derived from all four villages.

With reference to the features of the simulation resulting in the estimated $\bar{t}_o$, we wish to make three points.

(1) The high pre-reproductive mortality rates of men (35 per cent) and women (45 per cent) used as the input parameters in the simulation experiment are one of the major factors which cause the early extinction of the mutant allele. Ninety-four of the 133 cases where the mutant allele became extinct after the first generation are due to death of the carrier before reaching the reproductive age of 15.

(2) The high mortality rate of men between ages 15 and 45 (45 per cent), resulting from warfare and natural causes, together with the relatively late average age of paternity, due to a deficiency of women and competition for mates, further reduces the chances of survival of the mutant allele in the population. To a lesser degree, the 30 per cent mortality rate of women during reproductive age may also influence the early extinction of the mutant allele. For these reasons, we observed that 18 of the 133 cases where the mutant allele was lost in the first generation were caused by the death of the carrier between age 15 and 30 before transmitting the allele to the next generation. Clearly the average extinction time of a mutant allele in a population such as this will

be smaller than in a population with the present demographic characteristics of Europe or the United States, but precise estimates of $\bar{t}_o$ for these latter types of populations are not yet available.

(3) Despite allowance in the model for 16.6 per cent intervillage migration by women each generation, in only 23 of the 214 simulations did the mutation spread beyond the village of origin. Thus, by and large, the events which determine survival are village events. We argue from this that the N_e important to mutation survival is closely related to that of the primary breeding unit.

Earlier we have described some specific features of this population, not present in many other types of population, which must be borne in mind in evaluating the simulation $\bar{t}_o$. In addition, it also seems clear that some of the assumptions on which the Kimura-Ohta formulation is based are not met in our simulation model. The chief of these differences are as follows:

(1) Their model assumes a constant population size and absence of interactions between generations. Given a stationary finite population, as contrasted to a population of the same size whose net reproductive rate should result in expansion, we may expect greater mutant survival in the latter (because the average couple will have more children). The historical data, such as it is, suggests that the Yanomama are an expanding population (Neel *et al.* 1973), and this emerges from the simulation program of MacCluer *et al.* (1971), the numbers on the average approximately doubling in the course of 400 years. However, there were large variations in the rate of growth of the simulated populations (MacCluer *et al.* 1971), related to the importance of stochastic events in as small a population as this. There was no obvious relationship between mutant loss and whether the population appeared to be expanding or contracting at the time. Mutant loss occurs so early and under such circumstances in this simulation that the factor of population expansion

probably plays a very minor role in mutant survival. Nevertheless, we note that both populations in which the mutant persisted more than 400 years had doubled their numbers.

(2) Furthermore, although the concept of N_e as utilized in the formulation can in theory embrace many aspects of population structure (i.e., non-Poissonian distribution of children, fluctuations in population size, inbreeding), the standard derivations do not make adequate allowance for population subdivision of the type encountered here or structured mating patterns. The restrictions on intervillage migration undoubtedly influence the probability of mutant survival, and relatively more than they would influence the calculation of a variance effective number based on an established polymorphism with a gene frequency of $p = q = 0.5$.

(3) But perhaps the most important discrepancy between the simulation and the model is the absence of mortality in the Kimura model, the latter assuming that each individual born survives and on the average is the parent of two children, with number of children per couple following a Poisson distribution. In this situation, zero children is, broadly speaking, the operational equivalent of early death for a couple. In our simulation, 31 and 54 per cent of males and females respectively die prior to the age of reproduction, and there is failure of reproduction of 18 per cent of males and six per cent of females who reach maturity, whereas the Poissonian expectation of couples with no children is 14 per cent on the assumption of a mean of two children per couple.

We turn now to the problem of defining N. Our simulated population might well have included a fifth village. Let us assume it had 25 "couples" of reproductive age. N for the *five* villages would then be 250, and had these five villages been the base for the calculation, N_e would become approximately 261. On the other hand, earlier we noted that in only two cases did the mutation spread to all three of the other villages. Thus, the population of at least one of the villages was in all but two simulations irrelevant to mutant survival. N_e computed after subtracting an "average" village size of 50 from the 4-village size is 157. Although the migration matrix between villages does provide some basis for computing the N_e for $\bar{t}_o$, this alone is inadequate, since it fails to consider the effects of other aspects of population structure on N_e. The artificiality of a "population" of four villages is obvious. Among Indians, the most clearly defined population unit is the tribe. There are some 15,000 Yanomama, with an N of approximately 6,000-7,000. Use of any of these other values of N (and N_e) would of course alter our estimate of $\bar{t}_o$. Thus we suggest that unless one is willing to define a special "variance effective number" for this situation, namely, that which results from the simulation of $\bar{t}_o$ (which could only be confused with the usual definition), it would be preferable to refer to a "mutant loss N_e."

Fisher (1930) demonstrated that the probabilities of extinction of a mutant allele with one per cent selective advantage at any given generation are very close to those observed for an allele of neutral selective value in a population of infinite size. It is therefore probable that the average extinction time of a mutant allele with a slight advantage (or disadvantage) in this population will not be very different from our observed value of $\bar{t}_o$. In a subsequent study, we will use the observed value of $\bar{t}_o$ from this study and the data on the frequency of variants with respect to isozymes and serum proteins obtained from the Yanomama population for an indirect estimate of the mutation rate to genes assumed to be of neutral or nearly neutral selective value.

SUMMARY

In a simulation model based on four interbreeding villages of a tribe of American Indians, the Yanomama, the average survival time ($\bar{t}_o$) for a mutant gene of neutral selective value introduced into a newborn infant in a series of 214 simulations was 2.3 generations. For reasons stated in the text, we believe that approximately 3.3 is a better estimate of $\bar{t}_o$. The value of $\bar{t}_o$ for those mutations whose bearer reached adulthood in the first generation was estimated to be 4.7 generations.

REFERENCES

Cavalli-Sforza, L. L. and W. F. Bodmer 1971. The Genetics of Human Populations. San Francisco: W. H. Freeman.

Crow, J. F. and M. Kimura 1972. The effective number of a population with overlapping generations: a correction and further discussion, American Journal of Human Genetics 24: 1-10.

Fisher, R. A. 1922. On the dominance ratio, Proceedings of the Royal Society, Edin. 42: 321-341.

Fisher, R. A. 1930. The Genetical Theory of Natural Selection. Oxford: Clarendon Press.

Kimura, M. 1953. "Stepping stone" model of population, Annual Report of the National Institute of Genetics, Japan 3: 62-63.

Kimura, M. and T. Ohta 1969a. The average number of generations until fixation of a mutant gene in a finite population, Genetics 61: 763-771.

Kimura, M. and T. Ohta 1969b. The average number of

generations until extinction of an individual mutant gene in a finite population, Genetics 63: 701-709.

MacCluer, J. W., J. V. Neel and N. A. Chagnon 1971. Demographic structure of a primitive population: a simulation, American Journal of Physical Anthropology 35: 193-207.

Maruyama, T. 1970. On the rate of decrease of heterozygosity in circular stepping stone models of populations, Theoretical Population Biology 1: 101-119.

Neel, J. V. and N. A. Chagnon 1968. The demography of two tribes of primitive, relatively unacculturated American Indians, Proceedings of the National Academy of Sciences 59: 680-689.

Neel, J. V., T. Arends, C. Brewer, N. Chagnon, H. Gershowitz, M. Layrisse, Z. Layrisse, J. MacCluer, E. Migliazza, W. Oliver, F. Salzano, R. Spielman, R. Ward and L. Weitkamp 1973. Studies on the Yanomama Indians, Proceedings of the Fourth International Congress of Human Genetics, Amsterdam: Excerpta Medica.

Nei, M. and Y. Imaizumi 1966. Genetic structure of human populations. II. Differentiation of blood group gene frequencies among isolated populations, Heredity 21: 183-190, 344.

ACKNOWLEDGMENTS

We are indebted to Drs. W. J. Schull, R. Spielman, K. Weiss, P. Smouse and R. Ward for many helpful discussions. The financial support of the U.S. Atomic Energy Commission and the National Science Foundation is gratefully acknowledged. This study constitutes a contribution to the Integrated Research Project on the Population Genetics of the American Indian of the U.S. International Biological Program.

SIMULATING HUMAN REPRODUCTION: HOW COMPLICATED SHOULD A MODEL BE?

ALBERT JACQUARD
and
HENRI LERIDON

Elaboration of a model immediately raises the question of how much complexity is necessary and sufficient in order to arrive at a realistic representation of the phenomenon studied. The choice is important for several reasons:

(1) It restricts the possible methods of approach by eliminating those which can lead only to oversimplifications.

(2) If the model adopted is too unrealistic, it can lead to erroneous conclusions.

(3) If it is too complicated, there is a risk of misinterpretation, or to be more exact, of losing sight of important points (or even, if carried to the extreme, of losing sight of the problem itself).

But the choice of degree of complexity is itself *conditioned by*

(1) methodological possibilities (which are finite); and

(2) the state of existing knowledge about the number and value of the parameters involved in the phenomenon modeled.

For example, it is illusory for a model to include a variable about which nothing is known (except, of course, with the specific intention of studying that particular variable), or to include as an *independent* variable one which is known to be a function of another already included variable, simply because the nature of the relationship is unknown.

Our goal here will be to define, in the light

of empirical and analytical experience, the hypotheses which should be the bases of a model for the study of human reproduction. We shall examine successively:

(1) the most generally recognized basic hypotheses;
(2) problems of heterogeneity of various components of the model; and
(3) tentative conclusions which can be drawn from the model, considering only parameters of natural fertility.

BASIC HYPOTHESES

Fundamentally, the reproductive process in females is simply one of alternation between two states: one in which fertilization is possible, and one in which it is not.

The time spent in the first state is of variable duration, equal to the "delay to conception;" variability in this delay results from a single stochastic variable, the monthly risk of conception (or fecundability).

The second state follows a conception. Length of time in this state (the nonsusceptible period) is also variable, but to describe it exactly, we have to take two variables into account: pregnancy outcome (miscarriage, stillbirth, or live birth) and the length of the postpartum nonsusceptible period. These two variables are not independent: the mean duration of postpartum nonsusceptibility depends on the pregnancy outcome (as well as, following a live birth, on the condition of the newborn during the first months of its life). But in each case, there exists a distribution of the period of nonsusceptibility around some mean duration, which must be taken into account, at least in the case of a live birth.

All natality models agree on these points; most also assume that the mean conception delay and/or the risk of intra-uterine death are functions of maternal age. The increase in risk of intra-uterine mortality with maternal age has been demonstrated reliably; the increase is rapid from age 30-35 onwards. A decrease in fecundability beyond age 30 has long been assumed, but not always for valid reasons. In particular, evidence for an age dependent decrease in *fertility* or fecundity has not been distinguished adequately from evidence for a real decline in *fecundability*. The decrease in fecundity can be explained equally well either by a rise in intra-uterine mortality or by a lengthening of the postpartum nonsusceptible period.

By studying the change in the distribution of lengths of birth intervals occurring toward the end of reproductive life, we have been able to show (Léridon 1973), using deterministic models, that:

(1) Intra-uterine mortality which rises with age, and fecundability which decreases toward the end of reproductive life, play symmetric roles; but either the first must approach 100 per cent, or the second must tend toward zero (that is, the effective fecundability must be zero at the end of the reproductive age-span).

(2) A decrease in effective fecundability should occur whatever the age at which sterility begins; i.e., total sterility must be preceded by a period of reduced fecundity.

This can be expressed in concrete terms in the simulation process in the following way:

(1) intra-uterine mortality is assumed to be a function of age alone

(2) before simulation for the ith woman begins, the age, S_i, at which she will become sterile is drawn at random, and fecundability, P_i, is made a function of $(S_i - a)$, where a is the current age expressed in months.

Thus

$$P_i(a) = P_i \qquad \text{when} \qquad a \leq S_i - 60$$

$$P_i(a) = \frac{S_i - a}{S_i - 60} P_i \quad \text{when} \qquad S_i - 60 < a \leq S_i, \text{ and}$$

$$P_i(a) = 0 \qquad \text{when} \qquad a > S_i$$

In the process, we have introduced a fourth random variable: age at onset of permanent sterility. Although the distribution of this variable is poorly known, to assume that all women become sterile at the same age would seriously affect the realism of the model beyond ages 35 to 40.

The end of the reproductive period is thus characterized by a distribution of "losses." Logically, we must also take into account a distribution of entries into the reproductive period; this is generally estimated by the distribution of age at marriage.

PROBLEMS OF HETEROGENEITY

Our models as thus far constituted, lack an important source of variability: that resulting from heterogeneity within actual populations with respect to various factors. Proof of the existence of such heterogeneity exists for at least one variable. For example, in an attempt to reproduce demographic characteristics of the Hutterites, Bodmer and Jacquard (1968) were able to simulate only 40 per cent of the variance in completed family size, using a strictly homogeneous model.

Let us return to each of the basic variables: Proof that *fecundability* is heterogeneous is abundant. The consequences of this heterogeneity are important for the mean delay to conception, and even more so for the variance of this delay. Several authors have derived estimators of the mean and variance of conception delay under the assumption that fecundability follows a Beta distribution. When the resulting estimates are compared with those obtained when fecundability is assumed to be homogeneous and equal to the estimated mean, it can be shown that the mean delay calculated using a Beta distribution is generally longer by 2 to 4 months, and moreover, the variance is multiplied by a factor of at least four. We will return to this point.

No estimate of the distribution of *intra-uterine mortality* has yet been proposed, to our knowledge, although the idea is generally recognized as useful. This drawback is mitigated by the fact that it would probably be excessive to adopt two independent distributions for fecundability and intra-uterine mortality, since the two variables are certainly correlated - owing to the fact that the usual definition of fecundability takes into account the very high intra-uterine mortality in the first two weeks following conception. So long as the extent of this correlation is not clear, it is probably preferable to assume a single source of variability.

As for the duration of *nonsusceptibility*, the situation is more ambiguous. In all models, at the time of pregnancy, this interval is sampled from a distribution which is independent of such maternal characteristics as pregnancy order or age. Put another way, it is assumed that women are not characterized as having "long" or "short" nonsusceptible periods. Rather, the distributions used have been deduced from observations in such a way as to give estimates of the variance between women, rather than of the total variance. From a certain point of view, some heterogeneity is thereby taken into account, but since independent samples of the nonsusceptible period are taken at each successive pregnancy, it is a false heterogeneity. We may say, in summary, that even if it is not explicitly assumed that women are heterogeneous with respect to their nonsusceptible period, the variance of the distribution actually used does take this heterogeneity into account.

Under these conditions, why not proceed in the same way with fecundability? Nothing prevents sampling a "conception delay" from a distribution with sufficiently high variance to allow for heterogeneity. The difficulty with such a procedure would be that the hypothesis that some women have high, and others have low fecundity is discarded *de facto*, since none of the three fundamental functions would vary between women.

The reasons for choosing to consider fecundability as a truly heterogeneous variable are furnished by the study of Potter *et al.* (1965). For Punjabi women aged 20-29, the authors have estimated separately the variances of the duration of postpartum amenorrhea, and of the delay to conception. By then adding to these two values a theoretical estimate of the variance of an additional delay contributed by intrauterine mortality, as well as the variance of the length of gestation, they reached an estimate of the *total* variance of intervals between births:

	Mean length (months)	Variance ($months^2$)
Conception delay	10	75
Delay due to intra-uterine mortality	2	38
Gestation	9	1
Postpartum amenorrhea	10	49
Total	31	163

This estimate agrees with the observed variance (σ^2 = 180) reasonably well.

We return now to our own simulation model (Jacquard 1967). Taking into account the hypotheses of the model, it is possible to reconstruct theoretically the means and variances of the various components of the interval.

For conception delay (d_c):

$$P = 0.25 \quad \text{(between ages 20 and 29 years)}$$

from which

$$\bar{d}_c = \frac{1}{P} = 4 \quad \text{and} \quad \sigma^2_{d_c} = \frac{1 - P}{P^2} = 12$$

For the distribution of nonsusceptible periods

$$\bar{d}_m = 19 \quad \text{and} \quad \sigma^2_{d_m} = 39$$

Finally, the supplement to the interval resulting from intra-uterine mortality can be calculated, as Potter *et al.* have done, from formulae developed by Perrin and Sheps (1964), but with the values of the various parameters that follow from our own hypotheses.

We obtain

$$\bar{d}_s = 3 \quad \text{and} \quad \sigma^2_{d_s} = 41$$

Our overall mean birth interval is estimated to be 26 months, and its variance is 92. These results are consistent with those obtained from the simulation (Jacquard 1967).

	Mean length (months)	Variance (months^2)
Conception delay	4	12
Delay due to intra-uterine mortality	3	41
Gestation } Postpartum amenorrhea }	19	39
Total	26	92

Let us compare them with the observations made by Potter *et al.* Comparing means first, it can be shown that the estimate of the mean nonsusceptible period ($\bar{d}_m$) is equal to the sum of the mean lengths of gestation and of postpartum nonsusceptibility obtained by Potter *et al.* (1965), i.e., 19 months. The additional component due to intra-uterine mortality ($\bar{d}_s$) is one month longer (3 months, compared to 2), which is the logical consequence of our higher rate of intra-uterine mortality (25 per cent as opposed to 11 per cent). But the essential difference lies in the conception delay (4 months instead of 10).

The comparison leads to similar results with respect to variances. The greatest part of the total observed discrepancy (92 as opposed to 163) lies in the conception delay which has a variance equal to 12 in the simulation as opposed to 75 in the data. The difference in the component attributed to intra-uterine mortality is very small (41 in place of 38), nor is the difference large for postpartum infertility (39 to 50).

In other words, the total variance in birth intervals can be effectively simulated by including in the model a distribution of fecundabilities without having to consider other sources of heterogeneity.

We have made the comparison only for the age group 20-29 years; the 30+ group is manifestly too heterogeneous (because of age-effects) for us to be able to draw valid conclusions on heterogeneity in terms of cohorts.

PROVISIONAL CONCLUSIONS

In conclusion, it appears to us that in the current state of affairs the ideal simulation model should take into account the following:

(1) A distribution of fecundabilities;

(2) A homogeneous rate of intra-uterine mortality which is a function of age;

(3) A distribution of the duration of postpartum nonsusceptibility for each pregnancy outcome which could, eventually, also change with age;
(4) A distribution of age at the onset of permanent sterility; and
(5) A decrease in fecundability as each woman approaches the onset of permanent sterility.

We are currently working on a new version of our simulation model based on these considerations.

REFERENCES

Bodmer, W. F. and A. Jacquard 1968. La variance de la dimension des familles, selon divers facteurs de la fécondité, Population 23: 869-879.

Jacquard, A. 1967. La reproduction humaine en régime malthusien. Un modèle de simulation par la méthode de Monte-Carlo, Population 22: 897-920.

Léridon, H. 1973. Aspects des variations de la fécondité. I. Biométrie de la fécondité. I.N.E.D. - P.U.F. (Travaux et Documents no. 65).

Perrin, E. B. and M. C. Sheps 1964. Human reproduction: A stochastic process, Biometrics 20: 28-45.

Potter, R. G., J. B. Wyon, M. Parker and J. E. Gordon 1965. A case study of birth interval dynamics, Population Studies 19: 81-96.

RESEARCH AND EXPERIENCE WITH DEMOGRAPHIC SIMULATION MODELS

HANNES HYRENIUS

Research on demographic models at Gothenburg University was started in 1963 by an informal group within the Department of Statistics. In 1969, the group was given separate status as a Demographic Research Institute under the Swedish Social Science Council, located at the University of Gothenburg.

This paper includes:

(a) A brief report on the models developed so far (spring 1972), mainly dealing with fertility simulation. These models have been described in a number of Reports issued by the Demographic Research Institute as well as in several conference papers and journal articles.

(b) Plans for research on the labor force, using a combined macro- and micro-approach to separate the various factors involved in estimating the volume and structure of the labor force which corresponds to the population in working ages (15-75).

(c) Brief comments on a contemplated study of how the population sector of a "World Dynamic Model" might be expressed.

FERTILITY SIMULATION MODELS

The first study carried out dealt with the general approach to population dynamics through models which could allow artificial "experimentation" in areas in which we can usually make observations only under non-experimental conditions. A systematic catalogue of the main demographic and socio-economic variables and a general approach to the problems was presented at the UN Conference on the Application of Science and Technology for the Benefit of the Less Developed Areas in 1963. A revised version was published as the Institute's Report No. 3.

The first model was based on the so-called "biological approach." This involved the inclusion of the various physiological factors which in general determine fertility under conditions without any birth control measures. In the first model (DM 1) were included assumptions about fecundability, stipulated proportions of live births, stillbirths and abortions, distribution of the length of pregnancy for each outcome, and distribution of the duration of the temporary postpartum sterility for each outcome. In addition there were allowances for secondary definite sterility during those states of the reproductive life where this is appropriate. Finally there was an age distribution of the time for menopause.

It turned out that this type of model, with the numerical data chosen on the basis of available information, gave results in the form of age-specific marital fertility rates close to what have been observed in Sweden up to about 1870.

When these results had been obtained subsequent extensions were developed. Mortality of both spouses was included. In connection with infant mortality, the distribution of postpartum anovulatory periods was made differentially, according to the possible death of the first child in an interval. Nuptiality was introduced by way of predetermined age distributions at marriage. Together with this extension of the number of variables, certain technical improvements were also made (DM 2).

The second model, using a "demographic approach" and based on the conditions prevailing in Sweden during recent years, relies upon statistically observed information about the behavior of the population. Input parameters included the age distribution at marriage and estimates of the distribution of the number of children at the end of the fertile period. A further ingredient was the distribution of time intervals between marriage and first birth and between successive births. This approach gave rise to two models which described well the conditions prevailing in a population with a well-developed family planning system (DM 3, DM 4).

This approach for developing demographic fertility models may to a certain extent be described as a microsimulation. Subsequently, a combination of micro- and macrosimulation is contemplated, partly with the purpose of developing a dynamic model which will also take care of the transition of the reproduction from high levels down to low levels. As one result of these studies, it may be mentioned that a dynamic model for the population transition does not seem likely to be obtained merely through successive discrete steps from high to low levels of fertility and mortality. It seems necessary to introduce the time variable in a more complex way.

The development of micro-models of the reproductive process has been further extended to include heterogeneity of fecundability between women and marriages (couples), and also a more complex relation between fecundability and sterility on the one hand, and the previous reproductive history on the other.

Recently two reports have been published under the title Fecundity, Fertility and Family Planning. Modifications, which have been developed mainly by Dr. Ingvar Holmberg, aim at a structure and capability of the model such as to allow different kinds of changes in family planning. Fecundability may be influenced by the type of measure used to avoid pregnancy, and the desired number of births may change according to the outcome of the previous reproductive history.

The work going on at present is devoted to developing an integrated demographic model, using both macro- and micro-ingredients, and a combination of demographic and biological variables in order to obtain a model flexible enough to perform a dynamic analysis. This means above all that the various input variables must be functions of time. Time-dependence is achieved mostly by transforming the input into functions of which time is one of the variables. Parallel to this approach, parameters for the functions may in their turn be described as functions of time.

A complication of this technique is that some of the computer runs will have to be rather long and therefore expensive. A separate study has therefore been started in order to establish certain guide lines as to the dimensions of the runs of simulation series. Here again, a combination of micro- and macro-approaches seems useful, and it might be possible to reduce the number of runs considerably, by means of techniques developed in the art of experimental design.

The models described here were developed more or less independently of a number of other population models appearing at the same time, some of them with specific names like POPSIM, REPSIM etc. On comparison, it can be seen later on that a majority of the assumptions are common to the various models. At the same time, however, the techniques are to some extent different, the assumptions may vary and the models may differ in flexibility.

A comparison of the different models leads to the conclusion that much is to be gained from a collaboration in finding a new "generation" of population models, using the diversity of ideas developed by research workers in various parts of the world, and using a combination of macro- and micro-techniques.

A LABOR FORCE MODEL

All the models briefly presented here concentrate on reproductive behavior and are limited to demographic variables in a narrow sense. From a more general point of view this is not enough, even for the specific purpose of describing the behavior of the demographic factors involved in reproduction. The structure and variation of these demographic variables are influenced in different ways by external conditions and factors of an economic, social and psychological nature. In developing a more general model the demographic factors may be considered as the most important sector, but to a certain extent economic and social factors also must be included. Our purpose is not only to make it possible to describe the determinants of the demographic variables; we also need ways of analyzing the consequences of population changes.

In order to achieve this goal, one may first try to build more general models into which the interactions between the demographic variables in a narrow sense and various non-demographic factors can be built stepwise, starting with independent blocks and, one may hope, ending with an integrated system.

From such an integrated model one can take out the separate sections one may wish to concentrate on. Thus, for instance, it will be possible to obtain the reproductive process again, but now in a more integrated sense. Another sector of a demographic nature would include those variables - demographic as well as economic and social, health factors etc. - which determine the labor force of a population.

The goal of general models covering any aspect of population and society is evidently too ambitious to be attained in a near future. One can, however, approach the different parts of such a system according to approximately the same principles as the reproductive models constructed so far. With this intention, plans are being developed at the Demographic Research Institute in Gothenburg to concentrate on such factors as will enable us to analyze the labor force contained in a population between the ages of, say, 15 and 75. By separating the various components it will then be possible to reconstruct at will the levels, proportions and changes of these various components. The purpose of this plan is to develop instruments for socio-economic-demographic analysis and for decision makers in national and local policy.

The main factors to be put into such a labor force model are the following:

1. Health: acute illness
   invalidism

2. Age limitations: school attendance, old age pensioning
3. Quality: school attendance professional training professional experience
4. Ageing
5. Individual variations

It is easily seen that some of these factors can be taken care of in a classical macro-approach, using life-table techniques. For some others however, a simulation of an individual nature is necessary, not only for handling the factors as such, but also for obtaining the variation between individuals. This combination of macro- and micro-techniques can be manipulated, e.g. so as to keep the costs and the consumption of computer time to a minimum.

This project is at a preliminary stage. It is, however, considered important to develop, for other purposes also, the specific section dealing with morbidity. Special studies have therefore been started for finding a macro-micro way of dealing with the dynamics of morbidity in a population. In the past a number of approaches have been used to obtain methods for analyzing changes in structure profiles of morbidity and health. So far, however, these efforts have been scattered and uncoordinated. It is to be hoped that such a model of illness and health can be developed to meet the two following requirements:

(a) A sufficiently elaborate model is wanted for the specific needs of the administration of health and medical care; this requires a medically well-differentiated structure in order to allow experiments with different organizations of the medical activities in a society.
(b) Since morbidity is one important component in an integrated labor force model, the changes of health conditions over time, variations between various socio-economic groups, and the possibility of artificial experimentation within the socio-economic

frame are of importance.

The efforts to develop limited population models may serve a number of purposes. It is necessary in the long run to consider all the various factors which are exerting an influence on population changes and the effect of the feedback of the changes in population size and structure upon the external factors such as national resources, environmental conditions etc.

THE POPULATION SECTOR OF A GLOBAL MODEL

Some organizations and individual scientists have recently tried to develop so-called global models dealing with the general interrelations on a global level of population, economic structure and development, social conditions etc. These approaches have an added interest at the Demographic Research Institute in Gothenburg because it appears that the methods and techniques of demographic simulation models could be used to improve the population sector of a more general type of model. A few remarks may be made here, in particular about the model originally developed by Professor Jay Forrester at M.I.T. with a special view to applications in economic fields. It was later on used for a research project initiated and financed by the Club of Rome. This project, under the direction of Professor Dennis Meadows, has led to a model presented in *The Limits to Growth*.

The global dynamics model is a macro-model based on a limited number of variables. This means that some of the important factors and conditions in a global population system are not included, such as health and social conditions, institutional limitations, certain biological "laws" etc. Another remark which is especially relevant to the population sector is that the way in which the phenomena are expressed must be considered insufficient for the purpose for which they are used. It was therefore considered a challenge to the Demographic Research Institute in Gothenburg to try to improve the population sector.

This is not the place to make a critical appraisal

of the whole project. A few remarks should be made, however, about the way in which population has been included in the model. As an integrated system can never be stronger than the weakest link, it may be said that the value of the model as a whole depends heavily on the fact that the various demographic factors involved have been introduced in a rather crude and undifferentiated manner.

The age differentiation of the population is of paramount importance for various reasons. One is that both fertility and mortality vary closely with age. It will hence be impossible to make realistic assumptions about the development of the number of births and the number of deaths as influenced by changes in the non-demographic factors (e.g. pollution). Another reason is that the economic activities depend on the proportion of the population in the active ages and belonging to the labor force.

BIBLIOGRAPHY

Forrester, J. W. 1971. World Dynamics. Cambridge, Mass.: Wright-Allen Press.

Holmberg, I. 1968. Demographic models (DM 4), Demographic Institute Reports No. 8, Gothenberg, Sweden: Univ. of Gothenberg.

Holmberg, I. 1970. Fecundity, fertility and family planning I., Demographic Institute Reports, Gothenberg, Sweden: Univ. of Gothenberg.

Holmberg, I. 1972. Fecundity, fertility and family planning II., Demographic Institute Reports, Gothenberg, Sweden: Univ. of Gothenberg.

Hyrenius, H. 1965. New technique for studying demographic-economic-social interrelations, Demographic Institute Reports No. 3, Gothenberg, Sweden: Univ. of Gothenberg.

Hyrenius, H. and I. Adolfsson 1964. A fertility simulation model, Demographic Institute Reports No. 2, Gothenberg, Sweden: Univ. of Gothenberg.

Hyrenius, H., I. Adolfsson and I. Holmberg 1966. Demographic models (DM 2), Demographic Institute Reports No. 4, Gothenberg, Sweden: Univ. of Gothenberg.

Hyrenius, H., I. Holmberg and M. Carlsson 1967. Demographic models (DM 3), Demographic Institute Reports No. 5, Gothenberg, Sweden: Univ. of Gothenberg.

Meadows, D. H., D. L. Meadows, J. Randers and W. W. Behrens 1972. The Limits to Growth. A report for the Club of Rome's project on the predicament of mankind. New York: Universe Books.

THE EVALUATION OF FOUR ALTERNATIVE FAMILY PLANNING PROGRAMS FOR POPLAND, A LESS DEVELOPED COUNTRY*

A. V. RAO, Q. W. LINDSEY, R. C. BHAVSAR, B. V. SHAH, D. G. HORVITZ and J. R. BATTS

INTRODUCTION

This paper illustrates the application of a demographic microsimulation model (POPSIM) to the evaluation of four alternative family planning programs for a less developed country designated here as POPLAND. The four strategies are assumed to differ with respect to a) the rate of new (or repeat) acceptance of each of four contraceptive methods per 1,000 population and b) the age-parity distribution of acceptors for each method.

POPLAND hopes to reduce its crude birth rate to 25 per 1,000 population over the next 10 years or so, but there is concern that this goal will not be achieved with its present program. Therefore, there is need to explore alternatives with respect to cost, potential reduction in the birth rate and other demographic considerations. In this paper, a comparative evaluation of four strategies is carried out through computer simulation of each of the alternatives using the basic POPSIM model together with a family planning module.

OBJECTIVES OF THE STUDY

The primary objective of this study is a comparative evaluation of the following four alternative

*The data used in this study refer to an actual country. However, confidentiality requirements preclude identification of that country.

family planning strategies with respect to their respective impacts on the POPLAND population:

P_1-- The Present Program as Planned. This refers to POPLAND's integrated family welfare planning and maternal-child health program. Although not fully operational, it is the plan that is being implemented. For convenience here it will be called the *Present Plan*.

P_2-- The Present Program as Actually Operating. This refers to what is actually taking place with respect to the *Present Plan*, to what is actually functioning. It is designated in this study as the *Actual Program*. The intent has been to implement the *Present Plan*; the *Actual Program* is what is actually operational. In some respects they coincide; in others they do not.

P_3-- The Post-Partum Plan. This approach is a delivery-based family planning and maternal-child health plan similar to that recommended by Drs. Taylor and Berelson in a feasibility study for a worldwide program of this nature. Taylor and Berelson draw upon experience gained in the International Post-Partum Program sponsored by the Population Council that began in 1966, a program that currently is functioning in 14 countries.

P_4-- Another alternative, referred to as "A Fourth Alternative." Recognizing that other approaches are possible, the Fourth Alternative assumes that a delivery-based family planning and maternal-child health system similar to P_3 is implemented in urban communities, but that in rural communities the present POPLAND system is followed.

These strategies are expected to lead to different family planning acceptance levels. Some differences in the age-parity-method distribution of the acceptors are expected among the strategies. These differences, with respect to demographic characteristics of acceptors, are elaborated in the next section.

DESIGN OF THE STUDY

Significant differences exist between the urban and rural populations of POPLAND with respect to acceptance of family planning as well as with respect to the methods used. Because of these differences separate simulations were carried out for the rural and urban populations.

Simulations were replicated four times for each strategy-residence combination, with a population of 605 women for each urban population replication, and 963 women for each rural population replication. The population sizes were selected so that output data corresponding to rural and urban administrative population units could be obtained from the results for the simulated population without further calculations. Each simulation run was carried out for 13 years. The simulation runs were replicated in order to estimate the variances of the estimates obtained.

The mathematical model used in these simulations is the POPSIM model. A complete description of this model is given in the Appendix.

PARAMETERS FOR THE POPSIM MODEL

1. Demographic Parameters

The estimates of the demographic parameters used were collected in the 1964 POPLAND Census, for the most part. The 1964 census age distribution of POPLAND women by marital status is given in Table 1. The age-parity specific monthly probabilities of a live birth for currently married women are given in Table 2. These probabilities were calculated based on data which also corresponds to 1964. For the sake of brevity, estimates of the other demographic parameters required in the POPSIM model are not included here.

2. Parameters Related to Family Planning

The family planning parameters in the model are:

Age Group	Proportion of Women		
	Single	Married	Widowed
0-1	.08770		
1-5	.28569		
5-10	.29687		
10-15	.25213		
15-16	.05604 (15-20)	.01689	.00395 (15-20)
16-17		.02194	
17-18		.02628	
18-19		.02990	
19-20		.03285	
20-21	.01270 (20-25)	.03513	.01079 (20-25)
21-22		.03679	
22-23		.03788	
23-24		.03841	
24-25		.03849	
25-30	.00379	.18075	.02272
30-35	.00171	.14442	.04151
35-40	.00097	.10974	.05752
40-45	.00074	.08897	.09684
45-50	.00046	.06171	.10441
50-55	.00042	.04518	.15783
55-60	.00022	.02351	.09942
60-65	.00026	.01729	.16756
65-70	.00011	.00688	.07436
70-75	.00009	.00313	.07302
75-80	.00005	.00201	.04689
80-85	.00003	.00116	.02699
85+	.00002	.00069	.01619
Total	1.00000	1.00000	1.00000
Proportion of women in marital status group	.42576	.46543	.10881

Table 1. AGE-MARITAL STATUS DISTRIBUTION OF WOMEN, POPLAND, 1964

	Age Group					
Parity	15-19	20-24	25-29	30-34	35-39	40-44
0	.0185	.0308	.0301	.0215	.0101	.0011
1	.0246	.0321	.0298	.0215	.0116	.0039
2	.0253	.0272	.0288	.0238	.0127	.0034
3	.0267	.0230	.0273	.0252	.0142	.0039
4	.0282	.0188	.0258	.0267	.0158	.0044
5 & over	.0297	.0146	.0243	.0281	.0173	.0050

Table 2. MONTHLY PROBABILITY (ADJUSTED) OF LIVE BIRTH FOR CURRENTLY MARRIED WOMEN BY PARITY AND CONVENTIONAL AGE GROUPS*

*These probabilities are based on 1964 data and represent essentially non-contracepting or natural live-birth probabilities.

(a) Proportion of currently married women in different contraceptive status in each age-parity group.

The contraceptive categories considered are: 1) null state - no contraception; 2) conventional contraceptives; 3) intrauterine device (IUD); 4) sterilization; and 5) oral pills. The proportions used were derived from the results of a recent national survey of POPLAND contraceptive practices. Table 3 shows a breakdown of the contraceptors (current users) by method and residence.

The differences between the rural and urban

Method	Urban Population	Rural Population	Total Population
Sterilization	10.2	5.4	6.3
IUD	1.0	.6	.7
Oral	1.2	.1	.3
Conventional	8.2	1.2	2.4
All Methods	20.6	7.3	9.7

Table 3. CONTRACEPTIVE STATE OF THE POPLAND POPULATION BY TYPE OF CONTRACEPTION. (Per cent of Currently Married Couples Using Specified Method)

populations with respect to level of contraceptive use and the type of contraceptive used are quite significant. As pointed out earlier, because these are significant differences, separate simulations were carried out for the urban and rural populations. The rates shown in Table 3 when converted to per 1,000 population are 35.6 among the urban population and 13.1 among the rural population.

(b) Age-parity specific probability of acceptance of contraception among those currently not practicing contraception.

Three types of data, based on certain assumptions and some evidence regarding behavior under the four strategies, have been combined to generate these probabilities. The first set of data relate to the annual rate at which women not practicing contraception accept some method of contraception. These assumptions are summarized in Table 4. The expected numbers of new acceptors of contraceptives per 1,000 population plotted against year of simulation are shown in Figures 1 and 2.

Notice that the rate increases linearly, but at different rates, within each of three different time periods. The highest rate of increase is assumed to occur during the first three years of each program.

Year	Expected Number of Contraceptors							
	Urban Population				Rural Population			
	P_1	P_2	P_3	P_4	P_1	P_2	P_3	P_4
1	17.7	17.7	17.7	17.7	4.5	4.5	4.5	4.5
3	25.0	20.0	28.5	32.5	12.5	7.5	16.0	20.0
8	28.5	22.5	33.5	37.5	16.0	10.0	21.0	25.0
13	30.0	25.0	35.0	40.0	17.5	12.5	22.5	27.5

Table 4. EXPECTED NUMBER OF NEW (OR REPEAT) CONTRACEPTORS PER 1,000 POPULATION UNDER DIFFERENT STRATEGIES

The second set of data pertain to the age-parity distribution of new or repeat contraceptors for each contraceptive under each of the four strategies. The marginal distributions by age and by parity of the acceptors of each method are given in Tables 5a and 5b. It is noted that P_1 and P_4 have the same age and parity marginals for all methods.

The third set of data relate to the contraceptive mix, i.e., the expected proportion accepting each method under each strategy. The data are given in Table 6.

For all strategies, the per cent accepting sterilization among the rural population is equal to or

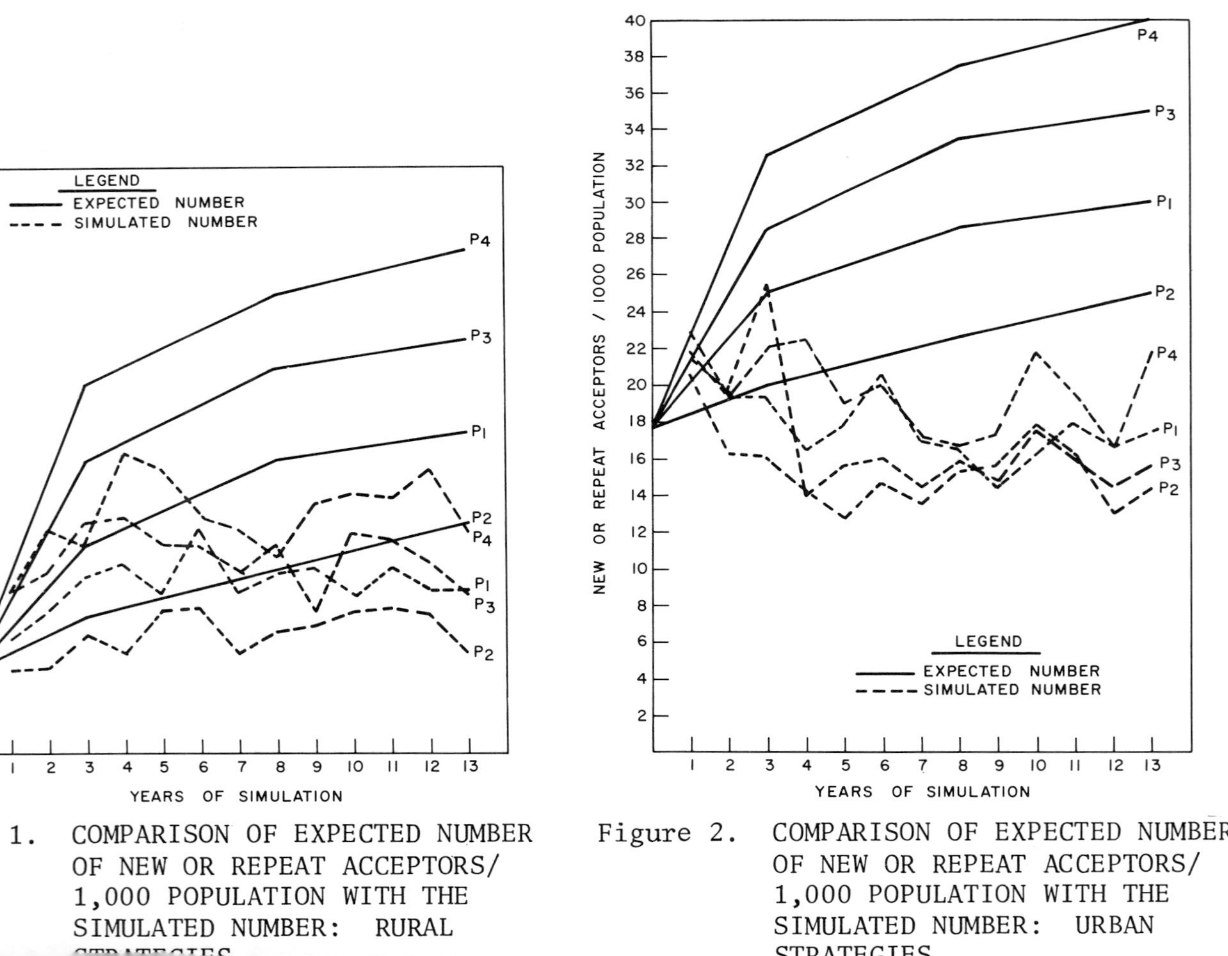

Figure 1. COMPARISON OF EXPECTED NUMBER OF NEW OR REPEAT ACCEPTORS/ 1,000 POPULATION WITH THE SIMULATED NUMBER: RURAL STRATEGIES

Figure 2. COMPARISON OF EXPECTED NUMBER OF NEW OR REPEAT ACCEPTORS/ 1,000 POPULATION WITH THE SIMULATED NUMBER: URBAN STRATEGIES

	Conventional Contraceptive			IUD			Sterilization		
	P_1^*	P_2	P_3	P_1^*	P_2	P_3	P_1^*	P_2	P_3
Age									
15-19	11	4	8	5	2	6	1	-	-
20-24	36	11	27	24	15	26	11	7	19
25-29	34	18	32	35	30	33	32	25	37
30-34	13	30	20	23	31	21	29	31	25
35-39	4	33	9	12	17	10	20	24	16
40-44	2	4	4	1	5	4	7	13	3
Total	100	100	100	100	100	100	100	100	100

Table 5a. AGE DISTRIBUTION OF NEW OR REPEAT ACCEPTORS OF CONTRACEPTIVES FOR EACH METHOD AND FAMILY PLANNING STRATEGY

*P_4 has the same distributions as P_1.

	Conventional Contraceptive			IUD			Sterilization		
	P^*_1	P_2	P_3	P^*_1	P_2	P_3	P^*_1	P_2	P_3
Parity									
0	9	2	2	-	-	1	-	-	-
1	19	16	26	10	5	16	-	-	-
2	27	33	22	24	16	24	16	3	6
3	25	26	21	30	25	19	32	29	22
4	16	18	12	20	23	14	25	25	27
5+	4	5	17	16	31	26	27	43	45
Total	100	100	100	100	100	100	100	100	100

Table 5b. PARITY DISTRIBUTION OF NEW OR REPEAT ACCEPTORS OF CONTRACEPTIVES FOR EACH METHOD AND FAMILY PLANNING STRATEGY

*P_4 has the same distributions as P_1.

Method	Urban Population P_1	P_2	P_3	P_4	Rural Population P_1	P_2	P_3	P_4
Sterilization	23	24	42	32	38	42	42	42
IUD	14	10	13	16	19	13	13	21
Orals	-	-	5	5	-	-	-	5
Conventionals	63	66	40	47	43	45	45	32
All acceptors	100	100	100	100	100	100	100	100

Table 6. EXPECTED DISTRIBUTION OF ACCEPTORS FOR EACH METHOD OF CONTRACEPTION AND STRATEGY

higher than for the urban population.

Thus the four strategies are assumed to differ on one or more of the following considerations:

(1) Number of new or repeat acceptors per 1,000 population,

(2) Age-parity distribution of acceptors for each method, and

(3) Proportion accepting each method.

The age-parity specific probabilities of non-contracepting women accepting some method of contraception during a period of one year were calculated using these three sets of data and the age-parity distribution of currently married women in the 15-44 age group. An example of these probabilities (strategy P_4, urban) is given in Table 7 for the third, fourth and last year of the simulation. For certain age-parity groups the probabilities for the fourth year are smaller than those for the third year (e.g., parity, age group 30-34 years). This occurs because there is a change in the age-parity-method probabili-

Parity	Year	Age Group 15-19	20-24	25-29	30-34	35-39	40-44
0	3	0.0050	0.0173	0.0260	0.0694	0.0000	0.0000
	4	0.0069	0.0590	0.1341	0.2378	0.0000	0.0000
	13	0.0083	0.0708	0.1609	0.2853	0.0000	0.0000
1	3	0.0289	0.0375	0.1284	0.3140	0.7283	0.0347
	4	0.0854	0.1250	0.1882	0.1334	0.0680	0.0074
	13	0.1024	0.1500	0.2259	0.1601	0.0816	0.0088
2	3	0.1515	0.0803	0.1429	0.6949	1.0000	0.1734
	4	0.3880	0.2241	0.3047	0.2610	0.3654	0.0735
	13	0.4656	0.2689	0.3656	0.3131	0.4385	0.0882
3	3	0.4640	0.1395	0.1841	0.4133	0.6380	0.3011
	4	0.9926	0.4112	0.3933	0.3501	0.1747	0.1147
	13	0.9949	0.4934	0.4719	0.4200	0.2096	0.1376
4	3	0.0000	0.3225	0.2310	0.2828	0.5416	0.1368
	4	0.0000	0.6405	0.3912	0.2471	0.2287	0.0812
	13	0.0000	0.7685	0.4693	0.2965	0.2743	0.0975
5+	3	0.0000	0.2590	0.1794	0.1332	0.1025	0.0579
	4	0.0000	0.2540	0.1827	0.1233	0.0872	0.0428
	13	0.0000	0.3048	0.2192	0.1479	0.1047	0.0513

Table 7. AGE-PARITY SPECIFIC PROBABILITY OF ACCEPTING SOME METHOD OF CONTRACEPTION: STRATEGY P_4, URBAN

ties of acceptors in the fourth simulation year for strategies P_1, P_3 and P_4.

(c) Probabilities of dropping out of other contraceptive states.

The annual probability of dropping out of the conventional state was arbitrarily assumed to be 0.5. The IUD and pill dropout have been derived by combining the actual experience of several less developed countries. The age-parity specific monthly probabilities of dropping from these non-null contraceptive states are given in Table 8.

(d) Switching patterns.

These are the conditional transition probabilities of switching to a new contraceptive given that the woman has dropped the method she was using. The model requires these conditional transition probabilities for parity 0, 1, 2, 3, 4 and 5+. The conditional probabilities for switching from the null state are based on the age-parity-method distribution of contraceptive users under each strategy. These have been arbitrarily derived on the assumption that a higher proportion of women of higher parity will adopt more effective methods such as IUD and sterilization. The only differences among the strategies with respect to switching patterns are in the transition probabilities from the null state to non-null states. The switching patterns are summarized in Tables 9a and 9b.

(e) Use-effectiveness of contraceptive states.

For each currently married woman 15-44 the model alters the live birth probability by multiplying by a factor determined by her current contraceptive state. This factor is assumed to be 1 for null state, .50 for conventionals, .85 for IUD, 0 for sterilization and .95 for orals.

RESULTS

Three kinds of program output measures were computed based on the four simulation runs for each strategy. These are:

(1) Birth rates for each simulation year, given

Parity	Age	Conventional	IUD	Sterilization	Orals
	15-19	0.056126	0.064942	0.000000	0.070883
	20-24	0.056126	0.079617	0.000000	0.060569
0	25-29	0.056126	0.097098	0.000000	0.051369
	30-34	0.056126	0.118468	0.000000	0.043056
	35-39	0.056126	0.144674	0.000000	0.035468
	40-44	0.056126	0.170688	0.000000	0.028486
	15-19	0.056126	0.049097	0.000000	0.053174
	20-24	0.056126	0.058292	0.000000	0.049123
1	25-29	0.056126	0.067448	0.000000	0.045253
	30-34	0.056126	0.075908	0.000000	0.041548
	35-39	0.056126	0.082602	0.000000	0.037994
	40-44	0.056126	0.086209	0.000000	0.034579
	15-19	0.056126	0.037320	0.000000	0.038497
	20-24	0.056126	0.043935	0.000000	0.039017
2	25-29	0.056126	0.050048	0.000000	0.039540
	30-34	0.056126	0.055226	0.000000	0.040066
	35-39	0.056126	0.058956	0.000000	0.040595
	40-44	0.056126	0.060761	0.000000	0.041128
	15-19	0.056126	0.027857	0.000000	0.025934
	20-24	0.056126	0.032967	0.000000	0.029960
3	25-29	0.056126	0.037493	0.000000	0.034178
	30-34	0.056126	0.041155	0.000000	0.038608
	35-39	0.056126	0.043666	0.000000	0.043276
	40-44	0.056126	0.044795	0.000000	0.048208
	15-19	0.056126	0.019897	0.000000	0.014935
	20-24	0.056126	0.024020	0.000000	0.021747
4	25-29	0.056126	0.027569	0.000000	0.029124
	30-34	0.056126	0.030355	0.000000	0.037175
	35-39	0.056126	0.032202	0.000000	0.046042
	40-44	0.056126	0.032974	0.000000	0.055920
	15-19	0.056126	0.012993	0.000000	0.005141
	20-24	0.056126	0.016418	0.000000	0.014229
5+	25-29	0.056126	0.019306	0.000000	0.024345
	30-34	0.056126	0.021523	0.000000	0.035765
	35-39	0.056126	0.022951	0.000000	0.048899
	40-44	0.056126	0.023505	0.000000	0.064395

Table 8. AGE-PARITY SPECIFIC MONTHLY PROBABILITY OF DROPPING OUT OF NON-NULL CONTRACEPTIVE STATES

Parity	Urban Conv.	Urban IUD	Urban Ster.	Urban Oral	Rural Conv.	Rural IUD	Rural Ster.	Rural Oral
				Actual Program (P_2)				
0	1.00	0	0	0	1.00	0	0	0
1	.93	.04	.03	0	.87	.09	.04	0
2	.91	.07	.02	0	.82	.12	.06	0
3	.65	.09	.26	0	.44	.12	.44	0
4	.59	.11	.30	0	.37	.14	.49	0
5+	.30	.18	.52	0	.09	.17	.74	0
				Present Plan (P_1)				
0	1.00	0	0	0	1.00	0	0	0
1	.90	.10	0	0	.82	.18	0	0
2	.71	.14	.15	0	.52	.20	.28	0
3	.58	.15	.27	0	.38	.20	.42	0
4	.54	.15	.31	0	.34	.19	.47	0
5+	.24	.21	.55	0	.12	.20	.68	0
				Post-Partum Program (P_3)				
0	.82	.18	0	0	.84	.16	0	0
1	.82	.16	.02	0	.85	.15	0	0
2	.59	.21	.19	.01	.63	.20	.17	0
3	.42	.12	.45	.01	.45	.12	.43	0
4	.28	.10	.62	0	.30	.10	.60	0
5+	.24	.11	.64	.01	.26	.11	.63	0
				Fourth Alternative (P_4)				
0	.92	0	0	.08	.88	0	0	.12
1	.73	.13	0	.14	.61	.21	0	.18
2	.56	.17	.23	.04	.40	.24	.32	.04
3	.43	.17	.37	.03	.28	.22	.47	.03
4	.40	.17	.42	.01	.26	.21	.52	.01
5+	.13	.18	.62	.07	.08	.20	.66	.06

Table 9a. PROBABILITY OF ACCEPTING DIFFERENT CONTRACEPTIVE METHODS AMONG THOSE WHO SHIFT FROM THE NULL STATE TO CONTRACEPTIVE STATE

Parity	Present Contraceptive State	Probability of Dropping Out or Shifting to Alternate State				
		Null	Conv.	IUD	Ster.	Oral
0	Conv.	.90	0	.10	0	0
	IUD	.90	.10	0	0	0
	Ster.	0	0	0	0	0
	Oral	.90	.10	0	0	0
1	Conv.	.80	0	.20	0	0
	IUD	.80	.20	0	0	0
	Ster.	0	0	0	0	0
	Oral	.80	.20	0	0	0
2	Conv.	.70	0	.20	.10	0
	IUD	.70	.15	0	.15	0
	Ster.	0	0	0	0	0
	Oral	.70	.15	0	.15	0
3	Conv.	.30	0	.40	.30	0
	IUD	.50	.15	0	.35	0
	Ster.	0	0	0	0	0
	Oral	.50	.15	0	.35	0
4	Conv.	.25	0	.35	.40	0
	IUD	.45	.10	0	.45	0
	Ster.	0	0	0	0	0
	Oral	.45	.10	0	.45	0
5+	Conv.	.20	0	.30	.50	0
	IUD	.40	.10	0	.50	0
	Ster.	0	0	0	0	0
	Oral	.40	.10	0	.50	0

Table 9b. PROBABILITY OF DROPPING OUT OF A CONTRACEPTIVE STATE AND RETURNING TO THE NULL STATE OR SWITCHING TO ANOTHER CONTRACEPTIVE STATE

below in Tables 10a for the urban population and 10b for the rural population.

(2) The per cent of contraceptive users among currently married women 15-45 at the end of each simulation year, given in Table 11a for the urban population and 11b for the rural population.

(3) The number of new (or repeat) acceptors of contraceptives for each simulation year. These figures are given in Table 12.

(4) Age and parity distributions of women using contraceptives during the thirteenth year of simulation for each method of contraception and each strategy. The distributions for the urban population are given in Tables 13a, b and c. Similar distributions for the rural population are not included in this report for the sake of brevity.

DISCUSSION OF RESULTS

The acceptance rates observed in the simulated population are considerably smaller than the overall acceptance rates provided as input parameters (Table 4). This is illustrated in Figure 1 for the rural population and in Figure 2 for the urban population. It should be noted here that the age-parity specific probabilities of acceptance used as inputs to the SIMRUN program were calculated based on the age-parity distribution of currently married women as it existed in the initial population. As the family planning programs advance through time, changes occur in the age-parity distribution of women due to the fact that the programs are oriented towards preventing high parity births. In general the higher parity cells have higher probabilities of acceptance. However, program activities result in a general decrease in the number of women available in the higher parity cells. There is also a depletion in the number of women eligible for acceptance since the per cent of currently married women 15-45 using a contraceptive increases over time.

Year	P_1	P_2	P_3	P_4
1	41.0	40.6	41.4	38.5
2	36.5	36.9	41.6	38.4
3	35.3	36.7	35.0	38.0
4	32.2	34.1	28.8	34.4
5	32.7	34.5	30.0	28.8
6	31.5	32.2	28.2	27.8
7	24.8	31.8	28.6	21.2
8	28.1	30.7	24.9	26.3
9	28.6	34.3	26.2	22.6
10	28.1	33.8	27.5	25.7
11	26.7	30.0	24.9	27.9
12	29.0	37.0	29.7	27.8
13	29.9	34.6	29.1	29.4

Table 10a. BIRTH RATES OBSERVED IN SIMULATION RUNS (URBAN BIRTH RATES BY STRATEGY)

Year	P_1	P_2	P_3	P_4
1	44.7	44.1	44.4	43.9
2	43.9	42.3	40.6	41.3
3	40.6	40.0	36.8	40.8
4	34.6	40.2	36.7	32.0
5	32.1	37.3	33.7	34.1
6	29.8	36.9	32.2	31.3
7	32.8	34.0	31.4	29.5
8	33.9	35.4	29.7	28.2
9	33.0	34.4	31.8	29.3
10	33.7	31.7	31.2	29.6
11	31.2	35.2	32.8	26.2
12	33.5	35.7	30.0	28.1
13	31.9	31.0	32.0	28.4

Table 10b. BIRTH RATES OBSERVED IN SIMULATION RUNS (RURAL BIRTH RATES BY STRATEGY)

Year	P_1	P_2	P_3	P_4
Initial Population	18.9	18.9	18.9	18.9
1	24.4	25.3	24.9	24.6
2	26.9	27.0	26.6	27.7
3	30.9	27.6	32.6	32.8
4	32.0	28.6	32.6	36.8
5	33.4	28.3	35.4	38.7
6	36.8	29.4	36.2	42.4
7	35.8	30.0	35.9	42.1
8	36.2	30.6	38.1	43.0
9	35.7	32.1	38.4	42.6
10	36.1	34.0	40.9	46.0
11	35.8	34.3	41.6	45.1
12	35.0	33.2	40.1	44.4
13	35.4	33.7	39.0	43.5

Table 11a. THE NUMBER OF CONTRACEPTIVE USERS PER 100 MARRIED WOMEN IN 15-44 AGE GROUP AT THE END OF EACH YEAR OF SIMULATION FOR EACH STRATEGY (URBAN CONTRACEPTORS PER 100 MARRIED WOMEN BY STRATEGY)

Year	P_1	P_2	P_3	P_4
Initial Population	6.9	6.9	6.9	6.9
1	8.8	8.1	10.1	10.2
2	11.1	9.5	13.2	13.4
3	14.3	11.3	16.7	17.0
4	17.3	12.7	20.4	22.9
5	18.3	14.7	21.5	26.3
6	21.5	16.7	23.7	29.1
7	22.6	17.3	25.6	30.7
8	24.9	17.7	27.1	32.7
9	26.5	19.1	26.4	33.9
10	27.5	20.4	28.8	36.7
11	27.6	21.3	29.7	37.7
12	27.4	21.3	30.0	38.9
13	26.9	20.8	30.0	38.0

Table 11b. THE NUMBER OF CONTRACEPTIVE USERS PER 100 MARRIED WOMEN IN 15-44 AGE GROUP AT THE END OF EACH YEAR OF SIMULATION FOR EACH STRATEGY (RURAL CONTRACEPTORS PER 100 MARRIED WOMEN BY STRATEGY)

	Number Per 1,000 Population							
	Rural				Urban			
Year	P_1	P_2	P_3	P_4	P_1	P_2	P_3	P_4
1	6.2	4.6	8.7	8.8	21.9	20.7	22.9	21.9
2	7.7	4.7	9.9	12.2	19.4	16.3	19.3	19.2
3	9.7	6.5	12.7	11.3	19.4	16.1	25.5	22.0
4	10.4	5.5	12.9	16.4	16.5	14.2	14.0	22.5
5	8.6	7.8	11.4	15.6	17.9	12.7	15.6	19.0
6	12.2	8.0	11.3	12.9	20.6	14.9	16.0	20.2
7	8.9	5.5	9.9	12.2	17.0	13.5	14.5	17.3
8	9.8	6.7	11.4	10.7	16.5	15.3	15.9	16.7
9	10.2	7.0	7.7	13.6	14.4	15.6	14.7	17.5
10	8.7	7.7	12.0	14.1	16.3	17.9	17.6	21.8
11	10.2	7.9	11.7	13.9	18.0	16.3	16.0	19.3
12	8.9	7.6	10.4	15.5	16.6	13.0	14.4	16.7
13	8.8	5.5	8.7	12.1	17.5	14.3	15.7	19.9

Table 12. SIMULATED NUMBER OF NEW (OR REPEAT) ACCEPTORS OF CONTRACEPTIVES PER 1,000 POPULATION BY URBAN-RURAL AND STRATEGY

Age Group	Conventional Strategy P_2	P_1	P_3	P_4	IUD Strategy P_2	P_1	P_3	P_4	Sterilization Strategy P_2	P_1	P_3	P_4
15-19	4	5	3	19	0	3	3	0	0	0	0	0
20-24	4	29	29	20	0	13	26	28	0	4	5	7
25-29	30	29	34	36	11	41	29	19	12	15	16	14
30-34	31	17	21	14	47	18	19	41	28	32	28	29
35-39	23	11	10	7	29	15	10	9	32	26	27	28
40-44	8	9	3	4	13	10	13	3	28	23	24	22
Total	100	100	100	100	100	100	100	100	100	100	100	100
Sample Size	74	89	67	73	38	39	31	32	222	224	291	316

Table 13a. DISTRIBUTION OF USERS OF EACH CONTRACEPTIVE METHOD DURING THE THIRTEENTH YEAR OF SIMULATION AMONG URBAN WOMEN BY AGE GROUP

Parity	Conventional Strategy P_2	P_1	P_3	P_4	IUD Strategy P_2	P_1	P_3	P_4	Sterilization Strategy P_2	P_1	P_3	P_4
0	0	25	10	22	0	5	0	0	0	0	0	0
1	5	17	33	12	5	15	19	9	1	0	0	1
2	38	26	25	34	3	23	42	25	11	16	13	19
3	31	12	13	19	30	31	19	41	24	29	27	30
4	15	12	12	7	34	13	16	9	24	25	27	23
5+	11	8	7	6	28	13	4	16	40	30	33	27
Total	100	100	100	100	100	100	100	100	100	100	100	100
Sample Size	74	89	67	73	38	39	31	32	222	224	291	316

Table 13b. DISTRIBUTION OF USERS OF EACH CONTRACEPTIVE METHOD DURING THE THIRTEENTH YEAR OF SIMULATION AMONG URBAN WOMEN BY PARITY

Method	Strategy P_2	P_1	P_3	P_4
Conventionals	22	25	17	17
IUD	11	11	8	7
Sterilization	66	63	74	72
Pill	1	1	1	4
Total	100	100	100	100
Sample Size	337	357	394	439

Table 13c. DISTRIBUTION OF USERS OF CONTRACEPTIVES BY METHOD AMONG URBAN WOMEN DURING THE THIRTEENTH YEAR OF SIMULATION

The combined effect of these related phenomena is to lower the overall acceptance rate. Program planning ignoring these phenomena will result in under-utilization of facilities.

Despite the differences in acceptance rates among strategies, there is no evidence to suggest that there are any significant differences in birth rates among P_1, P_3 and P_4. However, the current strategy, P_2, does appear to be leading to a higher birth rate in the urban area. The reasons for the apparent lack of differences in birth rates among strategies have been explored by analyzing the changes in number of births in different age-parity groups among urban women. Currently married women 15-44 are classified into two groups for this analysis: Group 1, women below 30 of parity two or less; Group 2, women above 30 or of parity greater than two. The changes in the contraceptive acceptance, and number of births for these two groups of women between the first year of simulation and the thirteenth year of simulation are shown in Table 14.

The changes in contraceptive usage are sizeable only among women over 30 or with parity greater than two. The percentage of women using contraceptives increased considerably among these women between the first year and thirteenth year of simulation; the birth rates have been reduced by more than 40 per cent for P_1, P_3 and P_4. On the other hand, among the women under 30 and with parity two or less there has been little or no change in acceptance of contraception; the reduction in birth rates has been less than 20 per cent. The impact of strategies P_1, P_3 and P_4 is fairly comparable, ranging from 14 to 20 per cent among the younger lower parity women and from 40 to 50 per cent among women over 30 or of higher parity. Among the three strategies, P_1 does appear to be more effective with the younger lower parity women and less effective with the older or higher parity women than P_2 and P_3. The latter two strategies have almost the same impact within each of the two groups of women. The net effect is similar birth rates for all three strategies by the thirteenth year.

The reader may wonder whether the small sample sizes used in this study have contributed to the apparent lack of discrimination among strategies. A natural question which arises is whether the results would have been different if a larger sample size had been used. This was investigated using an initial population of 10,000 women for urban strategy P_4. The strategy P_4 was chosen primarily because it has the largest acceptance probabilities. The results of the runs with two different sample sizes are compared in Tables 15, 16 and 17.

Description	Simulation Year	Strategy P_2	P_1	P_3	P_4
Currently married women under 30 and parity two or less					
Number of women	1	3,540	3,530	3,530	3,550
	13	4,480	4,890	4,790	4,890
Number and per cent of current users	1	450(13)*	560(16)	450(13)	430(12)
	13	190(4)	660(13)	620(13)	840(17)
Number of births per 1,000 women	1	288	303	303	284
	13	283	243	253	243
Currently married women over 30 and/or more than parity two					
Number of women	1	5,740	5,790	5,840	5,730
	13	5,600	5,190	5,310	5,210
Number and per cent of current users	1	1,840(32)	1,990(34)	1,890(32)	1,840(32)
	13	3,190(57)	2,870(55)	3,330(63)	3,560(68)
Number of births per 1,000 women	1	181	173	176	164
	13	134	100	86	81

*Numbers in parentheses are the corresponding percentages.

Table 14. CHANGES IN THE NUMBER OF BIRTHS AND CONTRACEPTIVE USAGE AMONG 50,000 URBAN WOMEN OBSERVED IN SIMULATED POPULATION

Year	Current Users Per 1,000 Population	
	Simulation with 2,420 Women	Simulation with 10,000 Women
1	24.6	22.8
2	27.7	26.8
3	32.8	30.2
4	38.8	35.1
5	42.4	38.6
6	42.0	40.4
7	43.0	42.0
8	42.6	42.1
9	43.0	44.0
10	46.0	44.5
11	45.1	44.3
12	44.4	44.8

Table 15. COMPARISON OF NUMBER OF CURRENT USERS OF CONTRACEPTIVES PER 1,000 POPULATION FROM TWO SIMULATION RUNS WITH URBAN STRATEGY P_4

Year	Acceptors Per 1,000 Population	
	Simulation with 2,420 Women	Simulation with 10,000 Women
1	21.9	18.9
2	19.2	19.4
3	22.0	20.4
4	22.5	22.5
5	19.0	20.5
6	20.2	19.3
7	17.3	18.0
8	16.7	17.2
9	17.5	18.7
10	21.8	19.6
11	19.3	17.7
12	16.7	19.4

Table 16. COMPARISON OF NUMBER OF NEW (OR REPEAT) ACCEPTORS PER 1,000 POPULATION IN TWO SIMULATION RUNS WITH URBAN STRATEGY P_4

Year	Birth Rates	
	Simulation with 2,420 Women*	Simulation with 10,000 Women
1	38.5 ± 2.7	35.9
2	38.4 ± 2.0	36.2
3	38.0 ± 2.3	33.2
4	34.4 ± 1.9	32.2
5	28.8 ± 1.3	30.4
6	27.7 ± 1.4	28.5
7	21.2 ± 2.0	25.7
8	26.3 ± 2.2	27.8
9	22.6 ± 1.9	25.8
10	25.7 ± 1.4	26.8
11	27.9 ± 1.4	26.8
12	27.8 ± 2.2	26.8

Table 17. COMPARISON OF BIRTH RATES FROM TWO SIMULATION RUNS WITH URBAN STRATEGY P_4

*Estimated standard deviations calculated from the four urban samples (605 women) run with this strategy.

With respect to current user level (Table 15) and the number of new or repeat acceptors per 1,000 population (Table 16), the differences between the runs (based on the two different sizes of population) are negligible. The observed differences in the birth rates (Table 17) between the two samples are attributable to stochastic variation. Thus there is no evidence to suggest that the small sample sizes used in this study have biased the results.

The age, parity and method distributions of users of contraceptives (Table 13) differ from those of new or repeat acceptors. This is due to the fact that the distribution of current users is affected by the switching patterns. The switching patterns result in a situation where higher parity women ultimately get sterilized.

CONCLUSION

This study suggests that a more dynamic change in the target populations than has been included in these simulations will be needed to achieve any significant changes in the birth rate over those expected from P_1. A simple increase in facilities or resources will not achieve the desired results without changes in program emphasis with respect to target groups.

ACKNOWLEDGMENTS

This research was partly supported by Contract NESA-460, USAID, with the Department of State, U.S. Government. The authors would like to thank Mrs. Kathryn Cameron for her assistance with computer processing.

APPENDIX

THE DEMOGRAPHIC MODEL (POPSIM)

GENERAL DESCRIPTION OF POPSIM

POPSIM is a dynamic demographic model designed for computer simulation of the principal demographic processes occurring in human populations (Horvitz *et al.* 1971; Shah 1970). It is classed as a microsimulation model because it generates a vital event history, including the dates of birth, marriage, divorce, widowhood, remarriage and death for each individual in the computer population. Although POPSIM is a two-sex model, it may be used for simulating cohort as well as period data.

POPSIM is a stochastic model in the sense that random sampling from probability distributions is used to determine which events occur to an individual and when they occur. It is a dynamic continuous time model, permitting the probabilities to change with time. The model can be made self-adjusting or recursive through the use of feedback mechanisms. For example, feedback models appropriate for POPSIM to account for the effect of changing marriage patterns on marriage rates are discussed in Shah and Giesbrecht (1969).

The demand in recent years for new techniques for studying complex demographic phenomena with fewer restrictive assumptions than has been possible with analytic models has led to the development of a variety of microsimulation models (Barrett 1967; Hyrenius and Adolffson 1964; Hyrenius *et al.* 1967; Holmberg 1968; Orcutt *et al.* 1961; Ridley and Sheps 1966). POPSIM is a laboratory research tool designed in response to that demand. It can be used to considerable advantage in a wide variety of simulated longitudinal studies. Further, it can be linked easily to other models (e.g. as the demographic component of models of economic, education, health or environmental systems), whether they be micro- or macro-models.

GENERATING THE INITIAL POPULATION (POPGEN)

The POPSIM computer program consists of two distinct parts or phases. The first, designated POPGEN, is used to create an initial population. The initial population is conceptualized as a random sample of individuals (stratified by age, sex and marital status) from a hypothetical population. The program, through the use of control cards, offers the user considerable flexibility in specifying the nature of the hypothetical population. For example, the user can choose to confine his population to a cohort of women x years of age in 1970, or to all persons 65 years of age and older in 1966, or to the civilian non-institutionalized U.S. population as of 1960. In practice, the input parameters required to create the initial population should be chosen such that the hypothetical population will be as similar to the real population of interest as possible.

The initial population can be considered usefully as a random sample of individuals selected from a population register, without regard to familial relationships. Thus, for example, a married female may be selected for the initial population, while her husband and children may not be chosen. Individuals in the computer population (initial sample plus births) are referred to as primary individuals, and marriage partners and children as secondary individuals. Since secondary individuals are not members of the computer population, information concerning them must be carried by the primary individual. In the simulation of vital event histories (second phase of POPSIM), all events which take place are considered as events to primary individuals. All tabulations produced are counts of primary individuals, or of events which happened to primary individuals. Secondary individuals enter the model only in the sense that they influence the vital event risks to which primary individuals are subject. For example, the risk of a married woman (primary individual) becoming a widow is a function of the age of her husband, a secondary individual.

The list of characteristics describing the primary individuals and the associated secondary individuals is shown in Table 1A. The list as initially developed for POPSIM consisted of the first 15 entries (Table 1A). The remaining five entries have been added recently, but were not used in the simulations comparing the alternative family planning programs. The nature of the entries in the list is dictated in part by the fact that POPSIM is a time-oriented simulation model, with continuous time. Consequently, rather than carry age as a characteristic and update periodically, date of birth in decimals is used.

RECORD(1)	=	sex of the individual
RECORD(2)	=	date of birth (decimal number)
RECORD(3)	=	current marital status (single, married, widowed, divorced)
RECORD(4)	=	parity
RECORD(5)	=	number of living children
RECORD(6)	=	current contraceptive method
RECORD(7)	=	number of marriages (0, 1, 2+)
RECORD(8)	=	date of current marital status
RECORD(9)	=	date of next event
RECORD(10)	=	next event
RECORD(11)	=	number of children (secondary individuals) for whom information on date of birth, sex and date of death (if appropriate) is available in a separate array for each mother
RECORD(12)	=	date of birth of spouse
RECORD(13)	=	previous contraceptive method
RECORD(14)	=	date of last birth
RECORD(15)	=	number of events which happen to the individual during a simulation
RECORD(16)	=	race (white or non-white)
RECORD(17)	=	residence (SMSA or non-SMSA)
RECORD(18)	=	family income deviate
RECORD(19)	=	family income (dollars)
RECORD(20)	=	date family income was computed

Table 1A. LIST OF CHARACTERISTICS OF EACH PRIMARY INDIVIDUAL IN THE SAMPLE POPULATION

The computer program to generate initial populations is written in FORTRAN for use on IBM 360 System/ Model 50 computers. The program is designed to generate a specified number of initial sample populations of a designated size in a single run and to write each population on a disk or on magnetic tape. The input to the program includes (in addition to parameters which control various options in the program and class limits used in the output tables) the following variables:

(1) The size of the initial population.
(2) The proportion of individuals in each of the eight sex-marital status groups.
(3) The proportion of individuals in specific (but arbitrary) age groups for each sex and marital status class.
(4) The probabilities with which married females are classified as remarried or not.
(5) Parameters to assign age of husband given age of wife.
(6) Parameters to assign age of wife given age of husband.
(7) Parameters to assign the date of current marital status.
(8) Monthly birth probabilities by age, parity and marital status (married or single), appropriate to three time points in the 30 year period prior to the date of the initial population. These values are used to generate a birth history, and hence the parity and date of last birth for each married or single female.
(9) Monthly death probabilities by age group, sex and marital status to determine number of living children for married or single females.
(10) Parameters to assign parity to widowed or divorced females.

The characteristics corresponding to RECORD(6), RECORD(9), RECORD(10), RECORD(13) and RECORD(15) are not assigned when the initial population is generated.

POPGEN creates each initial sample population in the computer by means of a series of subroutines which use random sampling of inverse probability distribution functions, for the most part, to assign a consistent set of characteristics to each individual. For example, a stratified random sampling procedure is used to assign age (date of birth), sex and marital status. Using the first three input variables listed above, a density function is fitted by the computer for each age-sex-marital status group. The distribution function and its inverse are then computed for each of these groups. The age assignment routine then sets up the records for the individuals in each age-sex-marital status group and assigns their ages by stratified random sampling of the associated inverse probability function. This is accomplished by first dividing the (0, 1) interval into n sub-intervals or strata of length 1/n, where n is the number of persons in the particular age-sex-marital status group, and then generating a uniformly distributed random number for each sub-interval to sample the appropriate inverse. This stratified sampling procedure distributes very effectively the ages of individuals over the entire age interval for each sex-marital status group.

The remaining characteristics are assigned to each individual by sampling the appropriate conditional distribution for the specific age, sex and marital status of the individual. For example, the age of husband is assigned by generating a random observation from the conditional distribution of age of husband given age of wife. Complete details regarding the functions and methods for deriving input parameters and the computer procedures used to assign each characteristic are given in Shah (1972).

POPSIM also permits the user the option of adding migrant individuals to the computer population at various points in time. While this occurs in the second phase, the program for creating the initial population is also used to create the additional individuals.

As the initial sample population is being generated, the computer program maintains a series of tables which are printed when the characteristics for the last individual have been determined. The exact series of tables produced depends in part on options selected by the user. For example, the POPGEN output tables might include:

(1) The distribution of primary individuals by sex, marital status and age group. The age groups are arbitrary and are determined by the user.

(2) The distribution of currently married women (primary) by age groups (as in 1) and parity (0, 1, ..., 6 or more).

(3) The distribution of never married women (primary) by age groups (as in 1) and parity (0, 1, ..., 6 or more).

(4) The distribution of currently married women by age at marriage and duration of marriage.

GENERATION OF VITAL EVENT HISTORIES (SIMRUN)

After creating an initial population of desired size and characteristics, a second program uses the Monte Carlo method to generate a vital event history or life pattern for each individual. This program advances the population forward through time in a series of time intervals or steps. At the end of each step, the program prints output tables and provides the user the option of updating the probabilities of the various events. The user must specify the total length of the simulation period and the time interval for each step. For example, one may simulate the vital events that occur to the initial population for a period of ten years in ten steps of one year each, or for a period of ten years in a single step, or 25 years in five steps of five years each.

The basic set of input data required by SIMRUN for generating vital event histories includes:

(1) Monthly birth probabilities for females by age group, marital status (married or not married) and parity (or number of living children).

(2) Monthly divorce probabilities by interval since marriage (or by age).
(3) Monthly death probabilities by age group, sex and marital status.
(4) Annual marriage probabilities for females by age and marital status.
(5) Parameters to determine the marital status of the groom given that of the bride.
(6) Bivariate distributions of ages of brides and grooms for first marriages and remarriages.

Additional input to the program, for controlling the operation of the model, is described in detail in Shah (1972).

At first glance, the list of required input parameters for both phases of POPSIM appears rather formidable. This is not a peculiarity of this or any other microsimulation model. The data required for any model increase rapidly with the degree of complexity of the model. However, POPSIM does not require all the input data for the model to be obtained entirely from one census or sample survey of the population of interest. Estimates of the various parameters used may be obtained from different prior studies on the population of interest and still be used in the model. Occasionally it may even be possible to use data from studies of different but similar populations and obtain valid results. Clearly, the data employed in a microsimulation model will have an important effect on the accuracy of predictions made with the model for particular populations. However, for most applications, the use of parameter values which have been estimated from data which do not pertain exactly to the population of interest will not hamper the usefulness of the model severely. In specific applications, simulation runs using upper and lower bounds for parameters whose values are in the questionable category may provide confidence bounds needed to accept the results from the model.

SIMRUN generates marriages, births, divorces and deaths using stored matrices of monthly transition (event) probabilities. A conditional probability approach is used which permits these event probabilities to depend on the current characteristics and prior history of the individual. For example, the monthly birth probabilities vary by parity and marital status within five year age groups for females between 15 and 45 years of age. Births are not permitted unless the interval since the last live birth is at least nine months.

An event-sequenced simulation procedure is used in which an individual is processed only when an event occurs to him. The first step in this procedure is to generate the time interval (and hence the date) of the next vital event for each individual in the initial population. Since the type of event to occur next (i.e., a birth or a change in marital status or a death) is not known, SIMRUN generates the time interval (or waiting time) separately for each of the competing events that can happen to the individual, under the assumption that nothing else does happen to him, and the event with the shortest generated time interval becomes the next event for that individual. Only this next event and its time of occurrence are carried in the record for each individual. This procedure for generating the next event is accurate under the assumption that the input parameters are independent probabilities for the competing events (or net rates) rather than crude rates.

The technique for generating the date of an event uses the inverse of the geometric distribution within time periods for which the monthly probabilities of the event remain constant. Consider, for example, the generation of the date of death of a married male who is exactly 42 years old. The monthly chance of dying for married males in the 40 to 44 age group is read from the stored table; this probability, denoted by $P_{mm}(11)$, refers to the 11th age group for married males. A uniform random number r between zero and one is generated and the quantity

$$t = \frac{\ln(1-r)}{\ln(1-P_{mm}(11))}$$

is computed. This is the randomly generated number of months (from the current month) until the death of the 42 year old male, provided $t \leq 36$. If $t > 36$, then the generated age at death of this man is greater than 45, in which case a new r and t must be generated using $P_{mm}(12)$, the monthly probability of dying for married males in the 45 to 49 age group. The month of death will have been determined if the new $t \leq 60$. Otherwise, the process is repeated again, using the appropriate monthly death probability, $P_{mm}(13)$, for the next age group (50-54). The process is continued until a time interval to death which does not extend into the next age group is obtained for this married male. The procedure is equivalent to using a sequence of independent, uniform (0, 1) random numbers and making a decision by comparing with the appropriate probability for each month. During intervals having constant probabilities, this assumes in effect, a Poisson process for the event, or a negative exponential distribution for the intervals between events.

An important point to note is that it is assumed that no other events happen to the individual in the interval. For example, it is assumed that the marriage of the 42 year old male does not end, due to divorce or death of his spouse, when calculating the time interval to his death. However, he is subject to having these competing events occur. To determine whether he becomes widowed before he dies, SIMRUN computes the date of death of his wife independently, using the monthly death probability for married females of her age class, and then compares the two death dates to determine which of these competing events is to occur first. Since divorce is also a possibility, the date of this event must be computed and compared with the two death dates to determine the next event for this 42 year old married male. Again, the time interval for each of the competing events is computed under the assumption that the other events do not occur.

For a female between the ages of 15 and 45, a competing risk is that of giving birth to a child.

Monthly probabilities of a live birth by age group, parity and marital status are used to generate the time interval to the next live birth by essentially the same method as explained above for computing the time interval to death.

Unmarried individuals are subject to the risk of marriage. Annual female marriage probabilities by age and marital status are read as input, while the male marriage probabilities are computed by SIMRUN in order to be consistent with those for the females. When a marriage occurs, the model uses bivariate distributions of ages of brides and grooms for first marriages and for remarriages to assign an age to the new spouse.

After the point in time for the next event is generated, it is checked to see if it falls within the interval chosen for that simulation step. If it is, time is advanced to that point and the event processed. If not, the individual is stored and not processed again until the beginning of the next simulation interval. Processing consists of recording the essential facts concerning the event and changing the status of individual characteristics affected by the event.

The processing required after the next event has been determined depends on the nature of the event. For example, if the event is death, the individual is marked as being dead and the event recorded in his history of vital events. Similarly, if the event is the death of the spouse or a divorce. In these cases, the individual's marital status code must also be changed. If the event is the death of a child, the only requirement is that the date of death of the child be recorded, and the count of living children be updated.

If the event happens to be marriage, some further processing is required. First, a decision must be made with respect to the marital status (single, widowed or divorced) of the partner. This choice is determined by means of 3 x 3 arrays of probabilities for six age groups (age of the primary individual involved). Once this has been done, the age of the marriage partner is obtained from the appropriate (first marriage or remarriage) bivariate distribution of ages of brides and grooms.

The remaining event which requires special treatment is the birth of a child. The date of birth and sex of the child is recorded in the list of secondary children associated with the mother. The sex of the child is determined by using a random number. The parity and count of the number of living children are both updated. Finally a special note is made of the birth in order to supply a sample of births (primary individuals) for the population.

When the event has been processed, a new next event is generated for the updated individual. This is continued until finally an event is obtained which is beyond the time allotted for the step in the simulation or the individual dies.

SIMRUN utilizes the series of births which occur to primary females as a random sample of births to add to the computer population. Thus, whenever a birth occurs to a primary female, the infant is entered as a member of the set of her associated children (secondary individuals), and the program also keeps a separate record of all these births. Then, after the female in question has been advanced beyond the time period specified for the simulation step and has been placed in a storage file, the program returns to the list of births and establishes a RECORD for a new primary individual for each birth. Each of these new primary individuals is immediately subjected to the various risks from the date of birth to the end of the simulation step, before being placed in the storage file. In subsequent steps of the simulation, these individuals are not distinguishable from other individuals who were generated for the initial sample population. It is important to note that no contact is maintained between the mother and her child, except as a secondary individual. Future events for the child as a primary individual are generated completely independently of those generated for the mother through the presence of the child as a secondary individual in her RECORD.

Three successive arrays of information are retained in the population file for each individual, when applicable. The first array is the basic set of of characteristics given in Table 1A. The second array contains the date of birth, sex and date of death for each of the secondary children associated with a primary female. The third array contains the history of events which have occurred to the individual during the simulation. The entries which are possible in the history of events array are shown in Table 2A . It is significant to note that the population or history file produced in any simulation run can be used as an initial population file in a subsequent run.

A series of tables are printed at the end of each step of the simulation. They include:

(1) The distribution of the population at the end of the interval by age, sex and marital status.
(2) The distribution of the deaths in the population (primary individuals only) by age (at death), sex and marital status.
(3) The distribution of births during the interval by age of mother (at the time of the birth) and the marital status of the mother.
(4) The distribution of marriages by age, sex and marital status of the primary individual involved.

The data in the population file at the end of a simulation period essentially constitutes a set of vital event histories for each individual in the computer population. The data in the file (stored on a disk or on magnetic tape) are equivalent to data collected from a sample of individuals in a longitudinal survey. This history feature of the SIMRUN output is very useful for special tabulation and analysis of the simulation data.

FAMILY PLANNING MODULE

The principal initial impetus for POPSIM was to provide demographers and population researchers with a computer model for studying the impact of alternative family planning programs on population growth and

Type of event	Code for event	Date of event	Marital status of primary individual	Descriptive information
Birth of a child	1	Date in months	Mother's marital status	Interval since previous birth
Divorce	2	Date in months	Married	Length of marriage in months
Death	3	Date in months	Marital status at death	Age at death in months
Marriage	4	Date in months	Marital status prior to marriage	Interval since last change in marital status
Widowhood	5	Date in months	Married	Interval since marriage
Death of a child	6	Date in months	(not assigned)	(not assigned)
Change in contraceptive technique	7	Date in months	Marital status	Code for both old and new contraceptive method

Table 2A. DETAILED ILLUSTRATION OF POSSIBLE ENTRIES IN THE HISTORY OF EVENTS ARRAY

vital rates. Accordingly, a family planning module has been developed for optional use with the basic POPSIM model. Although this family planning module is described separately here, it is physically a part of the event generation program (SIMRUN) and input data are required for both POPGEN and SIMRUN if family planning events are to be included.

The basic notion in the family planning module is that if a woman is practicing a given method of family planning, then the probability of her giving birth to a child in any given month will be reduced by a multiplicative factor. This factor will depend only on the method being used. Each woman is allowed to use any one of a number (limited to nine) of methods of birth control. The first method is considered equivalent to the null state, i.e., no contraceptive method is being used.

The family planning module consists of four parts or tasks. These are:

(1) Assigning the contraceptive method being used by women in the initial population.
(2) Generating the date at which a woman abandons a given family planning method.
(3) Assigning a new family planning technique to a woman, given that she has dropped a previous method.
(4) Modifying the basic birth probabilities according to the birth control technique practiced.

The first of these four tasks is carried out in the POPGEN program. Additional input to the basic program consists of the specific number of birth control techniques to be considered and parameters to assign one of these contraceptive methods to each woman by age group and parity. The POPGEN output includes a table of contraceptive methods by age.

The second, third and fourth tasks are carried out in the SIMRUN program. Additional input to the basic program consists of parameters to determine the date at which a change in contraceptive method occurs (the risk of change is a function of the current method, age and parity); parameters to determine the new contraceptive technique adopted at the time the previous method is abandoned (i.e., transition probabilities based on parity as well as the old and new contraceptive techniques); and parameters representing the use-effectiveness of each of the eligible birth control methods, where use-effectiveness is defined as one minus the ratio of the probability of conception while using a particular contraceptive to the probability of conception when no contraceptive device is being used, independent of age, parity and marital status of the woman.

The model assumes that the birth probabilities (age-parity-marital status specific net rates) available in the basic SIMRUN program are the result of the initial contraceptive mix in the simulated population. The net rates for women not practicing any of the contraceptive techniques to be included in the simulation are computed from the equation

$$p_0 = pf_1 + \sum_{i=2}^{k} pf_i(1-e_i),$$

where p_0 is the observed birth rate, p is the unknown birth rate for women not using any of the (k-1) contraceptive techniques under consideration, f_i is the proportion of women using the ith contraceptive method and e_i is its use-effectiveness. The explicit solution for the unknown birth probabilities (net rates) is

$$p = p_0[f_1 + \sum_{i=2}^{k} f_i(1-e_i)]^{-1}.$$

The model uses this equation for each parity and age group separately. The resulting probabilities are multiplied by $(1-e_i)$ to determine the appropriate birth probabilities for women using the ith contraceptive method.

REFERENCES

Barrett, J. C. 1967. A Monte Carlo study of reproduction, Presented at the Society for Human Biology Symposium, London, England.

Holmberg, I. 1968. Demographic models (DM 4), Report No. 8, Demographic Institute, Göteborg, Sweden: Univ. of Göteborg.

Horvitz, D. G., F. G. Giesbrecht, B. V. Shah and P. A. Lachenbruch 1971. POPSIM, A Demographic Microsimulation Model, Monograph No. 12. Chapel Hill, North Carolina: The Carolina Population Center, Univ. of North Carolina.

Hyrenius, H., I. Holmberg and M. Carlsson 1967. Demographic models (DM 3), Report No. 5, Demographic Institute, Göteborg, Sweden: Univ. of Göteborg.

Hyrenius, H. and I. Adolffson 1964. A fertility simulation model, Report No. 2, Demographic Institute, Göteborg, Sweden: Univ. of Göteborg.

Orcutt, G. H., M. Greenberg, J. Korbel and A. Rivlin 1961. Micro-analysis of Socioeconomic Systems. New York: Harper and Row.

Ridley, J. C. and M. C. Sheps 1966. An analytic simulation model for human reproduction with demographic and biological components, Population Studies 19: 297-310.

Shah, B. V. 1972. User's Manual for POPSIM. Preliminary Copy. Research Triangle Institute, North Carolina.

Shah, B. V. 1970. On the mathematics of population simulation models, Presented at the annual meetings of the Population Association of America, Atlanta, April 1970.

Shah, B. V. and F. G. Giesbrecht 1969. Mathematical models for changing marriage patterns, Paper presented at the meetings of the International Union for the Scientific Study of Population, London, September 1969.

APPLICATIONS OF POPREP, A MODIFICATION OF POPSIM

P. A. LACHENBRUCH
M. C. SHEPS
and
A. M. SORANT

INTRODUCTION

POPSIM is a stochastic microsimulation model which can be used to study either cohort or period populations. It was described at the 1969 IUSSP meetings, and in more detailed form in a series of working papers (Giesbrecht and Field 1969; Horvitz, Giesbrecht, Shah and Lachenbruch 1969). It is a two-sex model which allows for feedback mechanisms. In POPSIM, births are generated by using the probability of a live birth rather than generating a sequence of biological events such as conception, possible fetal loss, or sterility.

This paper will describe some modifications to POPSIM that incorporate these biological factors. We have retitled this version POPREP, but the major part of the model is identical to POPSIM. We also describe some studies that are in progress using POPREP.

BACKGROUND (POPSIM)

Although there are two versions of POPSIM available, we describe here only the "open" model which is used as the basis for POPREP.

> "The initial population can be thought of as a random sample of individuals selected from a population register, but without regard to familial relationships. Thus, a married female may be selected for the computer population, but her husband

> may not be chosen. Since marriage partners and offspring are not necessarily included when the sample is selected, the information concerning these individuals is carried in the computer records of the sample individuals. Just as the sample individuals constitute a valid sample of the population register, so also the simulated computer population at a future date is a random sample of individuals from a similar population register at the corresponding date.
>
> POPSIM creates initial populations in the computer by means of a series of subroutines which use random sampling of inverse probability distribution functions, for the most part, to assign a consistent set of characteristics to each individual. ...For convenience of programming and processing, each record also indicates the next event and the date of next event. A stratified random sampling procedure is used to assign ages" (Horvitz *et al.* 1969).

In POPSIM, the generation of the initial population is done by means of a separate computer program, but in POPREP, the initialization and vital event generation are performed in one program. To insure consistency for each individual alive at the start of simulation, we generate a history conditional on survival to that time. For example, if our initialization specifies that we have a 30 year old woman, we generate a history of marriages, births, divorces and widowhoods up to age 30, using the appropriate event probabilities.

> "[POPSIM] generates marriages, births, divorces and deaths for individuals using stored matrices of monthly transition (event) probabilities. A conditional probability approach is used which permits these event probabilities to depend on the current characteristics and prior history

of the individual.

An event-sequenced simulation procedure is used in which an individual is processed only when an event occurs to him. The first step in this procedure is to generate the date of the next vital event for each individual in the initial population. Since the type of event to occur next (i.e., a birth or a change in marital status or a death) is not known, a date for each of the eligible events for the individual is generated and the event with the earliest generated date is chosen as the next event for that individual. Only this next event and its date are carried in the record for each individual. This procedure for generating the next event is accurate under the assumption that the input parameters are independent probabilities for the competing events (or net rates) rather than crude rates" (*ibid.*).

To calculate the date of the next event, a hazard function technique is used. Thus, the conditional probability of an event occurring given that no event has yet occurred is assumed, say $\mu(t)$. It is known that $\mu(t) = f(t)/(1-F(t))$ where $f(t)$ is the unconditional density function of this particular event and $F(t) = \int_0^t f(y)dy$. Usually the value of $\mu(t)$ has been assumed to be piecewise linear.

"The second step in the event-sequenced simulation procedure is to process each individual on the date of their next event. Processing consists of recording the essential facts concerning the event, changing the status of individual characteristics affected by the event, and then generating the date of the next event for the individual.

The computer program which generates

vital events also provides tabulations of the initial population and of subsequent populations at the end of specified intervals of simulated time. These tabulations include the distribution of the computer population by age, sex and marital status and counts of the births, deaths, marriages and divorces that occurred during the time interval by various characteristics of the individual at the time of the event.

POPSIM [also] permits a vital event history tape to be written for each individual in the computer population. The data on this tape are equivalent to data collected from a sample of individuals in a longitudinal survey. Separate tabulation programs have been written for the history tape" (*ibid.*).

This program does not lend itself easily to experiments on contraception and abortion. For example, it has been shown (Sheps and Perrin 1964) that if women use a contraceptive with an effectiveness of 0.9, their birth rate is expected to be reduced by *less* than 0.9, because fecundability (which is reduced by contraceptives) is only one of the factors that affects birth rates (a contraceptive that is 90 per cent effective reduces the fecundability to 10 per cent of its natural value). Other important factors are the duration of pregnancy, the duration of the postpartum anovular (nonsusceptible) period and the proportion of pregnancies that end in spontaneous or induced fetal losses. The effect of a contraceptive (when used) depends on the distributions governing these functions.

Furthermore, the main feature of modern contraceptives such as the intrauterine devices (IUD) or hormones, is that they have fairly high discontinuation rates which vary with the woman's age and parity. It is awkward to provide for this eventuality in calculating birth probabilities.

Experience with a biological model, REPSIM, had shown that a more direct and satisfactory approach to these problems is provided by considering the biological functions in the model (Ridley and Sheps 1966). For these reasons, the birth routines in POPSIM were modified as described below.

POPREP, THE BIOLOGICAL VERSION OF POPSIM

POPSIM was modified by eliminating the birth subroutines and replacing them by a set of subroutines dealing with conception, fetal loss, induced abortion and live birth. One of the simplifications obtained was the elimination of special treatment of live births following widowhood or divorce.

The conception routines contain six parts:

1. Determination of age at menarche
2. Determination of age at sterility
3. Determination of maximum fecundability
4. Calculation of the date of next conception
5. Determination of the outcome of the pregnancy
6. Determination of the length of post-partum infecundability

Parts 1, 2, and 3 set parameters dealing with each woman and are determined once during initialization.

The age at menarche is chosen from a normal distribution with mean 13.2 and standard deviation 1. This fits the U.S. data fairly well. However, these parameters may be easily modified for other populations.

The age at sterility, S, is chosen from a distribution in which ln(50-S) has a normal distribution with mean 1.9 and standard deviation 0.5. Thus, the mean age at sterility is 42.4 with standard deviation 4. This too is modifiable at the user's option. If the age at sterility is less than the age at menarche, it is assumed that the woman never becomes fecund.

The maximum fecundability is chosen from a discrete distribution that is approximately Beta. It is given in Table 1, below. Its mean is approximately 0.2 and its harmonic mean 0.13. We originally planned to sample directly from the Beta distribution, but chose this distribution for simplicity of programming and speed of execution.

The pattern of fecundability for each woman by

Fecundability Level	Probability
.05	.1428
.10	.1700
.15	.1721
.20	.1506
.25	.1253
.30	.0839
.35	.0620
.40	.0933

Table 1. DISTRIBUTION OF MAXIMUM FECUNDABILITY

age has a trapezoidal shape. It is zero before age at menarche and after the age at sterility. Denote the length of the fecund period by L = (Age at sterility) - (Age at menarche). The fecundability of a woman rises linearly from 0 at age at menarche to its maximum level at L/6, remains at that level until L/2, and declines linearly to 0 at age of sterility. The fecundability function $\mu(t)$ is sketched in Figure 1.

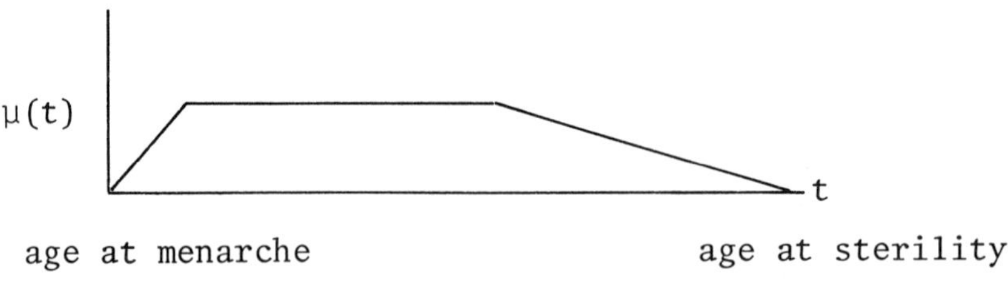

Figure 1. SHAPE OF FECUNDABILITY FUNCTION

The date of next conception is calculated by obtaining a random number R and solving the equation

$$R = 1 - \exp(-\int_{t_0}^{t_c} \mu(t)dt),$$

for t_c, where t_0 is the age at the time of the last event. If t_c is the earliest of all competing events, then the next event is a conception.

When conception is the next event, the outcome of the pregnancy must be determined. The possible "natural" outcomes are live birth or spontaneous abortion. When induced abortion is introduced, this also is an outcome of a pregnancy. The probability that a pregnancy ends in a spontaneous abortion is a function of the female's age

$$PFL = .000833 \text{ age}^2 - .0433 \text{ age} + .7625$$

where age is measured in years. This function has the value 0.23 at age 20, 0.20 at age 25 and 0.50 at age 45. A uniform (0,1) random number is compared with the probability of spontaneous abortion for the appropriate age of the woman. If the random number is less than this value, the woman has a fetal loss. In this case, the length of the pregnancy Q has an exponential distribution truncated at nine months:

$$f(Q) = \lambda\exp(-\lambda Q)/(1-\exp(-9\lambda))$$

We have assumed $\lambda = .5$ which gives Q a mean of 1.9 months and a variance of 3.08 months. A more realistic model might have been a mixture of exponentials to account for early and late fetal loss, but this was felt to be more complicated than we desired. If the pregnancy ends in a live birth, the length is assumed to be nine months.

The probability of induced abortion conditional on no spontaneous abortion occurring first is 1 - PLB, where PLB is an input function of parity. If an induced abortion occurs, the length of the pregnancy has an exponential distribution truncated at five months with the form:

$$f(t) = \frac{-5}{\ln PLB} \exp\left(\frac{\ln PLB}{5} t\right) / (1-PLB)$$

This length of pregnancy is compared with that generated for the natural outcome to determine what actually occurs. A separate value of PLB is input for each of parities 0, 1, 2, 3, 4, and 5+.

Post-partum anovulation lasts two months after a (natural or induced) fetal loss and follows an exponential distribution with a mean of five months after a live birth. If the child dies, the post-partum anovulation period cannot continue more than one month after the death.

Contraception is implemented in POPREP in two parts. If a woman is using contraceptive i (which may be no contraceptive), her fecundability is multiplied by the complement of the use-effectiveness to obtain the effective fecundability. Thus for non-users, the multiplier is 1.0, while for a device that is 0.95 effective, the multiplier would be 0.05. The second part of the contraception routines relates to changing contraceptive methods. This is treated exactly as other events are: a time to contraceptive change is computed; if it is the earliest event, then the next event is a change in contraceptive method. At present, the hazard function being used, if there has been no contraception state change since the last pregnancy (or marriage) is

$$h(t) = \begin{cases} A_i & t \leq 12 \\ A_i (t/12)^{K-1} & t > 12, \end{cases}$$

for t = time (months) since last pregnancy and, if

there has already been a contraceptive change:

$$h^*(t) = h(t+12)$$

for t = time since last change of state. In these functions,

$$A_i = C_i + D_i \cdot \text{Age (in Months)} + E_i \cdot \text{Parity},$$

and $$0 < K < 1.$$

K, C_i, D_i and E_i are determined by the user. The last three are specific for the ith contraceptive state. An option exists to set $A_i = 0$ for some contraceptive state. If $A_i \neq 0$, this function appears as in Figure 2.

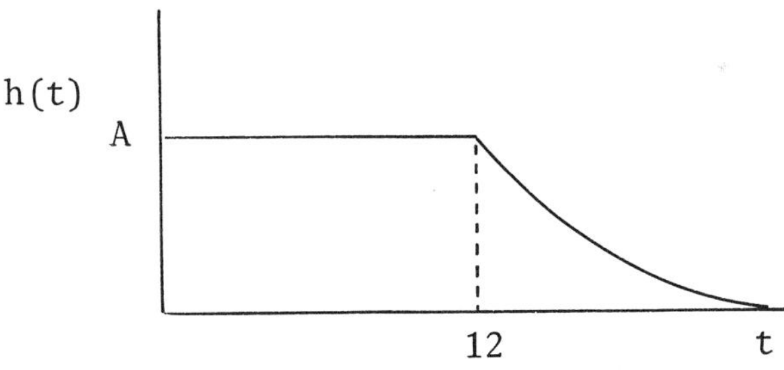

Figure 2. HAZARD FUNCTION FOR CONTRACEPTIVE CHANGE

If K = 1, the function is a horizontal line with $h(t) = A_i$, and the resulting distribution is exponential. Some examples of the coefficients, multipliers, and the probabilities of change within 12 months for a 30 year old, parity 2 woman are given in Table 2. If a contraceptive change is the next event, the new contraceptive state must be determined. A conditional

i	Type	C_i	D_i	E_i	P(Change in 12 Months)	Fecundability Multipliers
1	None	.215	-.00051	.0166	.54	1.00
2	Conventional	.172	-.00029	-.0124	.40	0.25
3	Modern	.167	-.00029	-.0112	.38	0.05

Table 2. COEFFICIENTS FOR A_i, FECUNDABILITY MULTIPLIERS, AND PROBABILITY OF CHANGE

transition matrix is used such that there are zeros on the main diagonal and the rows add to one. The matrix that has been used is given in Table 3.

		Final State		
		1	2	3
Initial State	1	0	.25	.75
	2	.50	0	.50
	3	.50	.50	0

Table 3. CONDITIONAL TRANSITION MATRIX

The transition matrix may be specified by the user. It may depend on parity, in which case there is a matrix for each relevant parity. Or it may be based on a desired stationary distribution among the states, depending on age and parity. A cumulative distribution technique is used to find the final state. At conception, a woman is placed in the non-using state.

FERTILITY MEASURES BASED ON BIRTH INTERVAL DATA

In recent years, various fertility rates have been used to study the births occurring to populations. They have been found unsuitable for rapid detection of changes in the reproductive performance of women. Some require large samples, some do not reflect changes rapidly, some pool groups of women whose performance is quite different. These considerations have led to the study of birth intervals as a potentially good measure for fertility. However, some drawbacks have been noted in literature; in particular, the truncation effect due to the limited length of time a woman has to complete her child-bearing has been studied by Sheps *et al.* (1970). Poole (1971) has developed a set of estimators based on birth intervals that consider the truncated nature of the data.

Given that there is an (i-1)th birth, the function $F_i(x)$ is defined as the probability (in the absence of competing risks) that there is an ith birth within x units of time (after the (i-1)th birth). $F_i(x)$ is assumed to be independent of age. $F_i(x|a)$ is the corresponding age-dependent probability that is conditional on an (i-1)th birth occurring at age a. The *first* birth is measured from the date of marriage, which may be called the 0th birth. Note that the F_i are defective, in that, in general, $F_i(\infty)$ or $F_i(\infty|a)$ is not equal to one.

Following Sheps and Menken (1972), Poole considered several schemes for ascertainment of the ith intervals to be measured, including prospective observations (which include data on all births occurring up to survey time, regardless of whether the women remain alive and married) and retrospective observations (which include data only on births occurring to "survivors," women who are still alive and married at survey time). Poole developed life table estimators $\hat{F}_i(x|a)$, appropriate for these schemes, using data on closed (completed) ith intervals (from the (i-1)th birth to the ith birth), open intervals (from the (i-1)th birth to survey time, in cases where women remain eligible but have no ith birth before the survey), and exposure intervals ended by death, divorce, or widowhood (from the (i-1)th birth until the woman becomes "ineligible"). Note that data on the last type of interval is unavailable in a retrospective study, as defined above.

Consideration was also given to developing indices from combinations of the estimators. For example, letting $w_i(a)$ be a suitable weighting factor for $\hat{F}_i(x|a)$, then

$$\hat{F}_i(x) = \frac{\sum_a w_i(a)\hat{F}_i(x|a)}{\sum_a w_i(a)}$$

and

$$\hat{B}(x) = \frac{\sum_{ia}\sum w_i(a)\hat{F}_i(x|a)}{\sum_{ia}\sum w_i(a)}$$

There is further work to be done in establishing suitable w_i.

TESTS OF FERTILITY MEASURES

Several limited tests of the life table estimators $\hat{F}_i(x|a)$ have been made as follows:

(a) In order to check the accuracy of the estimators, it was desired to make a comparison with the true (theoretical) distributions being estimated. Theoretical values could not easily be computed for birth intervals, so intervals between conceptions were considered instead (using estimators of the same form as for birth intervals). In two independent runs, life histories, including conceptions and births, were simulated for a cohort of 500 women having identical biological parameters, married at age 18, and using no contraception. Estimates $\hat{F}_1(x|18)$ and $\hat{F}_2(x|19)$ were determined from prospective data from surveys at age 24 (marital duration six years). These estimates were then compared with theoretical values $F_1(x|18)$ and $F_2(x|19)$. (These distributions refer to conception rather than birth intervals.) Graphs of the true distributions and estimates appear in Figures 3 and 4. The estimates were close to the theoretical results.

(b) From the same simulations, $F_1(x|18)$ for the first *birth* interval was estimated from prospective data and from retrospective data from surveys at age 21. The retrospective estimates compared well with the prospective estimates, which were taken as a standard. Graphs of these estimates appear in Figure 5.

(c) In order to test the value of the life table estimators for discriminating between different populations, two populations were simulated, beginning with the same cross-sectional distribution of ages, one with and one without contraception and induced abortion. (The former had 2000 females initially and the latter had 1000.) An index $\hat{B}(x)$ (combining the various estimates $\hat{F}_i(x|a)$) was computed for each population using retrospective data from a survey three years into the simulation. (Note that data from more than three years' history was available, since complete life histories were simulated for every individual alive at the beginning of the simulation.) The index $\hat{B}(x)$ discrim-

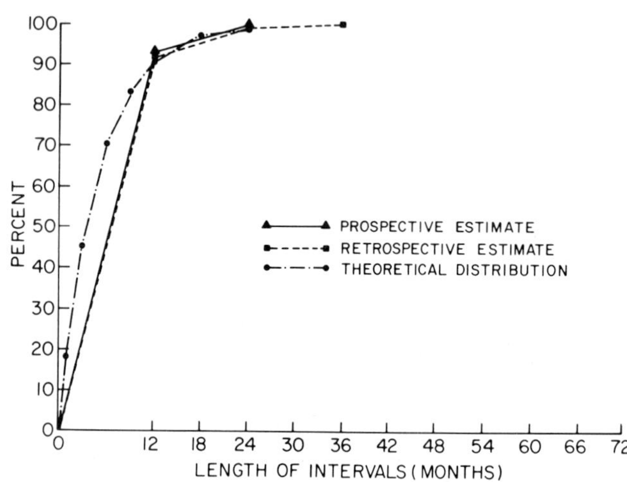

Figure 3. THEORETICAL AND LIFE TABLE ESTIMATES OF FIRST INTERCONCEPTION INTERVAL FOR WOMEN OF AGE 18 AT MARRIAGE (FROM POOLE)

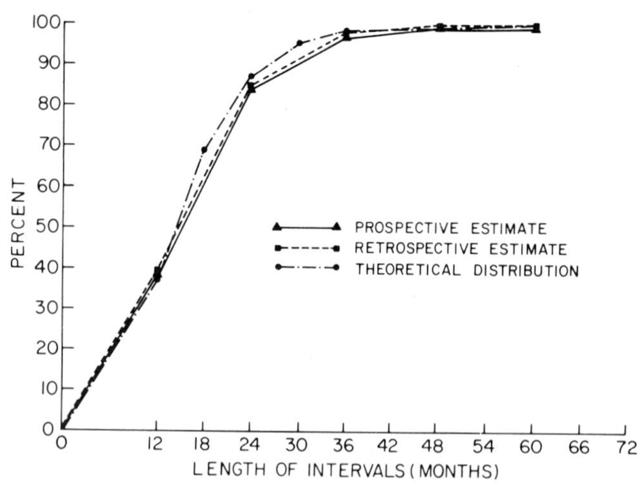

Figure 4. LIFE TABLE ESTIMATES OF SECOND INTER-CONCEPTION INTERVAL FOR WOMEN OF AGE 19 AT FIRST CONCEPTION (FROM POOLE)

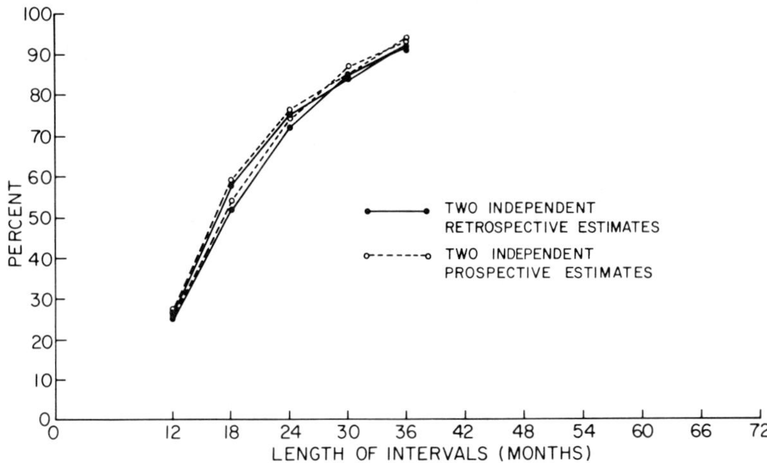

Figure 5. LIFE TABLE ESTIMATES OF FIRST BIRTH INTERVAL FOR WOMEN OF AGE 18 AT MARRIAGE (FROM POOLE)

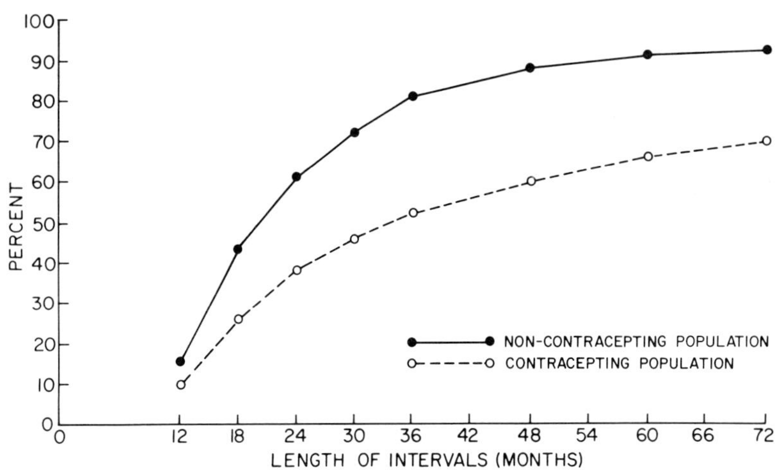

Figure 6. COMBINED LIFE TABLE ESTIMATES OF BIRTH INTERVALS FOR CONTRACEPTING AND NON-CONTRACEPTING POPULATIONS (FROM POOLE)

inated well between the two populations. Graphs of the two estimated distributions appear in Figure 6.

(d) Finally, the effect of sample size has been tested. An initial population of 4000 females of various ages was simulated for 30 years, with no contraception or abortion. Life table estimates $\hat{F}_i(x|a)$ for several i, a combinations were computed, first using all prospective data for the entire simulation (30 years plus previous experience of women alive at time zero), and then using prospective data beginning at the 25-year point. (Since the same population parameters were in effect throughout the simulation, the data from the five-year period was considered a valid subsample of the complete data.) There was close agreement between the large- and small-sample estimates. Graphs of a typical pair of estimates are shown in Figure 7.

One of the most important questions still to be investigated is the behavior of the life table estimators under changing conditions, such as initiation of a contraceptive program.

In a separate experiment, various birth interval measures of fertility were studied to determine their robustness to reporting errors. Errors were introduced in the following way. Given a 30-year simulation of a population not using contraception or abortion (described in part (d) above), each woman's history was modified by adding a random normal deviate to all birth dates, subject to the condition that the order among the events: marriage, first birth, second birth,..., and survey, was preserved. Note that the dates of marriage and survey were not changed. It was assumed that in practice, a religious or civil record of marriage date would be available, and so might be relatively accurately determined.

Three error models are considered here:

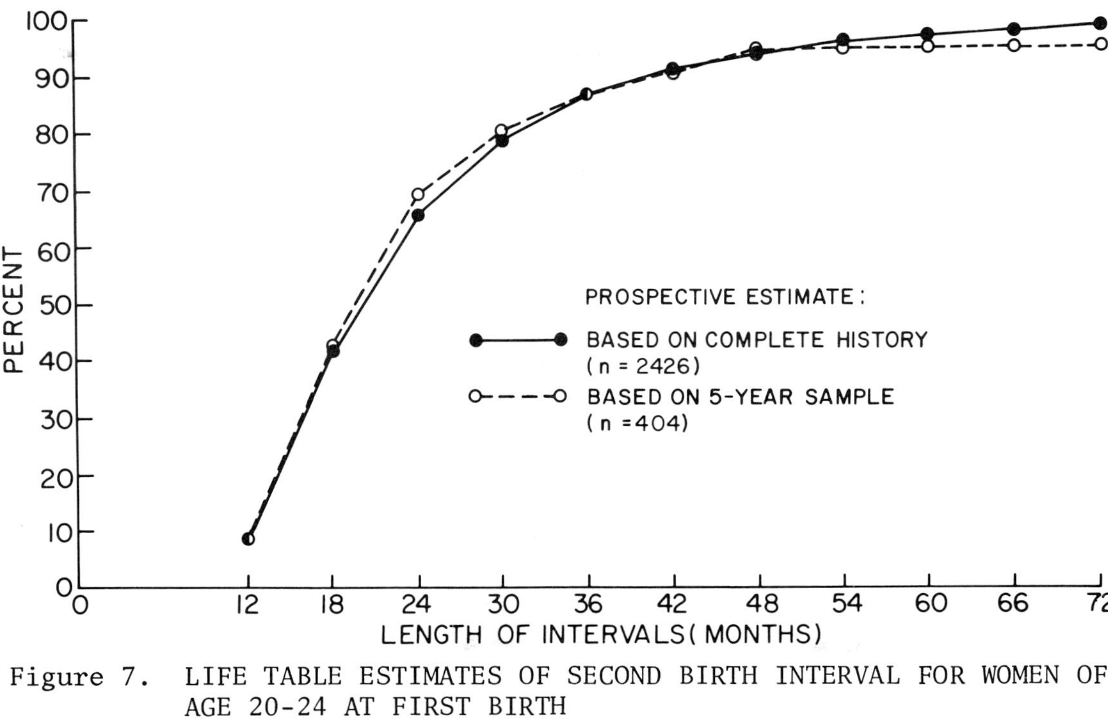

Figure 7. LIFE TABLE ESTIMATES OF SECOND BIRTH INTERVAL FOR WOMEN OF AGE 20-24 AT FIRST BIRTH

(a) $\mu=0$, $\sigma=6$ months
(b) $\mu=12$ months, $\sigma=6$ months (positive bias)
(c) $\mu=-12$ months, $\sigma=6$ months (negative bias)

The unbiased case ($\mu=0$) would arise from general uncertainty about dates, with no tendency to report dates earlier or later than the true ones. The positive bias case would arise if an interviewee reported all dates as occurring more recently than they actually did. The case of negative bias would arise when events were reported as occurring earlier than they actually did. Note that, in each model, the mean date adjustment is not actually the μ specified, because of the truncation effect of preserving the order of events.

The fertility measures considered were:

(a) The ith closed interval (the length of time from the (i-1)th to the ith birth), for women of age a at survey time.
(b) The open interval (from the last birth to the survey date), for women of age a and parity (i-1) at survey time.
(c) The life table estimators (described above), for women of age a at parity (i-1).

For the original, unmodified population history, and for two independent replicates of each of the three error models, all of these fertility measures were computed from retrospective data on all women who were alive and married at the 30-year point. The results of these experiments are summarized separately for each type of fertility measure.

Consider first the observed closed ith intervals. In the no-bias case ($\mu=0$, $\sigma=6$), there was a slight additional variability because of the random perturbations of the dates. In general, the mean intervals were quite similar to the true values. When a positive bias is included ($\mu=12$, $\sigma=6$), the *first* closed interval appears much longer than its true value, because the date of marriage is fixed, while the date of the first birth is increased by about 12 months, on the average. The *last* closed interval is shorter than the true value, in general. The next-to-last birth date tends to be increased by about 12 months, while the adjustment of the last birth date is limited, since it must precede the survey date, which is fixed. The intervals other than the first and last remain very close to their true values, since the (i-1)th and the ith birth dates tend to be adjusted by about the same amount. If a negative bias is included ($\mu=-12$, $\sigma=6$), the first interval is shortened by the same process accounting for the behavior of that interval in the positive bias case. All other closed intervals, including the last one, are unaffected except for increased variance. See Table 4 for a listing of some of the closed interval data.

The behavior of the open interval under reporting errors is affected by the same processes as the closed intervals. For the unbiased perturbation case, there is increased variability, but no observable trends. Generally the perturbed dates give mean intervals that are within one month of the true value. If positive bias holds, the open interval is decreased noticeably, as would be expected, since the last birth date tends to be increased while the survey date remains fixed. Similarly, the open interval increases, on the average, for the negative bias case. Open interval data is shown in Table 5.

The life table estimators of birth interval distributions are based in large part on closed intervals, so their behavior is not unlike that of the closed intervals. For unbiased perturbations, the estimates of the cumulative distribution are very close to those from the true data. For positive bias, the life table estimator for the first interval is stochastically greater than when there is accurate reporting. That is, there is a tendency for longer intervals to be estimated than in the unperturbed case. For other intervals, the estimated distributions are quite close. For the negative bias case, the distribution estimate for the first interval is stochastically smaller than the estimate from accurate data. Estimates for all other intervals are unchanged except for increased variance. An example of the distributions estimated

Parity	Number of Women	Interval Order 1		2		3		4	
1	169	$x=18.65$ $x_1=17.75$ $x_2=25.42$ $x_3=10.00$	$s=12.65$ $s_1=0.15$ $s_2=0.48$ $s_3=0.28$						
2	143	$x=17.97$ $x_1=18.47$ $x_2=28.92$ $x_3=9.16$	$s=10.58$ $s_1=1.07$ $s_2=0.06$ $s_3=0.54$	$x=21.10$ $x_1=19.33$ $x_2=16.19$ $x_3=18.20$	$s=8.59$ $s_1=1.10$ $s_2=0.49$ $s_3=0.39$				
3	89	$x=17.09$ $x_1=17.59$ $x_2=28.32$ $x_3=7.85$	$s=7.22$ $s_1=0.67$ $s_2=0.06$ $s_3=0.04$	$x=18.98$ $x_1=19.08$ $x_2=19.51$ $x_3=17.36$	$s=8.80$ $s_1=1.20$ $s_2=0.48$ $s_3=0.23$	$x=18.31$ $x_1=16.65$ $x_2=12.72$ $x_3=17.55$	$s=6.49$ $s_1=0.15$ $s_2=0.89$ $s_3=0.26$		
4	36	$x=14.54$ $x_1=14.63$ $x_2=26.79$ $x_3=6.58$	$s=4.78$ $s_1=0.12$ $s_2=1.97$ $s_3=0.47$	$x=20.24$ $x_1=18.99$ $x_2=21.17$ $x_3=16.72$	$s=6.42$ $s_1=1.17$ $s_2=3.37$ $s_3=1.43$	$x=17.40$ $x_1=19.09$ $x_2=15.52$ $x_3=17.61$	$s=7.79$ $s_1=0.21$ $s_2=1.06$ $s_3=0.95$	$x=18.00$ $x_1=16.25$ $x_2=11.45$ $x_3=18.41$	$s=6.73$ $s_1=2.00$ $s_2=0.56$ $s_3=1.54$

KEY

x = Mean interval from unperturbed data
x_1 = Combined mean interval from two replicates of $\mu=0$ model
x_2 = Combined mean interval from two replicates of $\mu=12$ model
x_3 = Combined mean interval from two replicates of $\mu=-12$ model
s = Standard deviation of intervals from unperturbed data
s_1 = Between sample s.d. of $\mu=0$ model
s_2 = Between sample s.d. of $\mu=12$ model
s_3 = Between sample s.d. of $\mu=-12$ model

All intervals measurements are in months.

Table 4. CLOSED BIRTH INTERVALS FOR WOMEN OF AGE 20-24 AT SURVEY

Parity	Number of Women	x	s
0	131	x =16.22 x_1=16.22 x_2=16.22 x_3=16.22	s =16.15 s_1= 0.00 s_2= 0.00 s_3= 0.00
1	169	x =13.80 x_1=14.69 x_2= 7.03 x_3=22.44	s = 9.34 s_1= 0.15 s_2= 0.48 s_3= 0.28
2	143	x =12.17 x_1=13.42 x_2= 6.12 x_3=23.87	s = 9.70 s_1= 0.02 s_2= 0.54 s_3= 0.15
3	89	x =11.26 x_1=12.31 x_2= 5.10 x_3=22.87	s = 8.74 s_1= 0.69 s_2= 0.45 s_3= 0.01
4	36	x = 8.08 x_1= 9.28 x_2= 3.32 x_3=18.93	s = 6.57 s_1= 1.17 s_2= 0.90 s_3= 0.40

KEY

x = Mean interval from unperturbed data
x_1 = Combined mean interval from two replicates of μ=0 model
x_2 = Combined mean interval from two replicates of μ=12 model
x_3 = Combined mean interval from two replicates of μ=-12 model
s = Standard deviation of intervals from unperturbed data
s_1 = Between sample s.d. of μ=0 model
s_2 = Between sample s.d. of μ=12 model
s_3 = Between sample s.d. of μ=-12 model

All intervals measurements are in months.

Table 5. OPEN BIRTH INTERVALS FOR WOMEN OF AGE 20-24 AT SURVEY

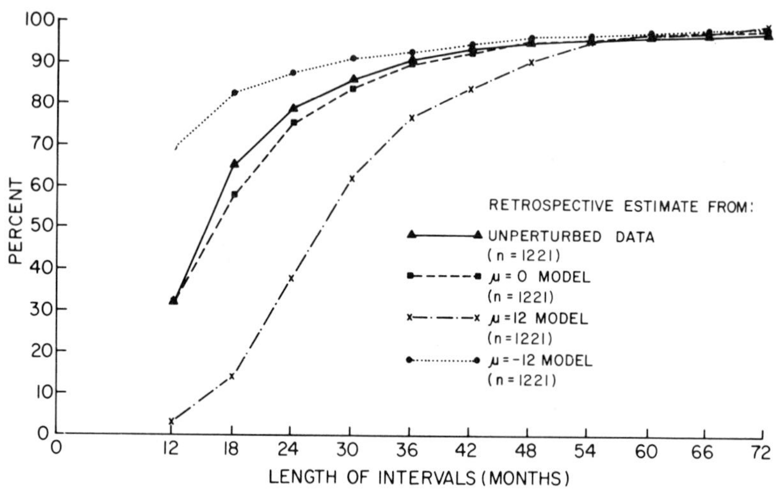

Figure 8. LIFE TABLE ESTIMATES OF FIRST BIRTH INTERVAL FOR WOMEN OF AGE 20-24 AT MARRIAGE

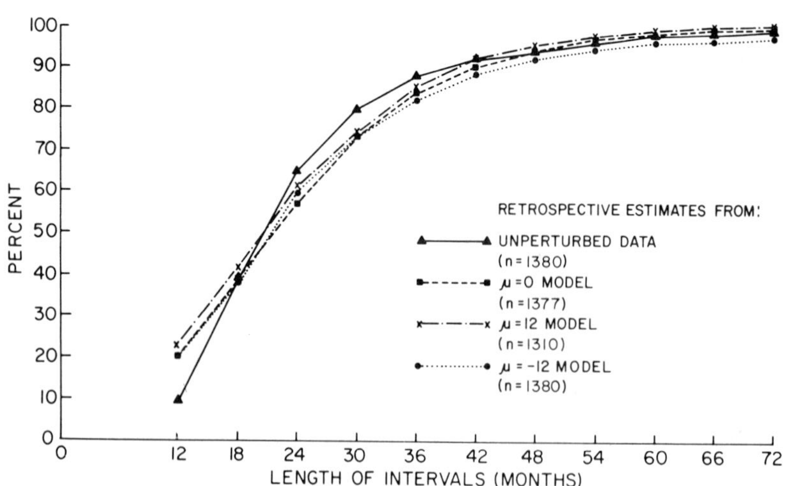

Figure 9. LIFE TABLE ESTIMATES OF THIRD BIRTH INTERVAL FOR WOMEN OF AGE 20-24 AT SECOND BIRTH

is shown in Figures 8 and 9.

Further studies of robustness should include different forms of reporting errors. A more realistic model of inaccuracies might have μ and σ as functions of the difference between survey date and event date. Another problem that could be considered is omission of births, possibly depending on whether the child has died. This was considered elsewhere in a pilot study and will be further investigated in the future.

REFERENCES

Giesbrecht, F. G. and L. Field 1969. Demographic microsimulation model POPSIM II, Manual for Programs to Generate Vital Events, Open Core Model, Technical Report No. 5, Project SU-285, Research Triangle Institute.

Horvitz, D. G., F. G. Giesbrecht, B. V. Shah and P. A. Lachenbruch 1969. POPSIM, a demographic microsimulation model, IUSSP General Conference Proceedings, London.

Poole, W. K. 1971. Fertility measures based on birth interval data, Final Report Project No. SU-587, Research Triangle Institute.

Ridley, J. C. and M. C. Sheps 1966. An analytic simulation model of human reproduction with demographic and biological components, Population Studies 19: 295-320.

Sheps, M. C. and E. B. Perrin 1964. Changes in birth rates as a function of contraceptive effectiveness: some applications of a stochastic model, American Journal of Public Health 53: 1031-1046.

Sheps, M. C., J. A. Menken, J. C. Ridley and J. W. Lingner 1970. Truncation effect in closed and open birth interval data, Journal of American Statistical Association 65: 678-693.

Sheps, M. C. and J. A. Menken 1972. Distribution of birth intervals according to the sampling frame, Theoretical Population Biology 3: 1-26.

ACKNOWLEDGMENTS

This research was supported by contract 70-2187 from NICHD and by Research Career Development Award HD-46,344. Part of the support for the development of POPREP was provided by Ford Foundation Grant number 68-576. The authors express their thanks to Serpil Yesilcay for her assistance in the data analysis.

THE ASSESSMENT OF THREE METHODS OF ESTIMATING BIRTHS AVERTED

ALICE S. CLAGUE
and
JEANNE CLARE RIDLEY

A crucial question encountered in family planning programs is the number of births averted by such programs. Estimation of births averted is not only of importance to the administrators of such programs but to governmental planners and officials who must justify these in face of the demands of other social and economic programs.

The task of estimating births averted, however, has proved to be no simple task (Mauldin 1968 and Chandrasekaran *et al.* 1971). To date, a number of workers have developed various methods for estimating births averted. These methods differ in terms of the types of assumptions made and in the kinds of data required. Yet, few guidelines exist as to which method will provide the most valid measure.

The objective of this paper is to present some limited results from utilizing a simulation model of human natality to assess three methods of estimating births averted by family planning programs. The three methods chosen for assessment are those developed by Lee and Isbister (1965), Potter (1969), and Wolfers (1969 and 1971). Estimates obtained by applying these methods to simulated data are compared with estimates obtained directly from an analytic micro-simulation model, REPSIM-B. In several respects, the results presented are quite limited and consequently, should be viewed as only a first step toward a thorough evaluation of these methods.

A secondary objective of this paper is to illustrate one potential use of simulation models.

To date, simulation models have been utilized to investigate a limited number of substantive and methodological issues[1] but, with one exception, (Barrett 1971), have not been utilized for the purpose of validating different methods of estimation.

In the first section of this paper the methods of Lee and Isbister, Potter, and Wolfers will be briefly reviewed. Subsequent sections of the paper will describe the simulation experiments and the application of the three methods to the simulated data, and discuss the results.

METHODS OF ESTIMATING BIRTHS AVERTED

Since the procedures of estimating births averted by Lee and Isbister, Potter, and Wolfers have been described in detail elsewhere, the description of these methods will be confined to contrasting them. The differences are particularly important since they influence the extent of their agreement with the "criterion measure" of births averted derived from the simulated data.

Lee and Isbister Method

The first attempt to estimate the reduction in fertility brought about by a family planning program was undertaken by Lee and Isbister. This procedure depends solely on the use of age-specific fertility rates in conjunction with component projection methods. Age-specific fertility rates are assumed to remain constant if no family planning program is initiated. To derive the number of births prevented by the program, an estimate is made of what the "potential" fertility rate of women in the program would have been, if they had not practiced contraception. For this estimate, they suggest that one may assume either that acceptors of contraception have the same fertility as all married women or that the fertility of acceptors is somewhat higher than that of married women.[2]

In their application, Lee and Isbister assumed that the fertility of acceptors would have been 20 per cent higher than that of all married women. The value, 20 per cent, is not, however, an integral part of their method and they suggest that the degree to which the fertility of acceptors is higher than that of all married women will vary with the population under consideration.

In developing estimates of "fertility foregone" by acceptors, the estimated fertility rate is time-lagged by one year under the assumption that births prevented by contraception would have occurred approximately a year after contraception begins. Accordingly, any contraceptive practice in the first year of the program is assumed to avert births in the second year. Consequently, if a five-year period is considered, births averted by contraception in the fifth year are ignored. The estimated age-specific fertility rate is then compared with the age-specific fertility rate of the base year before the family planning program existed. The difference between the rates produces an estimate of the total reduction in fertility resulting from the family planning program. In addition to estimating the total reduction in fertility, the Lee and Isbister method provides for the estimation of births averted by acceptors.

Potter's and Wolfers' Methods

Both Potter and Wolfers independently proposed alternative methods of estimating births averted with the stated purpose of refining Lee and Isbister's procedure. It should be noted, however, that unlike Lee and Isbister they do not develop a method for estimating the total impact of a family planning program on a population. Rather, they confine themselves to estimating only the births averted by women participating in a family planning program.

Potter took issue with Lee and Isbister for

using a constant for estimating the potential fertility of acceptors, for not correcting for accidental pregnancies, and for assuming unrealistic rates of retention of IUD's. In contrast, Wolfers criticized Lee and Isbister for using recent past fertility levels as an indication of what fertility would be in the absence of a program. Wolfers based his objection on the fact that since acceptors are more likely to have had a recent birth, their recent past fertility is likely to be higher than that of nonacceptors. In addition, he pointed out that marital fertility rates tend to be heavily weighted with first births and thus such rates bear no relation to the future potential fertility of acceptors. Thus, marital fertility rates would be particularly inappropriate as a basis for estimating births averted among young women. Yet, as will be discussed in more detail later in this paper, this same criticism may be applied when birth intervals regardless of order are used to estimate births averted.

In their methods, Potter and Wolfers included several other factors that Lee and Isbister omitted. Thus, corrections for sterility, for the overlap of contraceptive use and postpartum amenorrhea, acciden-pregnancies, and fetal loss were introduced. In addition, more detailed data regarding the length of use of contraceptives and life table continuation rates were utilized.

Potter built his method on two factors: the mean prolongation of the fecundable state (I) that results from contraceptive use; and the average duration per birth (D) that is required when contraception is not practiced. This latter factor, it should be noted, was derived from the previous age-specific fertility rates of acceptors. By dividing I by D, an estimate of the births averted per segment of contraceptive use was obtained. In contrast, Wolfers built his method by using the mean prospective birth intervals (births)[3] to adjust woman months of use. Life table techniques were employed to estimate the births averted for specified periods of time after a family planning program is introduced. This estimate of births averted was then corrected for the occurrence of accidental pregnancy and subsequent fetal loss.

THE SIMULATION EXPERIMENTS

Two simulations were performed to produce the data needed for calculating the births averted according to the procedures of Lee and Isbister, Potter, and Wolfers, and to produce the criterion values against which the three methods would be validated. These simulations were carried out with the microsimulation model, REPSIM-B. This model utilizes Monte Carlo methods and is an elaboration of the earlier model REPSIM-A (Ridley and Sheps 1966). Since REPSIM-B has not been described in detail previously, Appendix A presents a summary description of this computer simulation model.

Briefly, REPSIM-B simulates the detailed reproductive history of a hypothetical cohort of women. It provides for a woman's marrying, dying, becoming sterile, becoming pregnant and for varying outcomes of pregnancy, including induced abortion. Provision is also made for a woman to adopt contraception or become surgically sterilized. The dissolution of marriage by widowhood or divorce as well as remarriage is provided for. The probabilities of these events may vary with age and marital status. In many instances, the probabilities may also vary with parity, a woman's preference regarding the spacing between births, and the difference between a woman's desired family size and her number of surviving children.

Two cohorts of 3,000 women each were simulated from age 15 to age 40. In the first experiment, data were simulated that would be similar to what might be observed in a survey preceding a family planning program and to what might be observed if the acceptors in such a program were followed for a period of five years. No use of contraception prior to age 35 was postulated. A family planning program was assumed to begin operation when women attained age 35. Women were defined as eligible for the program only if they had achieved their desired family size or exceeded it.[4]

The probability of a woman beginning use of contraceptives was set at 0.25. This probability implies an expected average delay of four months between the time the family planning program began and the adoption of contraceptive practice by any particular eligible woman. A fairly high level of contraceptive effectiveness, i.e. 95 per cent, was assumed. Once practice was begun, women practiced according to a schedule of length of retention of IUD's for women ages 35 to 39 years, based on the experience reported by Potter for women in Taiwan (Potter 1971). In addition, women discontinued use when a child died if they no longer had as many children as they desired. Also, use was terminated if a marriage ended as a result of widowhood or divorce. Once a woman terminated practice, no resumption of practice was permitted.[5]

In the second experiment, data were simulated using exactly the same inputs with the exception that no family planning program was available. This latter cohort in comparison with the first cohort provides the criterion measure of births averted by the family planning program. Appendix B presents a summary of these and other inputs used in the two experiments.

CALCULATION OF THE THREE ESTIMATES AND THE CRITERION VALUES

To obtain the data necessary for calculating births averted according to the procedures of Lee and Isbister, Potter, and Wolfers, the complete reproductive history of each woman in the first simulated cohort was output. Each history included the month in which all events relevant to reproduction occurred. Although complete data were available, only the data specified by each method of estimation were utilized. In addition to the reproductive histories, data given in the output tables of the family planning cohort were used. In Appendix C the basic formulae for calculating each estimate are shown.

In calculating Lee and Isbister's estimate of the reduction in age-specific fertility rates, the pre-program fertility rates of acceptors and of ever married women of the family planning cohort were first compared. These rates were five-year averages of the fertility rates between ages 30 and 34. This provided a factor of 34 per cent that was used in the calculation of the potential fertility of acceptors had there been no family planning program. To estimate the number of women practicing totally effective contraception in each year of the program, the number of women accepting each year was adjusted for continuation of contraceptive use. To obtain continuation rates of contraceptive use, a life table based on the reproductive histories of the acceptors was calculated. In tabulating the months of contraceptive use, a monthly follow-up of all acceptors was assumed to be part of the hypothetical family planning program. Women dying or whose marriages were terminated were treated as withdrawals in the life table.

In their original application, Lee and Isbister did not rely on continuation rates derived from a life table. Rather, they utilized a constant continuation rate of 70 per cent since they did not have detailed data available for calculating more accurate continuation rates. They suggested, however, that if such detailed data were available they should be utilized in applying the method.

As an estimate of what the fertility rates would have been before the family planning program began, the age-specific fertility rates for all women ages 35 to 39 from the simulated cohort without family planning were used. Finally, the total number of women at the midpoint of each age was projected by applying the survival rates assumed in the simulated cohorts.

Lee and Isbister also provided a method for calculating births averted per acceptor. This measure is derived simply by applying the potential fertility of acceptors to the woman years of contraceptive use and dividing by the number of acceptors. The estimates of Potter and Wolfers, however, are based on woman years of contraceptive use. Therefore, to produce a more comparable measure for Lee and Isbister, the estimate of births averted derived from their procedure was calculated on the basis of woman years of use.

For calculating Potter's estimate, the distribution and mean interval in months between the acceptance of family planning and the preceding birth were calculated from the reproductive histories. The distribution of intervals was used in the calculation of the overlap between contraceptive use and amenorrhea. The mean interval was used in the estimation of the proportion of women who were fertile at the time of acceptance of contraception. From these data, the mean age at acceptance was also calculated. This mean age was part of the calculation of the average duration per birth that would have been required had contraception not been adopted. The other part necessary for the calculation of the average duration required per birth without use of contraception was derived by projecting the pre-family planning program fertility rates of acceptors.

Estimates of mortality and sterility were needed to calculate the mean length of contraceptive practice. Estimates of mortality were obtained from the same life table used as input in the simulations. The estimates of sterility, also used as input to the simulations, were based on those of Henry (1958). A correction factor for divorce based on the input data for the simulated cohorts was estimated since the cohorts had a significant risk of terminating marriage through divorce. The population to which Potter applied his method had an insignificant amount of divorce and thus he ignored this factor. In addition, the data needed for the calculation of the mean length of contraceptive practice were continuation rates of contraceptive use. These were obtained from the life table previously calculated for the Lee and Isbister method.

The months in which accidental pregnancies occurred were also tabulated. The proportion becoming accidentally pregnant was necessary for the calculation of the mean prolongation of stay in the fecundable state. Also needed was an estimate of fetal loss to be applied to correct the proportion becoming accidentally pregnant. For this the probability of fetal loss assumed in the simulations was used.

For calculating Wolfers' estimate of births averted, the mean and variance of prospective birth intervals (births) were tabulated from the reproductive histories. These intervals were computed only for women who had a birth during age 34. Since Wolfers ignored intervals longer than six years on the assumption that women with such long intervals could not be expected to accept contraception, such intervals were omitted.

Based on Wolfers' assumption, also, the length of postpartum amenorrhea was calculated from the variance of the prospective birth intervals (births). If the range of intervals between last birth and acceptance is small, one may assume that all women accept at the mean of this distribution. This is most likely the case in a postpartum family planning program. The period of overlap between the initial use of contraception and the end of the postpartum period would therefore be a simple calculation. Since, however, in the simulated experiments a different type of family planning program was stipulated and the range of the interval between delivery and acceptance could be up to 100 months, the overlap could not be calculated directly. Wolfers (1971) has recognized this problem and provided a technique for dealing with it. Since the procedure, however, involved elaborate and detailed calculations his method was followed for deriving the proportion no longer in the postpartum period for only the first month of overlap. Then a simple linear interpolation was followed for the approximately six months of postpartum amenorrhea that obtained in the simulations.

The final step for Wolfers was to calculate a life table that followed his procedures for correcting the woman months of contraceptive use by the mean prospective birth interval (births). The same continuation rates previously used for Lee and Isbister and Potter were applied. In deriving the woman months of contraceptive use, the probabilities of sterility, of overlap with postpartum amenorrhea, and of contraceptive continuation rates were utilized. Probabilities of accidental pregnancy and probabilities of fetal loss were used to correct the number of births averted. The same probabilities of sterility and fetal loss assumed in calculating Potter's method were also assumed in calculating Wolfers' method.

The criterion values for births averted were calculated directly from the output of the two simulated cohorts. From the reproductive histories of women in the family planning cohort months of contraceptive use were tabulated and summarized for each year and for the five-year period of the family planning program. From these two components births averted per woman year of use were calculated.

RESULTS

Table 1 compares the reduction in age-specific fertility rates resulting from the family planning program calculated by the Lee and Isbister method with the direct estimate derived from the simulated cohorts. As may be seen, the age-specific fertility rates with a family planning program estimated by the Lee and Isbister method do not fully reflect the impact of the family planning program (column b versus column e). The estimated rate for the entire

Age	Lee and Isbister			Simulated Cohorts		
	Fertility Rate Without Program*	Fertility Rate With Program	Per Cent Reduction	Fertility Rate Without Program	Fertility Rate With Program	Per Cent Reduction
	(a)	(b)	(c)	(d)	(e)	(f)
Total**	998.6	777.3	22	998.6	650.9	35
35	230.5	230.5	0	230.5	204.7	11
36	213.2	168.3	21	213.2	116.1	46
37	197.1	122.7	38	197.1	103.4	48
38	185.4	125.0	33	185.4	113.9	39
39	172.4	130.8	24	172.4	112.8	35

Table 1. COMPARISON BETWEEN AGE-SPECIFIC FERTILITY RATES FOR ALL WOMEN OBTAINED FROM LEE AND ISBISTER METHOD AND FROM THE SIMULATED COHORTS

*The pre-program fertility rates were obtained from the simulated cohort without family planning.

**Total = $\sum$ASFR.

five-year period is thus 19 per cent higher than the rates obtained directly from the simulated cohorts. Consequently, the method consistently underestimates the reduction in fertility (column c versus column f). The underestimate for the five-year period, however, is only 13 percentage points. The largest underestimate occurs in the second year of the family planning program. In the other years the underestimates vary from six to eleven percentage points.

The agreement between the Lee and Isbister method and the direct estimates obtained from the simulated cohorts is quite remarkable considering that some births averted in the five-year period are ignored. In fact, the results suggest that possibly an estimate closer to the direct estimate might have been obtained if the births averted in that year were not neglected.

In interpreting the above results, however, one must consider the basic assumption on which this method rests. Lee and Isbister assume that the age-specific fertility rates observed prior to a family planning program would remain unchanged in the future if no program existed. The data used here to test their method adhere perfectly to this assumption. Little imagination is required to conclude that if less accurate estimates of the age-specific fertility rates of the base period than postulated (Table 1, column a) are available, the estimates of the reduction of fertility could be changed greatly. Moreover, in an actual situation one would be utilizing the age-specific rates of women whose reproduction experience may have evolved quite differently from that of the women who are exposed to a family planning program. This would be particularly true in periods of rapid social and economic change. The only factor affecting the age-specific fertility rates assumed in this application is that of chance. Also, it must be emphasized that the other components of the estimates derived from the Lee and Isbister method are based on highly accurate and complete data. In many instances, such data are not readily available.

In Table 2, the births averted based on the three methods and the simulated cohorts are presented. Not unexpected is the fairly close agreement of the Lee and Isbister estimate for the total period of the program. As indicated above, such a close approximation may be attributed to having ideal data, a condition not likely to exist in the real world. As may be seen, no values are shown for the single years of the program since the Lee and Isbister method does not provide for obtaining such estimates.

The Potter and Wolfers procedures also produce underestimates of the births averted. For the total five-year period of the family planning program, the Potter and Wolfers methods underestimate the births averted by 59 per cent and 40 per cent, respectively. In terms of births averted in the various years of the program, the Wolfers procedure produces an overestimate for the first year and underestimates by an increasing amount each successive year. The Potter method for distributing births averted to the various years of the program also consistently produces underestimates. Like the Wolfers method, the underestimates become larger with each successive year. As may be noted, the Potter method attributes no births averted to the first year of the program under the assumption that women beginning contraceptive practice the first year avert only births in the second year.

In summary, only the Lee and Isbister method closely approximates the criterion value. Both the Potter and Wolfers methods give quite conservative estimates of births averted. This finding, in itself, is of importance since overestimates would be very serious.

DISCUSSION

This assessment of births averted presents only the first step in a comprehensive consideration of the problems of evaluating measures of births averted.

Period of Program and Age of Women		Lee and Isbister	Potter	Wolfers	Simulated Cohorts
Total:	35-39	1.07	.55	.81	1.34
First year:	35			.25	.10
Second year:	36		.20	.23	.30
Third year:	37		.14	.17	.32
Fourth year:	38		.10	.11	.30
Fifth year:	39		.06	.05	.32

Table 2. COMPARISONS OF BIRTHS AVERTED DERIVED FROM THE METHODS OF LEE AND ISBISTER, POTTER, WOLFERS, AND FROM THE SIMULATED COHORTS

By presenting this very limited assessment of various methods of estimating, it is hoped that an important use of fairly complex simulation models has been demonstrated.

For the limited test carried out, the Lee and Isbister method of estimating the reduction in age-specific fertility rates of all women resulting from a family planning program shows a rather close correspondence with the direct estimate. But as previously pointed out, this result appears to be almost entirely due to the extremely good data as to what the fertility rates would be without a family planning program. If, indeed, one has good evidence that fertility rates would remain unchanged in the absence of a program and also that in the past there has been little variation between cohorts in their fertility experience, one might be justified in using their method.

The estimates of births averted produced by the three methods is somewhat disappointing. Theoretically, both the Potter and Wolfers methods should approximate more closely the criterion values than the Lee and Isbister method since both methods attempt to take a large number of factors into account. For many of the factors, in fact, the same values used in the simulations were utilized in applying the Potter and Wolfers methods. More generally, neither the Potter nor Wolfers methods attempt to take into account the interaction between the various factors affecting fertility. While accounting for interaction, admittedly, would be extremely difficult, such interaction may be one reason for their lack of agreement with the criterion values. It is fortunate, however, that both methods produce underestimates of births averted.

The Potter method, it also should be remembered, is built on an assumption similar to that of the Lee and Isbister method, namely that, in the absence of a family planning program, fertility will remain unchanged. Central to Potter's method is the use of fertility rates of acceptors before the program began.

These rates are used to derive the average duration per birth required if contraception is not practiced. Criticisms similar to those applied to the Lee and Isbister method, therefore, may be applied to the Potter method. The results obtained with the Potter method suggest that the effect of the many refinements introduced over-corrects for births averted. It is difficult, however, without carrying out alternative calculations, to pinpoint exactly what factors are being over-corrected for in the Potter method.

In considering the Wolfers method a number of questions may be raised. It is apparent that the Wolfers procedure was designed to be applied to a postpartum family planning program. In the simulation experiment carried out, acceptance of contraception was not dependent on the length of birth intervals as assumed in the Wolfers method but on whether women had attained their desired family size. In reality, acceptance of contraception is probably dependent on both these factors. Thus, any procedure for estimating births averted should take both these factors into account.

Furthermore, there are a number of questions as to the appropriateness of the use of mean birth intervals (births). Wolfers' method as used in this paper was applied to data for women at a relatively late age in the reproductive period. As is well known, this is a period in which the birth intervals are truncated (Sheps *et al.* 1970). Moreover, birth intervals longer than six years are ignored. Some women in the simulated cohorts with long birth intervals actually accepted contraception. By not including the intervals of such women, the estimate of the mean birth intervals (births) is somewhat shorter than it would be if they were included.[6] This suggests that it may be more appropriate to derive the estimate of mean birth intervals (births) from acceptors only, rather than from a sample of recently delivered women as Wolfers' procedure specifies.

Another aspect that also should be considered is the fact that even recently delivered women are not a homogeneous group with respect to their birth intervals. By utilizing the mean, however, the Wolfers procedure implicitly makes this assumption. This suggests that attention should be paid to the distribution of the birth intervals and some correction for such heterogeneity should be introduced into his method. Related also is the averaging of all birth intervals regardless of order. Since first birth intervals tend to be shorter than subsequent intervals, application of the Wolfers method to a sample of young women would appear to be particularly inappropriate.

Also, it should be pointed out that there exists a correlation between a woman's birth interval and her length of use.[7] Women with higher fecundability tend to have shorter birth intervals than women with lower fecundability. Therefore, women with short birth intervals are also more prone to experience an accidental pregnancy when they are using a contraceptive and thus their length of use is likely to be short.

In addition to the criticisms that may be directed towards the use of birth intervals (births), the Wolfers method tends to assume too long a duration of postpartum period, data admittedly difficult to obtain. The Wolfers procedure depends on the variance of the birth interval (births) as the basis for estimating the mean length of the postpartum period. While the various factors affecting birth intervals (births) would tend to produce an overestimate of births averted, this latter factor would tend to produce an underestimate.

There are also several aspects that should be treated in a complete evaluation of the three methods. First, not considered here, is the question as to whether there would be variations in the results of the three methods for women at different ages. So far, the problem has been investigated only for

35-year old women. Moreover, the observation of these women was limited to a five-year period.

Another important aspect that should be considered is that of sampling variability. Another investigation could profitably be directed towards dealing with the sampling variability of the estimates produced by the three methods of estimating births averted. Simulation models, such as the one used here, provide an excellent vehicle for investigating this problem.

In addition, the effect of previous use of contraception was not considered. Nor was the effect of contraceptive use not directly attributable to a family planning program, commonly referred to as "the substitution effect," investigated. Also, the possible effects of abortion or sterilization were not considered. Moreover, the focus has been on only one segment of contraceptive use and not multiple segments of use. The use of different sets of parameters could possibly affect the results of the comparisons of the three methods. All of these aspects should eventually be considered in a complete evaluation of the various procedures for estimating births averted.

Lastly, it should be reiterated that ideal data were used in this application of the three methods. Accordingly, it was not necessary to make many of the unrealistic assumptions sometimes needed to apply these methods. Since both Potter's and Wolfers' methods have heavy data demands and involve considerable calculation, as contrasted with Lee and Isbister, the work reported on in this paper suggests the need for further investigation into the assessment of these methods.

FOOTNOTES

[1]For discussion of various microsimulation population models and a summary of results reported by various investigators, see Sheps (1971).

[2]Since acceptors tend to be selected on the basis of their higher past fertility and consequently their heightened interest in accepting family planning techniques, this latter assumption appears eminently reasonable.

[3]It should be noted that mean birth intervals (births) are different from mean birth intervals (women). The former are collected from women at the time they give birth while the latter are collected from women at any point in their reproductive cycle. Prospective intervals are counted at time x from the beginning of a specified age. (Wolfers 1969.)

[4]The number of surviving children of a woman had to be equal to or greater than her desired family size.

[5]There was one condition under which women ceased practice and then resumed practice. This occurred when women became accidentally pregnant and the pregnancy resulted in a fetal death. In such an instance, women resumed practice until they completed their previously assigned length of practice. In calculating length of practice for such women the months these women were pregnant were subtracted.

[6]This problem has been recognized by Wolfers. He estimates that the truncation effect shortens the mean length of the interval by about 10 per cent in age considered here. (Personal communication.)

[7]Jane A. Menken originally discussed this problem

with us.

REFERENCES

Barrett, J. C. 1971. Use of a fertility simulation model to refine measurement techniques, Demography 8: 481-490.

Chandrasekaran, C., D. V. R. Murty, and K. Srinivasan 1971. Some problems in determining the number of acceptors needed in a family planning program to achieve a specified reduction in the birth rate, Population Studies 25: 303-308.

Henry, L. 1953. Fécondité des mariages: nouvelle méthode des measure. Paris: Presses Universitaires de France.

Lee, B. M. and J. Isbister 1965. The impact of birth control programs on fertility, In Family Planning and Population Programs, B. Berelson, R. K. Anderson, O. Harkavy, J. Maier, W. P. Mauldin and S. J. Segal (eds.), Chicago: Univ. of Chicago Press.

Mauldin, W. P. 1968. Births averted by family planning programs, Studies in Family Planning 33: 1-7, New York: The Population Council.

Potter, R. G. 1969. Estimating births averted in a family planning program, In Fertility and Family Planning, S. J. Behrman, L. Corsa and R. Freedman (eds.), Ann Arbor: Univ. of Michigan Press.

Potter, R. G. 1971. Inadequacy of a one-method family planning program, Social Biology 18: 1-9.

Ridley, J. C. and M. C. Sheps 1966. An analytic simulation model of human reproduction with demographic and biological components, Population Studies 19: 297-310.

Sheps, M. C., J. A. Menken, J. C. Ridley and J. W. Lingner 1970. Truncation effect in closed and open birth interval data, Journal of the American Statistical Association 65: 678-693.

Sheps, M. C. 1971. Simulation methods and the use of models in fertility analysis, International Population Conference, London, 1969, Belgium: International Union for the Scientific Study of Population.

Wolfers, D. 1969. The demographic effects of a contraceptive programme, Population Studies 23: 111-140.

Wolfers, D. 1971. Contraceptive overlap with postpartum anovularity, Population Studies 25: 535-536.

ACKNOWLEDGMENTS

We are indebted to Mindel C. Sheps for comments on an earlier version of this paper. A number of colleagues discussed various aspects of this paper with us and provided statistical consultation. We wish to thank Mary Grace Kovar, Joan W. Lingner, Jane A. Menken and Mary Mittleman. Joseph C. Ott carried out the computer programming for the REPSIM-B model and Ilene Herz carried out the many detailed calculations necessary.

This work was supported in part by grants from the Ford Foundation.

APPENDIX A

SUMMARY DESCRIPTION OF REPSIM-B: A COMPUTER SIMULATION MODEL

REPSIM-B is an elaboration and extension of our work with an earlier computer model, REPSIM-A. In this appendix, REPSIM-B is described in detail. REPSIM-A has been described previously elsewhere (see references below).

Tables 1A and 2A have been prepared to summarize the differences in input and output of REPSIM-A and REPSIM-B. As may be seen, REPSIM-B is in many respects identical with REPSIM-A. In fact, REPSIM-B was designed so that the results from REPSIM-A would be directly comparable to the results obtainable from REPSIM-B. Identical experiments run on REPSIM-A may be run on REPSIM-B.

The major differences between REPSIM-A and REPSIM-B lie in the assumptions regarding various aspects of contraceptive practice, abortion, and sterilization. In addition, REPSIM-B provides the option of children dying. It should be noted that in both REPSIM-A and B the user has the option of making any state inoperative. For example, although there is a provision for women to become widowed in both REPSIM-A and B, the user may decide not to utilize this option since the particular concern is with women whose marriages are unbroken by widowhood. The differences in input between REPSIM-A and REPSIM-B are shown in Table 1A.

Another important difference between REPSIM-A and REPSIM-B is in the output. In REPSIM-A there were 10 tables of output. In REPSIM-B there is a total of 38 tables. The major changes are in terms of the calculation of various statistics by family planning status categories. The major differences in output tables are summarized in Table 2A. Also, in REPSIM-B the individual reproductive histories of women may be recorded on magnetic tape or printed as part of the print output. Such provisions allow the

EVENT	REPSIM-A May vary with:			REPSIM-B May vary with:			
	Age	Parity	Other	Age	Parity	GAP[a]	Other
Mortality							
Female	X			X			
Male	X			X			
Child	Not available						Age of child
Infant			X[b]				X[b]
Sterility							
Natural sterility	X			X			
Surgical sterility	Not available				X	X	Applies only after month of availability

Table 1A. REPSIM-A AND REPSIM-B PROGRAM INPUTS

EVENT	REPSIM-A May vary with:			REPSIM-B May vary with:			
	Age	Parity	Other	Age	Parity	GAP[a]	Other
Marriage							
First marriage	X			X			
Age difference between spouses			X[c]				Age of wife at marriage
Widowhood			Depends on male mortality (see above)				Depends on male mortality (see above)
Divorce	X		Order of marriage	X			Order of marriage
Remarriage from widowhood	X	X		X			
Remarriage from divorce	X		Order of marriage	X			Order of marriage

Table 1A. (cont'd.) REPSIM-A AND REPSIM-B PROGRAM INPUTS

EVENT	REPSIM-A May vary with:			REPSIM-B May vary with:			
	Age	Parity	Other	Age	Parity	GAP[a]	Other
Pregnancy and associated events							
Fecundability (conception)	X		Groups of women	X			Groups of women age of natural sterility
Outcome of pregnancy:							
Spontaneous fetal death	X		Death of woman in first six months of gestation	X			Death of woman in first six months of gestation
Induced abortion	Not available				X	X	Applies only after month of availability

Table 1A. (cont'd.) REPSIM-A AND REPSIM-B PROGRAM INPUTS

EVENT	REPSIM-A May vary with:			REPSIM-B May vary with:			
	Age	Parity	Other	Age	Parity	GAP[a]	Other
Live birth			Depends on not a fetal death				Depends on not a fetal death or induced abortion
Termination of pregnancy			Associated distributions of length of pregnancy depending on outcome				Associated distributions of length of pregnancy depending on outcome
Termination of postpartum nonsusceptibility			Associated distributions depending on outcome of pregnancy				Associated distributions depending on outcome of pregnancy

Table 1A. (cont'd.) REPSIM-A AND REPSIM-B PROGRAM INPUTS

EVENT	REPSIM-A May vary with:			REPSIM-B May vary with:			
	Age	Parity	Other	Age	Parity	GAP[a]	Other
Family planning and associated characteristics							
Month of availability	Not available						A constant
Desired family size		X[d]					Individual woman
Spacing preference		X[e]					Individual woman
Pattern I[f]							
Initial use of contraception		X			X	X	
Contraceptive effectiveness		X			X	X	Individual woman

Table 1A. (cont'd.) REPSIM-A AND REPSIM-B PROGRAM INPUTS

EVENT	REPSIM-A May vary with:			REPSIM-B May vary with:			
	Age	Parity	Other	Age	Parity	GAP[a]	Other
Length of practice		X			X	X	Spacing preference
Discontinuance of use	Not available					X	
Pattern II[g]							
Initial use of contraception	Not available					X	Length of open birth interval time since month of availability
Contraceptive effectiveness	Not available						
Length of practice	Not available					X	Spacing preference

Table 1A. (cont'd.) REPSIM-A AND REPSIM-B PROGRAM INPUTS

EVENT	REPSIM-A May vary with:			REPSIM-B May vary with:			
	Age	Parity	Other	Age	Parity	GAP[a]	Other
Discontinuance of use	Not available					X	
Resumption of contraceptive practice	Not available					X	Length of open birth interval

Table 1A. REPSIM-A AND REPSIM-B PROGRAM INPUTS

[a] the difference between desired family size and number of living children.

[b] with associated distribution of month of death depending on postulated level of infant mortality.

[c] a constant input in months.

[d] must be input via initial use of contraceptives.

[e] must be input via length of contraceptive practice.

[f] in REPSIM-B referred to also as Developed Country Pattern.

[g] in REPSIM-B referred to also as Developing Country Pattern.

MEASURE	COMMENT	REPSIM-A	REPSIM-B
Mortality			
Number of women dying	By age	X	X
Number of child and infant deaths	By age of mother	Only infant deaths	X
Number of women surviving	By exact age	NA	X
Number of women surviving	To end of simulation by order of marriage	X	X
Mean person years lived	For total cohort and women in unbroken marriages	X	X
Infant mortality rate		X	X
Surviving children Cumulative distribution Mean Variance Standard deviation Coefficient of variation	By desired family size and family planning status	NA	X

Table 2A. SUMMARY OF OUTPUTS OF REPSIM-A AND REPSIM-B PROGRAMS

MEASURE	COMMENT	REPSIM-A	REPSIM-B
Marriage			
Number of first marriages	By age	X	X
Number of divorces	By age	X	X
Number of marriages ending in widowhood	By age	X	X
Number of divorcees remarrying	By age	X	X
Number of widows remarrying	By age	X	X
Number single	By exact age	NA	X
Number in first marriage	By exact age	NA	X
Number in second marriage	By exact age	NA	X
Number currently married	By exact age	NA	X

Table 2A. (cont'd.) SUMMARY OF OUTPUTS OF REPSIM-A AND REPSIM-B PROGRAMS

MEASURE	COMMENT	REPSIM-A	REPSIM-B
Marriage			
Number divorced	By exact age	NA	X
Number widowed	By exact age	NA	X
Duration of marriage Mean Variance	For total cohort and women surviving to end of simulation	X	X
Duration of marriage Mean Variance	By order of marriage	NA	X
Pregnancy			
Number of pregnancies by outcome	By age	X	X
Number of women pregnant	By exact age	NA	X
Number of women pregnant	By planning status	NA	X

Table 2A. (cont'd.) SUMMARY OF OUTPUTS OF REPSIM-A AND REPSIM-B PROGRAMS

MEASURE	COMMENT	REPSIM-A	REPSIM-B
Natality			
Number of live births	By age	X	X
Births per person years lived	By order of marriage	NA	X
Births per person years married	By order of marriage	NA	X
Age specific birth rates: Single years Five-year intervals	For all women and various marital status and family planning groups	X NA family planning groups	X
Total fertility rates	For all women and various marital status and family planning groups	X NA family planning groups	X

Table 2A. (cont'd.) SUMMARY OF OUTPUTS OF REPSIM-A AND REPSIM-B PROGRAMS

MEASURE	COMMENT	REPSIM-A	REPSIM-B
Natality			
Cumulative birth rates: By marital duration and age at first marriage	For women in first marriages	X	X
By age	For total cohort and for various marital status groupings	X	X
Completed parity: Cumulative frequency distribution, Mean, Variance, Standard deviation, Coefficient of variation	For total cohort, for various marital status groups, family planning groups, by level of fecundability and by desired family size	X NA family planning, fecundability and desired family size	X
Gross reproduction rate		X	X

Table 2A. (cont'd.) SUMMARY OF OUTPUTS OF REPSIM-A AND REPSIM-B PROGRAMS

MEASURE	COMMENT	REPSIM-A	REPSIM-B
Natality			
Net reproduction rate		X	X
Length of generation: Mean Variance Standard deviation		X	X
Birth intervals by completed family size	For women surviving to end of simulation with first marriage unbroken	X	X
Birth intervals (Life table analysis): Mean Variance Standard deviation Third moment Fourth moment Quartiles	For women in first marriage	X	X

Table 2A. (cont'd.) SUMMARY OF OUTPUTS OF REPSIM-A AND REPSIM-B PROGRAMS

MEASURE	COMMENT	REPSIM-A	REPSIM-B
Family planning			
Number of women becoming family planners	By age	X	X
Number of family planners	By exact age and current family planning status	NA	X
Other			
Number of women in various states: Naturally sterile Surgically sterile Postpartum Nonsusceptible period	By age, by exact age and family planning status groups	NA for surgical sterility, exact age and family planning status	X

Table 2A. SUMMARY OF OUTPUTS OF REPSIM-A AND REPSIM-B PROGRAMS

*Abbreviations:

X = Available
NA = Not available

user to undertake further tabulations for the analysis of specific problems.

Both REPSIM-A and REPSIM-B computer programs were designed as generalized multipurpose models of human reproduction. REPSIM-A was written in the computer language MAD and thus its usefulness was restricted to a small number of computers. REPSIM-B is written in FORTRAN IV and may be run on computers having a minimum core size of 65,000 words or 262,000 bytes. Certain economies of core size may be achieved by segmenting the program. In addition, the REPSIM-B program requires a card reader, line printer, and a disk or tape to temporarily store approximately 3,000 words or 12,000 bytes. The program has been run on the following computers: CDC-6500, CDC-6600, Univac-1108, IBM 360-40, IBM 360-50, and IBM 360-91. Computer running time varies with the computer being used, the sample size, the number of states operating, the length of the period of observation, and the number of output tables requested. The running time for simulating 1,000 women on the CDC-6600 for the entire period of observation (i.e. ages 15 to 50) with all states operating and all output tables, is two minutes.

REPSIM-B is a microsimulation model that utilizes Monte Carlo methods to generate the reproductive histories of hypothetical cohorts of women from age 15 until age 50. That is, the individual woman is the unit of analysis and the occurrence of various events to each individual woman is treated stochastically. (The user may simulate any age period within these ages. For example, interest may focus on the reproductive histories of young women and thus only ages 15 to 20 or 20 to 25 may be simulated.) A random number (R) between zero and one is generated by a special programmed subroutine and is compared with a probability (P) of an event occurring. If R is $\leq$ P the event is assumed to occur at the particular point in time being considered. In most aspects, REPSIM-B may be characterized as a static or stationary model. Most of the probabilities do not change in terms of external time. Internally, however, it is dynamic in that many of the probabilities change with age, parity, or other features of a woman's history.

The reproductive history of each woman is generated sequentially. As each woman is processed, her age at death, age at first marriage, and age at natural sterility are first determined.

The probabilities of death, first marriage, and natural sterility are all dependent on age. If a woman's age at first marriage or age at natural sterility exceeds her age at death, this information is discarded.

Marriage is defined to include any type of sexual union. Inherent in the probabilities of marriage is the assumption of an available partner. Marriage may be dissolved by a woman's death, widowhood, or divorce The age difference between the spouses may vary with the age of the woman at the time of marriage. The probability of a woman becoming widowed depends on the probability of her husband dying. This latter probability in turn depends on the age of a woman's husband.

Divorce may depend on the age of the woman and the order of her marriage. If both widowhood and divorce occur in the same month, widowhood has priority over divorce. Remarriage from either widowhood or divorce may occur. The probability of remarriage from widowhood is a function of a woman's age. The probability of remarriage from divorce is a function of a woman's age and number of previous marital unions.

Exposure to the risk of pregnancy begins when a woman marries. As long as a woman is married and fecund, she is tested each month for conception. Natural fecundability, the monthly probability of conceiving, may vary among women. The program provides for up to five groups of women with different levels of fecundability. In addition, fecundability may vary with the age of a woman. Fecundability may also be adjusted to take into account a woman's previously determined age of natural sterility. Thus, the age at which a woman becomes naturally sterile may be preceded by a period of diminishing fecundability.

When a woman conceives, the outcome of the pregnancy is determined. Each pregnancy is tested independently for a spontaneous fetal death and an induced abortion. If neither occurs, the pregnancy ends in a live birth. The duration of a pregnancy depends on its outcome. If both a fetal death and an induced abortion are found to occur, the durations of pregnancy for both types of outcomes are compared and the shorter duration determines the outcome of pregnancy. If the durations are equal, the outcome is considered a spontaneous fetal death.

The probability of a fetal death may vary with the age of a woman. If a woman dies during her pregnancy, even if the outcome has been determined as a live birth, but the pregnancy has lasted seven months or less, the outcome is by definition a spontaneous fetal death. If, however, the pregnancy has lasted eight months or more, the outcome is defined as a live birth. If a woman is pregnant at the end of the simulation, the pregnancy is assumed not to have terminated.

At the termination of the pregnancy, a woman is considered nonsusceptible to conception for a period. The length of this period of postpartum nonsusceptibility depends on the outcome of pregnancy.

The program provides for three types of fertility control: (1) induced abortion; (2) surgical sterilization; and (3) family planning (defined as the use of contraceptives, rhythm, or coitus interruptus). All three types of fertility control may operate in any one simulation.

Probabilities of surgical sterility are applied only after a predetermined month of availability (by input). Surgical sterility may depend on a woman's parity or the difference between her desired family size and her number of surviving children. This difference is hereafter referred to as GAP.

Even if a woman is naturally sterile she may become surgically sterilized. If a woman is surgically sterilized before the time she would become naturally sterile, the monthly tests for natural sterility are discontinued. The previously determined month of natural sterility, however, is retained for output analysis.

The probabilities of induced abortion are applied only after a woman has become pregnant. The probability of a woman experiencing an induced abortion depends on the month of availability and her parity or GAP.

There are two different patterns of family planning defined in the program: (1) Developed Countries and (2) Developing Countries. Only one pattern of family planning may be utilized in any particular simulation.

A woman may become a family planner if she is currently married, not surgically sterile, and not currently pregnant. Women may use contraceptives even though they are naturally sterile or in the postpartum nonsusceptible state.

In both family planning patterns, desired family size is defined as the number of surviving children wanted by a woman. Desired family size may assume the value of 0, 1, 2,...n. The particular desired family size of a woman is defined at the beginning of a simulation from a distribution determined by input. Spacing preference is defined as the desired interval in months between births. The particular spacing preference of a woman is determined in the same way as desired family size.

In the Developed Countries Family Planning pattern, a woman may initiate the use of a contraceptive method at the time of her first marriage, or of any subsequent marriage, or the month following a live birth. The probability of beginning contraceptive practice may depend either on a woman's parity or on her GAP.

The effect of a woman using a contraceptive method is to reduce her natural fecundability by the postulated level of contraceptive effectiveness. Contraceptive effectiveness may vary with parity or GAP. Moreover, contraceptive effectiveness may vary over a range of values for each parity or GAP as determined by input.

The length of time a woman uses a contraceptive method may vary with parity, or GAP, or her desired interval between births (i.e. her spacing preference).

Three alternative methods for determining the length of contraceptive practice are provided for in the Developed Countries Family Planning pattern. The first method adjusts the length of practice after any live birth with the woman's spacing preference and the length of her previous birth intervals. The second method determines the length of practice on the basis of the spacing preference relative to the most recent birth. In the third method, length of practice depends only on parity or GAP.

In this family planning pattern, a woman terminates contraceptive use when she has an accidental pregnancy or she completes her assigned length of practice. It is also possible for a woman to discontinue use if her GAP changes. Accordingly, she may plan a birth if a child dies. Once a woman completes a pregnancy she immediately resumes contraceptive practice.

On the other hand, in the Developing Countries Family Planning pattern, women may begin contraceptive practice only at or after the specified month of availability. When this month occurs, probabilities of entering family planning are applied monthly.

The probability of initiating contraceptive use may depend either on GAP, the open birth interval, or the length of time since the specified month of availability. The length of time a woman practices contraception may depend only on GAP or on GAP and her spacing preference. Contraceptive effectiveness may vary only with GAP but as in the Developed Countries pattern may also vary over a range of values for each value of GAP. A woman may discontinue contraceptive use if her GAP changes. Once a woman terminates use as a result of an accidental pregnancy, reaching the end of her assigned length of practice, becoming surgically sterile, or if her GAP changes she does not automatically resume practice as in the Developed Countries pattern. Rather, resumption of contraceptive practice (if she is still eligible) depends on another set of probabilities. Such probabilities may depend on GAP or the length of the open birth interval of a woman.

Finally, the program summarizes the individual reproductive histories of women, calculates a number of natality statistics for purposes of output, and may, if specified, either write the individual histories on tape or print them.

REFERENCES

Ridley, J. C. and M. C. Sheps 1966. An analytic simulation model of human reproduction with demographic and biological components, Population Studies 19: 297-310.

Ridley, J. C., J. W. Lingner, M. C. Sheps and J. A. Menken 1967. Effects on natality of alternative family planning programs: estimation via simulation (abstract), Population Index 33: 304-305.

Ridley, J. C., M. C. Sheps, J. W. Lingner and J. A. Menken 1967. The effects of changing mortality on natality: some estimates from a simulation model, The Milbank Memorial Fund Quarterly 45: 77-97.

Ridley, J. C., M. C. Sheps, J. W. Lingner and J. A. Menken 1969. On the apparent subfecundity of non-family planners, Social Biology 16: 24-28.

Sheps, M. C. and J. C. Ridley 1967. Studying determinants of natality: quantitative estimation through a simulation model (summary), World Population Conference, Belgrade, 1965, Vol. III. New York: United Nations.

Sheps, M. C., J. C. Ridley and J. W. Lingner 1967. Effects of selected factors on natality: quantitative estimation through simulation, Proceedings of the Conference on Simulation in Business and Public Health. American Statistical Association.

Sheps, M. C., J. A. Menken, J. C. Ridley and J. W. Lingner 1967. Birth intervals - artifact and reality, Contributed Papers, Sydney Conference, Sydney, Australia: International Union for the Scientific Study of Population.

Sheps, M. C., J. A. Menken, J. C. Ridley and J. W. Lingner 1970. The truncation effect in closed and open birth interval data, Journal of the American Statistical Association 65: 678-693.

APPENDIX B

DESCRIPTION OF INPUTS IN RUNS 017 AND 018[a]

Event	Parameter		
Female mortality:	$\overset{o}{e}_o = 63.57$		
Male mortality:	$\overset{o}{e}_o = 58.92$		
First marriage:	Mean = 21.9		
	s.d. = 5.4		
Natural sterility:	Mean = 40.8		
	s.d. = 7.8		
		Probabilities	
Divorce:	Age	One Union	Two Unions
	15-19	.07	.00
	20-24	.12	.01
	25-29	.12	.03
	30-34	.10	.04
	35-39	.09	.05
	40-44	.10	.06
	45-49	.10	.06
Remarriage - Widows:	Age	Probabilities	
	15-19	.30	
	20-24	.30	
	25-29	.25	
	30-34	.20	
	35-39	.10	
	40-44	.05	
	45-49	.05	

[a]The basic inputs for these runs and initial runs of 1,000 women were carried out when the second author was Visiting Demographer at CELADE (Centro Latino-americano de Demografia) Santiago, Chile, in August-December 1971.

Remarriage - Divorce:	Age	Probabilities Number of Previous Unions	
		One	Two
	15-19	.90	.00
	20-24	.75	.25
	25-29	.25	.25
	30-34	.25	.25
	35-39	.20	.15
	40-44	.10	.15
	45-49	.10	.15

Length of pregnancy:

Live birth: Mean = 9.1 months
s.d. = 1.5 months

Spontaneous fetal death: Mean = 2.5 months
s.d. = 1.5 months

Spontaneous fetal death:	Age	Probabilities
	15	.26
	20	.20
	25	.24
	30	.33
	35	.40
	40	.47
	45	.50
	50	.55

Postpartum period:

Fetal death: Mean = 2.0 months
s.d. = .2 months

Live birth: Mean = 4.2 months
s.d. = 2.1 months

Child mortality:
Both sexes: $^{o}e_{o}$ = 61.2

Infant mortality rate: 85.0

Time of infant death: Mean = 4.7 months
s.d. = 3.4 months

Fecundability: Heterogeneous (5 groups)

Age	Mean Probabilities
15	.072
20	.153
25	.133
30	.117
35	.105
40	.093
45	.080
50	.000

Desired family size: Mean = 4.1 children
s.d. = 2.1 children

Probability of becoming a family planner:

GAP*	
≤ 0	.25
1	.00

Contraceptive effectiveness:

GAP*	
≤ 0	.95
1+	.00

*GAP: The difference between desired family size and number of living children.

Length of contraceptive practice:	Mean = 39.9	
	s.d. = 24.1	
Discontinuance of use:	GAP*	
	≤ 0	0.0
	1+	1.0

APPENDIX C

1. Lee and Isbister's Method

The following formula is used to estimate future age-specific fertility:

$$f_{i,t} = \frac{F_{i,t} \cdot f_{i,o} - Q_{i,t} \cdot g_i}{F_{i,t}}$$

where $f_{i,t}$ = the fertility rate of women at age i, in year t

$f_{i,o}$ = the fertility rate of women at age i in the base year, before the program is begun

$F_{i,t}$ = total women at age i, year t

g_i = "potential" fertility, which contraceptive users at age i would have experienced, were they not using contraceptives

$Q_{i,t}$ = number of women age i who were practicing totally effective contraception in year t-1.

Then

$$\frac{f_{i,o} - f_{i,t}}{f_{i,o}} \times 100$$ = per cent reduction in fertility due to use of contraception.

2. Potter's Method

This method estimates births averted by deriving an estimate of mean prolongations of stay in the fecundable state resulting from contraceptive use (I) and dividing this by the average duration per birth (D) where:

$I = F(R - A - PW)$, where all durations are in months and

I = average duration that childbearing is interrupted - i.e. mean prolongation of stay in the fecundable state

F = proportion of women fertile at time of acceptance

R = mean length of use among couples fertile at time of acceptance

A = allowance for amenorrhea

P = proportion becoming accidentally pregnant

W = penalty per accidental pregnancy

and

$B = \frac{I}{D}$, where I is defined above and

B = births averted per first segment of use

D = average duration per birth that would have been required if contraception had not been accepted.

3. Wolfers' Method

Wolfers constructs a life table (Table 1C) as shown on the next three pages. It may be constructed for as long a period as desired. In the illustration shown on the next page, the calculations are shown for only the first year. Column (c) contains the month after delivery and is used only when the range in the length of intervals between delivery and acceptors is small. In such an instance, all women are assumed to accept at the mean delivery acceptance interval. When the range of intervals is not small, the proportion of women accepting during each month after delivery is used. This was the case with the simulated data since women accepted up to

(a) Ordinal month	(b) Surviving fecund users at first of month	(d) Proportion ovulating	(e) Mean post-partum infe-cundity	(f) Effective popula-tion	(g) Continu-ation rate to end of month	(i) Sterility factor	(j) Women months of use in months
1	91,585	.5050	5.7	46,250	.8685	.865657	43,143
2	79,281	.6000	10.0	47,569	.9780	.974799	46,970
3	77,283	.7000	10.0	54,098	.9722	.969018	53,260
4	74,889	.8000	10.0	59,911	.9736	.970413	59,025
5	72,673	.9000	10.0	65,406	.9816	.978387	64,699
6	71,103	1.0000	10.0	71,103	.9796	.976394	70,264
7	69,424	1.0000	10.0	69,424	.9792	.975995	68,591
8	67,757	1.0000	10.0	67,757	.9787	.975497	66,927
9	66,097	1.0000	10.0	66,097	.9773	.974101	65,241
10	64,385	1.0000	10.0	64,385	.9839	.980680	63,763
11	63,141	1.0000	10.0	63,141	.9854	.982173	62,578
12	62,015	1.0000	10.0	62,015	.9852	.981975	61,456

Table 1C. COMPUTATION OF CUMULATIVE BIRTHS AVERTED PER 100,000 WOMEN ACCEPTING CONTRACEPTION
(Women aged 35; Mean prospective birth interval, 27.6; Monthly probability of sterility, .996727)

Ordinal month	(k) Corrected mean birth interval	(1) Births averted (100% effect)	(m) Probability of pregnancy	(n) Probability of pregnancy x live birth proportion	(o) Births	(p) Corrected births averted	(q) Cumulative births averted	(r) Number sterile or discontinued in month
1	23.3	1,852	.00506	.00286	286	1,566	1,566	12,304
2	24.2	1,941	.00253	.00143	143	1,798	3,364	1,998
3	25.1	2,122	.00316	.00178	178	1,944	5,308	2,394
4	26.0	2,270	.00126	.00071	71	2,199	7,507	2,216
5	26.8	2,414	.00190	.00107	107	2,307	9,814	1,570
6	27.6	2,546	.00190	.00107	107	2,439	12,253	1,679
7	27.6	2,485	.00379	.00214	214	2,271	14,524	1,667
8	27.6	2,425	.00126	.00071	71	2,354	16,878	1,660
9	27.6	2,364	.00253	.00143	143	2,221	19,099	1,712
10	27.6	2,310	.00126	.00071	71	2,239	21,338	1,244
11	27.6	2,267	.00316	.00178	178	2,089	23,427	1,126
12	27.6	2,227	.00126	.00071	71	2,156	25,583	1,118

Table 1C. COMPUTATION OF CUMULATIVE BIRTHS AVERTED PER 100,000 WOMEN ACCEPTING CONTRACEPTION
(Women aged 35; Mean prospective birth interval, 27.6; Monthly probability of sterility, .996727)

100 months after delivery. A further calculation, therefore was necessary, which utilizes the proportion accepting in each month after delivery for purposes of adjusting the proportions ovulating, mean infecundity and number of fecund women. A summary of these calculations provided the entries in Table 1C for month 1 in Columns (b), (d) and (e), respectively. In addition, Column (h) contains a modifying factor correcting the continuation rates for variation in subgroups of a population. This we omitted since we had a population homogeneous in terms of contraceptive continuation rates.

As stated by Wolfers:

Column (a) designates the months after acceptance serially.

Column (b) records the number of surviving fecund users of 100,000 original acceptors. Deductions are made monthly from Column (r) for discontinuations, including pregnancies, and women expected to have become sterile during the previous month. In symbols, Column (b) may be written: $b_a = b_{a-1} - r_{a-1} = b_{a-1} i_{a-1}$

Column (d) records the proportion ovulating.

Column (e) shows the corresponding mean postpartum sterility.

Column (f) represents the average number of women who are not in a state of postpartum sterility during the month. It is obtained by multiplying nonsterile surviving acceptors (Column (b)) by the probability integral (Column (d)) for the middle of the month.

Column (g) records the proportion of acceptors surviving to the beginning of the month who continue use to the end of the month. As these rates are common to all groups it is necessary to adjust them to the specific group for which the table is constructed.
On the assumption that sterility will develop at the same rate among continuers and discontinuers, continuation rates are then multiplied by the sterility factor (C) to give:

Column (i) = (g)xC, the proportion neither discontinuing nor becoming sterile during the month.

Column (j) gives women-months of effective use during the month, assuming that discontinuers and those becoming sterile contribute half a month of use each, and other women a full month. Only the effective population, Column (f) is considered. In symbols, (j) = 1/2(f) (I + i).

Column (k) shows the corrected mean birth interval for the women in Column (f) or (j). It is derived by subtracting from the general mean interval for the group (A), the difference between the value of mean postpartum sterility in Column (e) and the general mean postpartum sterility. In symbols, (k) = A - (F-(e)).

Column (l) gives the number of births prevented on the assumption of zero pregnancy rates for users. It is found by dividing Column (j) by Column (k).

Column (m) shows pregnancy rates for month a per initial acceptor.

Column (n) shows the probability of a live birth resulting from a pregnancy occurring during the month. (n) = 0.7(m), where 0.7 is the live birth proportion.

Column (o) shows live births expected to occur to women using contraception during the month. (o) = 100,000(n).

Column (p) is obtained by subtracting the births in Column (o) from the births prevented in Column (l). It gives the true number of births prevented by contraceptive use during month a.

Column (q) cumulates Column (p) to show the number of births prevented by contraceptive use to the end of the month a.

Column (r) shows the number of surviving nonsterile acceptors at the beginning of the month who discontinue or become sterile during month a. (r) = b(1-(i)).

THE TIME RESPONSE IN AVERTED BIRTHS*

J. C. BARRETT

A calculation of the timing of births that are averted may seem a curious exercise, when not only do the births in question not occur, but the corresponding conceptions may never have existed. However, such a calculation may have considerable use. In order to assess the likely direct impact of a contraceptive program on birth rates it is useful to estimate the number of births that would, in the absence of the program, have occurred among the couples who accept it. Moreover, some time would necessarily elapse before a new 'steady state' in fertility could be reached, even if the program and the potentially fertile population did not change in any way; and it is worthwhile to seek to find the times (for a few years after the start of a program) when the (averted) births would have occurred in its absence, and to examine any inherent oscillations produced in birth rates by it. This question is considered below only for groups of women aged 20 at marriage (a state which is taken to be the start of regular exposure to the risk of conception), but the same methods are applicable to other ages (possibly allowing for mortality), and appropriate combinations of age groups and cohorts in the fertile range may be used to estimate changes in fertility and reproduction rates expected from a program, subject to given conditions, for several years after its start. The methods can also be generalized, by means of convolution, to contraceptive programs that change with time, but these are not considered further.

The demographic effects of contraceptive programs

*Reprinted from *Population Studies*, Vol. XXVI, No. 3, pp. 507-514, by permission of the publisher.

have been treated in various ways by Lee and Isbister (1965); Potter (1969, 1970); Wolfers (1969a, 1969b, 1970, 1971); Fisek (1968); Enke and O'Hara (1969); Chandrasekaran, Murty and Srinivasan (1971); Venkatacharya (1971); and others. Lee and Isbister suggested that births averted could be found by calculating how many women would have given birth, according to age-specific fertility rates of the married population, after making an allowance of about 20 per cent for the presumption that couples adopting family planning are those who have had more children and are accordingly more fecund. Such a method is open to the criticism that women do not enter and leave family planning programs at random points in the various states of the reproductive cycle. Those who enter (often shortly after a birth) are typically not at the same stage, even of the infecund state, as others in that state. On the other hand, several available methods providing more realistic models have been mainly concerned with averages over time. There has been scope for a method that that takes account of variations in the separate components of reproduction, and particularly of heterogeneity of fecundability. It should also be noted that it has been found, in results (Brass 1970) of runs of the computer simulation model with heterogeneity of fecundability used here, that especially for short durations of marriage, high fertility is the result far more of chance than of high fecundability, and this finding has been corroborated by other simulations (Ridley *et al.* 1969). As Chandrasekaran *et al.* (1971) have noted: 'data are required for the specific periods for which changes in births are to be estimated: (i) for all acceptors from the initiation of the program, the number of births which would have occurred during the period if the method had not been accepted from the program; (ii) for all acceptors from the initiation of the program, the number of births which would occur during the period in spite of acceptance of the method. These may be accidental births or births expected to occur after discontinuation of the use of the method.'

The sudden introduction of a contraceptive

program in a population may sometimes be expected to produce, like an impulse response in a servomechanism, transient oscillations in fertility rates. We ask how soon these disappear, and find the numbers of births directly averted in the first few years after acceptance of the program, in relation to the times of the reproductive cycle at which women (or their husbands) become acceptors. No cognizance is taken of losses and failures of contraceptive devices, which are assumed to be 100 per cent effective and lasting. Thus the chief concern is with the first problem posed by Chandrasekaran *et al.*, and furthermore, in the most simple situation, no contraception occurs apart from the program. The results should apply more directly to sterilization programs (which is not to say that sterilization is necessarily the most desirable method) or to programs of contraception of high use-effectiveness. But the results are also intended as a guide in situations that are less extreme, and as a prerequisite to more comprehensive analyses, since if the relatively small number of births referred to in the second problem of Chandrasekaran *et al.* has any measurable effect on the nature of the oscillations, it will be to decrease rather than to increase their magnitude.

In the Appendix a simplified macro-analytical model is described and a transform (6) is derived for the fraction of women who are fecund at any time. Similar macro-analytical methods have been used to find means and variances of birth intervals by Perrin and Sheps (1964), and by Srinivasan (1966). However, it is generally found that the use of a formula such as (6) is attended by several disadvantages. First, it does not allow for the finite duration of reproductive life (not more than a few decades); this factor produces 'truncation effects' which become increasingly apparent at higher ages and parities (Sheps *et al.* 1970). Secondly, for more realistic models than we treat macro-analytically, we wish to use parameters (e.g. for the durations of states) that vary with women's ages, parities, etc. Thirdly, though advantage may be taken of the greater generality offered by macro-analysis, it may not be convenient for obtaining numerical results. These difficulties can be largely overcome by simulation. I have given a detailed specification of the simulation model used here (Barrett 1971). It is perhaps sufficient to repeat that the parameters have been chosen either to fit fertility data for the Census of Ireland, 1911, or to be, as far as possible, reasonably representative of an unselected population of women. Incorporated stochastically in the computer program is the possibility that couple sterility may occur at any time, e.g. earlier than the menopause, together with a β-distribution of ages at menopause, a Pascal distribution for the duration of post-partum infecundity between births, and age-dependent probabilities of foetal death and of stillbirth. Live birth pregnancies occupy ten lunar months (10/13 year), and stillbirths nine.

Results obtained for runs representing the reproductive histories of 1,000 women (which is about the minimum number, if these runs are not to be vitiated by sampling errors) are shown in the graphs. Figure 1 shows the births occurring among a cohort of women who married at t = 0 at age 20. Consequently no births occur sooner than at 10 lunar months, when there is a wave attributable to conceptions in the first month of marriage (assumed to commence in the fecund state). After a scarcely discernible under-shoot the graph of birth rates settles to around 28.2 births per 1,000 women per month (the reciprocal of the mean live birth interval), later falling very slightly.

In Figure 2 is shown the birth rate for a cohort of women who instead give birth at t = 0. (There are often a number of practical reasons for preferring to begin a contraceptive program close to this point in the cycle; see Wolfers 1970.) After the minimum interval of post partum infecundity, conception and pregnancy, the rate begins to rise and eventually reaches the same level as in Figure 1.

The run for Figure 3 is similar to that for Figure 2, except that second births were not included in the birth rate, which accounts for its slower rise.

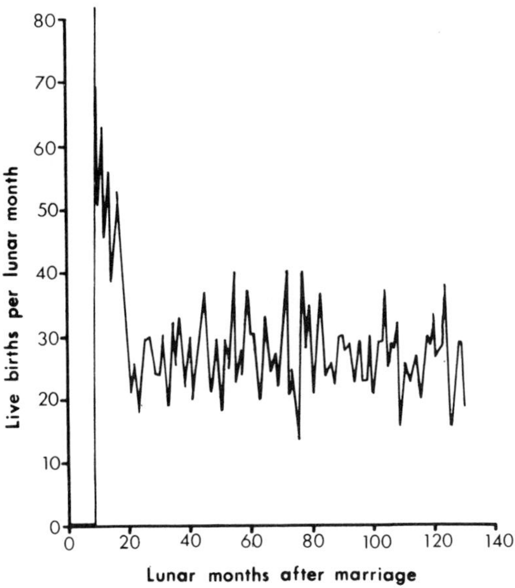

Figure 1. BIRTH INTERVALS FOR A COHORT OF 1,000 WOMEN WHO MARRIED AT t = 0 AT AGE 20

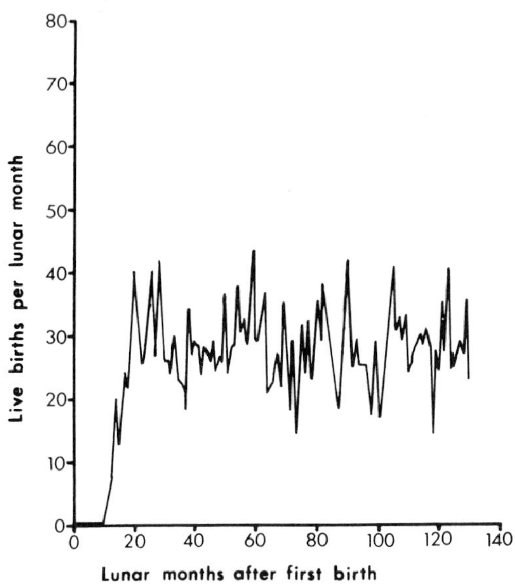

Figure 2. BIRTH INTERVALS FOR A COHORT OF 1,000 WOMEN WHO GAVE BIRTH AT t = 0

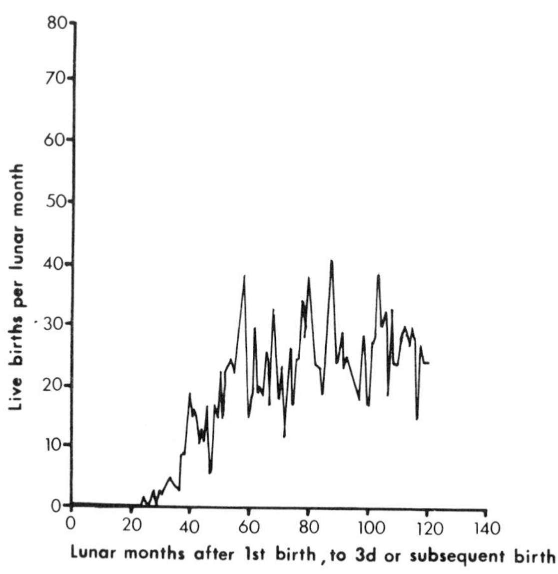

Figure 3. INTERVALS FROM 1ST TO 3RD OR SUBSEQUENT BIRTH, FOR A COHORT OF 1,000 WOMEN WHO GAVE BIRTH AT t = 0

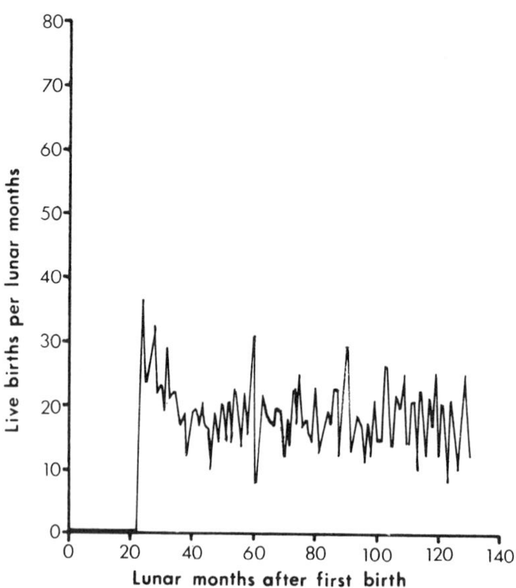

Figure 4. BIRTH INTERVALS FOR A COHORT OF 1,000 WOMEN WHO GAVE BIRTH AT t = 0 AND WERE STERILIZED AFTER THE SECOND PREGNANCY IF t < 12

Figure 4 shows the subsequent birth rate for a cohort of women who give birth at $t = 0$ as in Figure 2. However, in this hypothetical cohort, women (or their husbands) who conceive within 12 months of the first birth (i.e. for $t<12$) are assumed to become sterilized very soon afterwards (irrespective of which of the three possible outcomes was otherwise fated to occur as a result of the pregnancy) and therefore contribute no births at all. The mean level to which the birth rate tends to fall (after a wave following twelve months fecund interval plus ten months gestation) is markedly reduced, not only because a proportion (which forms about 29 per cent in this case) of women (or men) are sterilized, but also because the remaining ones tend here to be selected from among the least fecund, in view of their relatively long interval (over twelve months) preceding conception. The latter factor contributes also to the slower fall in the mean level of the birth rate following the peak.

The birth rate fluctuates irregularly from month to month in these runs for only 1,000 women, due to random sampling. It is in some ways more informative, therefore, to show instead the percentage of women who are pregnant, in pregnancies leading to a live birth. This is depicted in Figure 5 for a cohort of 4,000 women who conceive at $t = 0$. This graph is somewhat analogous to 'percentage labelled mitoses' curves which are used in cell population kinetics (Barrett 1966).

The graphs shown here have a number of features in common which may be noted. Generally the first wave can be discerned, but any subsequent waves are too highly damped to have any practical effect. It is concluded that after at most three years after the start of the program any oscillations have in effect ceased, no matter at what stage of the reproductive cycle women become acceptors. From theoretical considerations the damping is produced by variations in the lengths of post partum infecundity, by variations in the length of the fecund interval, and by pregnancy wastage. The numerical results have been derived for

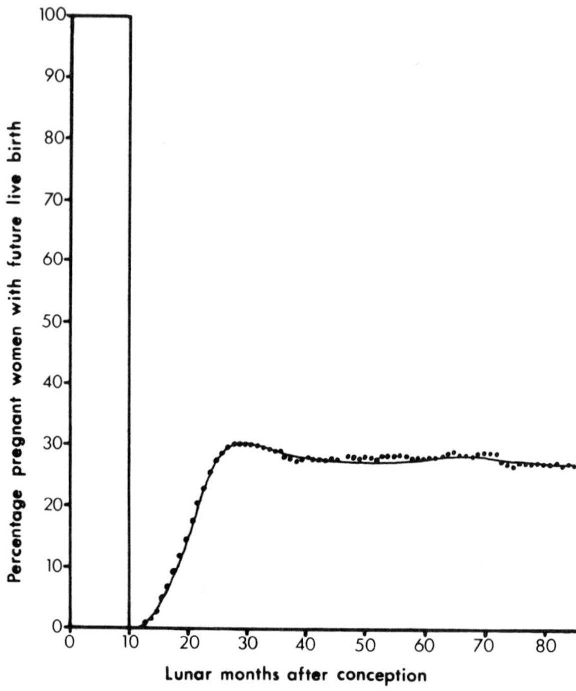

Figure 5. PERCENTAGE OF WOMEN PREGNANT, IN PREGNANCIES LEADING TO A LIVE BIRTH, IN A COHORT OF 4,000 WOMEN

typically the same population of married women in each case, and no account has been taken of the selection for fecundability which may exist to a small extent among some acceptors (but see above). One can predict, however, that the damping factor would be somewhat less, and a further wave perhaps discernible, in a population of women whose infecund intervals were not so varied (Sheps and Menken 1971), who had experienced less pregnancy wastage, or whose fecundabilities were greater. Even so, consideration of the macro-analytical model leads to the conclusion that the main features derived from these simulation runs should be substantially unaffected when extended to natural populations. And the finding that oscillations in the number of averted births are damped out relatively soon after the start should help to simplify the problem of assessing the direct effects of contraceptive programs.

REFERENCES

Barrett, J. C. 1966. A mathematical model of the mitotic cycle and its application to the interpretation of percentage labelled mitoses experiments, Journal of the National Cancer Institute 37: 443-450.

Barrett, J. C. 1970. Optimized parameters for the mitotic cycle, Cell and Tissue Kinetics 3: 349-353.

Barrett, J. C. 1971. Use of a fertility simulation model to refine measurement techniques, Demography 8: 481-490.

Bellman, R. and J. M. Danskin 1954. A survey of the mathematical theory of time-lag, retarded control and hereditary processes, Report 256, RAND Corporation, Santa Monica, California.

Brass, W. 1970. Outline of a simple birth distribution model for the study of systematic and chance components of variation, Proceedings of 3rd Conference on the Mathematics of Population, Chicago.

Chandrasekaran, C., D. V. R. Murty and K. Srinivasan 1971. Some problems in determining the number of acceptors needed in a family planning programme to achieve a specified reduction in the birth rate, Population Studies 25: 303-308.

Churchill, R. V. 1944. Modern Operational Mathematics in Engineering. New York: McGraw-Hill.

Enke, S. and D. J. O'Hara 1969. Estimating fertility changes from birth control measures, Studies in Family Planning 46: 1-5.

Fisek, N. H. 1968. Births averted by family planning programmes, Studies in Family Planning 33: 1-7.

Lee, B. M. and J. Isbister 1965. The impact of birth control programs on fertility, In Family Planning and Population Programs, B. Berelson, *et al.* (eds.), Chicago: Univ. of Chicago Press, pp. 737-758.

Perrin, E. B. and M. C. Sheps 1964. Human reproduction: a stochastic process, Biometrics 20: 28-45.

Potter, R. G. 1969. Estimating births averted in a family planning program, In Fertility and Family Planning: A World View, S. J. Behrman *et al.* (eds.), Ann Arbor: Univ. of Michigan, pp. 413-434.

Potter, R. G. 1970. Births averted by contraception: an approach through renewal theory, Theoretical Population Biology 1: 251-272.

Ridley, J. C., M. C. Sheps, J. W. Lingner and J. A. Menken 1969. On the apparent subfecundity of non-family planners, Social Biology 16: 24-28.

Sheps, M. C., J. A. Menken, J. C. Ridley and J. W. Lingner 1970. Truncation effects in closed and open birth interval data, Journal of American Statistical Association 65: 678-693.

Sheps, M. C. and J. A. Menken 1971. A model for studying birth rates given time dependent changes in reproductive parameters, Biometrics 27: 325-343.

Srinivasan, K. 1966. An application of a probability model to the study of inter-live birth intervals, Sankhya B 28: 175-182.

Venkatacharya, K. 1971. A model to estimate births averted due to IUCD's and sterilizations, Demography 8: 491-505.

Wolfers, D. 1969a. The means of measurement of the impact of a family planning program, Proceedings of Pakistan International Family Planning Conference, Dacca, pp. 451-460.

Wolfers, D. 1969b. The demographic effect of a contraceptive program, Population Studies 23: 111-140.

Wolfers, D. 1970. Post Partum Intra-Uterine Contraception in Singapore. Amsterdam: Exerpta Medica.

Wolfers, D. 1971. The Singapore family planning programs: further evaluation data, Proceedings of International Population Conference, London, Liège: International Union for the Scientific Study of Population.

ACKNOWLEDGMENTS

I am indebted to Mr. W. Brass for helpful suggestions.

APPENDIX

MACRO-ANALYTICAL MODEL

The reproductive history of a woman consists of a series of alternations between states. The first is taken to be the fecund state, and the frequency function for its duration t is denoted by $f_1(t)$. The next state (pregnancy) is entered with probabilities θ_2, θ_3, θ_4 (where $\theta_2 + \theta_3 + \theta_4 = 1$), with frequency functions $f_2(t), f_3(t), f_4(t)$ respectively for the durations associated with stillbirth, foetal death and live birth. Following the first two types of pregnancy the woman soon returns to the fecund state, but following a live birth a state of infecundity with duration $f_5(t)$ intervenes. For convenience, any infecundity after foetal death or stillbirth is included in $f_2(t)$ or $f_3(t)$. The durations of states are taken to be independent.

If these frequency functions and any parameters associated with this renewal process are constant with time, age, parity, etc., we can formulate the probability $H_i(t)$ that a woman who is in the fecund state at $t = 0$ will be for the ith time at some point in a fecund state again at time t. Denoting Laplace transforms by asterisks,

$$f_i^*(s) = \int_0^{\infty} e^{-st} f_i(t)dt \tag{1}$$

$$sH_0^* = 1-f_1^*, \tag{2}$$

and

$$sH_1^* = [\theta_2 f_2^*+\theta_3 f_3^*+\theta_4 f_4^* f_5^*]\,[1-f_1^*]\,f_1^* \tag{3}$$

since the convolution $\int_0^t f_5(x)f_4(t-x)dx$ is the frequency function for the length of the infecund state plus the gestation interval for a live birth. Also,

$$sH_2^* = [\theta_2 f_2^* + \theta_3 f_3^* + \theta_4 f_4^* f_5^*]^2 \, [f_1^*]^2 \, [1-f_1^*] \, . \qquad (4)$$

And in general,

$$sH_n^* = [\theta_2 f_2^* + \theta_3 f_3^* + \theta_4 f_4^* f_5^*]^n \, [f_1^*]^n \, [1-f_1^*] \, . \qquad (5)$$

Now,

$$|(f_1^*)(\theta_2 f_2^* + \theta_3 f_3^* + \theta_4 f_4^* f_5^*)| < 1.$$

Therefore, by d'Alembert's ratio test, the infinite series $s(H_0^* + H_1^* + H_2^* + \ldots)$ is absolutely convergent, and can be summed to give the transform of the probability that the woman is in the fecund state at time t after the original entry to the fecund state (e.g. just married):

$$sH^* = s(H_0^* + H_1^* + H_2^* + \ldots)$$

$$= \frac{1-f_1^*}{1-[\theta_2 f_2^* + \theta_3 f_3^* + \theta_4 f_4^* f_5^*] \, f_1^*}. \qquad (6)$$

Furthermore, if the numerator is multiplied by f_5^*, the formula applies to the fecund fraction in a cohort of women who instead give birth at $t = 0$; and the omission of f_1^*, from the numerator of sH^* is appropriate for a cohort who instead conceive at $t = 0$. Other cohorts may be treated in similar ways.

This formula is equivalent to that derived by Barrett (1966, 1970) in the solution of a problem analogous to the present one, namely to find the probability that a cell is in the state of synthesizing deoxyribonucleic acid, DNA (a process that, interestingly enough, also appears to occupy a discrete phase of a cycle in all types of cells except certain bacteria) at a time differing by t from the time of cell division (in mitosis).

The Laplace transform H^* can generally be inverted (Churchill 1944) to provide the fraction $H(t)$ of women who are fecund at time t, and the birth rate can be obtained by similar means. Cauchy's theorem of residues shows that $H(t)$ is the sum of residues of $e^{st}H^*(s)$ at the poles of $H^*(s)$. The functions f_i^* must be replaced by forms which depend on the data available. For example, the following corresponds to a simplification of the fertility model of Barrett (1971), replacing geometric distributions by similar exponential distributions for convenience, and replacing the β-distribution of fecundability by a constant probability of 1/9 per lunar month:

$$f_1^* = \frac{1}{1+9s},$$

$$\theta_2 f_2^* = \frac{0.19\, e^{-3s}}{1+0.45s},$$

$$\theta_3 f_3^* = 0.02\, e^{-9s} e^{-2s},$$

$$\theta_4 f_4^* = 0.79\, e^{-10s},$$

and

$$f_5^* = \left(\frac{1}{1+5s}\right)^2 e^{-s}. \tag{7}$$

In this case the poles of (6) are located at the roots of the transcendental equation:

$$1+9s = \frac{0.19\, e^{-3s}}{1+0.45s} + 0.02\, e^{-11s} + \frac{0.79\, e^{-11s}}{(1+5s)^2}. \tag{8}$$

The two smallest roots (apart from $s = 0$) are $s = -0.11 \pm 0.21i$, giving a period of $2\pi/0.21$ lunar months, or about 2.3 years, after which time the amplitude of the wave of fecundable women (as distinct from the birth rate) is reduced to a fraction $e^{-2\pi 0.11/0.21}$ or about 3 per cent of its former value.

Similar combinations of fixed time lags and exponential decays occur in control systems associated with 'hereditary' processes (Bellman and Danskin 1954).

A MIGRATION MODEL

ARTHUR S. BOUGHEY,
JAMES B. PICK
and
GORDON N. SCHICK

Demographers are traditionally reluctant to predict population trends. One reason for this is the rapid change which can occur in fertility rates. A second is the necessity to anticipate population *mobility*. In this century there has been a continuation of the mass migration from rural to urban areas which began as a consequence of the Industrial Revolution. More recently there has occurred a massive exodus from the inner city to the suburbs, and a vast regional redistribution of populations. The last American census revealed that more than half the counties in the United States suffered a net migration loss of population. In approximately one third of the counties this migration loss was so high that it exceeded the natural increase, and the county suffered an overall decline in population. Reflecting these instances of declining county populations, dramatic rises have occurred in the population of a number of other counties.

In underdeveloped countries too, in- and out-migration is becoming of greater significance. The flight to urban areas parallels the movement which began over a century ago in the developed countries. It also is associated with mass movements from less favorable to more favorable regions. Although fewer demographic statistics are available for these underdeveloped countries, it is nevertheless important to try to construct predictive models of mobility patterns for them also.

PREVIOUS MIGRATION MODELS

Much of the previous work on population mobility has stressed the desirability of utilizing *net* rather than *gross* migration rates. That is, it was the balance of movement rather than individual in- or outmigration which was emphasized. In many cases what was studied was not so much total in- and out-migration as its type, that is migration according to race, socio-economic class, or occupation. Studies of the so-called 'brain drain' are an example of these specific types of investigation. Morrison (1972) has recently provided a critical appraisal of population movement in the United States of a specific nature. He identifies four key factors which are likely to influence future trends in mobility behavior. First, there is the effect of the apparent recent and rapid decline in fertility. Second, there is a reduction in rural-urban migration; net migration from rural counties has declined during the last decade by about 13 per cent of what it was in the previous decade of the 1950's. Third, there is an accentuation of the already uneven distribution of population because of intermetropolitan migration. Fourth, Morrison notes a marked decline in the preference for city life.

One of the more important analyses of general migration was undertaken by Stouffer (1960). His formulas allowed for in- and outmigration but ignored age distribution. Lee (1966) summed up migration hypotheses with emphasis on a two-region system. Age-specific migration in a multiregional system was treated by Rogers (1968) by a large matrix which included separate submatrices for projection of population change due to vital rates and to in- and out-migration. Tabah (1968) presented an expanded matrix similar to that of Rogers which further divided the population into urban-rural, employed-unemployed and male-female. A system similar to the closed model presented in this paper was used by the U.S. Census Bureau (1967) to project state and regional migration;

the main difference lies in their use of a vector for the calculation of outmigrants.

The predictive mobility model described here does not attempt a further analysis of the factors to which Morrison and others have directed attention. It is concerned simply with the construction of a computer model capable of the empirical forecasting of the amount of mobility to be anticipated within the U.S. population over 15 years starting from 1967.

In the closed model in the present paper, a modified Leslie matrix is used. In recent analyses of inter-SMSA migration, Greenwood and Sweetwood (1972) used a complicated regression formula which takes into account economic variables but ignores age structure.

One change from the previous models cited lies in the modification of the open model, such that vital rates for inmigrants are made dependent on duration of residence in the arrival area. Estimates of duration were made by Morrison (1971). Another change in the open model is the choice of an algorithm for estimation of inmigrants.

DESCRIPTION OF THE MODEL

In this empirical predictive model one key element is the treatment of outmigration as a demographic factor producing effects essentially similar to those of mortality. Individuals leave a population either by dying or by migrating. Just as mortality tables express the expectation of dying, so similar tables may be constructed to express the expectation of migration.

The mobility model has been designed to predict age-specific migration in the United States. The terms *open* and *closed* to migration are defined as follows: in a region closed to migration, there is no net movement across the borders of the region (or group of regions combined) in a given time period; an open region can have either positive or negative net movement across its boundaries. The net regional population movement, summed over all regions, can be chosen either as open or closed migration, but migrants are not separated by destination.

The two sub-models (closed and open) are implemented in separate 500-statement FORTRAN programs. The life table and projection subroutines are modified from standard routines (Keyfitz and Fleiger 1971). LIFE is called to construct all life tables and PROJECT to perform the five-year projections.

Treatment of Outmigration

Outmigration is calculated similarly whether for a closed or open total region. The Leslie population projection matrix is modified by equating the deceased with outmigrants. In other words once a person has left a region he is assumed never to return (equivalent to death). Rates of outmigration are calculated for one year (they are averaged by the program for longer periods if yearly statistics are unavailable). The rates are computed in the same way as in the standard definition of mortality rates (outmigration during one-year period divided by mid-year population).

One-year mortality rates (M_x) are converted to death probabilities [v] over time period t by the formula

$$_t v_x = \frac{(t) \cdot (M_x)}{1 + (t - S_v)\, M_x}$$

where S_v is the death separation factor for interval t, that is, the mean number of years lived in the interval by persons dying in the interval.

Similarly one-year outmigration rates (N_x) are converted to probabilities of occurrence of outmigration by

$$_t n_x = \frac{(t) \cdot (N_x)}{1 + (t - S_n)\, N_x}$$

where S_n is the outmigration separation factor defined analogously to S_v.

For estimation of ${}_5r_x$, the probability of a person aged x to x + 5 neither outmigrating nor dying ("surviving"), the relationship is:

$${}_5r_x = 1 - {}_5v_x - {}_5n_x$$

This is so because the three possibilities, remaining alive within the region, outmigration, and death, are mutually exclusive.

Once ${}_5r_x$ for all age groups is calculated, standard techniques can be used to obtain life tables for the combined risks. Calculation of life years "lived" for interval 0 - 1 uses an S_n of .45 (as compared to S_v of .11). For interval 1 - 4, S_n is set at 1.8 (compared to S_v of 1.5) and for interval 5 - 9 both S_n and S_v are 2.5 (Long 1972).

In the output of the life tables, S_c, the separation factor for the combined probability ${}_5b_x = {}_5v_x + {}_5n_x$, is printed. It is set at .196 for age group 0 - 1, 1.8 for age group 1 - 4, 2.5 for age group 5 - 9; for all other age groups S_c is computed by the modified subroutine LIFE and generally assumes a value of 2.5 ± .1.

Tables 1, 2 and 3 show an unmodified life table, a life table modified for outmigration by the normal population, and a life table modified for outmigration by the highly mobile segment of the population (see below). These charts use the standard life table headings (see Keyfitz 1968). For the case with no outmigration, the column labeled Q(X) represents ${}_5v_x$, the column A(X) represents S_v, and M(X) represents M_x.

AGE	PP	DD	Q(X)	L(X)	D(X)	LL(X)	AGE
0	1681748	33586	0.019620	100000	1962	98242	0
1	6727000	5855	0.003474	98038	341	391301	1
5	9787751	3618	0.001847	97697	180	488036	5
10	10198731	2914	0.001428	97517	139	487255	10
15	9436501	5121	0.002714	97378	264	486264	15
20	8453752	5400	0.003194	97114	310	484813	20
25	6855426	5138	0.003755	96803	363	483160	25
30	5834646	6730	0.005782	96440	558	480921	30
35	5694428	10910	0.009537	95882	914	477287	35
40	6162141	17384	0.014013	94968	1331	471715	40
45	6264605	25476	0.020141	93637	1886	463754	45
50	5756102	34202	0.029337	91751	2692	452420	50
55	5207206	44943	0.042363	89060	3773	436375	55
60	4589812	56733	0.060212	85287	5135	414401	60
65	3869542	76983	0.095318	80151	7640	382839	65
70	3128831	100054	0.149073	72512	10810	336920	70
75	2271173	117808	0.231687	61702	14296	273878	75
80	1408727	115198	0.340060	47406	16121	197140	80
85	968522	137081	1.000000	31285	31285	221042	85

AGE	M(X)	A(X)	TT(X)	R(X)	E(X)	MM(X)	AGE
0	0.019971	0.104	7527762	0.0000	75.278	0.019971	0
1	0.000870	1.500	7429520	0.0000	75.782	0.000870	1
5	0.000370	2.500	7038219	0.0000	72.041	0.000370	5
10	0.000286	2.625	6550183	0.0000	67.170	0.000286	10
15	0.000543	2.635	6062928	0.0000	62.262	0.000543	15
20	0.000640	2.567	5576664	0.0000	57.424	0.000639	20
25	0.000752	2.642	5091851	0.0000	52.600	0.000749	25
30	0.001160	2.706	4608691	0.0000	47.788	0.001153	30
35	0.001916	2.676	4127770	0.0000	43.050	0.001916	35
40	0.002821	2.652	3650484	0.0000	38.439	0.002821	40
45	0.004067	2.650	3179769	0.0000	33.948	0.004067	45
50	0.005950	2.646	2715015	0.0000	29.591	0.005942	50
55	0.008646	2.635	2262595	0.0000	25.405	0.008631	55
60	0.012392	2.657	1826220	0.0000	21.413	0.012361	60
65	0.019956	2.655	1411819	0.0000	17.614	0.019895	65
70	0.032283	2.628	1028980	0.0000	14.191	0.031978	70
75	0.052197	2.577	692059	0.0000	11.216	0.051871	75
80	0.081775	2.525	418182	0.0000	8.821	0.081775	80
85	0.073579	7.065	221042	0.0000	7.065	0.141536	85

Table 1. LIFE TABLE OF UNITED STATES FEMALES, UNMODIFIED (NO MIGRATION)

AGE	PP	DD	Q(X)	L(X)	D(X)	LL(X)	AGE
0	96942	1935	0.041812	100000	4181	96864	0
1	387780	337	0.089191	95819	8546	366183	1
5	560132	207	0.078133	87273	6819	419316	5
10	572207	163	0.073047	80454	5877	387621	10
15	534015	289	0.094315	74577	7034	356304	15
20	493951	315	0.158400	67543	10699	311191	20
25	390391	292	0.142478	56844	8099	262978	25
30	318024	366	0.111538	48745	5437	229293	30
35	319529	612	0.093860	43308	4065	205899	35
40	358391	1011	0.079813	39243	3132	188089	40
45	373527	1519	0.072998	36111	2636	173839	45
50	355251	2110	0.075406	33475	2524	161055	50
55	317534	2740	0.083578	30951	2587	148345	55
60	281841	3483	0.098660	28364	2798	135003	60
65	239140	4757	0.134776	25566	3446	119476	65
70	206979	6618	0.183175	22120	4052	100742	70
75	154751	8027	0.262207	18068	4738	78674	75
80	97848	8001	0.367583	13331	4900	54445	80
85	68551	9702	1.000000	8431	8431	59564	85

AGE	M(X)	A(X)	TT(X)	R(X)	E(X)	MM(X)	AGE
0	0.043166	0.196	3854778	0.0000	38.548	0.019971	0
1	0.023339	1.800	3757914	0.0000	39.219	0.000870	1
5	0.016262	2.500	3391731	0.0000	38.864	0.000370	5
10	0.015161	2.508	2972416	0.0000	36.946	0.000286	10
15	0.019741	2.643	2584795	0.0000	34.659	0.000543	15
20	0.034380	2.521	2228490	0.0000	32.994	0.000639	20
25	0.030809	2.365	1917300	0.0000	33.729	0.000749	25
30	0.023712	2.345	1654422	0.0000	33.940	0.001153	30
35	0.019742	2.382	1425129	0.0000	32.907	0.001916	35
40	0.016652	2.405	1219230	0.0000	31.068	0.002821	40
45	0.015164	2.452	1031141	0.0000	28.555	0.004067	45
50	0.015673	2.496	857302	0.0000	25.610	0.005942	50
55	0.017438	2.522	696247	0.0000	22.495	0.008631	55
60	0.020728	2.564	547902	0.0000	19.317	0.012361	60
65	0.028840	2.576	412898	0.0000	16.150	0.019895	65
70	0.040221	2.566	293423	0.0000	13.265	0.031978	70
75	0.060219	2.537	192683	0.0000	10.664	0.051871	75
80	0.090002	2.509	114009	0.0000	8.552	0.081775	80
85	0.082913	7.065	59564	0.0000	7.065	0.141536	85

Table 2. LIFE TABLE OF NEW ENGLAND REGION FEMALES, MODIFIED (OUTMIGRATION OF NORMAL POPULATION INCLUDED)

AGE	PP	DD	Q(X)	L(X)	D(X)	LL(X)	AGE
0	96944	1935	0.078867	100000	7887	94085	0
1	387778	337	0.219557	92113	20224	328005	1
5	560132	207	0.196958	71889	14159	324048	5
10	572207	163	0.184850	57730	10671	261317	10
15	534015	289	0.234099	47059	11016	208341	15
20	493951	315	0.374491	36042	13498	145755	20
25	390391	292	0.336895	22545	7595	91755	25
30	318024	366	0.266929	14950	3990	63696	30
35	319529	612	0.222168	10959	2435	48202	35
40	358391	1011	0.182789	8524	1558	38447	40
45	373527	1519	0.157392	6966	1096	31948	45
50	355251	2110	0.149797	5870	879	27079	50
55	317534	2740	0.150591	4990	752	23033	55
60	281841	3483	0.161448	4239	684	19475	60
65	239140	4757	0.199334	3555	709	16001	65
70	206979	6618	0.239532	2846	682	12519	70
75	154751	8027	0.313023	2164	677	9114	75
80	97848	8001	0.412469	1487	613	5885	80
85	68551	9702	1.000000	874	874	6172	85

AGE	M(X)	A(X)	TT(X)	R(X)	E(X)	MM(X)	AGE
0	0.083826	0.196	1754877	0.0000	17.549	0.019970	0
1	0.061658	1.800	1660792	0.0000	18.030	0.000870	1
5	0.043695	2.500	1332787	0.0000	18.539	0.000370	5
10	0.040837	2.439	1008739	0.0000	17.473	0.000286	10
15	0.052877	2.553	747422	0.0000	15.883	0.000543	15
20	0.092604	2.447	539081	0.0000	14.957	0.000639	20
25	0.082777	2.239	393327	0.0000	17.446	0.000749	25
30	0.062648	2.231	301572	0.0000	20.173	0.001153	30
35	0.050512	2.292	237875	0.0000	21.706	0.001916	35
40	0.040527	2.321	189674	0.0000	22.251	0.002821	40
45	0.034319	2.371	151226	0.0000	21.709	0.004067	45
50	0.032471	2.418	119278	0.0000	20.321	0.005942	50
55	0.032628	2.446	92199	0.0000	18.475	0.008631	55
60	0.035141	2.487	69166	0.0000	16.317	0.012361	60
65	0.044282	2.499	49691	0.0000	13.980	0.019895	65
70	0.054453	2.491	33690	0.0000	11.838	0.031978	70
75	0.074337	2.479	21171	0.0000	9.782	0.051871	75
80	0.104201	2.475	12057	0.0000	8.109	0.081775	80
85	0.097690	7.065	6172	0.0000	7.065	0.141536	85

Table 3. LIFE TABLE OF NEW ENGLAND REGION FEMALES, MODIFIED (OUTMIGRATION OF HIGHLY MOBILE SEGMENT OF POPULATION INCLUDED)

In the modified Tables (2 and 3), the column Q(X) represents ${}_5r_x$, A(X) represents S_c, and M(X) represents the average of M_x and N_x. In Table 2, the column Q(X), which is the probability of either dying or outmigrating, seems to be higher in value for all age groups and, through averaging with survivorship probabilities, has partly assumed the standard distribution of outmigration probabilities, with characteristic bulges noticeable in ages 0 - 5 and 20 - 35. The E(X) column of life expectancy in Table 2 is lowered greatly to 38.548, that is, one has only 38 years to live and stay within the Pacific states. In Table 3, outmigration rates have more greatly influenced the Q(X) column and E(X) is only 17.549.

After construction of the altered life table, projection is accomplished by a modified Leslie matrix. This matrix is the standard means of projecting future population by age groups where age intervals are of a fixed size (in this case, 5 years) and are equal to the length of projection time intervals. A more complete explanation is available in standard sources (Keyfitz 1968, Keyfitz and Fleiger 1971).

The values of the matrix responsible for mortality losses (the sub-diagonal elements) are based on the ${}_tL_x$ column of a particular life table. Thus by using a Leslie matrix based on the above modified and unmodified life tables, projection can be accomplished which either includes or does not include losses of outmigrants. In Figure 1, the complete closed model is diagrammed. In going from Box 1 to Box 2, Matrix M uses ${}_sL_x$ values from an unmodified life table, and hence no outmigrants are lost. In proceeding from Box 1 to Box 3, however, since matrix A uses values based on a modified life table, the resultant population in 1972 does not include the past five years' outmigrants. Thus the difference of persons in Box 2 minus persons in Box 3 is the past five years' outmigrants (shown in Box 4a). A similar subtraction is done with Boxes 7 and 8 to obtain Box 10a, and with

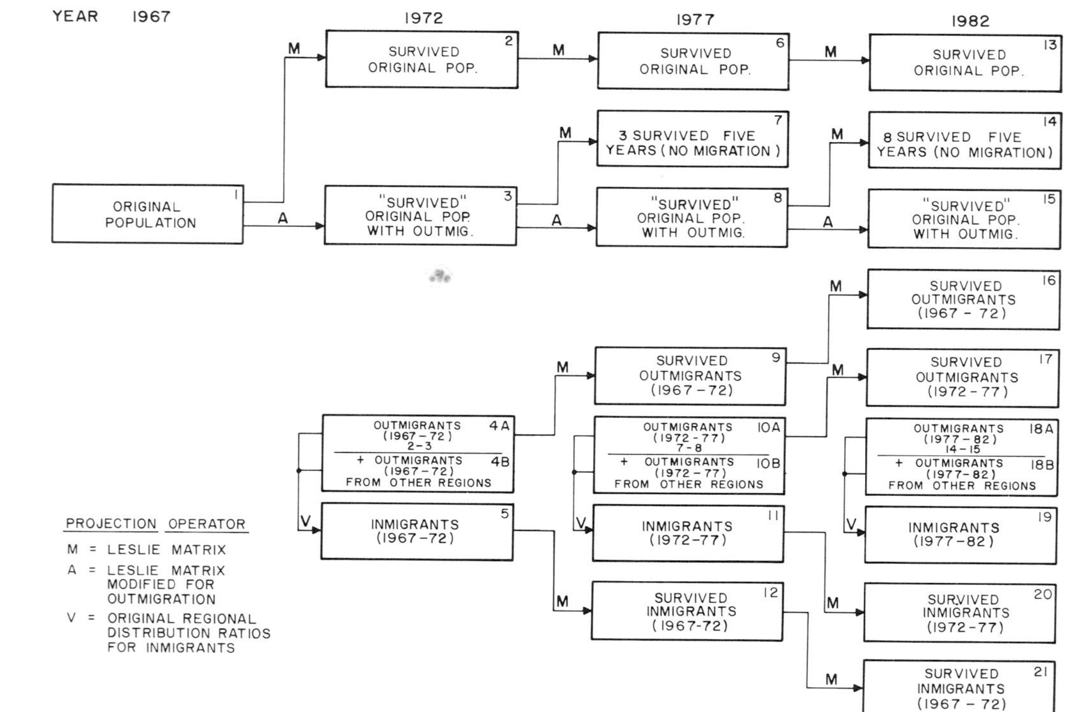

Figure 1. CLOSED MIGRATION MODEL FOR ONE REGION

Boxes 14 and 15 to obtain Box 18a.

An important aspect of this subtraction process is that subtraction takes place at the end of a time period and so the past five years' outmigrants have survived up to the end of the interval. This means that the quantity of outmigrants in Box 4a includes the children of the outmigrants born after departure and before 1972, but does not include outmigrants who died after departure and before 1972. This procedure of including as outmigrants children of outmigrants, and excluding outmigrants who die, is used for all tabulations of outmigrants. For instance, Box 16 includes 20 years' births, and excludes 20 years' deaths involving the original 1967-72 outmigrants.

Treatment of Inmigration

Unlike its antithesis, inmigration is handled differently in the closed and open models. In the first, the outmigrants are taken as the basis for migration flux both ways. Since in any five-year projection period the total number of outmigrants for all the regions equals the total number of inmigrants, the age-specific number of inmigrants can be estimated by redistribution of total outmigrants of the past five years according to initial regional and age-specific inmigration rates. For each five-year period

$$M(x,r,p) = [J(x,p)] \cdot [1(x,r,i)]$$

where: M(x,r,p) is the number of inmigrants of age group x to x + 5, region r, and for time p - 5 to p.
1 (x,r,i) is the initial rate of inmigration, by age group x to x + 5, region r, and initial period i - 5 to i per total number of outmigrants of age group x to x + 5 in all regions of this period.
J(x,p) is the total of outmigrants in all regions for time p - 5 to p.

This can be expressed as

$$J(x,p) = \sum_{r} n(x,r,p)$$

where n(x,r,p) is the number of outmigrants. Thus the closed method bases inmigration on initial rates in relation to outmigration, and simply redistributes the outmigrants of each five-year period. Since in this case the prime objective is that the system be balanced, and since outmigrants cannot return (as outmigration is treated analogously to mortality), inmigrants are not allowed to leave. Because inmigrants have been shown to have heightened outmigration (Morrison 1971) this assumption necessarily introduces an error. Since last year's inmigrants are the last five years' outmigrants redistributed, they represent inmigrants who survive up to the end of the time period. Similarly, when they are projected forward, they include children and exclude the deceased from among the original inmigrants.

In the open case a different method is employed. This second sub-model (Figure 2) is intended for the special instance in which the location is attractive to inmigrants in such a way that numbers of inmigrants (in any age group) are a linear function of total population size. An area which has not reached its limits of growth, such as the Pacific or Mountain states, is best fitted by this second sub-model. Before applying it, past trends must be analyzed to determine if this relationship has previously held true. The program can be altered to operate with non-linear variation with total size, or with other algorithms.

Here inmigrants are calculated by

$$M(x,r,p) = [R(x,r,i)] \; . \; [P(r,p) - \sum_{x} M(x,r,p)]$$

where: M(x,r,p) is the number of inmigrants for one region by age over period p - 5 to p "survived" to time p.

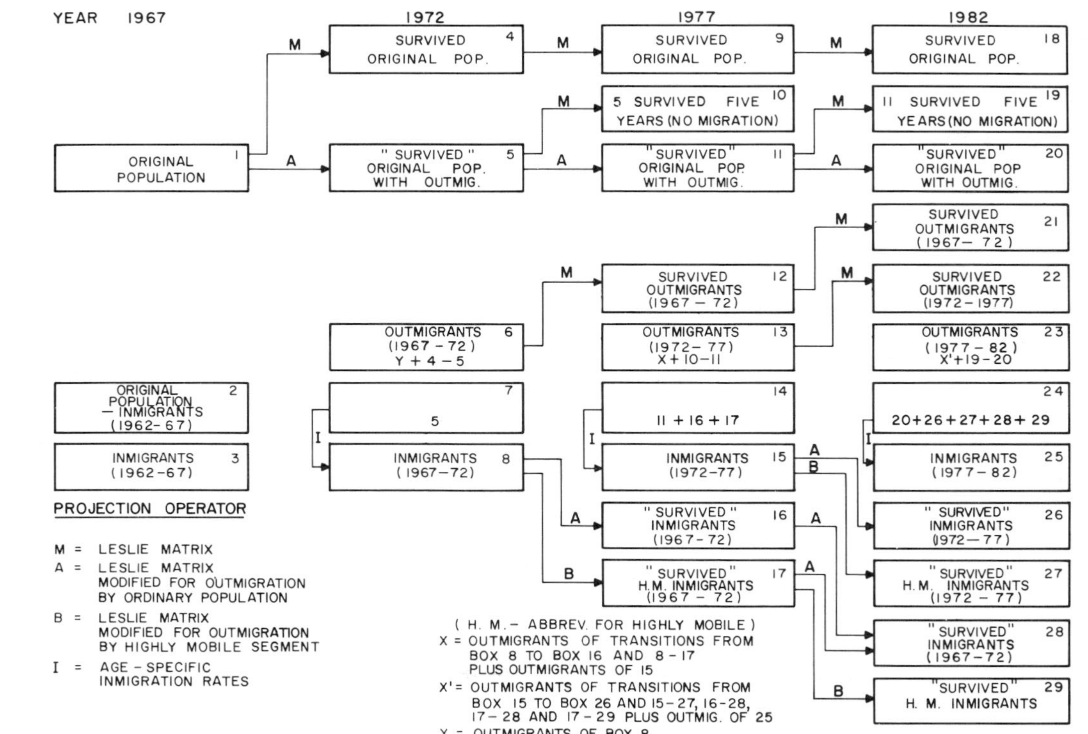

Figure 2. OPEN MIGRATION MODEL FOR ONE REGION

$P(r,p)$ is the total population of a region at time p.
$R(x,r,i)$ is the age-specific rate of in-migration determined by the initial year solution to the above equation.

Instead of solving this equation for $M(x,r,p)$, the right hand term of the above product is determined by looking at the components of population at a particular time. For example in Figure 2 for the year 1977, $P(r,p)$ is represented by boxes 11, 15, 16, and 17. $\sum_x M(x,r,p)$ is represented by Box 15. Thus the difference $P(r,p) - \sum_x M(x,r,p)$ is simply Boxes 11, 16, and 17. $M(x,r,p)$ is estimated as follows. Let $G(x,r,p)$ be the number of inmigrants of a particular age group who arrived during a five-year period. Then a good approximation to $M(x,r,p)$ (assuming a linear arrival of inmigrants with time over the five-year period) is

$$\frac{G(x,r,p) + G^1(x,r,p)}{2}$$

where $G^1(x,r,p)$ is $G(x,r,p)$ projected 5 years. Since data from the U.S. Census is closest to $G(x,r,p)$ (deceased inmigrants and inmigrant children are not included in the count of inmigrants), this approximation is necessary. In the program the projection to obtain $G^1(x,r,p)$ assumes outmigration at standard rates for 18 per cent of the arriving group and heightened outmigration (2.7 times the normal rates) for the remainder (Morrison 1971). This method of calculation is not applicable to unusually high migration rates, because the right hand term in the above product becomes small or possibly zero for certain age groups.

In this second sub-model, inmigrants, having arrived, are more realistically treated. Following the general results of a recent study (Morrison 1971) each inmigrant group is split into two segments for the next five years (see Figure 2 for the preceding and following points). One, consisting of 91 per cent of the newly arrived inmigrants, assumes outmigration rates in accordance with the normal population. The remainder, a highly mobile group, has greatly increased outmigration rates (2.7 times the normal). Five years after the end of the arrival period, the survivors of the majority group above are continued with the same rates, whereas survivors of the highly transient minority are split in two. Half of these remain highly mobile; half are returned to normal rates. In the program the age, sex-specific composition of the various inmigrant groups (at any time point) can be printed out.

In the open model inmigrants who later outmigrate (after arrival) are collected and added to the outmigrants for the period. The added outmigrants are represented by Y in Box 6, X in Box 13, and X^1 in Box 23 of Figure 2.

APPLICATIONS OF THE MODEL

Application of this model was made to nine regions of the United States (Table 4). The sources of data were as follows: population figures (1970 Census), birth and death rates (1967 Census), and state migration rates for in- and outmigration (1960 Census). Total out- and inmigrants were calculated for a state and distributed in accordance with 1955-60 national age-specific rates (Bogue 1969) to the age groups, which were then totalled regionally and nationally. The results of the main projection routine give age- and sex-specific regional projections. Total population, inmigrants, outmigrants, and net migrants are graphically portrayed by the computer program for each region (summarized in Tables 5 and 6).

Table 5 shows, under the headings "1967 Population" and "1982 Population," the population affected by both in- and outmigration under the closed model, for the first and last years of the projection process. These totals are represented in Figure 1 by Box 1 (for 1967) and Boxes 15 + 19 + 20 + 21 (for 1982). Totals for the two intermediate years of the projection process are represented in Figure 1 by Boxes 3 + 5 (for 1972) and Boxes 8 + 11 + 12 (for 1977). The column labeled "In Migration" represents the total number of inmigrants from 1967 to 1982 (Boxes 19 + 20 + 21 in Figure 1). The column labeled "Out Migration" is computed exactly like "In Migration," and "Net Migration" is "In Migration" minus "Out Migration."

Table 6 for the open model represents the above quantities in exactly the same manner. The "In Migration" column again represents the sum of all inmigrant groups survived with no outmigration up to 1982. The "Out Migration" column includes the outmigrants of inmigrant groups which were present five years before. However, it does not include outmigrants of the previous five years' inmigrants. The reason for not including these in the total is that these rapid outmigrants are not included as inmigrants either.

Interaction Between Fertility and Migration

The interaction of fertility and migration was examined by adjusting age-specific birth rates to a replacement level (our assumption here is that replacement is a reasonable lower limit of fertility). This is accomplished by dividing fertility rates used above by the present Net Reproduction Rate. Table 7 shows (in column 1) populations of each region projected to 1982, based on our standard fertility estimates, compared with projections based on replacement fertility (column 2). An interesting question is how the marked reduction in 1982 population (column 3) which results from lowered fertility can be compared in its effects with the effects of possible variations in migration rates.

Column 5 shows the ratio of loss due to lowered

Region	States
New England	Maine, New Hampshire, Vermont, Massachusetts, Rhode Island
Mid Atlantic	New York, New Jersey, Pennsylvania
E.N. Central	Ohio, Indiana, Illinois, Michigan, Wisconsin
W.N. Central	Minnesota, Iowa, Missouri, N. Dakota, S. Dakota, Nebraska, Kansas
S. Atlantic	Delaware, Maryland, District of Columbia, Virginia, W. Virginia, N. Carolina, S. Carolina, Georgia, Florida
E.S. Central	Kentucky, Tennessee, Alabama, Mississippi
W.S. Central	Arkansas, Louisana, Oklahoma, Texas
Mountain	Montana, Idaho, Wyoming, Colorado, New Mexico, Arizona, Utah, Nevada
Pacific	Washington, Oregon, California, Alaska, Hawaii

Table 4. KEY TO REGIONAL DISTRIBUTION SUB-DIVISIONS IN TERMS OF COMPONENT STATES

fertility, and the absolute value of net migration for each region at the lower fertility figure. This comparison shows that a reduction of fertility to replacement levels would be of relatively little importance in the Pacific, Mountain, E.S. Central, and W.N. Central regions. This is in keeping with the traditional large inmigration to the Pacific states, recent inmigration to the Mountain states, and outmigration

Closed Region	1967 Population	1982 Population	Change 1967-82 Population	Natural Increase[1]	Net Migration	In Migration	Out Migration
N. England	11841663	12998622	1156959	1559512	-402553	2865974	3268526
Mid Atlantic	37199040	39252686	2053646	4462959	-2409313	5801267	8210580
E.N. Central	40252476	44058606	3806130	6136150	-2330020	8071840	10401861
W.N. Central	16319187	16888416	569229	2133959	-1564730	4094597	5659327
S. Atlantic	30671337	38224522	7553185	4822893	2730292	13001291	10270999
E.S. Central	12800470	13489850	689380	1991836	-1302456	2962045	4264501
W.S. Central	19320560	21476863	2156303	3135196	-978893	5067624	6046517
Mountain	8281562	11175003	2893441	1488236	1405205	5174262	3769057
Pacific	26522631	35586526	9063895	4211544	4852351	11822592	6970242
Total	203208926	233151094	29942168	29942285	-117	58861492	58861610

[1] Estimated by subtracting net migration from population change 1967-82

Table 5. FIFTEEN YEAR REGIONAL MIGRATION PROJECTIONS FOR CLOSED MODEL

Open Region	1967 Population	1982 Population	Change 1967-82 Population	Natural Increase[1]	Net Migration	In Migration	Out Migration
N. England	11841663	12877959	1036296	1579941	-543645	3034215	3577861
Mid Atlantic	37199040	39005140	1806100	4661277	-2855177	6135948	8991126
E.N. Central	40252476	43836748	3584272	6284484	-2700212	8681655	11381868
W.N. Central	16319187	16448780	129593	2157180	-2027587	4047707	6075294
S. Atlantic	30671337	38344136	7672799	4743891	2928958	14458867	11529908
E.S. Central	12800470	13250473	450003	1987100	-1537097	3015755	4552852
W.S. Central	19320560	21266983	1946423	3116595	-1170172	5374219	6544391
Mountain	8281562	11186132	2904570	1479407	1425163	5710885	4285723
Pacific	26522631	36791122	10268491	4106835	6161656	14337013	8175357
Total	203208926	233007473	29798547	30116660	-318113	64796265	65114381

[1]Estimated (approximately) by subtracting net migration from population change 1967-82

Table 6. FIFTEEN YEAR REGIONAL MIGRATION PROJECTIONS FOR OPEN MODEL

Region	(1) Population 1982	(2) Population 1982 with Replacement Fertility	(3) Change in Population (1) - (2)	(4) Net Migration with Replacement Fertility	(5) % (3)/(4) (Absolute Value)
N. England	12998622	12665456	333166	-391906	.850
Mid Atlantic	39252686	38270466	982220	-2350584	.418
E.N. Central	44058606	42907231	1151375	-2273005	.506
W.N. Central	16888416	16450642	437774	-1519612	.288
S. Atlantic	38224522	37226175	998347	2663948	.375
E.S. Central	13489850	13137585	352265	-1264120	.279
W.S. Central	21476863	20910317	566546	-950545	.596
Mountain	11175003	10868331	306672	1360599	.225
Pacific	35586526	34653962	932564	4725110	.197
Total	229081821	223354213	5727603	-115	

Table 7. RELATIVE MAGNITUDE OF POSSIBLE FERTILITY AND MIGRATION EFFECTS, 1962

from the rural states in the E.S. Central and W.N. Central areas. Lowered fertility would have the greatest relative effect in the New England and W.S. Central states.

SUMMARY AND CONCLUSIONS

(1) Closed and open computer models providing a 15-year projection of in- and outmigration have been constructed for regions of the continental United States.

(2) The programs of the two models follow and print out the entire age structure of all regional and migration categories within the population at all time points.

(3) If age-specific migration data are unavailable, a preliminary sorting program can distribute inmigrants (and outmigrants to subregion age groups) according to subregion total rates and the national age distribution of migrants.

(4) The programs were implemented for the 1967 U.S. population and show trends in nine regions.

(5) The relative loss to the population through the lowering of fertility to the replacement value is compared with total net migration for the regions.

(6) In the present version of the model, initial birth, death, and migration rates apply for the entire length of prediction. Future modifications to the programs will incorporate the inconstant case, in which rates vary in estimated ways. It is also possible to incorporate into the framework of the computer programs more complex determinants of migration, such as economic, geographical and social factors.

REFERENCES

Bogue, D. J. 1969. Principles of Demography. New York: Wiley.

Greenwood, M. J. and D. Sweetwood 1972. The determinants of migration between standard metropolitan statistical areas, Demography 9: 665-681.

Keyfitz, N. 1968. Introduction to the Mathematics of Population. Reading, Mass.: Addison Wesley.

Keyfitz, N. and W. Fleiger 1971. Population, Facts and Methods of Demography. San Francisco: Freeman.

Lee, E. S. 1966. A theory of migration, Demography 3: 47-57.

Long, L. H. 1972. New estimates of migration expectancy in the United States, paper presented at the annual meeting of the Population Association of America, Toronto, Canada, April 13-15, 1972.

Lowry, I. S. 1966. Migration and Metropolitan Growth: Two Analytical Models. San Francisco: Chandler.

Morrison, P. A. 1971. Chronic movers and the future redistribution of population: a longitudinal analysis, Demography 8: 171-184.

Morrison, P. A. 1972. Population Movements and the Shape of Urban Growth: Implications for Public Policy, (WN-7497-1-CPG). Santa Monica: Rand Corporation.

Morrison, P. A. 1967. Duration of residence and prospective migration, Demography 4: 553-561.

Rogers, A. 1968. Matrix Analysis of Interregional

Population Growth and Distribution. Berkeley: Univ. of California Press.

Stouffer, S. A. 1960. Intervening opportunities and competing migrants, Journal of Regional Science 2: 1-26.

Tabah, L. 1968. Representation matricielle des perspectives de population active, Population 23: 437-476.

United States Bureau of the Census 1967. Illustrative projections of the population of states, 1970 to 1985, Series P-25 (No. 326).

ON MATHEMATICS OF POPULATION SIMULATION MODELS

B. V. SHAH

INTRODUCTION

A life history of an individual consisting of all vital events (birth, marriage, divorce, death) can be considered to be a stochastic process. In general, the probabilities of occurrence of a vital event will depend on many characteristics (age, sex, race, marital status, parity) of an individual describing the "state" to which the individual belongs. Models using discrete time intervals utilize transition probability matrices where element (ij) represents the probability that an individual in state i at the beginning of the period will be in state j at the end of the period. Continuous time models use instantaneous intensities of probability, such as force of mortality, and generate events accordingly.

In this paper, a general mathematical model underlying most demographic models is described. Interrelationships between the parameters used for discrete and continuous time models, and also between "macro" and "micro" models are derived.

The results presented in this paper are not new. These have been derived by many individuals and are scattered in the demographic literature. Keyfitz (1969) gives a summary of population mathematics with an excellent bibliography. An attempt has been made here to consider different types of demographic simulation models and to compare them.

A variety of mathematical techniques have been used to construct population simulation models. Almost all population models start out with an initial population of individuals and their characteristics; the models simulate the events that happen to the individuals and predict the nature of the population at a future date. The models differ in the way they handle events, time and individual members of the population:

(1) Some models treat large groups of individuals at a time; these are called "macro" models. Some models simulate life histories of each individual separately; these are called "micro" models.
(2) A model may treat time as a continuous or a discrete variable. The classical integral equation of Sharpe and Lotka (1911) treats time as a continuous variable, whereas the matrix model of Leslie (1945) deals with discrete time points.
(3) A model may be stochastic or deterministic. In a deterministic model, probabilities are entered for each group of individuals, but the population is assumed to evolve at exactly its expected values. Stochastic models utilize individual probabilities and the theory of Markov processes or branching processes, to give a more realistic picture of the true variation in population changes.

In the next three sections, we shall consider mathematical aspects of these differences.

MACRO- AND MICRO-MODELS

In all models, individuals are identified by their characteristics, such as sex, age, race, marital status, etc. The probabilities with which different events such as death, divorce, marriage, birth, occur in each individual's life depend on his characteristics. As the events happen, the individual's characteristics may change. An account over time of individuals by their characteristics, and by the events that happen to them, provides a picture of population dynamics. Each distinct combination of characteristics of an individual is called a distinct state of the individual. The events then are equivalent to a change in the state of an individual.

Macro-models consider a group of individuals

having the same state at the beginning of a period and simulate how many of these will be in the different possible states at the end of a period. Micro-models consider one individual at a time. By repeatedly simulating individuals with the same characteristics as many times as the size of the group, micro-models can achieve the same expected results as macro-models. It may be noted that in deterministic models, this simply means multiplication by the proper weight. Thus, there is hardly any difference between micro- and macro-deterministic models. Stochastic models may appear to require more work than deterministic models, but this is not the case if the number of attributes is large. Mathematically, it is possible to produce (stochastically) identical results by either type of model, provided sufficient computer time and storage are available. In a sense, a micro-model can take on some of the characteristics of a macro-model if each individual is assumed to represent a cluster of individuals. The stochastic aspect then reflects the appropriate variation between clusters, but is deterministic regarding the within-clusters variability. One could then use smaller population sizes in the computer but must arrange to weight the individual results according to the cluster size.

CONTINUOUS AND DISCRETE TIME MODELS

The major difference between continuous and discrete time models arises in the treatment of the events. Consider an individual that is capable of being in a finite or denumerable number of states, which may be labelled by integers 1, 2, ... For each time t, define a discrete random variable $X(t)$ whose value indicates the state of the individual; that is the event "$X(t) = j$" is the same as the event "the individual is in the j-th state."

Denote by $P_{ij}(\tau,t)$ the conditional probability that an individual is in state j at time t, given that he was in state i at time τ; that is

$$P_{ij}(\tau,t) = \Pr\{X(t) = j \mid X(\tau) = i\}$$

If the process is assumed to be Markovian, then it can be shown that

$$P_{ik}(\tau,t) = \sum_j P_{ij}(\tau,r)\, P_{jk}(r,t) \qquad i,\ k = 1,2,\ldots, \quad \tau < r < t;$$

With some regularity assumptions, if the intensity functions (Chiang 1968) $\gamma_{ij}(\tau)$ are given by

$$\gamma_{ij}(\tau) = \left\{ \frac{\partial}{\partial t} P_{ij}(\tau,t) \right\}_{t=\tau}, \qquad i \neq j$$

and

$$\gamma_{ij} = - \sum_{j \neq i} \gamma_{ij}$$

then it can be shown that

$$\frac{\partial}{\partial t} P_{ik}(t) = \sum_j P_{ij}(t)\, \gamma_{jk} = \sum_j \gamma_{ij}\, P_{jk}(t).$$

If $\underset{\sim}{P}$ and $\underset{\sim}{\gamma}$ are matrices defined as

$$\underset{\sim}{P}(\tau,t) = \begin{bmatrix} p_{11}(\tau,t) & p_{12}(\tau,t) & \cdots \\ p_{21}(\tau,t) & p_{12}(\tau,t) & \cdots \\ \vdots & \vdots & \vdots \end{bmatrix},$$

$$\underset{\sim}{\gamma}(t) = \begin{bmatrix} \gamma_{11}(t) & \gamma_{12}(t) & \cdots \\ \gamma_{21}(t) & \gamma_{22}(t) & \cdots \\ \vdots & \vdots & \vdots \end{bmatrix},$$

and if $\underset{\sim}{V}(t)$ is assumed to be independent of t, then the solution of the equations is given by

$$\underset{\sim}{P}(\tau,t) = e^{(t-\tau)\underset{\sim}{V}}$$

Of course, the solution is derived assuming the following obvious restrictions:

$$\sum_j P_{ij}(\tau,t) = 1$$

$$\sum \gamma_{ij}(t) = 1$$

and $$\underset{\sim}{P}(\tau,\tau) = \underset{\sim}{I},$$

where $\underset{\sim}{I}$ is an identity matrix.

These differential equations were first derived by Kolmogorov (1931); detailed discussions may be found in Feller (1957) and Chiang (1968). Explicit solutions and the extensions of the results to a nondenumerable infinity of states may be found in the references.

If the parameters γ_{ij} for continuous time models were obtained by solving the known $P_{ij}(\tau,t)$ of a discrete model, then the simulation results from both models will be the same. In discrete time models the results will be available only at discrete time intervals, whereas in continuous models, results can be obtained for any time point.

DETERMINISTIC AND STOCHASTIC MODELS

The differences between the mathematical treatment of stochastic and deterministic models are great, since the two approaches are quite different. In a deterministic model, the objective is to express mathematically the numbers of individuals in various subgroups of a given population consequent to events which happen to members of the population. The objective with a stochastic model is to obtain the frequency, or probability, distributions of the subgroup sizes when events occur in some random fashion to population members, either individually or in groups.

Deterministic continuous time models were the first ones to be used in demographic analysis. Lotka (1922) considered such models based on integral equations similar to

$$B(t) = \int_0^\infty B(t-x)\, p(x)\, i(x)\, dx$$

where

$B(t)$ = total female births per annum at time t

$p(x)$ = probability of survival from birth to age x

$i(x)$ = female births per annum at age x.

Extensive work has been done on methods for obtaining algebraic and numerical solutions of integral equations by Lotka (1939), Feller (1941), Coale (1957) and Keyfitz and Flieger (1968). However, because of mathematical complexities, the treatment has been primarily limited to age-specific death and birth rates. Considerations of factors such as marital status, parity, and family planning practices are not found in the literature.

Discrete time deterministic models, commonly known as matrix multiplication models, have been used extensively in population projections. The mathematical theory is based on the writing down of expected values for a simple branching process (Galton and Watson 1874).

Discrete time stochastic macro-models have been considered by Pollard (1966), Goodman (1967) and Thomas (1969). Pollard (1966) has derived relations for the higher moments of branching processes; these turn out to be mathematically similar to the expected value equations of Leslie (1945).

Only a simple modification is required to convert a matrix multiplication deterministic type model to a purely stochastic model that will simulate a random realization for the given population. Assume there are N_i individuals in the i-th state at the start of the period and P_{ij} is the probability that an individual in the i-th state at the beginning of the period is in the j-th state at the end of the period. Then the number of individuals in the j-th state at the end of the period in the deterministic model is:

$$M_j = \sum_i N_i P_{ij}.$$

With a stochastic model, one can generate M^*_{ij}, $j = 1, 2, \ldots$; for each i, these quantities have a multinomial distribution with parameters $P_{i1}, P_{i2}, \ldots$ and N_i. Then

$$M^*_j = \sum_i M^*_{ij}.$$

Computationally, calculation of M^*_j will involve only a few more steps than that of M_j. Both models will be identical except for stochastic variation that will be present even in real life populations.

Recently, Orcutt *et al.* (1961), Hyrenius *et al.* (1964, 1966, 1967) and Horvitz *et al.* (1967) have developed stochastic microsimulation models. A common procedure adopted in these models is to generate a life history as a random process for each individual in the computer population, and then to compute appropriate aggregates for various subgroups of population as desired.

In theory, it is possible to derive higher order moments (Pollard 1966) for expected value models, and thus provide reasonable knowledge of likely variation. With many runs stochastic models will give good estimates of expected values and distribution of any desired characteristics of a population. The results derived under two models with appropriate parameters will be mathematically equivalent, because, under very general regularity conditions, there is a one to one correspondence between the distribution and all its moments.

COMPARISON OF TWO TYPES OF MODELS

In the previous sections, we discussed the equivalence of some aspects of population models. In this section, we compare two special groups of population models: discrete time, deterministic (expected value) macro-models and continuous time, stochastic, micro-models. For the sake of convenience we shall refer to these as 'macro-' and 'micro-' models respectively.

Macro-models, such as those by Leslie, Beshers, Potter and Sakoda, are often called matrix multiplication models. Micro-models have been discussed by Hyrenius *et al.* (1964, 1966, 1967), Horvitz *et al.* (1967) and Ridley and Sheps (1966).

In a macro-model, it is necessary to evaluate the number of population members in each of the possible states, and to consider all feasible transitions from one state to another in order to calculate expected values or higher moments of number of individuals in various subgroups of population. In a micro-model, on the other hand, one starts with a sample of individuals, in which some states may not be represented, and only those transitions between states which take place in the life of each individual in the sample are considered. Several simulation runs with the same hypothesis are therefore required to obtain reliable expected values and standard errors of estimates of desired characteristics of the population. It is important to note that a macro-model can obtain unbiased estimates of only linear functions of numbers in various subgroups of the population, at different times, without any sampling error. Stochastic micro-models make possible unbiased estimation of any function of the numbers in various subgroups of the population; these estimates are subject to some sampling errors.

In addition to the basic difference in the approach, the two models differ widely in the actual handling of data and storage. Let us assume that there are v variables or attributes (of each individual) that are considered important. These attributes have N_1, N_2, ..., N_v distinct states or levels and so they make $M = N_1 \times N_2 \times \ldots N_v$ possible states. Let us also assume that one needs to consider a total population of size P.

In a micro-model, for each of the individuals, a record of v characteristics is maintained. Total storage required is equal to vP words. The events that happen to each of the P persons will be processed separately.

In a macro-model, the information about the number of individuals having each combination of attributes is kept. This requires M words of storage. It is also necessary to compute probabilities for persons in each possible combination for transitions that may be possible, and then to arrive at the numbers at the end of the period.

As an example, consider a population model with 20 age levels, 2 sex levels and 2 marital status levels. The macro-deterministic model will require storage of 80 words. A similar micro-model with 10,000 individuals will require 30,000 words of storage. In this case, a macro-deterministic model is preferable.

Alternatively, consider a population model with education and income as follows: 80 age levels, 16 education levels, 20 income levels, 2 race levels, 2 sex levels, 3 residence levels, 4 marital status levels and 9 numbers of children levels. The macro-model will require storage and processing of 11,059,200 states, whereas a micro-model with 10,000 individuals will require 80,000 words of storage and processing of 10,000 states. In this case, a microsimulation model should prove to be advantageous.

The second major difference in the two models is in the definition of vital rates. As an example, let us consider death rates for single males 30 to 34 years of age. Assuming the death rate to be constant over this age group, each individual in the group should be subject to the same death rate. Now, consider two individuals aged 30.2 years and 33.5 years at the beginning of the simulation period. In a macro-model with five-year groups, these two individuals will belong to the same age group (30-34 years) and will not be treated separately. They will be subject to the same death rate for the next five years; that is for the actual age 30.2 to 35.2 for the first individual and 33.5 to 38.5 for the second individual. Hence, the appropriate input death rate for the model should be an average death rate for individuals aged 30 to 34 weighted according to their proportions in the population. In practice, one may use the equivalent death rate (survival rate) according to life table proportions of these individuals.

In contrast, a micro-model considers each individual separately. The first individual aged 30.2 years will be subjected to the death rate for the age group 30 to 34 years for the next 4.8 years and to the death rate for the age group 35 to 39 years for the next 0.2 years or the remaining time for the five-year period. Similarly, the second individual aged 33.5 years will be subject to the death rate for single males aged 30 to 34 years for the first 1.5 years and to the death rate pertaining to the 35 to 39 year age group for the next 3.5 years. Thus the input death rate for the 30 to 34 age group in a micro-model should be the "cohort" death rate applicable for the next five years to individuals aged exactly 30 years. This distinction is true for all vital rates, and hence all vital rates used in a micro-model should be cohort rates, applicable to the age group of individuals at the minimum age of the specified age interval.

The third major difference arises because of the required input probabilities. In the case of micro-models, the basic parameters required are net probabilities of each vital event that can occur to an individual. It is essential to derive these from available data and also state assumptions in relation to the net probabilities.

The macro-models require probabilities of transition from one state to another over a unit time. For example in a model with age, sex and marital status, for unmarried males one would need probabilities of survival and remaining single and also the probabilities of surviving and being married.

Even if the assumptions are made with respect to changes in only death rates (or marriage rates), it will be necessary to recalculate all the transition probabilities. If one is dealing with many states this will involve considerable effort. To simplify the calculation of the transition probability matrix $\underset{\sim}{P}(\tau,t)$, it is often assumed that at most one of the feasible events occurs to an individual during the interval $(t-\tau)$. This is not too bad if $(t-\tau)$ is sufficiently small.

In the case of micro-models, the basic parameters required are net probabilities of each vital event that can occur to an individual. It is essential to derive these from available data and also state assumptions in relation to the net probabilities.

In conclusion, the models will yield identical results in the limiting cases, that is, the limit as $(t-\tau) \to 0$ in macro-models and the limit as the number of persons in the computer population, $P \to \infty$ in the equivalent micro-model.

SOME REMARKS

The proponents of macro-models have claimed that macro-models are simple, inexpensive and easy to use compared to micro-models, while those favoring micro-models have argued that micro-models are more versatile, flexible and realistic than macro-models. For simple cases involving only a few characteristics, for example, age and sex only, macro-models are known to be less expensive than micro-models. However, for complex situations involving 15 or 20 characteristics with about a million distinct states, it is doubtful if macro-models will be less expensive or less complex than micro-models.

Until someone designs macro-models that can handle complex situations, it will be impossible to reach a conclusive decision. Meanwhile, individuals who need models for investigating complex situations must turn to micro-models.

REFERENCES

Beshers, J. M. 1965. Birth projections with cohort models, Demography 2: 593-599.

Chiang, C. L. 1968. Introduction to Stochastic Processes in Biostatistics. New York: Wiley.

Coale, A. J. 1957. A new method for calculating Lotka's r - the intrinsic rate of growth in a stable population, Population Studies 11: 92-94.

Feller, W. 1941. On the integral equation of renewal theory, Annals of Mathematical Statistics 12: 243-267.

Feller, W. 1957. An Introduction to Probability Theory and its Applications. Second Edition. New York: Wiley.

Galton, F. and H. W. Watson 1874. On the probability of extinction of families, Journal of the Anthropological Institute 6: 138-144.

Goodman, L. A. 1967. On the reconciliation of mathematical theories of population growth, Journal of Royal Statistical Society, A, 130: 541-553.

Horvitz, D. G. *et al.* 1967. Microsimulation of vital events in a large population, Paper presented at meeting of Population Association of America, Cincinnati.

Hyrenius, H. and I. Adolfsson 1964. A fertility simulation model, Demographic Institute Reports No. 2, Göteborg, Sweden: Univ. of Göteborg.

Hyrenius, H., I. Adolffson and I. Holmberg 1966. Demographic models, Demographic Institute Reports No. 4, Second Report (DM 2), Göteborg, Sweden: Univ. of Göteborg.

Hyrenius, H., I. Holmberg and M. Carlsson 1967. Demographic models, Demographic Institute Reports No. 5 (DM 3), Göteborg, Sweden: Univ. of Göteborg.

Keyfitz, N. and W. Flieger 1968. World Population: An Analysis of Vital Data. Chicago: Univ. of Chicago Press.

Keyfitz, N. 1969. Population mathematics, Paper presented at the International Union for the Scientific Study of Population, London: General Conference, September 1969.

Kolmogorov, A. M. 1931. Über die analytischen Methoden in der Wahrscheinlichkeitsrechnung, Mathematische Annalen 104: 415-548.

Leslie, P. H. 1945. On the use of matrices in certain population mathematics, Biometrika 33: 183-212.

Lotka, A. J. 1922. The stability of the normal age distribution, Proceedings of the National Academy of Sciences 8: 339-345.

Lotka, A. J. 1939. Théorie Analytique des Associations Biologiques. Part II. Analyse démographique avec application particulière à l'espèce humaine (Actualités Scientifiques et Industrielles, No. 780). Paris: Hermann and Cie.

Orcutt, G. H., M. Greenberger, J. Korbel and A. M. Rivlin 1961. Microanalysis of Socio-economic Systems: A Simulation Study. New York: Harper and Row.

Pollard, J. H. 1966. On the use of the direct matrix product in analysing certain stochastic population models, Biometrika 53: 397-415.

Potter, R. G. and J. M. Sakoda 1966. A computer model of family building based on expected values, Demography 3: 450-461.

Ridley, J. C. and M. C. Sheps 1966. An analytic simulation model for human reproduction with demographic and biological components, Population Studies 19: 297-310.

Sharpe, F. R. and A. J. Lotka 1911. A problem in age-distribution, Philosophical Magazine, Series 6, 21: 435-438.

Thomas, V. J. 1969. A stochastic population model related to human populations, Journal of the Royal Statistical Society, 132, Part I, 89-104.

FOOTNOTES ON IMPLICATIONS OF AGGREGATED DATA USED IN POPULATION SIMULATION

PETER KUNSTADTER

Distinctions have been made between macrosimulation and microsimulation, depending on whether events occur to individuals or to the simulated group as a whole (MacCluer 1973). A further distinction may be required, especially among microsimulations, depending on the proposed uses of the simulation output. For some purposes the intent is to look neither at traits of individuals, nor at rates amongst the group as a whole, but rather to examine the distributions within subgroups of the population which are defined as part of the simulation.

My concern in this paper is with the form in which data are used to establish rates or probabilities which are applied to simulated events. I am particularly interested in the implications of the choice of bases for rates in simulations which allow an examination of interrelationships between demographic variables and social structural variables, but the suggestions outlined below should have implications for the interaction of genetic and demographic variables as they are mediated through, or depend on *interaction* within families (i.e., parents and their sets of children). Uncritical use of aggregate figures may distort simulated distributions as compared with real ones.

Examples illustrate the types of problems I have in mind. Suppose one wishes to determine the effect of natural increase or decrease in population size on the distribution of land among heirs, given various systems of inheritance or property transmission. An answer to this question requires information on age, sex, and numerical distribution of offspring within kinship groupings (families), relationship of time of death of parents to time of death of offspring, etc. This problem is analogous to questions of growth and extinction of lineages, for which historical data may be available. Or suppose one wishes to determine the relationship between population size, growth or decline of a population with given birth and death rates, and customary restrictions on choice of marital partners. Hammel and Hutchinson discuss this type of problem in their contribution to this volume.

An answer to either of these kinds of questions requires information on the *distribution* of individuals within and between families or other genealogically defined groupings. *Averages* are not adequate to answer these questions. How might the distribution of family size (number of children surviving to age x) vary depending on the choice of rates which are used, and how, in turn, would the distribution of family size influence the outcome of the simulation of choice of marriage partners?

There has been an unfortunate tendency to argue from the general to the specific. An illustration, slightly out of context, may be found in Hammel and Hutchinson's paper. They argue that the populations of early man "were small and they increased very slowly in the aggregate, so that on the average they were on the knife edge between demographic success and failure most of the time." No one seriously debates the average smallness of the early human groups, nor the apparent fact that as a whole, measured in the long run, the early human population grew at a very slow rate. But what might this mean regarding socio-demographic conditions in any one group at any given time, or over the short run? I see no reason to assume that long run averages are an adequate description of short run processes, especially in small and inherently variable populations.

Low overall growth rates can be achieved in a number of ways. All that is required is a small difference between birth and death rates measured over the appropriate length of time. Vital rates may be approximately balanced at high or low levels, or may fluctuate, for example, so that a substantial surplus of births over deaths is wiped out by an occasional very high incidence of deaths. The choice of demographic model is important because of its influence on distributions within groupings in the population. High birth rates would commonly produce large sibling sets, low birth rates would very rarely do so. Under conditions of high birth and high death rates, a few of the large sibling sets might survive. In spite of the fact that on the average the size of surviving sibling sets under high birth and death rates or low birth and death rates could be the same, the distribution of family size could be different.

So far as I know, the simulation game has not been played systematically with these different demographic models, but the effect of using long term average rather than short term fluctuating rates would be to reduce the variance of the distribution of family sizes. A similar effect would be created by using low birth and death rates as compared to high birth and death rates. These effects may be important if distribution of sibling set size is the subject of study through simulation.

A series of increasingly complicated simulation programs operating on a short run illustrates other dimensions of the problem. If we assume the mean family size of the simulated population is 2.3, and the sex ratio is approximately 1:1, a simple (but very unrealistic) way of creating family groups would be to allow each married couple to have either two or three children, assigning a probability of .3 for the three-child families, all others being considered to be two-child families. Sex might be assigned in such a way that half the sibships contain males, and the other half only females. This program would generate a distribution with *mean* values similar to the average desired, but the range in distribution of family size, and the distribution of children by sex within each family would not be like any real population, since we know that in real populations with mean completed family size of 2.3, couples may have zero, one, two, three, up to 10 or more children, and it is extremely unlikely that all children in each family would be of the same sex.

How can a more realistic distribution of family size and composition be generated? A more complicated program would assign live births to women on the basis of their simulated age, using age-specific (annual) birth rates, and updating the simulation after each simulated annual change of the population's status. The effect of this program would be to give everyone the same birthday, i.e., to allow births to take place only once per year. In terms of the total number of children born, this should have no effect in a sufficiently large population. The rates upon which the probabilities are derived are determined from simply the number of births in a calendar year to women of age x, and this number would be reproduced more or less accurately, depending on the size of the cohort in question. But the distribution of births among families might be distorted by this procedure since two kinds of events are excluded: plural births (twins, triplets, etc.), and multiple birth outcomes in a 12-month period.

What implications might there be for an error of this type, and how serious might the error be? The rate of plural births, as a proportion of total live births, is said to be relatively constant; approximately 20 per 1,000 live births are born in plural births, or, to put it another way, on the average, 1,000 live births require no more than 980 mothers, if plural births are considered. This rate seems relatively unchanged over the past 20 years in the United States, despite the purported effect of birth control pills in causing plural deliveries. Rates in non-whites are five or six per 1,000 higher than in whites, according to the Vital Statistics of the United States (Statistical Abstracts of the United States 1971, Table 63; Vital Statistics of the United States 1966, Table 1-37; Vital Statistics of the United States 1960, Table 2-6; Vital Statistics of the United States 1950, Tables 23 and 24). Textbooks citing foreign sources give similar figures.

Equivalent figures are not readily available on the frequency of multiple pregnancies in the same woman within a single 12-month period. There is an extensive literature on child spacing and on estimating the effects of birth control, but I have not seen figures presented in quite this way. As a first step in determining empirically the total number of multiple pregnancies I have looked at the data from the 1971 Korean Fertility Survey, a collection of reproductive histories from 6,269 women between the ages of 15 and 54 (data collected by the Korean Institute of Family Planning, cited with permission of Dr. Lee-Jay Cho).

The calendar year starts in January, but 12-month periods starting January 1 are only samples of all possible 12-month periods into which a time series might be divided. If we examine the experience of women over 12-month periods starting January 1, February 1, March 1, etc., we can arrive at an estimate of the distortion implied in annual rates as a result of the fact that pregnancies are neither conceived nor terminated on an annual basis. Births are seasonally distributed, thus one would expect multiple pregnancy outcomes for a given woman within a 12-month period to be seasonally variable. We find this to be the case in the Korean materials with the lowest number occurring in 12-month periods starting in January (equivalent to the calendar year) and the highest occurring in 12-month periods starting in April (Table 1). If this finding is generally correct, an estimate based only on *calendar* years (as opposed to a broader sample of 12-month periods) would be too low an estimate of the *clustering* of births among some women. Simulation based on such an estimate would tend to spread out the births among all women, rather than to cluster them among the most fertile women. In other words, the distribution of family sizes would tend to be distorted, becoming less skewed than it should be.

The magnitude of this effect is suggested by preliminary figures from the Korean data, where an average of about 5.35 per cent of livebirths took place within 12 months of a previous livebirth (Table 2). This figure may be a bit low, because the search for plural births revealed that only 0.45 per cent of the live born children were born in plural births, as compared with the average of about two per cent in the U.S. Obviously the 5.35 per cent should not be taken as anything but a preliminary estimate for one sample of one population. The figure might be expected to change depending on the general level of fertility, lactation patterns, etc.

If we assume that the magnitude of multiple births in a single year is around five per cent or more, how might the simulation program be adjusted to handle this? There are several possible ways. If pregnancy completion is to be updated on a simulated annual basis, the age-specific probabilities of *being a mother* one or more times per year might be substituted for the age-specific birth rate. Then the probability of having two (or more) children in a 12-month period could be applied to each of the women identified as being a mother in any given year. The difficulty with this scheme is that the probability of having one or more children in the next year of simulation should be affected by the event of having had one or more children in the first year. What is required is a more sophisticated method of spacing the simulated children.

An alternative method is to assign, at random, completed family size to women in the simulated population, with the distribution of family size based on some empirical or theoretical distribution. There are several drawbacks to this approach, depending on the purpose of the simulation:

(a) The method could tell you nothing of the spacing of children, which might be important if age distribution is a necessary aspect of the simulation in the next generation.

(b) The method could tell you nothing of sex distribution by age in the next generation.

(c) The method would be inadequate to deal with changes in birth rates or death rates which occurred

Starting Month	Number of Mothers	Number of Livebirths	Number of Livebirths Minus Number of Mothers
January	2,198	2,207	9
February	2,175	2,201	26
March	2,190	2,222	32
April	2,309	2,558	249
May	2,399	2,627	228
June	2,255	2,456	201
July	2,136	2,292	156
August	2,894	2,008	114
September	1,979	2,085	106
October	2,088	2,217	129
November	2,147	2,255	108
December	2,178	2,286	108

Table 1. DISTRIBUTION OF LIVEBIRTHS BY MONTH, AND DISTRIBUTION OF LIVEBIRTHS WITHIN TWELVE MONTHS OF PREVIOUS LIVEBIRTH, BY MONTH[a]

[a]Data from 1971 Korean Fertility Survey, cited by permission of Dr. Lee-Jay Cho. The assistance of Mr. James Modecki in calculation of these figures is gratefully acknowledged.

The 6,269 women covered in this survey had an average of 4.1405 livebirths. An average of 5.35 per cent of livebirths took place within 12 months of previous livebirths. The total plural livebirths recorded in this survey was 124, or 0.45 per cent, probably an underestimate.

Women's Age in 1971	Number of Women in 1971	Woman-Years in Reproductive Histories at Specified Ages	Total Age-Specific Livebirths	Number of Livebirths Minus Number of Mothers	Per cent Difference
15	2	6,269	32	0	0.0
16	1	6,267	107	1	0.93
17	5	6,266	336	15	4.46
18	14	6,261	602	25	4.15
19	24	6,247	918	42	4.58
20	46	6,223	1,269	77	6.07
21	63	6,177	1,515	80	5.28
22	110	6,114	1,703	106	6.22
23	138	6,004	1,858	115	6.19
24	199	5,866	1,921	117	6.09
25	191	5,667	1,893	123	6.50
26	210	5,476	1,836	112	6.10
27	231	5,266	1,744	104	5.96
28	208	5,035	1,648	90	5.46
29	243	4,827	1,424	67	4.71
30	233	4,584	1,335	71	5.32
31	218	4,351	1,212	57	4.70
32	252	4,133	1,086	56	5.16
33	246	3,881	914	43	4.70
34	256	3,635	812	38	4.68
35	250	3,379	717	38	5.30
36	227	3,129	584	27	4.62
37	260	2,902	495	17	3.43
38	188	2,642	406	21	5.17
39	232	2,454	353	9	2.55
40	210	2,222	246	7	2.85
41	187	2,012	158	4	2.53
42	167	1,825	142	3	2.11
43	166	1,658	75	0	0.0
44	187	1,492	41	1	0.0
45	172	1,305	23	0	0.0
46	139	1,133	2	0	0.0
47	141	994	4	0	0.0
48	131	853	0	0	0.0
49	147	722	1	0	0.0
50	141	575	1	0	0.0
51	139	434	0	0	0.0
52	98	295	1	0	0.0
53	111	197	0	0	0.0
54	86	86	0	0	0.0
Total	6,269	138,858	27,414	1,466	5.3476

Table 2. AGE SPECIFIC RATES OF MULTIPLE BIRTHS WITHIN TWELVE-MONTH PERIODS

within a generation.

(d) The method might have to be modified to allow women to "die" before completing their reproductive years (or might allow the husband to die), etc. In other words, anything which depended on the timing of events during the woman's reproductive years would be distorted or obscured, but the system might be satisfactory if the interest were primarily in number of offspring.

Another approach would be updating on a monthly basis (which more closely resembles the period within which a woman can conceive a child), working through a series of subroutines which would include the variables of age of woman, whether or not she is presently pregnant, how long she has been pregnant, probability of miscarriage, stillbirth, or livebirth at a given month of pregnancy (and age of mother, parity of mother, etc., if necessary), time since termination of previous pregnancy, type of termination of pregnancy (livebirth, stillbirth, miscarriage at month m, etc.), and present status of liveborn child (alive or dead, nursing or not nursing). Such a series of routines might come closer to simulating the temporal spacing and familial distribution of childbirth than a simple application of age-specific fertility rates, but is expensive in computer time. The degree of improvement in quality of simulation cannot be predicted without comparing the different systems. The example of use of annual birth rates may be considered trivial because ever since Sheps and Perrin's studies of birth as a stochastic process, many population simulations have involved monthly rather than annual rates. Nonetheless, the general conclusions stated above may be valid even if monthly rates are used. Simulation based on monthly rates might be skewed unless the monthly probabilities are seasonally adjusted, are modified to allow for plural births, and use rates based on number of *mothers* for a given number of children at given age of mother.

If probabilities were assigned randomly, this pattern of simulation still would not handle the objection that some women give the appearance of being more fecund than others (although we might ask how much of this apparent difference might be due to "chance" in a sufficiently complex model). A further adjustment (or tuning) of the simulation might be made by designating a proportion of the women or of couples as sterile, or by assigning different probabilities of fecundability to each woman - an increasingly difficult and complicated job.

My general plea in this discussion has been to look for places where aggregating events or failing to differentiate amongst them results in altering distributions such as number of children in completed families.

I want to mention several other problems which have yet to be investigated. I believe population simulation has been relatively negligent in the unstated assumption that social regulation of mating behavior (or inheritance, or what have you) remains stable. In general, this represents the failure to use simulation systematically to look for homeostatic mechanisms.

The question of "sufficient size," or the effect of random variation in small populations, is important to anthropologists because many of the populations we study are relatively small. Kunstadter *et al.* (1963) and Hammel and Hutchinson (1973) have suggested some of the effects of size on the operation of mating systems, but the question has not yet received the systematic investigation it deserves. Size is undoubtedly an important determinant of patterns of population growth and the interaction of growth with effect of various mechanisms commonly applied in societies which directly or indirectly impinge on population growth. It is clear that all population groups must cope with problems of size: become too small and face extinction, become too large and face Malthusian controls. Perhaps simulation is a good way to suggest points at which people need to modify their rules in order to perpetuate their society.

One hypothesis, testable only by simulation, is that in small population aggregates it is essential to have relatively high birth rates, because of the probability of a maldistribution of sexes and ages, at least where monogamy, close age matching, and adherence to the incest and exogamy taboos are norms in mate selection. Simulation would allow us to look, for example, at the minimum size of self-perpetuating units, given different marriage rules and fertility schedules, and might suggest the critical sizes within groups with specified rules, at which point the people might have to relax the rules in order to prevent extinction, or tighten them up to reduce population growth. Systematic investigation of this type might point to the extreme importance for group survival of what might be considered by anthropologists to be rare, exceptional, non-normative events: recruitment of mates from outside, or outmigration.

Polygyny might be examined in this context as a social device which allows populations to survive with reduced fertility while maintaining incest rules (since it does not require one male of proper age and kinship distance for each eligible female). It thus helps to insure that every woman may have a mate, so there may be less pressure to maintain high fertility in order to assure an adequate age-sex distribution to allow choice of marital partners and thus allow adequate reproduction in a small population. Furthermore, the custom of polygyny may itself reduce fertility (by decrease in frequency of intercourse for fecundable women). I simply do not know what the interaction between polygyny and restriction on marriage choice in future generations might be, because a larger proportion of the population might be half-siblings or the descendants of half-siblings, and thus ineligible as marriage partners.

The polygynous marriage system thus may be seen as a more complex self-regulating mechanism which contains within it the possibility of controlling population growth or decline, with minimal rearrangement of rules. In an initial generation the system increases choice of marriage partners, and thus insures a higher possible level of reproduction; in later generations it might reduce the number of eligible partners, thus lowering the potential level of reproduction.

As a final footnote to this paper, I wonder at the meaning or propriety of applying average rates to small samples. In any given simulated short period it is probable that rare events will not occur. What distortion is implied in taking few, short-run, small samples? We have suggested in this paper that rates or the frequency distributions they generate in the simulations may vary in part due to the size of the population involved (sampling error), in part due to the characteristics of the processes which are summarized in the rates, and in part due to modifications in the behavior of the individuals in the population, as they are affected by their past history. The challenge for simulators is to develop models which allow for these sources of variability.

REFERENCES

Hammel, E. A. and D. Hutchinson 1973. Two tests of computer microsimulation: the effect of an incest tabu on population viability, and the effect of age differences between spouses on the skewing of consanguineal relationships between them, In Computer Simulation in Human Population Studies, B. Dyke and J. W. MacCluer (eds.), New York: Seminar Press.

Kunstadter, P., R. Buhler, F. F. Stephan and C. F. Westoff 1963. Demographic variability and preferential marriage patterns, American Journal of Physical Anthropology 21: 511-519.

MacCluer, J. W. 1973. Computer simulation in anthropology and human genetics, In Methods and Theories in Anthropological Genetics, M. H. Crawford and P. L. Workman (eds.), Albuquerque: Univ. of New Mexico Press.

Perrin, E. B. and M. C. Sheps 1964. Human reproduction: a stochastic process, Biometrics 20: 28-45.

COMPUTER GENERATION OF RANDOM VARIATES

WILLIAM M. STITELER, III

The generation of observations on random variables is based on the fact that if you take any random variable, say X, and operate on it by some function to produce a quantity Y (e.g. $Y=X^3$, $Y=\sqrt{X}$), then Y will also be a random variable and will have a different probability distribution. So if one has at his disposal a routine for generating some random variable he might be able, with a little ingenuity, to generate some other random variable of interest. Fortunately it is possible, at least approximately, to generate on a computer a random variable, say U, having a uniform distribution with probability density function

$$f(u) = 1/(b-a) \qquad a \le u \le b$$
$$= 0 \qquad \text{elsewhere.}$$

This random variable can serve as a basis for generating any other random variable once you discover a way in which to operate on U to obtain a random variable having the desired probability distribution. This is usually not too difficult because of some fundamental properties which relate the uniform distribution to other probability distributions.

The inverse technique is sometimes useful for generating random variates having a continuous density function over some interval, say (a,b) (where a and b are not necessarily finite). This technique is based on the fact that if X is a random variable having distribution function F(x) then the random variable defined by U = F(X) will have a uniform distribution over the interval (0,1) regardless of the density function of X. That this is true can be shown by finding the distribution function of the new random variable U and noting that it is the distribution function of a uniformly distributed random variable over (0,1).

Denoting the distribution function of U by G(u) we have

$$G(u) = P(U \le u) = P(F(X) \le u) = P(F^{-1}(F(X)) \le F^{-1}(u))$$
$$= P(X \le F^{-1}(u)) = F(F^{-1}(u)) = u$$

for $0 \le u \le 1$, where the existence of the inverse is insured by the conditions imposed on the density function of X.

So the complete definition of G(u) is

$$G(u) = \begin{matrix} 0 & u < 0 \\ u & 0 \le u \le 1 \\ 1 & u > 1 \end{matrix}$$

which is the desired distribution function.

Several other "standard" techniques which relate the uniform distribution to other distributions are available. They all have a common goal - to assist us in finding a function of one or more uniformly distributed random variables which has some other specific probability distribution.

One fact which is often overlooked is that once one has a routine to generate some random variable other than the uniform he may be able to use this as a "building block" in generating many other random variables. To illustrate this idea let us suppose that we have at our disposal a routine for generating observations on a random variable, say Z, having a standard normal distribution with probability density function

$$f(z) = \frac{1}{\sqrt{2\pi}} e^{-z^2/2} \qquad -\infty < z < \infty$$

One approach to generating this random variable employs the Central Limit Theorem which states roughly that the average of n observations on *any* random variable with a finite variance will be approximately normally distributed as n gets large. If we start with the uniform random variable the distribution of the average converges very rapidly to normality. For many purposes a value of n as small as 10 is quite adequate. Since the variance of a uniform distribution over the interval (0,1) is 1/12 a value of n = 12 greatly simplifies the arithmetic since the standardized random variable $\frac{\bar{u}-\mu}{\sigma}$ becomes $\Sigma u_i - 6$. Therefore, a FORTRAN subroutine for generating a standard normal random variable would be:

```
      SUBROUTINE CLTNOR(Z)
      SUM = 0.
      DO 1 I = 1,12
    1 SUM = SUM + RAND(1.)
      Z = SUM - 6.
      RETURN
      END
```

The inverse technique can also be applied to generating a standard normal random variable by employing a numerical approximation to the inverse of the distribution function. One such approximation is given by Hastings (1955).

```
      SUBROUTINE STDNOR(Z)
      N = RAND(2.)
      ETA = SQRT(ALOG(1./RAND(.5)**2))
      X = (ETA - (2.515517 + ETA*(.802853 + .010328
     1* ETA))/(1. + ETA*(1.432788 + ETA*(.189269
     2+ .001308*ETA))))*(-1.)**N
      RETURN
      END
```

The standard normal generator can be used to generate any other normal distribution by using the transformation $X = \mu + \sigma Z$ which results in X having a normal distribution with mean μ and variance σ^2.

```
SUBROUTINE NORMAL(X,AVE,STDEV)
CALL STDNOR(Z)
X = AVE + STDEV*Z
RETURN
END
```

The gamma distribution with p.d.f.

$$f(x) = \frac{1}{\Gamma(\alpha)\beta^{\alpha}} x^{\alpha-1} e^{-x/\beta} \qquad \begin{array}{l} 0 < x < \infty \\ 0 < \alpha < \infty \\ 0 < \beta < \infty \end{array}$$

which might be a suitable model if the random variable takes only positive values, is related to the standard normal random variable for certain values of the parameters and can be generated using STDNOR. If one takes k independent standard normal observations, say $Z_1, Z_2, \ldots, Z_k$, and forms the sum

$$X = Z_1^2 + Z_2^2 + \ldots + Z_k^2,$$

then X has the p.d.f.

$$f(x) = \frac{1}{\Gamma(\frac{k}{2})\, 2^{k/2}} x^{\frac{k}{2} - 1} e^{-x/2} \qquad 0 < X < \infty$$

This is called a chi-square distribution with k degrees of freedom and it is clear that this distribution is a special case of the gamma distribution with $\alpha = \frac{k}{2}$ and $\beta = 2$.

```
      SUBROUTINE CHISQ(X,K)
      X = 0.
      DO 1 I = 1,K
      CALL STDNOR(Z)
    1 X = X + Z**2
      RETURN
      END
```

Other gamma distributions can be obtained by using the fact that if X has a gamma distribution with parameters α and β then cX, where c is a positive constant, will have a gamma distribution with parameters α and $c\beta$. This means that we can generate any gamma distribution so long as the parameter α is some multiple of 1/2.

```
SUBROUTINE GAMMA(X,ALPHA,BETA)
CALL CHISQ(X,2*ALPHA)
X = (BETA/2.)*X
RETURN
END
```

If one needs a model with a p.d.f. which is bell shaped but has heavier tails than the normal distribution a good choice might be the Student's t distribution with p.d.f.

$$f(x) = \frac{\Gamma[(k+1)/2]}{\sqrt{\pi k}\,\Gamma(k/2)} \frac{1}{(1+x^2/k)^{(k+1)/2}} \qquad -\infty < x < \infty$$

It is quite easy to generate a Student's t random variable using STDNOR and CHISQ. This follows from the fact that if Z has a standard normal distribution and X has a chi-squared distribution with k degrees of freedom, and if Z and X are stochastically independent, then $Y = Z/\sqrt{X/k}$ has a Student's t distribution with k degrees of freedom.

```
SUBROUTINE STUDNT(Y,K)
CALL STDNOR(Z)
CALL CHISQ(X,K)
Y = Z/SQRT(X/K)
RETURN
END
```

The Cauchy distribution with p.d.f.

$$f(x) = \frac{1}{\pi(1+x^2)} \qquad -\infty < x < \infty$$

is a special case of the Student's t distribution with degrees of freedom equal to one.

Other distributions which are now easy to obtain include the F distribution and the Beta distribution. The F distribution with degrees of freedom k_1 and k_2 has the p.d.f.

$$f(x) = \frac{\Gamma((k_1+k_2)/2)(k_1/k_2)^{k_1/2}}{\Gamma(k_1/2)\,\Gamma(k_2/2)} \frac{(x)^{k_1/2 - 1}}{(1+k_1x/k_2)^{(k_1+k_2)/2}} \qquad 0 < x < \infty$$

$$= \quad 0 \qquad \text{elsewhere}$$

A random variable having the F distribution is easily generated using the fact that if V and W are stochastically independent chi-squared random variables with k_1 and k_2 degrees of freedom, respectively, then $X = (V/k_1)/(W/k_2)$ has an F distribution with k_1 and k_2 degrees of freedom.

```
SUBROUTINE F(X,K1,K2)
CALL CHISQ(V,K1)
CALL CHISQ(W,K2)
X = (V/K1)/(W/K2)
RETURN
END
```

The Beta distribution is closely related to the F distribution. If Y has an F distribution with k_1 and k_2 degrees of freedom then $X = (1+(k_1/k_2)Y)^{-1}$ has a Beta distribution with p.d.f.

$$f(x) = \frac{\Gamma(k_1+k_2)}{\Gamma(k_1)\,\Gamma(k_2)} x^{k_1-1}(1-x)^{k_2-1} \qquad 0 < x < 1$$

$$= \quad 0 \qquad \text{elsewhere}$$

```
SUBROUTINE BETA(X,K1,K2)
CALL F(Y,K1,K2)
X = 1/(1+(K1/K2)*Y)
RETURN
END
```

It is also illuminating to fix our attention on some one distribution and to look at the variety of ways in which one can "construct" this distribution from others. To illustrate this, we will consider the discrete random variable having probability density function

$$f(x) = \frac{\Gamma(x+k)}{x!\Gamma(k)} p^x q^k \qquad x = 0,1,2,3\ldots$$

$$0 < k < \infty$$

$$p + q = 1$$

This is the well known negative binomial distribution which is probably best known as a model describing the number of failures before the kth success in a series of independent repeated Bernoulli trials. This suggests one way in which one can generate the negative binomial distribution. A Bernoulli trial is easily generated by truncating a uniform random variable. For example, the statement M = RAND(2.) will assign to M either the value 0 or 1 with equal probability. An easy modification will allow any probability of success. One has only to keep a running total of the M's as they are generated, stopping when they total k. Then if X is set equal to the number of trials minus M, X will have a negative binomial distribution. This approach could be quite slow if p (probability of success) is small and k is large. One solution might be to think of the negative binomial random variable X as being the sum of k independent random variables each distributed as a geometric random variable. Since a geometric random variable is easily generated from a single uniform random variable, the computer time could be reduced considerably. There are, in addition, a number of other ways in which the negative binomial distribution can arise. Boswell and Patil (1970) list about twelve different chance mechanisms giving rise to the negative binomial distribution. Some of these suggest ways of generating the negative binomial distribution.

One such mechanism is a model for clumping behavior. That is to say, one can consider individuals which tend to aggregate in clumps or colonies where the number of individuals in a colony is a random variable, say Y. The number of colonies occupying a region would also be a random variable, say N. Therefore the total number of individuals in a region could be expressed as

$$X = Y_1 + Y_2 + \ldots + Y_N.$$

Now, if the random variable Y (size of colony) has a logarithmic distribution and the random variable N (number of colonies) has a Poisson distribution, the resulting probability distribution for X will be a negative binomial. This means that the negative binomial can be generated by first generating a value for N using a Poisson generator and then calling a routine to generate logarithmic random variables N times and taking the total.

Another mechanism generating the negative binomial arises as a model for heterogeneity. Here we assume that the individuals of some population are randomly distributed over some region so that when the individuals in some selected area are counted we get an observation from a Poisson distribution with parameter λ. Now, if the region varies in density so that the value of λ can be considered to be a random variable and if we assign to that random variable a gamma distribution, then the resulting distribution will be a negative binomial. This suggests another method for generating the negative binomial: First generate a value for λ by using a generator for the gamma distribution and then generate a value from a Poisson generator using that value of λ.

As these examples illustrate, this "building block" approach not only simplifies the task of generating random variables in some cases, but it can provide valuable insight into the mechanisms operating to produce a particular probability distribution as a model.

REFERENCES

Boswell, M. T. and G. P. Patil 1970. Random Counts in Models and Structures. The Penn State Statistics Series, University Park, Pa.: The Pennsylvania State Univ. Press.

Hastings, C. 1955. Approximations for Digital Computers. Princeton, N.J.: Princeton Univ. Press.

Hollingdale, S. H. (ed.) 1967. Digital Simulation. New York: American Elsevier.

Knuth, D. E. 1969. The Art of Computer Programming. II: Reading, Mass.: Addison Wesley.

Maisel, H. and G. Gnugnoli 1972. Simulation of Discrete Stochastic Systems. Chicago: Science Research Associates, Inc.

Naylor, T. H., J. L. Balintfy, D. S. Burdick and K. Chu 1966. Computer Simulation Techniques. New York: Wiley.

THE USE OF DYSTAL IN SIMULATION

JAMES M. SAKODA

The use of computers in simulation presents special problems. In this paper I review some of the requirements of computer simulation and alternative methods of meeting them. This is followed by a more detailed discussion of the use of DYSTAL, a FORTRAN programming subroutine package.

REQUIREMENTS OF SIMULATION

Mathematical Simulation. Simulation can be classified into three categories: mathematical, expected value computer simulation and Monte Carlo computer simulation. In addition there are other miscellaneous types of simulation possible. Mathematical simulation involves writing equations predicting such phenomena as population growth as a function of birth and death rates. Its advantage is elegance, and the ability frequently to obtain analytical solutions to a problem. For example, the end state of population distribution as a result of a Markov chain process can be calculated analytically without finding population distributions for intervening years. The disadvantage of mathematical solutions is that restrictions must be placed on the types of variables introduced - for example, variables must be additive, linear, continuous, etc.

Programming for Mathematical Simulation. Computer programs for mathematical simulation can generally be written in a straightforward manner in an algebraic language such as FORTRAN or ALGOL. Many models call for standard mathematical routines for which computer programs can be found. IBM's scientific subroutine package, for example, contains routines for matrix operations, solution of polynomial equations, solution of characteristic equations, etc. For the scientific subroutine package the programmer needs to provide for allocation of arrays, input of the data, call to the subroutines, and the output of the answers. The subroutine package is written in dimension-free form, and it is necessary for the programmer to write his input routines to meet this specification. In general two-dimensional arrays must be simulated by single-dimensioned ones. For example, the two-dimensional subscript, X(I,J), can be calculated for a single dimensioned array as

$$IJ = (J - 1) * NR + I$$

where NR is the maximum value of subscript I. One would then write X(IJ) in place of X(I,J). DYSTAL's dynamic storage allocation system operates in a similar manner. Hence, its dynamic storage allocation and input-output routines can be used to advantage with the scientific subroutine package.

<u>Computer Simulation</u>. Greater flexibility and less reliance on mathematical sophistication is possible by using computer simulation. Here the need is for computer skills. Two basic concepts in computer simulation are entities and events. Entities are the objects being processed. In a population growth model, for example, the entities may be women of child-bearing ages. These entities are passed through processes or events, such as pregnancy, miscarriage, birth, post-birth delay before return to a fecundable state. A common programming tool in simulation is the waiting line. Entities are frequently described by arrays, and these arrays are placed on waiting lines to await processing. When the processing is completed they are removed from that waiting line and usually placed on another one. Statistical calculations, such as average length of time on a waiting line or the mean and standard deviation describing a distribution, are

generally required in simulation.

Expected Value vs. Monte Carlo Simulation. Computer simulation can be classified as expected value or Monte Carlo. In expected value simulation probabilities of occurrences are applied to categories of individuals. For example, the probability of becoming pregnant during any month can be applied to women with specified parity. Since each category can contain large numbers of individuals, in expected value models the computation time need not be great, and only a single run is necessary to obtain reliable results. However, it is necessary to keep track of each category separately. Addition of a single variable will multiply the storage requirement by the number of categories in that variable. Hence, the complexity of the model is limited by the available space for data.

Monte Carlo simulation, on the other hand, handles individuals, who are usually described individually by an array of values. Addition of a variable simply increases the length of each individual array. Probabilities are applied individually by using a table of random numbers so that processing time is apt to be a factor to be taken into account as a limitation of the approach. In addition, because the number of cases which can be handled is limited by the available storage, several runs are necessary to study the variance to which results are subject. However, it has the advantage of being able to handle more complex models within the limit of available memory.

Computer Simulation Programming Requirements. Computer simulation requires some flexibility in creation of arrays and data structuring. Entities are generally represented by arrays, and sometimes these vary in the number required and length and are best created dynamically, i.e., as they are needed. Their processing generally involves use of waiting lines, which can best be done by placing names of arrays on other arrays, and inserting and deleting these names as needed. It can also be done by chaining arrays, and using list-processing procedures to insert or delete arrays. There is also need for efficient use of secondary memory, such as disk storage, to augment core memory. It is useful to have arrays which are expandable so that space is not wasted by using a maximum size. It is also necessary to be able to input and output data easily, and to make statistical calculations.

Other Types of Simulation. Other types of simulation are possible. One might depict a mechanical model, for example, using a computer. My checkerboard model of social interaction moves pieces on a checkerboard, which is represented by a matrix. Another commonly used device is the tree structure. It can be used to represent company organization, a family tree, possible moves in a game, combinations of probabilities.

ALTERNATIVE SOLUTIONS

Canned Programs. The methods of achieving a desired simulation vary in degrees of generality. The more specific the solution the more likely that labor is saved at the cost of limitation in what can be simulated. The most specific is the canned program, such as REPSIM, POPSIM, FERMOD, etc., which have already been written and can be used for specific purposes. In addition to the consideration of whether the program can do the job in question, one needs to see whether it is available on one's own machine. Canned programs themselves will vary in degree of generality, with mathematical models being the most restrictive and the Monte Carlo model usually being most general. For the nonprogrammer canned programs are a God-sent gift. Even for a person who can program, a canned program which he can modify to fit his own needs is better than starting from scratch.

Simulation Language. A second alternative is the

use of a simulation programming language or a subroutine package. Because programming for simulation can be complex and many of the routines needed are common to many simulations, the use of a simulation language can save a programmer a great deal of programming effort. Here again, unless the package is written in a common language such as FORTRAN, the programming language may not be available. Generally speaking, the most fortunate are those with large IBM computers. Computer languages include GPSS, SIMSCRIPT, and others such as GASP II by Pritsker and Kiviat, which has the advantage of possible implementation on most computers. GASP provides dynamic storage allocation of fixed length arrays, and can be improved by use of DYSTAL's dynamic storage allocation system.

General Purpose Language. A third alternative is to write one's own routines and programs. Assembly language provides complete flexibility, but requires excessive dependence on a programmer and on a particular machine. So-called list-processing languages, such as IPL-V, LISP, SLIP, provide both dynamic storage allocation and ability to create data structures, but have other limitations. Except for SLIP, which is written in FORTRAN, list-processing languages are generally weak on input-output and mathematical calculation capabilities. PL/I is a general purpose language and possesses a combination of mathematical, commercial and list-processing capabilities. It may be the best language for writing one's own simulation programs. Its main disadvantage is that it is available mostly only on larger IBM computers, and also its excessive complexity.

FORTRAN is the most commonly used scientific programming language, and hence some programmers may prefer it to PL/I in spite of FORTRAN's limitations. (A show of hands at the conference indicated that the bulk of the attendees were programming in FORTRAN.) FORTRAN does not provide dynamic storage allocation or two-level store and its data-structuring ability is limited. However, many of these limitations can be overcome and the fruit of this programming put in the form of FORTRAN subroutines. A simple method of achieving both dynamic storage allocation and data structuring is to create a large matrix and treat each column of this matrix as an array. Each array can be referenced by a column number, which can be used as a pointer to the array. This pointer can be placed on other arrays or used to chain one array to another. In GASP II arrays are chained to one another to form a list of available arrays, and list-processing techniques are used to build up chains of arrays as needed, borrowing arrays from the available list. To use this approach a short lesson in list-processing techniques is helpful. The main disadvantage of this approach is that arrays are fixed in length and no provision is made for the use of secondary storage.

DYSTAL. DYSTAL is written as a set of Basic FORTRAN IV subprograms which provide general purpose programming capabilities. These include:

(a) Dynamic storage allocation
(b) Data structuring capability
(c) Two-level store
(d) Parameters stored with arrays
(e) Basic routines in the following areas:
    (1) Statistical operations
    (2) Matrix operations
    (3) Sorting and ranking
    (4) List processing with chained arrays
    (5) Tree structure operations
    (6) String processing

Arrays can be created to be of any length within the limitation of the available dynamic storage area. Arrays are relocatable and can be expanded, if necessary. DYSTAL's distinctive feature is the two-level store or virtual memory, which permits arrays to be moved from core memory to a disk file to make room for other arrays. Its advantage over PL/I is that it can be implemented on smaller and non-IBM machines. Its disadvantage is that access to arrays by use of functions is both more awkward for the programmer and slower in execution. Its use in writing XTAB8, a cross-tabulation program, demonstrates that it can be used effectively for production work.

SELECTED DYSTAL COMMANDS

DYSTAL consists of a collection of some 90 Basic FORTRAN IV subprograms (mostly functions). Those that are needed should be compiled and stored in the system or user's library. When an argument of a subprogram is underlined it can either be a list name or a location. Unless specified as a subroutine a DYSTAL command is a function which returns a value, which is often a list name.

Creation of Arrays

INLOT (NPARM,MAPN,MAX). Subroutine. Sets up the dynamic storage area with number of public locations = NPARM, capacity of MAP (the directory) = MAPN, and length of dynamic storage area = MAX.

MAPL (MOD,MAX). Creates an array of Mode = MOD and length = MAX. Returns the name of that array. Modes: 1 = name list, 2 = integer list, 3 = real list, 4-7 = others.

MAPM (MOD,NROW,NCOL). Returns the name of an NROW x NCOL matrix with a Mode of MOD. (DYSTAL's row corresponds to FORTRAN's column - i.e. locations within rows are stored consecutively.)

ICOPY (LSTA). Copies Array LSTA and returns the name of the copy.

Input-Output

LRD (NFILE,I,N,LSTA). Inputs from Device NFILE into Positions I to N of Array LSTA. Returns LSTA as its value. Format for integer array: (5(6XI8)); for real arrays: (5(1XF13.5)).

LWR (NFILE,I,N,LSTA). Outputs on Device NFILE from Positions I to N of Array LSTA.

IDUMP (LSTA). Prints out the head as well as the content of Array LSTA.

Storage and Retrieval

IPUT (WD,I,LSTA). Stores WD in the Ith position of LSTA. Returns LSTA.

LOAD (WD,LSTA). Stores WD in the next available position of LSTA, increments the counter and returns LSTA. Expands LSTA when full.

ITEM (I,LSTA). Returns the Ith item (integer) of LSTA.

FITEM (I,LSTA). Returns the Ith item (real) of LSTA.

Array Processing

INSET (WD,I,LSTA). Inserts WD in the Ith position of LSTA and returns LSTA. Increases the counter by one and expands LSTA if it is full.

ITAKE (I,LSTA). Deletes and returns the Ith item of LSTA. If I = -9 deletes and returns the last item of the array.

TAKE (I,LSTA). Real version of ITAKE.

IHUNT (WD,LSTA,I). Makes a linear search for WD in LSTA beginning with the Ith position. Returns the position of the first occurrence of WD or a zero, if unsuccessful.

Matrix Operations

MDIM (NR,NC,MATA). Subroutine. Stores the number of rows and columns of MATA in NR and NC, respectively.

LINE (J,MATA). Returns the location of the Jth row of Matrix MATA. (Actually one location before the line begins.)

MITEM (I,J,MATA). Returns the item (integer) on the Ith row and Jth column of MATA.

XITEM (I,J,MATA). Real version of MITEM.

MPUT (WD,I,J,MATA). Stores WD in the Ith row and Jth column of MATA.

LADD (N,LSTA,LSTB,LSTC). Adds N real items of LSTA to corresponding items of LSTB and stores them in corresponding positions of LSTC.

MTRAN (MATA). Replaces MATA by its transpose and

returns MATA.

MATMP (MATA,MATB,MATC). Matrix multiplies MATA by MATB and stores it in MATC and returns MATC. If MATC is zero, it creates a new array; if too small it is enlarged.

MPTRA (MATA,MATB,MATC). Matrix multiplies MATA by the transpose of MATB (row by row multiplication). Otherwise, same as MATMP.

MINV (MATA). Replaces MATA with its inverse and returns MATA. MATA must be a real symmetric matrix.

Chained Arrays

LPULL (LCHN). Deletes and returns the first array chained on Array LCHN. Returns a zero if the chain is empty.

LPUSH (LSTA,LCHN). Pushes down or inserts LSTA after Array LCHN and returns LSTA.

ILINK (LSTA,LCHN). Links LSTA to the end of the chained array, LCHN. Replaces this name with LSTA and returns LSTA.

Sublist Operations

LOCAL (LSTA). Returns the location of LSTA or if LSTA is not a list name returns LSTA itself.

KCHEK (LSTA,LSTB, LOCA, LOCB). Subroutine. Checks to see that LSTA and LSTB are both in core memory and stores their locations in LOCA and LOCB.

CHEK3 (LSTA,LSTB,LSTC,LOCA,LOCB,LOCC). Subroutine. Same as KCHEK except for application to three arrays.

LOT (IA), FLOT (IA). Subscripts LOT or FLOT directly to store or retrieve an item in Location IA. To access the Ith item of LSTA, IA = LOCAL (LSTA) + I.

SETTING UP THE DYNAMIC STORAGE AREA

DYSTAL provides a single large storage area called LOT or FLOT. Space for data is allotted to LOT/FLOT with three specification statements:

```
     DIMENSION LOT(3000), FLOT(3000), GLOT(3000)
     COMMON GLOT
     EQUIVALENCE (LOT(1), FLOT(1), GLOT(1))
```

GLOT is placed in COMMON to override a Basic FORTRAN prohibition against FORTRAN functions changing values stored in COMMON. Additional equivalences for the card reader (NRD), the printer (NPR) and the array counter (NCTR) are provided by the following card:

```
     EQUIVALENCE (LOT(27),NRD), (LOT(29),NPR),
       (LOT(20),NCTR)
```

These are followed by an instruction to create a disk file, No. 4:

```
     DEFINE FILE 4 (1000,80,U,JFI)
```

The first executable statement is generally a call to INLOT to initialize the dynamic storage area for use:

```
     CALL INLOT (10,50,3000)
```

INLOT stores system parameters in LOT(1) to LOT(39). It also provides 10 public locations in LOT(50) to LOT(59), which are available to the user for communication among subprograms he writes. The number of array names that can be stored on the directory, MAP, is specified here as 50. The length of the dynamic storage area, LOT/FLOT is 3000.

DYSTAL PROGRAMMING

Most of the DYSTAL commands are functions which return a value and hence can be nested when that value can be used in a command which follows immediately after it. Also, dimensions of arrays are stored in the head of each array and need not be included as arguments. For example,

```
     MATC = MATMP (MATA,MATB,0)
     MATD = ICOPY (MATC)
     MATD = MINV (MATD)
```

can be written on a single line:

```
     MATD = MINV (ICOPY (MATMP (MATA,MATB,0)))
```

MARKOV CHAIN CALCULATION - AN EXAMPLE

The following program performs a repeated multiplication of an array, MATA, by a matrix, MATB, in Markov chain style. At each step IDUMP is called to print out the head and content of MATC, which holds the result of the multiplication. The output values stabilize after about the 30th multiplication.

```
    5 READ (NRD,10) NROW, KTIME
   10 FORMAT (10I5)
      MATA = IDUMP (LRD (NRD,1,N,MAPM (3,1,N)))
      MATB = IDUMP (LRD (NRD,1,N*N,MAPM (3,N,N)))
      MATC = MAPM (3,1,N)
      DO 50 I = 1,KTIME
C ***   MULTIPLY MATA BY MATB AND STORE IN MATC.
C ***     PRINT MATC.
        CALL IDUMP (MATMP (MATA,MATB,MATC))
C ***   SWITCH NAMES MATA AND MATC.
        ITEMP = MATA
        MATA  = MATC
        MATC  = ITEMP
   50 CONTINUE
      STOP
      END
```

The output for a run for which NROW = 4 and KTIME = 4 is shown in Table 1.

CALLING OTHER SUBROUTINES

It is possible to allow DYSTAL to provide the array creation and input-output and then call a subroutine written in FORTRAN or one of the subroutines in the IBM Scientific Subroutine Package. The steps involved are:

1. Create and input arrays LSTA, LSTB, LSTC.
2. Call LOCAL, KCHEK or CHEK3 to make sure arrays are in core memory and to find their locations. For example,

   ```
   CALL CHEK3 (LSTA,LSTB,LSTC,LOCA,LOCB,LOCC)
   ```

```
LOCA       123 NSTA          2 NMAP         69 NREF          1 NDSK          0
NIDE           NODE         -4 NMOD          3 NMAX          4 NCTR          4

   1000.00012      1000.00012      1000.00012      1000.00012

LOCA       134 NSTA          2 NMAP         70 NREF          1 NDSK          0
NIDE           NODE         -4 NMOD          3 NMAX         16 NCTR         16

      0.90000         0.05000         0.03000         0.02000
      0.10000         0.80000         0.07000         0.03000
      0.15000         0.10000         0.70000         0.05000
      0.20000         0.15000         0.05000         0.60000

LOCA       157 NSTA          2 NMAP         71 NREF          1 NDSK          0
NIDE           NODE         -4 NMOD          3 NMAX          4 NCTR          4

   1349.99951      1099.99975       849.99987       700.00000

LOCA       123 NSTA          2 NMAP         69 NREF          1 NDSK          0
NIDE           NODE         -4 NMOD          3 NMAX          4 NCTR          4

   1592.49878      1137.49927       747.49963       522.49987

LOCA       157 NSTA          2 NMAP         71 NREF          1 NDSK          0
NIDE           NODE         -4 NMOD          3 NMAX          4 NCTR          4

   1763.62305      1142.74878       676.77441       416.84973

LOCA       123 NSTA          2 NMAP         69 NREF          1 NDSK          0
NIDE           NODE         -4 NMOD          3 NMAX          4 NCTR          4

   1886.42114      1132.58472       627.48547       353.50341
```

Table 1. OUTPUT OF MARKOV CHAIN CALCULATION

3. Then call the subroutine with FLOT (LOCA+1), FLOT (LOCB+1), FLOT (LOCC+1) in place of array names.

For example, to call EIGEN (A,R,N,MV) in the Scientific Subroutine Package we create and input A as MATA and create R as MATR. Then we write:

```
CALL KCHEK (MATA,MATR,LOCA,LOCR)
CALL EIGEN (FLOT (LOCA+1), FLOT (LOCR+1),N,MV)
CALL IDUMP (MATA)
CALL IDUMP (MATR)
```

By writing subroutines in FORTRAN it is possible to overcome the handicap of subscripting found in DYSTAL. If adjustable dimensions are available even subscripting of two-dimensional arrays can be done in FORTRAN.

TWO-LEVEL STORE

The operation of two-level store is not always apparent at the programming level. When arrays are created and there is insufficient room in core memory, arrays are moved to the disk file to make space for the new array. When an array is needed, LOCAL is usually called to make sure it is in core or brought in from the disk file. The problem in managing two-level store is to make the operation as efficient as possible. The ideal strategy is to keep the most distantly needed array on the disk file, while keeping those needed the soonest in core. This ideal cannot be met without looking ahead at the program. In an effort to meet this goal, the programmer is allowed to specify arrays as permanent, semi-permanent or temporary. Permanent arrays remain in core and are not allowed to move to the disk file. To accomplish this

```
CALL LPERM (LSTA)
```

is used. This makes LSTA and all other semi-permanent arrays created before it permanent. Semi-permanent arrays represent the default condition and are brought into core on a first-in, first-out basis. Arrays which have remained in core for a long time are put on the disk file before those which have been brought in recently. Temporary arrays are created by LTEMP (MOD) when creating an array:

```
     LSTA = MAPL (LTEMP (MOD),N)
```

Temporary arrays are handled on a last-in, first-out basis so that the last temporary array created or brought into core memory is the first candidate for the disk file. Sequentially accessed records of a file are best handled as temporary arrays, since once they have been used they will not be needed until other arrays in the same file have been accessed.

DATA STRUCTURING

One of DYSTAL's capabilities is the structuring of data by using the names of arrays as pointers. There are two ways of creating data structures. The first is to place array names on another array. The second is to place a pointer in the head of an array (in Position -3) to the next array, thus setting up a system of chain of arrays. The chain of arrays is processed using list-processing concepts of pushdown and pop-up. Both methods can be applied to the waiting line situation.

Waiting Line Using a Sequential Array. A sequential waiting line of Length LEN can be created by calling MAPL:

```
     LWAIT = MAPL (1,LEN)
```

The mode of the array here is 1 because it is to contain names of arrays. This array must be created with a finite length, but if LOAD is used to store arrays on it it will automatically be moved and increased in length by 1/5 LEN + 5 when it becomes full.

One can add an array, LSTA, to the waiting line, LWAIT, by calling LOAD (LSTA,LWAIT). LOAD checks the array counter and stores LSTA, the name of the array, in the next available position of LWAIT and increases the counter by one. When several arrays are created and loaded on the same waiting line it is not necessary to provide explicit names for each array.

```
     DO 10 I = 1, N
        CALL LOAD (MAPL (3,M),LWAIT)
  10 CONTINUE
```

will create N arrays of Length M and place them on LWAIT in turn.

LOAD stores arrays on a waiting line in positions 1, 2, 3, etc. For example, LSTA, LSTB and LSTC stored in that order would appear on the waiting line as

LWAIT--LSTA, LSTB, LSTC.

To remove an array from the waiting line ITAKE (I,LWAIT) is used. ITAKE deletes the Ith item of LWAIT, and moves the remaining arrays to fill in any gap that is created. If the array is empty ITAKE returns a zero. To operate the waiting line on a first-in, first-out basis one sets I to 1, thus removing the first item, LSTA. This requires, of course, the movement of the remaining arrays one position each. We then have:

```
          Before:  LWAIT--LSTA, LSTB, LSTC.
     LRET = ITAKE (1,LWAIT)
          After:   LWAIT--LSTB, LSTC.
```

Last-in, first-out operation calls for removal of the last word on the array. This can be accomplished by setting I to ITEM (0,LWAIT), which retrieves the counter content or by convention by setting I to -9:

```
          Before:  LWAIT--LSTA, LSTB, LSTC.
     LRET = ITAKE (-9,LWAIT)
          After:   LWAIT--LSTA, LSTB.
```

Operation of a last-in, first-out waiting line does not require moving the remaining items.

An advantage of the sequential waiting line is that it is possible to access the Ith name on LWAIT directly. In FERMOD, for example, miscarriage takes place on the third month. It is a simple matter to access the third array on LWAIT by writing:

```
     L3 = ITEM (3,LWAIT)
```

In the list-processing approach it is necessary to trace linkages down through the chain until the desired array name is found.

<u>Waiting Line Using Chained Arrays</u>. Working with

chained arrays has certain advantages, such as ability to create a waiting line of unlimited length and to make insertions and deletions simply by changing a link. To start a waiting line the anchor array, LCHN, is created with at least one word:

```
     LCHN = MAPL (2,N)
```

This is followed by storage of LCHN in the first position if the array is to be used for first-in, first-out operation:

```
     CALL LOAD (LCHN,LCHN)
```

Other words can be stored on the rest of the array, but they should be integers, since the array is an integer array.

Now, to build up the chain of arrays on a first-in, first-out basis ILINK (LSTA,LCHN) is called. This results in LSTA being added to the end of the chain of arrays. If LSTA, LSTB and LSTC had been added to the chain in that order, the appearance of the chain would be as follows:

```
     LCHN (LSTA)--LSTC.
     LSTA (LSTB)--
     LSTB (LSTC)--
     LSTC (    )--
```

The pointers are stored in the -3 position of the head of each array and are shown in parentheses. LCHN has a pointer to LSTA, LSTA has one to LSTB, and LSTB to LSTC. The lack of a pointer in LSTC indicates that it is the end of the chain. LSTC is also the first word of LCHN.

To build up the chain on a last-in, first-out or pushdown stack basis, LPUSH (LSTA,LCHN) is used. This reverses the order in which arrays are stacked:

```
     LCHN (LSTC)--
     LSTC (LSTB)--
     LSTB (LSTA)--
     LSTA (    )--
```

Storage of LSTA on LCHN initially is not necessary, since it is not used.

To remove an array from a chain LPULL is called:

```
     LRET = LPULL (LCHN)
```

In the first-in, first-out chain LSTA would be removed,

and in the push-down stack LSTC would be taken out. The result would be:

First-in, First-out	Last-in, First-out
LCHN (LSTB)--LSTC	LCHN (LSTB)--
LSTB (LSTC)--	LSTB (LSTA)--
LSTC ( )--	LSTA ( )--

The Sorted Waiting Line. In the expected value model the clock can be moved one unit at a time and each of the processes called in turn. Since each entity represents a group of individuals, there is a good chance that each of the events will take place at each movement of the clock. For example, pregnancy, miscarriage, stillbirth, live birth, move back to the fecundable state can all be expected to take place each month, after the processes get underway. Hence, the clock can be run under a DO loop:

```
      CLOCK = 0.0
      DO 100 ICLOK = 1, NCLK
        CLOCK = CLOCK + 1.0
        CALL PREG
        CALL MISS
        CALL STILL
        CALL BIRTH
        CALL BACK
  100 CONTINUE
```

In the Monte Carlo approach it is customary to place arrays representing individuals on various waiting lines and then check to see which event is scheduled to occur next. For this purpose it is desirable to set up a sorted file of events. An event would have as one of its descriptions the time of next occurrence of that event, and its position in the event file would be determined by this. Events could then be removed without having to search through the file.

JFILE is not a standard DYSTAL routine, but is shown here to illustrate how such routines are written. The list-processing approach is used here, but insertions and deletions in a finite length linear array also would have been possible.

```
      FUNCTION JFILE (LSTA,I,LCHN)
C *** A SORTED FILE ROUTINE.  FILES LSTA BY SIZE OF
C *** THE ITH WORD (REAL) OF LSTA FROM SMALL TO LARGE
C *** IN CHAIN LCHN.  RETURNS LCHN AS THE VALUE OF
C *** JFILE.  USE LPULL TO REMOVE THE ARRAY WITH THE
C *** SMALLEST VALUE OF THE ITH WORD.
C *** XWD IS THE COMPARISON WORD.
      XWD  = FITEM (I,LSTA)
      LSTB = LCHN
   10 LSTC = ITEM (-3,LSTB)
C *** IS THE CHAIN EMPTY.  IF SO STORE IMMEDIATELY.
      IF (LSTC) 30,30,20
   20   IF (XWD - FITEM (I,LSTC)) 25,25,30
   25     LSTB = LSTC
          GO TO 10
C *** INSERT LSTA BETWEEN LSTB AND LSTC.
   30 CALL LPUSH (LSTA,LSTB)
      KFILE = LCHN
      RETURN
      END
```

To file an event LSTQ in sorted order by time of next occurrence stored in Position 1,

```
     CALL JFILE (LSTQ,1,LEVNT)
```

is used. To remove the event with the smallest time of occurrence, one simply writes

```
     LIST = LPULL (LEVNT)
```

LIST then represents the event which is to occur and the time clock is moved up to the time of this event:

```
     CLOCK = FITEM (1,LIST)
```

STATISTICS

One of the necessary functions in simulation is the collection of statistics. This may take the form of frequency distributions, means, and standard deviations. In FERMOD the statistics required were the mean, standard deviation and skewness of parity at different points along the time dimension. DYSTAL's arrays are linear in arrangement and hence the calculation of statistics is relatively straightforward. There are some DYSTAL routines for statistical operations. SUM (N,LSTA) will return the sum of N items of an array or line of a matrix. VAR (N,LSTA) will similarly calculate the variance of an array or line of a matrix. LADD (N,LSTA,LSTB,LSTC) will add columnwise items of LSTA to items of LSTB and store them in corresponding positions of LSTC. LHIST (LSTX,XLO,STEP,N) will take an array, LSTX, and form a frequency distribution.

RECURSION AND TREE STRUCTURE

A recursive routine is one which is capable of calling itself. FORTRAN does not permit recursion and employs iteration using a DO loop instead. Recursion calls for temporary storage of parameters until an end state is reached and then using the parameters in reverse or pushdown order. In DYSTAL the dynamic storage allocation capability permits the creation of an array on which parameters can be stored and used as needed and then deleted. Hence, it is possible to write a subroutine which in essence accomplishes the job done by recursive subroutines.

The use of a tree-structure is sometimes helpful in simulation. It has been used in modeling thought processes, lining up strategies in playing chess, and in binary tree sorting routines. It can be used in combination of probabilities; the mechanical creation of the binomial distribution by dropping steel balls on a network of pins is a binary tree operation. The family tree is generally represented in tree structure form.

In DYSTAL the ability to place names of arrays on other arrays permits creation of a tree structure. Not all of the arrays need to be in core memory at the same time. Each branch can have any number of subbranches. The nodes of the tree will consist of name lists, while terminal branches will hold data of some sort. Instead of creating a tree structure it is possible to read one in using LSRD, a list-structure read routine, which is capable of reading in any number of arrays.

To search through a tree structure a recursive process is used. INDEX (INDX,MAX,LSTS) is first called to create a pushdown stack to store three words for each level of the tree. Each time NEXTX (INDX,LIST, NFLAG) is called the name of the next array is stored in LIST and an indicator placed in NFLAG to show whether the movement was down, up or across the tree. The action the user wants to take is dependent upon the nature of the array and on NFLAG.

OTHER CONVENIENCES

Random Number Generation. A frequently needed operation is random number generation. MAPR (MOD,N) will create an array with N random numbers. These numbers will be real values between 0.0 and 1.0 if MOD = 3 or randomly arranged integers from 1 to N.

Sorting. ISORT (LSTA) will sort an array of words in ascending order, unless LSTA is negative, in which case the sorting is from large to small. IRANK (LSTA,LSTB) stores ranks in LSTB to reflect the rank of numbers on LSTA. This routine is convenient for writing nonparametric statistical routines. MSORT (NAME,LKEY) will sort records whose names are on NAME by keys specified on LKEY.

KDUMP. CALL KDUMP will result in printing out of the head and content of every array whose name remains on the directory. This constitutes a convenient diagnostic tool. This dump includes the first array which holds system parameters and content of the user's public locations. The error routine, when called, also calls on KDUMP.

DISADVANTAGES

There are, of course, costs in using DYSTAL. The first is the need to compile and store routines in a library. Since DYSTAL is not in common usage this is most likely to be a private matter. DYSTAL II is distributed on a small reel of magnetic tape, and the FORTRAN source programs need to be dumped onto cards and then compiled and stored.

The second problem is the learning of a new language. While DYSTAL is written in FORTRAN, it still has language features of its own, in addition to the commands themselves. Hence, there is a definite start-up problem. There is a DYSTAL II Manual available to aid in learning.

A third problem has to do with storage and retrieval. Access functions, such as IPUT or ITEM, make program writing easier, but slow down execution. Direct subscripting of LOT and FLOT using calculated subscripts is more efficient, but somewhat cumbersome. A compromise procedure is first to write programs with access functions and later to replace them with direct subscripts. Another alternative is to pass array locations to a subroutine written in straight FORTRAN.

CONCLUSION

I would venture to say that FORTRAN and COBOL have proven to be much hardier than expected and that languages such as PL/I and APL are not likely to replace them soon. Other special languages such as GPSS and SIMSCRIPT do not appear to have captured a large following, partially because languages tend to become obsolete as computers change and implementation lags behind computer hardware changes. GASP II, which is FORTRAN-based, appears to me like a good compromise. By rewriting it in DYSTAL, it should be possible to provide it with greater flexibility and power.

BIBLIOGRAPHY

Green, B. F., Jr. 1963. Digital Computers in Research. New York: McGraw-Hill.

Katzan, H., Jr. 1970. Advanced Programming. New

York: Van Nostrand.

Martin, F. F. 1968. Computer Modeling and Simulation. New York: Wiley.

Potter, R. G., Jr. and J. M. Sakoda 1966. A computer model of family building based on expected values, Demography 3: 450-461.

Potter, R. G., Jr., J. M. Sakoda and W. E. Feinberg 1968. Variable fecundability and the timing of births, Eugenics Quarterly 15: 155-163.

Potter, R. G., Jr., B. McCann and J. M. Sakoda 1970. Selective fecundability and contraceptive effectiveness, Milbank Memorial Fund Quarterly, Vol. XLVIII, No. 1, 91-102.

Pritsker, A. A. B. and P. J. Kiviat 1969. Simulation with GASP II: A FORTRAN Based Simulation Language. Englewood Cliffs, N.J.: Prentice-Hall.

Sakoda, J. M. 1965. DYSTAL Manual, Dynamic Storage Allocation Language in FORTRAN. Brown Univ., Sociology Computer Laboratory.

Sakoda, J. M. 1968. DYSTAL: dynamic storage allocation language in FORTRAN, In Symbol Manipulation Languages and Techniques, D. G. Bobrow (ed.) North Holland Publishing Company, pp. 302-311.

Sakoda, J. M. 1970. DYSTAL II Manual. Brown Univ., Sociology Computer Laboratory.

Sakoda, J. M. 1971. The checkerboard model of social interaction, Journal of Mathematical Sociology 1: 119-132.

AUTHOR'S NOTE

DYSTAL II is available on a 200-foot magnetic tape in FORTRAN source program form. Also available is a *DYSTAL II Manual* (1970) coordinated with the tape. This replaces the old *DYSTAL Manual* (1965) and the shorter *User's Introduction to DYSTAL II* (1963). The author will supply further information upon request.

SPECIAL PURPOSE SIMULATION LANGUAGES FOR POPULATION STUDIES

F. PAUL WYMAN

INTRODUCTION

Although the title of this paper is "Special Purpose Simulation Languages for Population Studies," I would like to correct any impression that I am going to attempt an overview of all simulation languages relevant to population research. Rather, I would like to briefly review two simulation languages with which I am somewhat familiar, and hope that they will stimulate some fresh ideas as to how one might apply simulation to population studies.

A great many tasks that are common to all simulations are simplified with special purpose simulation languages. There are several such computer languages, as Professor Sakoda has pointed out in this volume. The two languages, SIMSCRIPT and DYNAMO, represent "discrete state" versus "continuous" approaches to computer simulation. In this paper an example of a non-fatal contagious disease epidemic is illustrated in both SIMSCRIPT and DYNAMO. Let us compare and contrast these languages in order to point out their various advantages and disadvantages.

The majority of simulation models are programmed in FORTRAN. At a simulation conference in 1971, 275 papers were delivered, and approximately 90 per cent of these papers were based on FORTRAN simulations. GPSS and DYNAMO accounted for about 5 per cent, while one or two SIMSCRIPT models along with 8 or 9 other miscellaneous languages represented the remaining 5 per cent. Thus, FORTRAN is really the primary simulation language and the growth and development of special purpose simulation languages has been somewhat slow. Although they have been in existence for several years at this point, the basic factor impeding their adoption is the existing familiarity with FORTRAN. There is a pervasive confidence in the FORTRAN user that virtually any type of simulation task can be programmed in FORTRAN. And this is technically valid. Nevertheless, if we have several common simulation tasks such as time-keeping, computing descriptive statistics, and generating pseudorandom numbers, would we not benefit from languages which have such features automatically available so that we can save programming time? Special languages do not necessarily save substantial amounts of computer time, but the overall cost of a project is certainly reduced if we significantly decrease the number of man-months of programming required to develop a simulation model.

SIMSCRIPT vs DYNAMO

Let us proceed to compare SIMSCRIPT and DYNAMO. Our comparison of these languages is summarized in Table 1. First, the world view of SIMSCRIPT involves some concepts that we call *entities*, *attributes*, *sets* and *events*. In DYNAMO the world view consists primarily of *levels* and *rates*. We have special types of equations in DYNAMO for auxiliaries and functions, but most important are the level and rate equations. SIMSCRIPT facilitates modeling discrete state changes whereas DYNAMO facilitates modeling continuous state changes. Related to this distinction, we note that SIMSCRIPT is designed to be a variable time increment simulation. Between successive events, the amount of time can vary randomly. In other words, the time between birth and death might be 87.3 years, or the time between birth and marriage might be 18.9 years, as generated from a random process. In DYNAMO, we have a fixed-time increment between changes in the system's status equations. This is equivalent to the case in a FORTRAN "do-loop" where elements within the loop change state in discrete steps each time the increment

SIMSCRIPT	DYNAMO
(1) World View: Entities; Attributes; Sets; Events	(1) World View: Levels; Rates; Auxiliaries; Functions
(2) Facilitates modeling of discrete state changes (micro-focus)	(2) Facilitates modeling of continuous state changes (macro-focus)
(3) Variable time increment (Fixed time possible)	(3) Fixed time increment
(4) Fortran-English syntax	(4) Differential Equation syntax
(5) Event-oriented computation (Time-oriented possible)	(5) Time-oriented computation
(6) General purposes Procedure-oriented Compiler language	(6) Specific scope Problem-oriented Interpreter language
(7) Advantages/Disadvantages . Flexible input/output . Flexible programming . Difficult to learn . Difficult for novice to debug . Compilation costly . Execution inexpensive	(7) Advantages/Disadvantages . Restricted but attractive input/output . Restricted programming . Easy to learn . Diagnostics clear . Execution very inexpensive

Table 1. A COMPARISON OF SIMSCRIPT AND DYNAMO

is updated. DYNAMO advances its simulation clock in this fashion.

SIMSCRIPT is event-oriented rather than time-oriented. In other words, we first determine the next most imminent event to be executed, next update the clock, and then make the relevant status changes. In DYNAMO (as usual in continuous simulation languages) first we update the clock in constant increments and upon each update of the clock, we scan the entities in the system to determine the amount of change in each level, rate, and auxiliary for that particular time period. Thus DYNAMO is said to be "time-oriented."

The two languages also differ in syntax. The syntax of SIMSCRIPT is very similar to FORTRAN, but also permits a bit more "free-English" style than FORTRAN, as can be seen from the example in Appendix A. On the other hand, DYNAMO has a differential-equation syntax as illustrated in Appendix B. The differential equation notions are really quite elementary: if DYNAMO seems forbidding or intimidating at first, one need not be concerned since it is a very straightforward language once one understands levels and rates.

SIMSCRIPT is a general purpose language, as is FORTRAN. In fact, SIMSCRIPT is more powerful than FORTRAN, in that it features dynamic storage allocation and list processing. SIMSCRIPT is similar to PL/1 in this regard, since PL/1 also has a list processing feature. However, SIMSCRIPT is a bit more attractive than PL/1 for simulation purposes because it has a built-in next-event timing mechanism as well as pseudo-random number generators for several distributions, including the uniform (both integral and continuous), beta, gamma, normal, exponential, Weibull, Erlang, and so forth. About a dozen random process generators are built into the language. The basic generator was written up in the Communications of the ACM (Gorenstein 1967). It is a multiplicative congruential generator with ten possible seeds. You sample from the ten streams by specifying an integer between 1 and 10 as an argument to the process generator you are using. To use antithetic sampling one may specify a negative integer from -1 to -10.

Since SIMSCRIPT is a general purpose language, it has much more flexible input and output than DYNAMO. It has an option of free or formatted READ and WRITE statements so that you can read from or write on disk, binary file, etc. Flexible programming also means that you can program special statistical functions, such as auto-correlation of time series data, if you so desire. This capability again makes it similar to FORTRAN.

SIMSCRIPT is a compiler language, being first translated into assembly code, and then into object code prior to execution, a feature which of course increases total computation time. Compilation is very costly in SIMSCRIPT, but execution is frequently shorter and less expensive than compilation. For example, it might cost twenty dollars to get a compilation, while execution of that run might cost only two dollars. Execution of a program in SIMSCRIPT will cost about one and one half times the amount required to do the same simulation in FORTRAN. DYNAMO, however, is an interpreter language which may be thought of as one big computer program. What you "program" in DYNAMO are merely input data cards. The interpreter accepts the data, goes through some initialization of the DYNAMO input cards, and then starts the simulation. Therefore, we find that since a true compilation is not required, DYNAMO is very inexpensive to operate. The little program in Appendix B cost about eighty-eight cents to run on an IBM 360/67, whereas the SIMSCRIPT model in Appendix A cost about eighteen dollars.

The languages differ in degree of learning difficulty. I would estimate that it takes about 60 hours in the classroom, plus individual study time, to learn the SIMSCRIPT language. FORTRAN is usually estimated to require somewhere in the neighborhood of 20 to 30 hours, while DYNAMO requires about 5 to 6 hours. In fact, DYNAMO is a very easy language to learn even without instruction, if you have already had exposure to several other languages.

Over the past three years, the Pennsylvania Transportation and Traffic Safety Center has been commissioned by the Army Corps of Engineers to develop a simulation model of the St. Lawrence Seaway. The first project used FORTRAN and simulated the movement of vessels up and down a single series of four locks and canals. This is a fairly complicated system because one must provide for queues developing on each side of each lock; provide for sequencing of lock gates opening; properly raise or lower the lock water level; etc. To make a long story short, it required about two man-years of programming time and about $2000 of computer time for the FORTRAN model. We have recently duplicated this simulation in SIMSCRIPT with some additional features: we now have the ability to read in at execution time any network of locks and canals desired. In other words, we read in the structure of the system at execution time, thus avoiding costly reprogramming delays for minor modifications. Therefore, once a SIMSCRIPT model is developed and programmed, it is very inexpensive to evaluate alternative configurations of a system. The costs of programming the St. Lawrence Seaway in SIMSCRIPT include six months of programmer time, and $2500 of computation time. So this is one case in which we feel that SIMSCRIPT is more effective than FORTRAN. Conceivably, there are several other instances in which it would be superior to FORTRAN. However, I am not about to argue that SIMSCRIPT is superior to FORTRAN in all cases. It depends upon the situation, and especially upon how important it is to represent discrete state changes. Likewise, if the phenomena of interest merit the assumption of continuity, then you probably should use a continuous simulation language approach. Let me proceed to develop in some detail the concepts of SIMSCRIPT: the entities, sets, attributes, and events.

SIMSCRIPT EXAMPLE

In Figure 1 it can be seen that I have designated *entities* as the circles and *sets* as the oval shapes. A *set* is conceptually a collection of entities. We see that an entity CITY can *own* a set BOYS and it can *own* a set ELKS. This illustrates how entities may own sets. Entities may also *belong to* sets, so that the MAN entities may *belong to* MASONS, BOYS, or ELKS. In SIMSCRIPT we can define entities, sets, entity-set membership relations, and ownership relations. Using this member-owner feature, we can build up a fairly complex tree structure in SIMSCRIPT, which is a very attractive capability, perhaps the most attractive feature of the language. For example, each of the MAN entities could own a set named FAMILY. And to the set named FAMILY could belong entities named CHILD. Furthermore, we could say that each CHILD will own its own set FAMILY so that in a hierarchical fashion, we develop a genealogical structure. This is a fairly simple concept.

One might ask how this tree-structure is really accomplished by the computer. Note that I have only discussed entities and sets to this point. The owner and member relationships are implemented in the machine by means of *attributes*. An entity is defined as a group of attributes while an attribute is merely a computer storage word in which we store *list pointers*. For example, if we declare that MAN is to belong to the set MASONS, SIMSCRIPT will automatically define two special attributes, one whose name has the prefix letter P, another that has the prefix letter S. Figure 2 shows P.MASONS and S.MASONS for each MAN entity. The P attribute stands for *predecessor* in the set MASONS, while the S stands for *successor* in the set MASONS. The first MAN may be stored at location 100, the second MAN at location 300, and the third at location 423. Once we have established a set of MAN entities belonging to the set MASONS, the second MAN would have as the content of his P.MASONS attribute the value 100, denoting (or

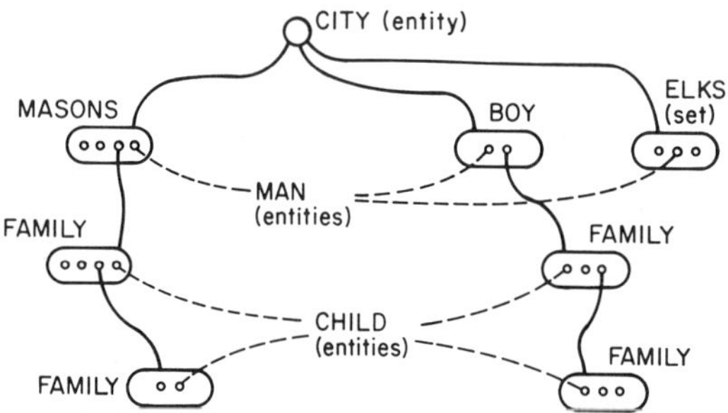

Figure 1. RELATIONSHIPS OF ENTITIES AND SETS IN SIMSCRIPT

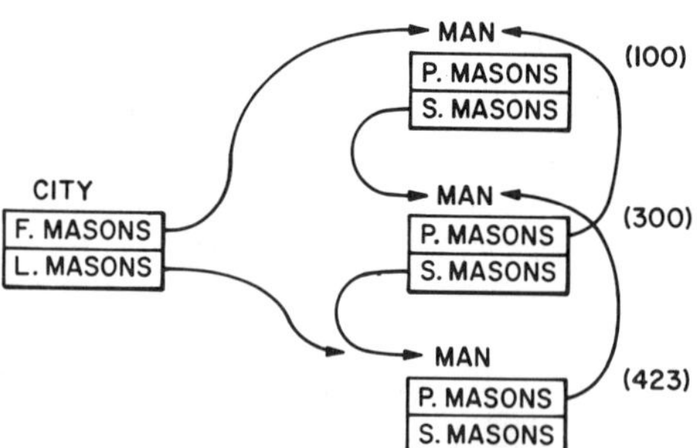

Figure 2. ATTRIBUTES AS SET-POINTERS IN SIMSCRIPT

"pointing" back to) the predecessor of the second MAN. Similarly, the predecessor attribute of the third MAN would contain the value 300, so that the P.MASONS attribute points back to the second MAN. In a similar fashion we link up the "list" through successor attributes (technically we call this a doubly-linked list). S.MASONS points to the successor of the current MAN. Thus, the S.MASONS attribute of the second MAN points to that second MAN's successor, which of course would be the third MAN, stored at 423.

We designate *ownership* of sets by having two special purpose attributes of an owner entity which are F and L prefixed to the set name (F meaning first, L meaning last). Thus the owner entity has two special purpose attributes: F.set-name pointing to the first MAN in the set; and L.set-name pointing to the last MAN in the set. An entity may own or belong to more than one set; sets may be empty at any point in simulated time. The fact that entities do not have to be stored consecutively makes possible their creation and elimination without changing the positions of other entities in storage.

When entities are created, SIMSCRIPT reserves the attributes necessary to represent their set membership and their set ownership relations. Every time we specify that a MAN is to be created, the computer automatically generates a P.MASONS and S.MASONS, a P.BOYS and S.BOYS, a P.ELKS and an S.ELKS, and so forth for the new MAN entity. These attributes are automatically defined by SIMSCRIPT, which creates and reserves the proper storage locations when you execute a command to create an entity. The actual command used is: CREATE A MAN. In response to this command SIMSCRIPT scans the core storage; it reserves a block of five or six, or however many words are needed for set linkages; and it initializes the possibility of set linkages. You may then carry out several operations such as FILE MAN INTO ELKS, or REMOVE MAN FROM BOYS, which are examples of SIMSCRIPT statements. REMOVE MAN FROM BOYS would take the entity MAN out of a set by resetting the appropriate P and S attributes. All list processing routines are carried out in this fashion. Note that articles are synonymous: A, THE and SOME have exactly the same meaning to the computer. The reason for this is simply to facilitate writing the statements in grammatically correct English.

Let us now take a look at how we actually go about defining the syntax of this example in SIMSCRIPT. We have a PREAMBLE which is the first section in the computer program. To establish this structure we would write: EVERY CITY OWNS SOME ELKS, SOME BOYS, AND THE MASONS. This syntax communicates to the computer the necessary set pointers to be defined and reserves in core storage the pattern for every entity CITY that will be specified. We then say: EVERY MAN MAY OWN A FAMILY AND CAN BELONG TO THE ELKS, THE MASONS, AND THE BOYS. Similarly we can say: EVERY CHILD MAY BELONG TO A FAMILY AND CAN OWN A FAMILY. I would like to stress the last statement because this type of statement has potential for genealogical studies which exhibit a hierarchy of generations: we can have in a genealogical sequence a CHILD, owning a set FAMILY; to that set FAMILY belong other CHILD entities; each of these entities can own its own FAMILY; and then the entities in these FAMILIES may also own other CHILD entities, etc. This illustrates the potentially "understandable" English-oriented syntax that we can use in SIMSCRIPT.

A "PLAGUE" IN SIMSCRIPT vs DYNAMO

Let us examine a "Plague" model in order to see another example of an entity-set structure. As shown in Figure 3, each entity TOWN owns four sets. These sets are WELL, INFE (infected), SICK, and IMMUNE. PERSON entities may belong to these sets. This structure is established in the PREAMBLE which is shown in the program listing page 1 in Appendix A. The relevant statements are EVERY TOWN OWNS A WELL, AN INFE, A SICK, AND AN IMMUNE, and EVERY PERSON BELONGS TO A WELL, AN INFE, A SICK, AND AN IMMUNE.

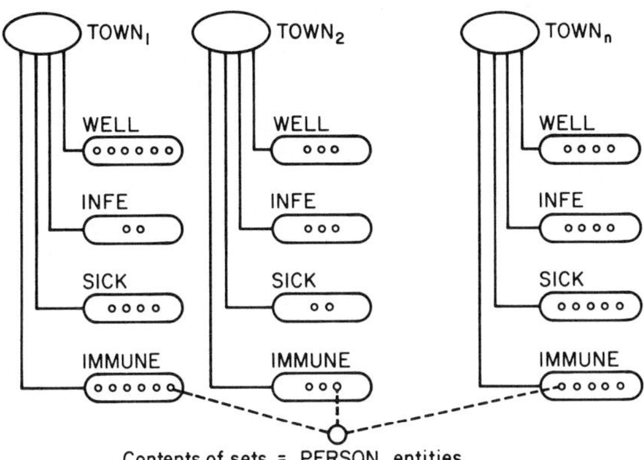

Figure 3. SIMSCRIPT PLAGUE MODEL

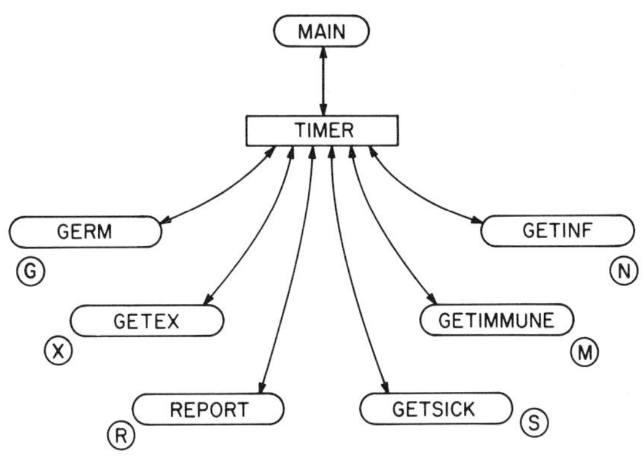

Figure 4. SIMSCRIPT TIMING CONTROL

Other declarations of a similar nature are made in the PREAMBLE.

The MAIN routine (listing page 2) reads a data card containing the population size of each town; specifies N.TOWN, the number of towns; calculates N.PERSON, the total population; CREATES all the PERSON and TOWN entities; and files each PERSON in the set WELL(TOWN). After printing a heading, the statement START SIMULATION is encountered, which passes control to a timing routine (TIMER) built into SIMSCRIPT. This routine is responsible for determining the order and timing of events.

Before continuing with the plague simulation, let us look at the operation of these "events" which are represented in SIMSCRIPT by special subroutines. You will recall that in FORTRAN, transfer of control to a subroutine is accomplished by a specific CALL statement each time it is to be used. In SIMSCRIPT, on the other hand, control is transferred from one routine to the next at some future time, specified in advance. Unlike FORTRAN, SIMSCRIPT allows a subroutine to call itself.

The first special purpose subprogram executed is named GERM, which is an exogenous event and which has causation linkages to other event routines. The exogenous events are scheduled by reading in a data card. At the back of the program deck would be a data card which says GERM and then specifies the time at which GERM is to be executed. It so happens in this case that the first data card says that GERM is to be executed at time zero of the simulation. When this happens the computer reserves storage space for a special *entity* also named GERM. This entity has an attribute in which is stored that event's time of future occurrence. Next the entity GERM is filed in a special set by the name of EV.S (events set). The timer routine then examines the events set to determine which is the next event to be executed, i.e., which entity has the lowest time-of-occurrence value. At first this will be the GERM event, so the timer takes the GERM entity out of the set EV.S and then transfers control to the subroutine named GERM as shown in Figure 4. Let us examine the printout of event GERM in Appendix A. First comes the statement CAUSE A REPORT NEXT. This means REPORT will be scheduled to occur as soon as GERM is finished. We show in Figure 5 that GERM causes REPORT after a time increment Δt equal to zero, which means no delay. CAUSE is a key word which creates a special entity for the pending event and files this entity into the set EV.S. The next statement in event GERM is CAUSE A GETINF NOW. The two words NEXT and NOW are synonyms. CAUSE A GETINF NOW means that an *entity* GETINF is filed into the events set. The final statement in GERM is RETURN. But to where does control return? It returns to the master timing routine as shown in Figure 4. The master timing routine now re-examines the events set. It again determines the next event, i.e. the event with the most imminent occurrence time. Now TIMER sees that the pending REPORT and GETINF both have a value of 0, meaning that both are to be executed at time 0. Therefore the timer picks the first event that was filed into the set, which happens to be REPORT. Control is transferred to event REPORT. Now examine the printout of event REPORT in Appendix A. As you can see, output capabilities are fairly flexible. When we say PRINT 3 LINES WITH TIME.V THUS we essentially have a "free field" output statement, putting asterisks in the columns where we want the output to be printed. In the event REPORT note that we "bootstrap," in other words, we always schedule the next report ten time units hence, so that one report is always pending future execution. This aspect is accomplished by line 16 of REPORT in Appendix A as SCHEDULE THIS REPORT AT TIME.V + 10. After REPORT is finished, control comes back to the timing mechanism.

The next event is a GETINF (get infected). What happens in GETINF? The infected person randomly contacts from one to five persons who are not sick. There is a 90 per cent chance that the PERSON who is infecting others is going to contact someone in his

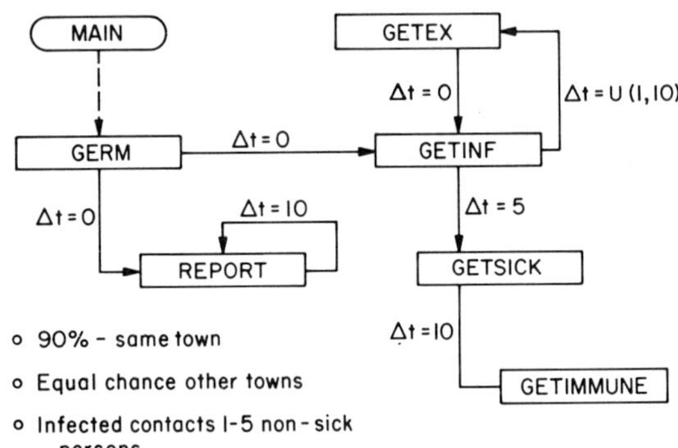

Figure 5. EVENT LINKAGE IN SIMSCRIPT

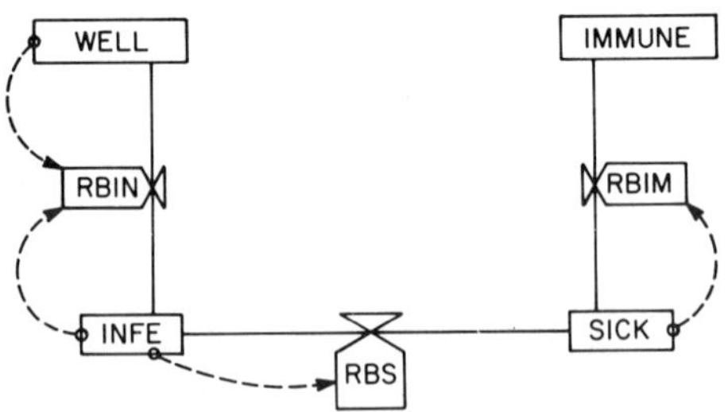

Figure 6. DYNAMO PLAGUE MODEL

own town, and a 10 per cent chance that he will contact a person in one of the other four towns. The probabilities of choosing one of the four towns are equally distributed. RANDI symbolizes a uniformly distributed discrete variate. Next, a GETEX (get exposed) event is scheduled for each of the contacted persons. Let us suppose the first infected person is going to contact three other persons. The GETEX events might be scheduled to occur at times 3, 5, and 6. The three GETEX entities are filed in proper order in EV.S. Next control is returned to the timer routine which proceeds in the same fashion, scanning the event set to see which is the next most imminent event. When control is transferred to one of the event routines the clock is automatically updated. A fairly interesting feedback process has begun to occur: the more people infected, the more exposures there will be; the more exposures there are, the more people will then become infected. After a person is infected he will become sick (GETSICK) after a delay of five days. Upon becoming sick we assume that he will be a good citizen and will not contact other persons who are in the WELL set. After a delay of ten days the sick person will be filed into the set IMMUNE. Each of the events GETSICK and GETIMMUNE are simply set-manipulation events. They take an entity out of one set and put it into another set.

Let us review the tabulated results on the last page of Appendix A. On day 0 we start off with 1500 people all in the set WELL. On day 10 we have a few people who are exposed, a couple of people who are sick, and a couple who are already immune. We observe that the process starts to move quite rapidly on day 20, and it grows more rapidly still by day 30. On day 40 it continues and on day 50 it looks as though most people have become sick or immune. Note here that by day 60 the plague has almost completely passed through the entire population of entities. They have all been shifted from one set WELL, to the next set EXPOSED, to the next set SICK, and finally to the set IMMUNE. After the 70th day about 10 per cent of the population have not been contacted by any sick persons; they are still in the set WELL.

Of course this model is a purely illustrative device, and I do not claim that it corresponds very closely to real-life processes. Nevertheless, the fact that there exists a certain number of persons who remain uninfected is interesting in itself. Perhaps this is due to the randomness built into the system, or possibly to the discrete time-advance nature of this simulation.

In contrast to SIMSCRIPT, DYNAMO approaches the process in a somewhat different fashion. Rather than dealing with discrete entities which are moved from membership in one set to membership in another (i.e., from WELL to INF, to SICK, to IMMUNE), DYNAMO simply establishes a set of interrelated equations whose solutions represent either *levels* (sizes of various classes of entities), or *rates* (quantities by which the various levels are changed at each increment of time). In the plague example shown in Figure 6 and in the listing in Appendix B, four level equations, corresponding to the sets in the SIMSCRIPT program, are established. These are denoted as levels by the L in the first column of the relevant statements in the listing. Statements preceded by an R in the first column are rate equations: RBIN (rate of becoming infected), RBS (rate of becoming sick), and RBIM (rate of becoming immune). *Auxiliaries*, denoted by an initial A, are intermediate equations which are used to establish relationships such as feedback between levels and rates. Suffixes J, K, and L associated with levels denote preceding, present, and next time period, respectively. The suffixes JK and KL associated with rates indicate the time period over which the given rate is to be applied (in the level equations), or computed (in the auxiliary equations). Statements preceded by an N are those in which levels are initialized; an initial C denotes statements in which a constant is set, while NOTE indicates a non-executable comment. The SPEC statement specifies time increment (here DT = 0.5 days), duration of the simulation (LENGTH = 50), as well as print and plot intervals. I/O statements are preceded by PRINT or PLOT.

The tabular output in Appendix B shows the results. Those unaffected by the plague are shown in the WELL column. Starting at 1999 at the end of Day 0 (remember, DT = 0.5 day), this group is essentially depleted by the end of Day 25. Those infected (INFE) begin to increase, and peak by Day 20, etc. The plot on the next page shows one of DYNAMO's most attractive features: a graphical representation of the WELL time path may be obtained by connecting the W's in the plot, etc. The ease with which this can be done can be seen by looking at the PLOT statements in the listing.

Let me refer again to Table 1 as a summary of the advantages and disadvantages of SIMSCRIPT and DYNAMO. SIMSCRIPT has flexible programming and I/O, but it is relatively expensive to run, and relatively difficult for the novice to learn. Once you have made the investment, however, you have a powerful tool for microsimulation at your disposal. DYNAMO is very attractive if you are dealing with large numbers of entities, and you wish to specify complex interactions. That is to say, it is intended for macrosimulation. I should also mention that there is available what is essentially a FORTRAN version of SIMSCRIPT called GASP (Pritsker and Kiviat 1969). This language allows you to write part of the routines in FORTRAN, but the simulation timing mechanism is already written for you. I should think that DYSTAL (Sakoda, this volume) would also be attractive to FORTRAN users who did not want to make the transition to SIMSCRIPT. In any case, there are a number of possible alternatives to FORTRAN which may prove advantageous in simulation.

APPENDIX A. SIMSCRIPT LISTING

```
LINE  CACI SIMSCRIPT II.5  REL/VERS 6B                          02/21/73   PAGE   1

 ''               PLAGUE SIMULATION
               PREAMBLE
       LAST COLUMN IS 80
               PERMANENT ENTITIES.....
               EVERY TOWN OWNS A WELL, AN INF, A SICK, AND AN IMMUNE
               EVERY PERSON BELONGS TO A WELL, AN INF, A SICK AND AN IMMUNE
               DEFINE WELL, INF, SICK, IMMUNE AS SETS WITHOUT
                    FF,FA,FB,RF,RL ROUTINES

               EVENT NOTICES INCLUDE REPORT
               EVERY GETINF
               HAS A NAME IN WORD 6 AND A MTOWN IN WORD 7
               EVERY GETEX
               HAS A NAME IN WORD 6 AND A MTOWN IN WORD 7
               EVERY GETSICK
               HAS A NAME IN WORD 6 AND A MTOWN IN WORD 7
               EVERY GETIMMUNE
               HAS A NAME IN WORD 6 AND A MTOWN IN WORD 7
               DEFINE NAME, MTOWN AS INTEGER VARIABLES
               EXTERNAL EVENTS ARE GERM
       DEFINE POPULATION.PER.TOWN AS A REAL VARIABLE
               DEFINE I,FPERSON,LPERSON,          LIMIT  AS INTEGER VARIABLES
               END

LINE  CACI SIMSCRIPT II.5  REL/VERS 6B                          02/21/73   PAGE   2

               MAIN
       READ POPULATION.PER.TOWN
               LET N.TOWN=5
       LET N.PERSON = N.TOWN * POPULATION.PER.TOWN
               CREATE EACH PERSON
               CREATE EACH TOWN
               FOR EACH TOWN DO
       FOR PERSON = POPULATION.PER.TOWN *(TOWN-1)+1 TO
             POPULATION.PER.TOWN*TOWN   DO
               FILE PERSON IN WELL(TOWN)
               LOOP
               LOOP
               START NEW PAGE
               PRINT 1 LINE THUS
                                  PLAGUE SIMULATION
               SKIP 5 LINES

               START SIMULATION
               PRINT 1 LINE WITH TIME.V THUS
         END OF SIMULATION AT TIME ****.**
               STOP
               END

LINE  CACI SIMSCRIPT II.5  REL/VERS 6B                          02/21/73   PAGE   3


               EVENT GERM
               CAUSE A REPORT NEXT
               CAUSE A GETINF NOW
               LET NAME(GETINF)=F.WELL(1)
               LET MTOWN(GETINF)=1
               RETURN
               END

LINE  CACI SIMSCRIPT II.5  REL/VERS 6B                          02/21/73   PAGE   4


               EVENT GETINF
               LET PERSON = NAME(GETINF)
               LET TOWN=MTOWN(GETINF)
               REMOVE PERSON FROM WELL(TOWN)
               FILE PERSON IN INF(TOWN)
               LET LIMIT=RANDI.F(1,05,1)
               FOR I=1 TO LIMIT DO
               SCHEDULE A GETEX AT TIME.V+UNIFORM.F(1.0,10.0,1)
               LET MTOWN(GETEX)=TOWN
               LOOP
               SCHEDULE A GETSICK AT TIME.V+5.0
               LET NAME(GETSICK)=PERSON
               LET MTOWN(GETSICK)= TOWN
               RETURN
               END
```

```
LINE   CACI SIMSCRIPT II.5  REL/VERS 6B                          02/21/73   PAGE    5

                    EVENT GETEX
                    LET TOWN=MTOWN(GETEX)
      'TOP'         LET I=RANDI.F(1,10,1)
                    IF I¬=1 GO TO INTOWN ELSE
      'REPEAT'      LET I = RANDI.F(1,5,1)
                    IF I=TOWN GO TO REPEAT ELSE
                    LET TOWN = I

      'INTOWN'      IF N.SICK(TOWN) = POPULATION.PER.TOWN
                                 RETURN ELSE
                  LET FPERSON=POPULATION.PER.TOWN *(TOWN-1)+1
                  LET LPERSON=POPULATION.PER.TOWN *TOWN
      'REP'         LET PERSON = RANDI.F(FPERSON,LPERSON,1)
                    IF PERSON IS IN SICK      GO TO REP ELSE
                    IF PERSON IS NOT IN WELL RETURN ELSE
                    CAUSE A GETINF NOW
                    LET NAME(GETINF)=PERSON
                    LET MTOWN(GETINF)=TOWN
                    RETURN
                    END

LINE   CACI SIMSCRIPT II.5  REL/VERS 6B                          02/21/73   PAGE    6

                    EVENT GETSICK
                    LET PERSON = NAME(GETSICK)
                    LET TOWN=MTOWN(GETSICK)
                    REMOVE PERSON FROM INF(TOWN)
                    FILE PERSON IN SICK(TOWN)
                    LET SICKTIME = 10.0
                    IF RANDI.F(1,2,1)=1 LET SICKTIME=0. ELSE
                    SCHEDULE A GETIMMUNE AT TIME.V+SICKTIME
                    LET NAME(GETIMMUNE)=PERSON
                    LET MTOWN(GETIMMUNE)=TOWN
                    RETURN
                    END

LINE   CACI SIMSCRIPT II.5  REL/VERS 6B                          02/21/73   PAGE    7

                    EVENT GETIMMUNE
                    LET PERSON=NAME(GETIMMUNE)
                    LET TOWN=MTOWN(GETIMMUNE)
                    REMOVE PERSON FROM SICK (TOWN)
                    FILE PERSON IN IMMUNE (TOWN)
                    RETURN
                    END

LINE   CACI SIMSCRIPT II.5  REL/VERS 6B                          02/21/73   PAGE    8


                    EVENT REPORT SAVING THE EVENT NOTICE
                    PRINT 3 LINES WITH TIME.V THUS
        DAY ***.*

TOWN              WELL       EXPOSED    SICK       IMMUNE
         LET K = 0
         SKIP 1 LINE
                    FOR EACH TOWN DO
                    PRINT 1 LINE WITH
                          TOWN,N.WELL(TOWN),N.INF(TOWN),N.SICK(TOWN), N.IMMUNE(TOWN)
                                THUS
**                ***         ***        ***        ***
         IF N.INF(TOWN) + N.SICK(TOWN) = ZERO AND  N.IMMUNE(TOWN) GT ZERO
                    ADD 1 TO K   OTHERWISE
                    LOOP
                    SKIP 5 LINES
         IF K EQ N.TOWN RETURN ELSE
      'NE'          SCHEDULE THIS REPORT AT TIME.V + 10.0
                    RETURN
                    END
```

PLAGUE SIMULATION

DAY 0.

TOWN	WELL	EXPOSED	SICK	IMMUNE
1	300	0	0	0
2	300	0	0	0
3	300	0	0	0
4	300	0	0	0
5	300	0	0	0

DAY 10.0

TOWN	WELL	EXPOSED	SICK	IMMUNE
1	288	8	2	2
2	300	0	0	0
3	297	3	0	0
4	300	0	0	0
5	298	2	0	0

DAY 20.0

TOWN	WELL	EXPOSED	SICK	IMMUNE
1	202	58	17	23
2	295	5	0	0
3	271	15	6	8
4	295	5	0	0
5	277	14	2	7

DAY 30.0

TOWN	WELL	EXPOSED	SICK	IMMUNE
1	53	56	74	117
2	250	34	6	10
3	154	74	27	45
4	218	57	11	14
5	170	68	24	38

DAY 40.0

TOWN	WELL	EXPOSED	SICK	IMMUNE
1	17	9	33	241
2	71	90	69	70
3	21	44	89	146
4	54	76	70	100
5	42	42	73	143

DAY 50.0

TOWN	WELL	EXPOSED	SICK	IMMUNE
1	14	1	7	278
2	10	7	72	211
3	8	3	24	265
4	11	10	49	230
5	15	2	37	246

DAY 60.0

TOWN	WELL	EXPOSED	SICK	IMMUNE
1	14	0	1	285
2	10	0	5	285
3	8	0	3	289
4	9	0	6	285
5	12	1	2	285

DAY 70.0

TOWN	WELL	EXPOSED	SICK	IMMUNE
1	14	0	0	286
2	10	0	0	290
3	8	0	0	292
4	9	0	0	291
5	12	0	1	287

DAY 80.0

TOWN	WELL	EXPOSED	SICK	IMMUNE
1	14	0	0	286
2	10	0	0	290
3	8	0	0	292
4	9	0	0	291
5	12	0	0	288

APPENDIX B. DYNAMO LISTING

```
* PLAGUE DIFFUSION MODEL

L       WELL.K=WELL.J+(DT)(-RBIN.JK)
L       INFE.K=INFE.J+(DT)(RBIN.JK-RBS.JK)
L       SICK.K=SICK.J+(DT)(RBS.JK-RBIM.JK)
L       IMMU.K=IMMU.J+(DT)(RBIM.JK)
NOTE
NOTE      RATE EQUATIONS
NOTE
NOTE      INFECTED RATE  NEVER EXCEEDS NUMBER IN THE WELL LEVEL
NOTE
A       NCT.K=((CPI)(INFE.K)(WELL.K)/(WELL.K+INFE.K+IMMU.K))(PROB)
A       NUIN.K=DELAY3(NCT.K,MDCT)
R       RBIN.KL=MIN(WELL.K,NUIN.K)
NOTE
NOTE      SICK RATE NEVER EXCEEDS LEVEL INFECTED
NOTE
A       RBSN.K=DELAY3(INFE.K,IFD)
R       RBS.KL=MIN(INFE.K,RBSN.K)
NOTE
NOTE      IMMUNE RATE NEVER EXCEEDS SICK LEVEL
C       MDCT=5 DAYS MEAN DELAY FOR INFECTED TO CONTACT WELL PERSONS
NOTE
A       RNIM.K=DELAY3(SICK.K,SKD)
R       RBIM.KL=MIN(RNIM.K,SICK.K)
NOTE
NOTE      INITIAL VALUES OF LEVELS
NOTE
N       WELL=TOTAL-ONE
N       INFE=ONE
N       SICK=ZERO
N       IMMU=ZERO
NOTE
NOTE     CONSTANTS
NOTE
C       IFD=5  DAYS FOR INFECTION DELAY
C       SKD=10 DAYS FOR SICKNESS DURATION
C       PROB=5E-1    0.5 CHANCE OF INFECTION
C       CPI=5  CONTACTS MADE BY EACH INFECTED PERSON
C       TOTAL=2000    PERSONS IN THE SYSTEM
C       ONE=1    PERSON(S) INITIALLY INFECTED
C       ZERO=0 PERSON(S) INITIALLY SICK AND IMMUNE
NOTE
PRINT 1)WELL/2)INFE/3)SICK/4)IMMU/5)RBIN/6)RBS/7)RBIM
PLOT   WELL=W,INFE=N,SICK=I,IMMU=M(0,4000)
PLOT   RBIN=N,RBS=S,RBIM=M(0,2500)
PLOT   NUIN=N,RBSN=S,RNIM=M
SPEC   DT=0.5/LENGTH=50/PRTPER=1/PLTPER=1
RUN     1 BASIC PLAGUE MODEL
/*
```

TIME	WELL	INFE	SICK	IMMU	RBIN	RBS	RBIM
.0	1999.0	1.00	.0	.0	2.50	1.00	.00
1.	1996.5	2.50	1.0	.0	2.50	1.00	.00
2.	1994.0	4.00	2.0	.0	2.55	1.02	.00
3.	1991.4	5.57	3.0	.0	3.01	1.21	.02
4.	1988.1	7.52	4.3	.0	4.15	1.66	.08
5.	1983.6	10.26	6.0	.1	6.02	2.41	.21
6.	1976.9	14.23	8.4	.4	8.63	3.46	.41
7.	1967.5	19.89	11.7	.9	12.14	4.87	.73
8.	1954.3	27.81	16.2	1.7	16.89	6.79	1.18
9.	1935.9	38.80	22.3	3.0	23.44	9.44	1.81
10.	1910.3	54.04	30.6	5.0	32.54	13.14	2.68
11.	1874.9	75.16	42.0	8.0	45.17	18.31	3.87
12.	1825.7	104.37	57.7	12.2	62.61	25.53	5.50
13.	1757.6	144.66	79.5	18.2	86.52	35.57	7.72
14.	1663.6	199.93	109.9	26.7	119.02	49.50	10.75
15.	1534.4	275.15	152.1	38.4	162.70	68.79	14.90
16.	1358.2	376.40	210.8	54.6	220.39	95.41	20.61
17.	1120.4	510.40	292.2	77.0	294.55	132.00	28.47
18.	804.1	683.23	404.8	108.0	385.79	181.93	39.33
19.	392.8	896.93	559.5	150.7	392.79	249.40	54.37
20.	98.2	921.22	770.7	209.9	98.20	339.26	75.20
21.	24.5	628.18	1055.5	291.7	24.55	454.97	104.04
22.	6.1	212.62	1376.3	404.9	6.14	212.62	143.89
23.	1.5	56.22	1380.8	561.4	1.53	56.22	198.76
24.	.4	14.82	1207.3	777.4	.38	14.82	272.51
25.	.1	3.90	924.2	1071.8	.10	3.90	363.15
26.	.0	1.02	539.5	1459.5	.02	1.02	461.81
27.	.0	.27	154.8	1844.9	.01	.27	154.81
28.	.0	.07	38.8	1961.1	.00	.07	38.84
29.	.0	.02	9.7	1990.2	.00	.02	9.74
30.	.0	.00	2.4	1997.5	.00	.00	2.45

```
WELL=W,INFE=N,SICK=I,IMMU=M

    0.                     1000.                    2000.
  .0N - - - - - - - - - - - - - - - - - - - - - - - - W -
    N                        .                        W
    N                        .                        W
    N                        .                        W
    N                        .                        W
    N                        .                        W
    N                        .                       W.
    N                        .                       W.
    IN                       .                       W.
    MN                       .                      W .
 10.MN- - - - - - - - - - - - - - - - - - - - - - - W - -
    MIN                      .                     W  .
    MI N                     .                    W   .
    M I N                    .                  W     .
    .M I N                   .                W       .
    .M  I  N                 .            W           .
    .M   I   N               .        W               .
    . M    I     N           .  W                     .
    .  M      I      N  W    .                        .
    .   M     W   I       N  .                        .
 20.- W -M- - - - - - -I- -N- - - - - - - - - - - - - - -
    .W     M        N        .I                       .
    W    N    M              .        I               .
    WN            M          .         I              .
    W                  M     .    I                   .
    W                      I . M                      .
    W            I           .          M             .
    W   I                    .                    M   .
    WI                       .                       M.
    W                        .                        M
 30.W - - - - - - - - - - - - - - - - - - - - - - - - M -
```

REFERENCES

Forrester, J. W. 1968. Principles of Systems. Cambridge: Wright-Allen Press.

Gorenstein, S. 1967. Testing a random number generator, Comm. of the ACM 10, 2: 111-118.

Kiviat, P. J., R. Villaneuva and H. M. Markowitz 1968. The SIMSCRIPT II Programming Language. Englewood Cliffs, N.J.: Prentice-Hall.

Pritsker, A. A. B. and P. J. Kiviat 1969. Simulation with GASP II: A FORTRAN Based Simulation Language. Englewood Cliffs, N.J.: Prentice-Hall.

Pugh, A. L. 1970. DYNAMO II User's Manual. Cambridge: MIT Press.

Sakoda, J. M. 1973. The use of DYSTAL in simulation. In Computer Simulation in Human Population Studies, B. Dyke and J. W. MacCluer (eds.), New York: Seminar Press.

Wyman, F. P. 1970. Simulation Modeling: A Guide to Using SIMSCRIPT. New York: Wiley.

BIBLIOGRAPHY

The bibliography listed below is maintained in a computerized information retrieval system (BAG, General Purpose Bibliographic and Grouping System) developed by Dr. John B. Smith of The Pennsylvania State University. We have included primarily references to microsimulation models and techniques in anthropology and social systems, human genetics, and demography.

Abelson, R. P., 1968. Simulation of social behavior. In G. Lindzey and E. Aronson (Eds.) *The Handbook of Social Psychology,* Vol. II. Reading, Massachusetts: Addison Wesley, pp. 274-356.

Anderson, W. W. and C. E. King 1970. Age-specific selection. *Proceedings of the National Academy of Sciences* **66:** 780-786.

Apter, M. J. 1970. *The Computer Simulation of Behavior.* New York: Harper and Row.

Barrett, J. C. 1967. A Monte Carlo simulation of reproduction. In W. Brass (Ed.) *Symposium on Biological Aspects of Demography.* London: Society for the Study of Human Biology.

Barrett, J. C. 1969. A Monte Carlo simulation of human reproduction. *Genus* **25.**

Barrett, J. C. 1971. Use of a fertility simulation model to refine measurement techniques. *Demography* **8:** 481-490.

Barrett, J. C. 1972. The time response in averted births. *Population Studies* **26:** 507-514.

Beshers, J. M. 1965. Substantive issues in models of large-scale social systems. In J. M. Beshers (Ed.) *Computer Methods in the Analysis of Large-Scale Social Systems.* Cambridge, Massachusetts: M.I.T.-Harvard Joint Center for Urban Studies. Pp. 85-91.

Beshers, J. M. 1967. Computer models of social processes: the case of migration. *Demography* **4:** 838-842.

Bodmer, W. and A. Jacquard 1968. La variance de la dimension des familles selon divers facteurs de la fécondité. *Population* **23:** 869-878.

Bongaarts, J. P. and W. D. O'Neill 1972. A systems model for the population renewal process. *Demography* **9:** 309-320.

Boughey, A. S., J. B. Pick, and G. N. Schick 1973. A migration model. In B. Dyke and J. W. MacCluer (Eds.) *Computer Simulation in Human Population Studies.* New York: Academic Press.

Brown, L. A. 1963. The Diffusion of Innovation: a Markov Chain Approach. *Discussion Paper Series* No. 3. Evanston: Northwestern Univ.

Brown, L. A. 1965. Models for Spatial Diffusion Research: A Review. *Technical Report* No. 3. Evanston: Northwestern Univ., Department of Geography.

Brown, L. A. and E. G. Moore. 1968. Diffusion Research In Geography: A Perspective. *Discussion Paper* No. 9. Iowa City: Univ. of Iowa.

Brues, A. M. 1954. Selection and polymorphism in the ABO blood groups. *American Journal of Physical Anthropology* **12:** 559-598.

Brues, A. M. 1963. Stochastic tests of selection in the ABO blood groups. *American Journal of Physical Anthropology* **21:** 287-299.

Brues, A. M. 1973. Models applicable to geographic variation in man. In B. Dyke and J. W. MacCluer (Eds.) *Computer Simulation in Human Population Studies.* New York: Academic Press.

Cannings, C. and M. H. Skolnick. Homeostatic mechanisms in human populations: a computer study. Oxford: International Congress of Cybernetics and Systems. In press.

Cannings, C. and M. H. Skolnick 1973. A study of human evolution by computer simulation. Fourth International Congress of Human Genetics, Paris.

Carroll, T. W. 1969. SINDI 2: Simulation of Dairy Innovation Diffusion in a Brazilian Rural Township. *Technical Report* No. 8, Project of Diffusion of Innovations in Rural Societies. East Lansing: Michigan State Univ.

Cavalli-Sforza, L. L. and W. F. Bodmer 1971. *The Genetics of Human Populations.* New York: W. H. Freeman. Pp. 455-459, 841-848.

Cavalli-Sforza, L. L. and G. Zei 1967. Experiments with an artificial population. In J. F. Crow and J. V. Neel (Eds.) *Proceedings of the Third International Congress of Human Genetics.* Baltimore: Johns Hopkins Press. Pp. 473-478.

Cavalli-Sforza, L. L. 1969. "Genetic drift" in an Italian population. *Scientific American* **221**(2): 30-37.

Clague, A. S. and J. C. Ridley 1973. The assessment of three methods of estimating births averted. In B. Dyke and J. W. MacCluer (Eds.) *Computer Simulation in Human Population Studies.* New York: Academic Press.

Coe, R. M. 1964. Conflict, interference, and aggression: computer simulation of a social process. *Behavioral Science* **9:** 186-196.

Coleman, J. S. 1961. Analysis of social structures and simulation of social processes with electronic computers. *Educational and Psychological Measurement* **21:** 203-218.

Coleman, J. S. 1964. *Introduction to Mathematical Sociology.* New York: Free Press.

Deutschmann, P. J. 1962. *A Machine Simulation of Information Diffusion in a Small Community.* San Jose, Costa Rica: Programma Interamericano de Informacion Popular.

Dutton, J. M. and W. H. Starbuck 1971. Computer simulation models of human behavior: a history of an intellectual technology. *IEEE Transactions on Systems, Man, and Cybernetics* **SMC-1:** 128-171.

Dutton, J. M. and W. H. Starbuck 1971. *Computer Simulation of Human Behavior.* New York: Wiley.

Dyke, B. 1973. Estimation of changing rates by simulation. In B. Dyke and J. W. MacCluer (Eds.) *Computer Simulation in Human Population Studies.* New York: Academic Press.

Dyke, B. and J. W. MacCluer 1973. Estimation of vital rates by means of Monte Carlo simulation, *Demography* **10.** 383-403.

Dyke, B. and J. W. MacCluer (Eds.) 1973. *Computer Simulation in Human Population Studies.* New York: Academic Press.

Edwards, J. H. 1960. The simulation of Mendelism. *Acta Genetica et Statistica Medica* **10:** 63-70.

Emshoff, J. R. and R. L. Sisson 1970. *Design and Use of Computer Simulation Models.* New York: Macmillan.

Finkner, A. L. and B. G. Greenberg 1969. Some applications of POPSIM, a computerized demographic microsimulation model. Paper prepared for Inaugural Conference, The Scientific Computation Center, Institute of Statistical Studies and Research, Cairo Univ.

Forrester, J. W. 1968. *Principles of Systems.* Cambridge, Massachusetts: Wright-Allen Press.

Forrester, J. W. 1971. *World Dynamics.* Cambridge, Massachusetts: Wright-Allen Press.

Fraser, A. S. and D. Burnell 1970. *Computer Models in Genetics.* New York: McGraw-Hill.

Fraser, A. S. 1957. Simulation of genetic systems by automatic digital computers. *Australian Journal of Biological Science* **10:** 484-499.

Funkhouser, G. R. 1968. A General Mathematical Model of Information Diffusion. *Report.* Stanford: Institute for Communication Research, Stanford Univ.

Funkhouser, G. R. 1970. A probabilistic model for predicting news diffusion. *Journalism Quarterly* 47(1): 41-45.

Garrison, W. L. 1962. Toward simulation models of urban growth and development. *Proceedings of the IGU Symposium in Urban Geography, Lund Studies in Geography, B,* **24:** 91-108.

Giesel, J. T. 1971. Inbreeding in a stationary, stable population as a function of age and fecundity distribution. *Genetics* **66:** s21.

Gilbert, J. P. and E. A. Hammel 1966. Computer simulation and analysis of problems in kinship and social structure. *American Anthropologist* **68:** 71-93.

Guetzkow, H. (Ed.) 1962. *Simulation in Social Science: Readings.* Englewood Cliffs, New Jersey: Prentice-Hall.

Gullahorn, J. T. and J. E. Gullahorn 1964. Computer simulation of human interaction in small groups. *1964 Spring Joint Computer Conference, Proc.* **25:** 103-113.

Gullahorn, J. T. and J. E. Gullahorn 1965. The computer as a tool for theory development. In D. H. Hymes (Ed.), *The Use of Computers in Anthropology.* The Hague: Mouton, pp. 427-448.

Gullahorn, J. T. and J. E. Gullahorn 1971. Social and cultural system simulations. In H. Guetzkow and P. Kotier (Eds.), *Simulation in Social and Administrative Science.* Englewood Cliffs, New Jersey: Prentice-Hall.

Hägerstrand, T. 1953. *The Propagation of Innovation Waves.* Royal Universities of Lund: Lund Studies in Geography.

Hägerstrand, T. 1965. Aspects of the spatial structure of social communication and the diffusion of information. *Regional Science Association Papers* **16:** 27-42.

Hägerstrand, T. 1965. Quantitative techniques for analysis of the spread of information and technology. In C. J. Anderson and M. J. Bowman (Eds.), *Education and Economic Development.* Chicago: Aldine. Pp. 244-280.

Hägerstrand, T. 1967. On the Monte Carlo simulation of diffusion. In W. L. Garrison and D. F. Marbles (Eds.), *Quantitative Geography, Part I, Economic and Cultural Topics.* Evanston, Illinois: Northwestern Univ. Press.

Hainline, J. 1963. Genetic exchange: model construction and a practical application. *Human Biology* **35:** 167-191.

Hajnal, J. 1963. Concepts of random mating and the frequency of consanguineous marriages. *Proceedings of the Royal Society, Part B,* **159:** 125-177.

Hammel, E. A. and D. Hutchinson 1973. Two tests of computer microsimulation: the effect of an incest tabu on population viability, and the effect of age differences between spouses on the skewing of consanguineal relationships between them. In B. Dyke and J. W. MacCluer (Eds.), *Computer Simulation in Human Population Studies.* New York: Academic Press

Handler, P. and J. Sherwood 1972. The PLATO system population dynamics course. In T. N. E. Greville (Ed.), *Population Dynamics.* New York: Academic Press. Pp. 419-434.

Hanna, J. 1970. Information-theoretic techniques for evaluating simulation models. In J. M. Dutton and W. A. Starbuck (Eds.), *Computer Simulation in Human Behavior.* New York: Wiley.

Hanneman, G. J. 1971. Stimulating diffusion processes. *Simulation and Games* **2:** 387–404.

Hanneman, G. J. 1973. Simulating information and innovation diffusion processes. In B. Dyke and J. W. MacCluer (Eds.), *Computer Simulation in Human Population Studies.* New York: Academic Press.

Hanneman, G. J. and T. W. Carroll 1970. SINDI 1: Simulation of Information Diffusion in a Peasant Community. *Technical Report* No. 7 of the Project on Diffusion of Innovations in Rural Societies. East Lansing, Michigan: Department of Communication, Michigan State Univ.

Hanneman, G. J., T. W. Carroll, E. M. Rogers, J. D. Stanfield, and N. Lin 1969. Computer simulation of innovation diffusion in a peasant village. *American Behavioral Scientist* **12:** 36-45.

Hays, D. G. 1965. Simulation: an introduction for anthropologists. In D. H. Hymes (Ed.), *The Use of Computers in Anthropology.* The Hague: Mouton. Pp. 401-426.

Heer, D. M. and D. O. Smith 1968. Mortality level, desired family size, and population increase. *Demography* **5:** 104-121.

Heer, D. M. and D. O. Smith 1969. Mortality level, desired family size and population increase: further variations on a basic model. *Demography* **6:** 141-149.

Heinmets, F. 1969. *Concepts and Models of Biomathematics: Simulation Techniques and Methods.* New York: Marcel Dekker.

Holland, J. H. 1973. A brief discussion of the role of co-adapted sets in the process of adaptation. In B. Dyke and J. W. MacCluer (Eds.), *Computer Simulation in Human Population Studies.* New York: Academic Press.

Holmberg, I. 1968. Demographic models (DM 4). *Demographic Institute Reports* No. 8. Gothenberg, Sweden: Univ. of Gothenberg.

Holmberg, I. 1970. Fecundity, fertility and family planning I. *Demographic Institute Reports.* Gothenberg, Sweden: Univ. of Gothenberg.

Holmberg, I. 1972. Fecundity, fertility and family planning II. *Demographic Institute Reports.* Gothenberg, Sweden: Univ. of Gothenberg.

Horvitz, D. G., F. G. Giesbrecht, B. V. Shah, and P. A. Lachenbruch 1971. POPSIM, a demographic microsimulation program. Monograph 12, Carolina Population Center, Univ. of North Carolina.

Horvitz, D. G., T. D. Hartwell, and J. R. Batts 1970. Simulation of hospital utilization. *Proceedings of the American Statistical Association* 1970: 129-138.

Hovland, C. I. 1963. Computer simulation in the behavioral sciences. In B. Berelson (Ed.), *The Behavioral Sciences Today.* New York: Basic Books.

Howell, N. 1973. An empirical perspective on simulation models of human populations. In B. Dyke and J. W. MacCluer (Eds.), *Computer Simulation in Human Population Studies.* New York: Academic Press.

Hurtubise, R. A. 1969. Sample sizes and confidence intervals associated with a Monte Carlo simulation model possessing a multinomial output. *Simulation* 1969: 71-77.

Hyrenius, H. 1965. New technique for studying demographic-economic-social interrelations. *Demographic Institute Reports* No. 3. Gothenberg, Sweden: Univ. of Gothenberg.

Hyrenius, H. 1973. Research and experience with demographic simulation models. In B. Dyke and J. W. MacCluer (Eds.), *Computer Simulation in Human Population Studies.* New York: Academic Press.

Hyrenius, H. and I. Adolfsson 1964. A fertility simulation model. *Demographic Institute Reports* No. 2. Gothenberg, Sweden: Univ. of Gothenberg.

Hyrenius, H., I. Adolfsson, and I. Holmberg 1966. Demographic models (DM 2). *Demographic Institute Reports* No. 4. Gothenberg, Sweden: Univ. of Gothenberg.

Hyrenius, H., I. Holmberg, and M. Carlsson 1967. Demographic models (DM 3). *Demographic Institute Reports* No. 5. Gothenberg, Sweden: Univ. of Gothenberg.

Imaizumi, Y., N. E. Morton, and D. E. Harris 1970. Isolation by distance in artificial populations. *Genetics* **66:** 569-582.

Jacquard, A. 1967. La reproduction humaine en régime malthusien. Un modèle de simulation par la méthode de Monte-Carlo. *Population* **22:** 897-920.

Jacquard, A. 1970. Panmixie et structure des familles, *Population* **25:** 69-76.

Jacquard, A. and H. Léridon 1973. Simulating human reproduction: how complicated should a model be? In B. Dyke and J. W. MacCluer (Eds.), *Computer Simulation in Human Population Studies.* New York: Academic Press.

Johnston, F. E. and M. E. Albers 1973. Computer simulation of demographic processes. In M. H. Crawford and P. L. Workman (Eds.), *Methods and Theories in Anthropological Genetics.* Albuquerque: Univ. of New Mexico Press.

Keyfitz, N. 1968. *Introduction to the Mathematics of Population.* Reading, Massachusetts: Addison-Wesley. Pp. 357-359, 374-375, 397-398.

Kibel, B. M. 1972. Simulation of the Urban Environment. *Commission on College Geography Technical Paper* No. 5. Washington: Association of American Geographers.

King, C. E. and W. W. Anderson 1971. Age-specific selection II. The interaction between "r" and "K" selection during population growth. *American Naturalist* **105:** 137-156.

Kiviat, P. J., R. Villaneuva, and H. M. Markowitz 1968. *The* SIMSCRIPT II *Programming Language.* Englewood Cliffs, New Jersey: Prentice-Hall.

Kunstadter, P. 1973. Footnotes on implications of aggregated data used in population simulation. In B. Dyke and J. W. MacCluer (Eds.) *Computer Simulation in Human Population Studies.* New York: Academic Press.

Kunstadter, P., R. Buhler, F. Stephen, and C. F. Westoff 1963. Demographic variability and preferential marriage patterns. *American Journal of Physical Anthropology* **21:**511-519.

Lachenbruch, P. A., M. C. Sheps, and A. M. Sorant 1973. Applications of POPREP, a modification of POPSIM. In B. Dyke and J. W. MacCluer (Eds.), *Computer Simulation in Human Population Studies.* New York: Academic Press.

Lee, C. F. 1972. Asymptotic implications of fluctuating nuptiality and fertility considering both sexes together. *Demography* **9:** 549-567.

Levin, B. R. 1967. The effect of reproductive compensation on the long term maintenance of the Rh polymorphism: the Rh crossroad revisited. *American Journal of Human Genetics* **19:** 288-302.

Levin, B. R. 1969. Simulation of genetic systems. In N. E. Morton (Ed.), *Computer Applications in Genetics.* Honolulu: Univ. of Hawaii Press. Pp. 38-46.

Li, F. H. F. and J. V. Neel 1973. A simulation of the fate of a mutant gene of neutral selective value in a primitive population. In B. Dyke and J. W. MacCluer (Eds.), *Computer Simulation in Human Population Studies.* New York: Academic Press.

Livingstone, F. B. 1969. The founder effect and deleterious genes. *American Journal of Physical Anthropology* **30:** 55-60.

Livingstone, F. B. 1969. Gene frequency clines of the hemoglobin locus in various human populations and their simulation by models involving differential selection. *Human Biology* **41:** 223-236.

Livingstone F. B. 1969. Polygenic models for the evolution of human skin color differences. *Human Biology* **41:** 480-493.

MacCluer, J. W. 1967. Monte Carlo methods in human population genetics: a computer model incorporating age-specific birth and death rates. *American Journal of Human Genetics* **19:** 303-312.

MacCluer, J. W. 1973. Avoidance of incest: genetic and demographic consequences. In B. Dyke and J. W. MacCluer (Eds.), *Computer Simulation in Human Population Studies.* New York: Academic Press.

MacCluer, J. W. 1973. Computer simulation in anthropology and human genetics. In M. H. Crawford and P. L. Workman (Eds.), *Methods and Theories in Anthropological Genetics.* Albuquerque: Univ. of New Mexico Press.

MacCluer, J. W. Monte Carlo simulation: the effects of migration on some measures of genetic distance. In J. F. Crow, C. Denniston, and P. O'Shea (Eds.), *Genetic Distance.* New York: Plenum Press. In press.

MacCluer, J. W., J. V. Neel, and N. A. Chagnon 1971. Demographic structure of a primitive population: a simulation. *American Journal of Physical Anthropology* **35:** 193-208.

MacCluer, J. W. and W. J. Schull 1970. Frequencies of consanguineous marriage and accumulation of inbreeding in an artificial population. *American Journal of Human Genetics* **22:** 160-175.

MacCluer, J. W. and W. J. Schull 1970. Estimating the effective size of human populations. *American Journal of Human Genetics* **22:** 176-183.

Maisel, H. and G. Gnugnoli 1972. *Simulation of Discrete Stochastic Systems.* Chicago: Science Research Associates.

Martin, F. F. 1968. *Computer Modeling and Simulation.* New York: Wiley.

Martin, F. G. and C. C. Cockerham 1960. High-speed selection studies. In O. Kempthorne (Ed.), *Biometrical Genetics.* New York: Pergamon Press,. Pp. 35-45.

Meadows, D. H., D. L. Meadows, J. Randers, and W. W. Behrens 1972. *The Limits to Growth. A Report for the Club of Rome's Project on the Predicament of Mankind.* New York: Universe Books.

Meier, R. L. 1961. Explorations in the realm of organization theory. IV. The simulation of social organization. *Behavioral Science* **6:** 232-248.

Mihram, G. A. 1972. *Simulation: Statistical Foundations and Methodology.* New York: Academic Press.

Morgan, K. 1969. Monte Carlo simulation of artificial populations: the survival of small, closed populations. Paper presented at the Conference on the Mathematics of Population. Berkeley and Asilomar, California.

Morgan, K. 1973. Computer simulation of incest prohibition and clan proscription rules in closed, finite populations. In B. Dyke and J. W. MacCluer (Eds.), *Computer Simulation in Human Population Studies.* New York: Academic Press.

Morrill, R. L. 1963. The development of spatial distributions of towns in Sweden: an historical-predictive approach. *Annals of the Association of American Geographers* **53:** 1-14.

Morrill, R. L. 1965. Migration and the spread and growth of urban settlement. Royal Universities of Lund: Lund Studies in Geography, **B,** 26.

Naylor, T. H. (Ed.) 1969. *The Design of Computer Simulation Experiments.* Durham, North Carolina: Duke University Press.

Naylor, T. H. 1971. *Computer Simulation Experiments with Models of Economic Systems.* New York: Wiley.

Naylor, T. H., J. L. Balintfy, D. S. Burdick, and K. Chu 1966. *Computer Simulation Techniques.* New York: Wiley.

Orcutt, G. H. 1963. Views on simulation and models of social systems. In A. C. Hoggatt and F. E. Balderston (Eds.), *Symposium on Simulation Models.* Cincinnati: South-Western. Pp. 221-236.

Orcutt, G. H. 1965. Data needs for computer simulation of large-scale social systems. In J. M. Beshers (Ed.), *Computer Methods in the Analysis of Large-Scale Social Systems.* Cambridge, Massachusetts: M.I.T.-Harvard Joint Center for Urban Studies. Pp. 230-239.

Orcutt, G. H., M. Greenberger, J. Korbel, and A. M. Rivlin 1961. *Microanalysis of Socio-economic Systems: A Simulation Study.* New York: Harper and Row.

Perrin, E. B. and M. C. Sheps 1963. A Monte Carlo investigation of a human fertility model. Paper presented at the annual meeting of the American Public Health Association.

Pitts, F. R. 1963. Problems in computer simulation of diffusion. *Papers of the Regional Science Association,* **II:** 111-122.

Pitts, F. R. 1965. Hager III and Hager IV: two Monte Carlo computer programs for the study of spatial diffusion programs, Spatial Diffusion Study. *Technical Report* No. 4. Evanston, Illinois: Northwestern Univ.

Pollard, J. H. 1969. A discrete-time two-sex age-specific stochastic population program incorporating marriage. *Demography* **6:** 185-221.

Potter, R. G. and J. M. Sakoda 1966. A computer model of family building based on expected values. *Demography* **3:** 450-461.

Pugh, A. L. 1970. DYNAMO II *User's Manual.* Cambridge, Massachusetts: MIT Press.

Rainio, K. 1961. A stochastic model of social interaction. *Transactions of the Westermarck Society,* Vol. 7, Copenhagen: Munksgaard.

Rainio, K. 1965. Social interaction as a stochastic learning process. *Archives of European Sociology* **6:** 68-88.

Rainio, K. 1966. A study on sociometric group structure: an application of a stochastic theory of social interaction. In J. Berger, M. Zelditch, Jr., and B. Anderson (Eds.), *Sociological Theories in Progress.* New York: Houghton Mifflin. Pp. 102-123.

Rao, A. V., Q. W. Lindsey, R. C. Bhavsar, B. V. Shah, D. G. Horvitz, and J. R. Batts 1973. The evaluation of four alternative family planning programs for Popland, a less developed country. In B. Dyke and J. W. MacCluer (Eds.), *Computer Simulation in Human Population Studies.* New York: Academic Press.

Raser, J. R. 1969. *Simulation and Society. An Exploration of Scientific Gaming.* Boston: Allyn and Bacon.

Ridley, J. C. and M. C. Sheps 1965. Marriage patterns and natality: preliminary investigations with a simulation model. *Abstracts of contributed papers. Population Association of America, Chicago, Illinois, April 1965.*

Ridley, J. C. and M. C. Sheps 1966. An analytic simulation model of human reproduction with demographic and biological components. *Population Studies* **19:** 297-310.

Ridley, J. C., J. W. Lingner, M. C. Sheps, and J. A. Menken 1967. Effects on natality of alternative family planning programs: estimation via simulation. *Abstracts of contributed papers, Population Association of America, Cincinnati, Ohio, April 1967.*

Ridley, J. C., M. C. Sheps, J. W. Lingner, and J. A. Menken 1967. The effects of changing mortality on natality: some estimates from a simulation model. *The Milbank Memorial Fund Quarterly.* Pp. 77-97.

Rogers, E. M. 1962. *Diffusion of Innovations.* New York: Free Press.

Rogers, E. M. 1969. Computer simulation of innovation diffusion in a peasant village. In E. M. Rogers (Ed.), *Modernization among Peasants.* New York: Holt. Pp. 343-359.

Rohlf, F. J. and G. D. Schnell 1971. An investigation of the isolation by distance model. *American Naturalist* **105:** 295-324.

Rossmann, D. L. and W. J. Schull 1973. Recessive lethals and the birth interval. In B. Dyke and J. W. MacCluer (Eds.), *Computer Simulation in Human Population Studies.* New York: Academic Press.

Sakoda, J. M. 1973. The use of DYSTAL in simulation. In B. Dyke and J. W. MacCluer (Eds.), *Computer Simulation in Human Population Studies,* New York: Academic Press.

Schull, W. J. 1969. Discussion of Monte Carlo simulation. In N. E. Morton (Ed.), *Computer Applications in Genetics.* Honolulu: Univ. of Hawaii Press. P. 47.

Schull, W. J. and B. R. Levin 1964. Monte Carlo simulation: some uses in the genetic study of primitive man. In J. Gurland (Ed.), *Stochastic Models in Medicine and Biology.* Madison: Univ. of Wisconsin Press. Pp. 179-196.

Shah, B. V. 1968. Open and closed models for microsimulation of vital events in a large population. *Working Paper* No. 22. Research Triangle Institute, North Carolina.

Shah, B. V. 1973. On mathematics of population simulation models. In B. Dyke and J. W. MacCluer (Eds.), *Computer Simulation in Human Population Studies.* New York: Academic Press.

Sheps, M. C. and J. C. Ridley 1967. Studying determinants of natality: quantitative estimation through a simulation model (summary). *World Population Conference, Belgrade, 1965.* Vol. III. New York: United Nations.

Sheps, M. C., J. C. Ridley, and J. W. Lingner 1967. Effects of selected factors on natality: quantitative estimation through simulation. *Proceedings of the Conference on Simulation in Business and Public Health.* American Statistical Association.

Shubik, M. 1967. Transfer of technology and simulation studies. In D. L. Spencer and A. Woroniak (Eds.), *The Transfer of Technology to Developing Countries.* New York: Praeger. Pp. 119-140.

Skolnick, M. H. and C. Cannings 1972. The natural regulation of population size for primitive man. *Nature* **239:** 287-288.

Skolnick, M. H. and C. Cannings 1973. Simulation of small human populations. In B. Dyke and J. W. MacCluer (Eds.), *Computer Simulation in Human Population Studies.* New York: Academic Press.

Stanfield, D. J., N. Lin, and E. M. Rogers 1965. Simulation of Innovation Diffusion. Project of Diffusion of Innovations in Rural Societies, *Working Paper* No. 7. East Lansing: Michigan State Univ.

Starbuck, W. H. 1961. Testing case-descriptive models. *Behavioral Science* **6:** 191-199.

Stiteler, W. M. 1973. Computer generation of random variates. In B. Dyke and J. W. MacCluer (Eds.), *Computer Stimulation in Human Population Studies.* New York: Academic Press.

Sved, J. A. 1968. The stability of linked systems of loci with a small population size. *Genetics* **59:** 543-563.

Talwar, P. P. 1969. Effect of changes in age at first marriage on fertility: a case study of the U.S. population using a microsimulation model. *Working Paper* No. 33. Research Triangle Institute, North Carolina.

van de Walle, E. and J. Knodel 1970. Teaching population dynamics with a simulation exercise. *Demography* **7:** 433-448.

Venkatacharya, K. 1971. A Monte Carlo model for the study of human fertility under varying fecundability. *Social Biology* **18:** 406-415.

Venkatacharya, K. 1972. Reduction in fertility due to induced abortions: a simulation model. *Demography* **9:** 339-352.

Watt, K. E. F. 1968. *Ecology and Resource Management.* New York: McGraw-Hill.

Williams, A. V., J. Longfellow, and C. Monroe 1973. Simulation over space. In B. Dyke and J. W. MacCluer (Eds.), *Computer Simulation in Human Population Studies.* New York: Academic Press.

Williams, B. J. 1965. A Model of Hunting-Gathering Society and Some Genetic Consequences. Doctoral Thesis, Univ. of Michigan.

Wolpert, J. 1967. A regional simulation model of information diffusion. *Public Opinion Quarterly* **30**: 597-608.

Wyman, F. P. 1970. *Simulation Modeling: A Guide to Using* SIMSCRIPT. New York: Wiley.

Wyman, F. P. 1973. Special purpose simulation languages for population studies. In B. Dyke and J. W. MacCluer (Eds.), *Computer Simulation in Human Population Studies.* New York: Academic Press.

Zellner, A. 1965. Estimation of parameters in simulation models of social systems. In J. M. Beshers (Ed.), *Computer Methods in the Analysis of Large-Scale Social Systems.* Cambridge, Massachusetts: M.I.T.-Harvard Joint Center for Urban Studies. Pp. 137-157.

Zubrow, E. B. W. 1971. Adequacy criteria and prediction in archaeological models. Paper presented at the meetings of the American Anthropological Association, New York.

Zubrow, E. B. W. 1971. A Southwestern Test of an Anthropological Model of Population Dynamics. Doctoral Thesis, Univ. of Arizona.

SUBJECT INDEX

B
C 8
D 9
E 0
F 1
G 2
H 3
I 4
J 5